HONORIFICS EXPLAINED

Throughout the Kodansha Comics books, you will find Japanese honorifics left intact in the translations. For those not familiar with how the Japanese use honorifics and, more important, how they differ from American honorifics, we present this brief overview.

Politeness has always been a critical facet of Japanese culture. Ever since the feudal era, when Japan was a highly stratified society, use of honorifics—which can be defined as polite speech that indicates relationship or status—has played an essential role in the Japanese language. When addressing someone in Japanese, an honorific usually takes the form of a suffix attached to one's name (example: "Asuna-san"), is used as a title at the end of one's name, or appears in place of the name itself (example: "Negi-sensei," or simply "Sensei!").

Honorifics can be expressions of respect or endearment. In the context of manga and anime, honorifics give insight into the nature of the relationship between characters. Many English translations leave out these important honorifics and therefore distort the feel of the original Japanese. Because Japanese honorifics contain nuances that English honorifics lack, it is our policy at Kodansha Comics not to translate them. Here, instead, is a guide to some of the honorifics you may encounter in Kodansha Comics books.

-san: This is the most common honorific and is equivalent to Mr., Miss, Ms., or Mrs. It is the all-purpose honorific and can be used in any situation where politeness is required.

-sama: This is one level higher than "-san" and is used to confer great respect.

-dono: This comes from the word "tono," which means "lord." It is an even higher level than "-sama" and confers utmost respect.

-kun: This suffix is used at the end of boys' names to express familiarity or endearment. It is also sometimes used by men among friends, or when addressing someone younger or of a lower station.

-chan: This is used to express endearment, mostly toward girls. It is also used for little boys, pets, and even among lovers. It gives a sense of childish cuteness.

Bozu: This is an informal way to refer to a boy, similar to the English terms "kid" and "squirt."

Sempai/
Senpai: This title suggests that the addressee is one's senior in a group or organization. It is most often used in a school setting, where underclassmen refer to their upperclassmen as "sempai." It can also be used in the workplace, such as when a newer employee addresses an employee who has seniority in the company.

Kohai: This is the opposite of "sempai" and is used toward underclassmen in school or newcomers in the workplace. It connotes that the addressee is of a lower station.

Sensei: Literally meaning "one who has come before," this title is used for teachers, doctors, or masters of any profession or art.

-[blank]: This is usually forgotten in these lists, but it is perhaps the most significant difference between Japanese and English. The lack of honorific means that the speaker has permission to address the person in a very intimate way. Usually, only family, spouses, or very close friends have this kind of permission. Known as *yobisute*, it can be gratifying when someone who has earned the intimacy starts to call one by one's name without an honorific. But when that intimacy hasn't been earned, it can be very insulting.

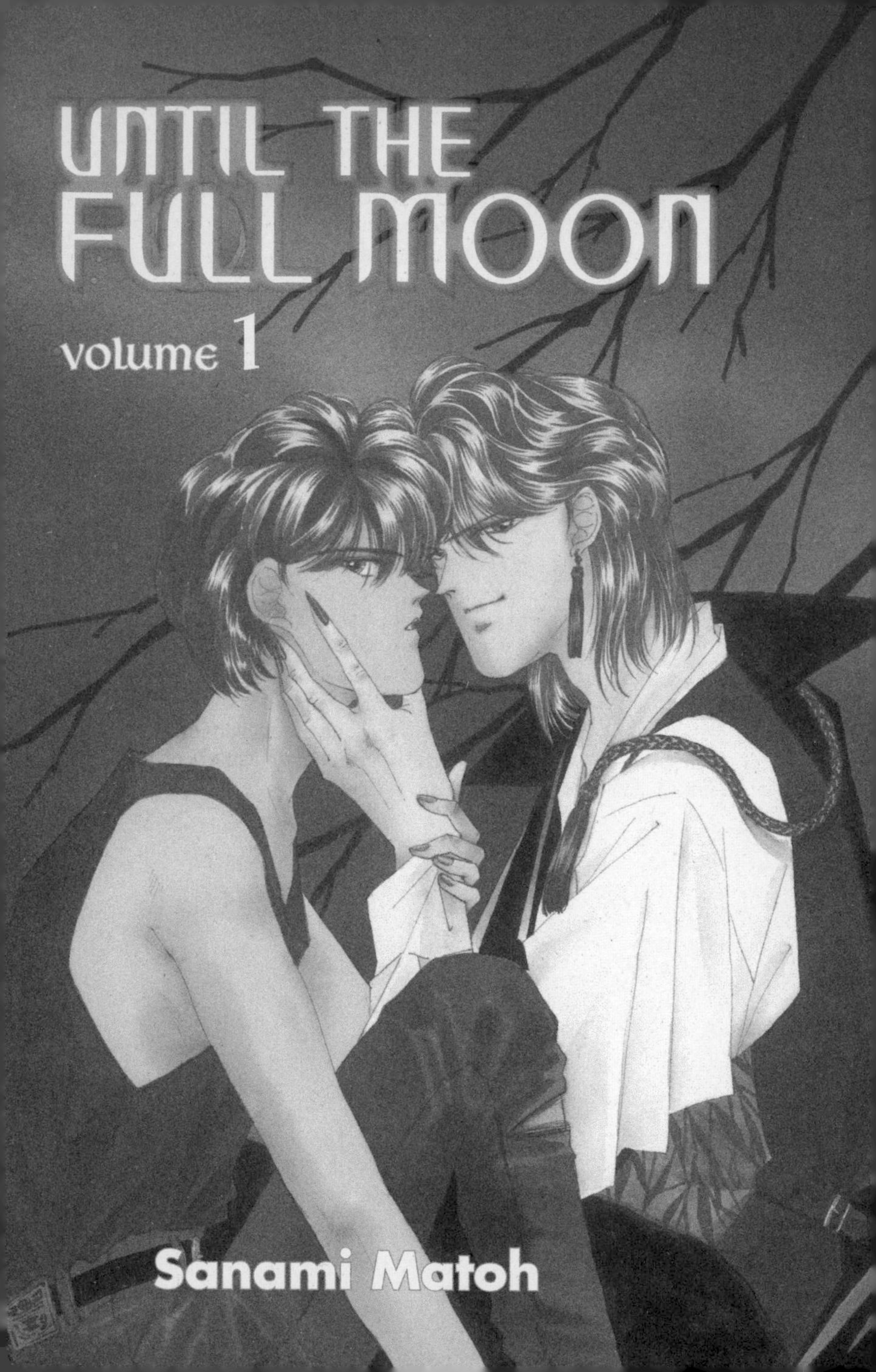
UNTIL THE FULL MOON
volume 1
Sanami Matoh

UNTIL THE FULL MOON

volume 1

Chapter 1: Whisper To Me On A Full Moon Night   3

Chapter 2: Embrace Me On A Full Moon Night   43

Chapter 3: Smile At Me On A Full Moon Night   103

Chapter 4: Kiss Me On A Full Moon Night   155

Special Chapter: The Dragon And The Witch (Part 1)   205

chapter 1

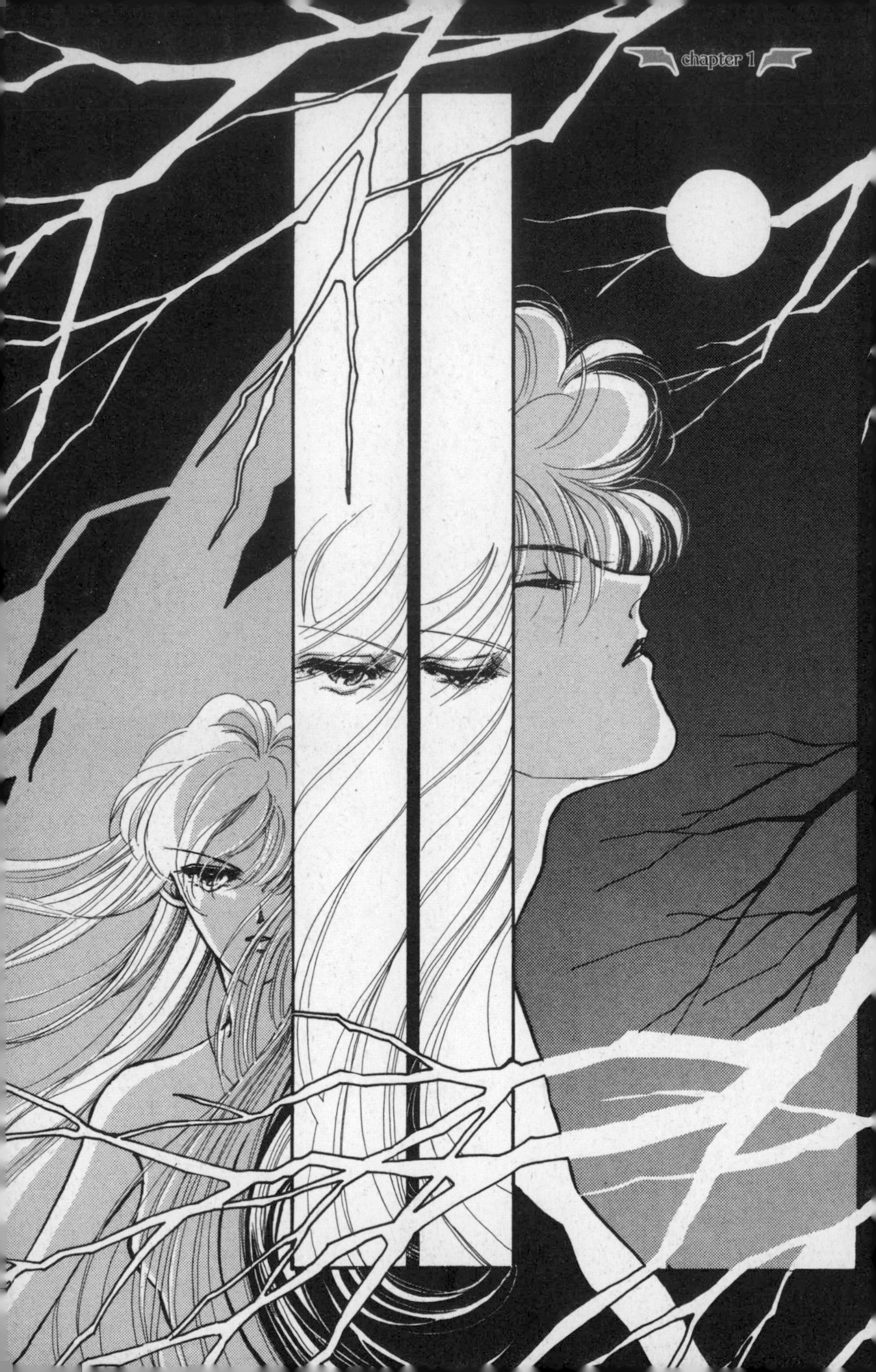

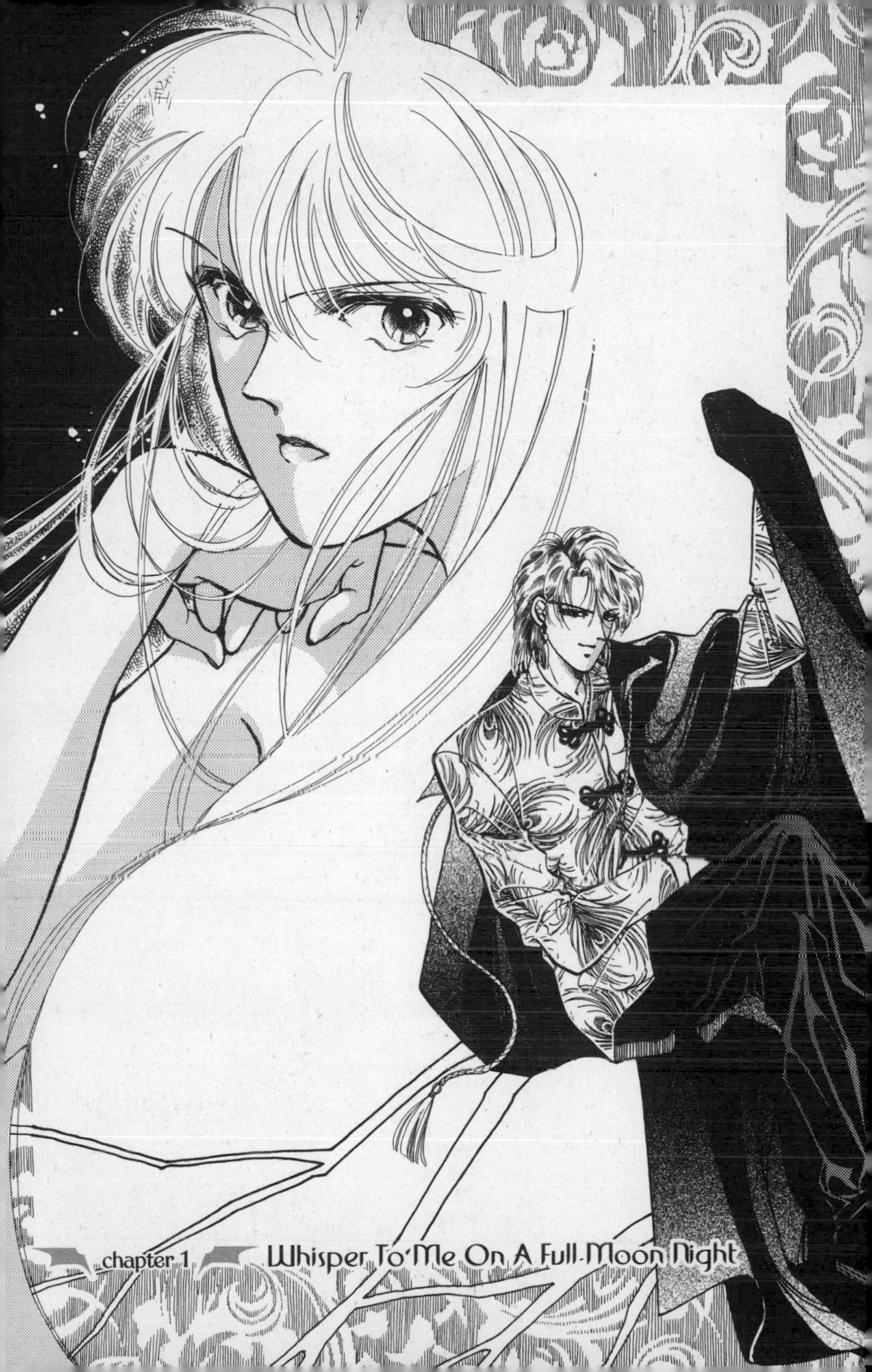
chapter 1
Whisper To Me On A Full Moon Night

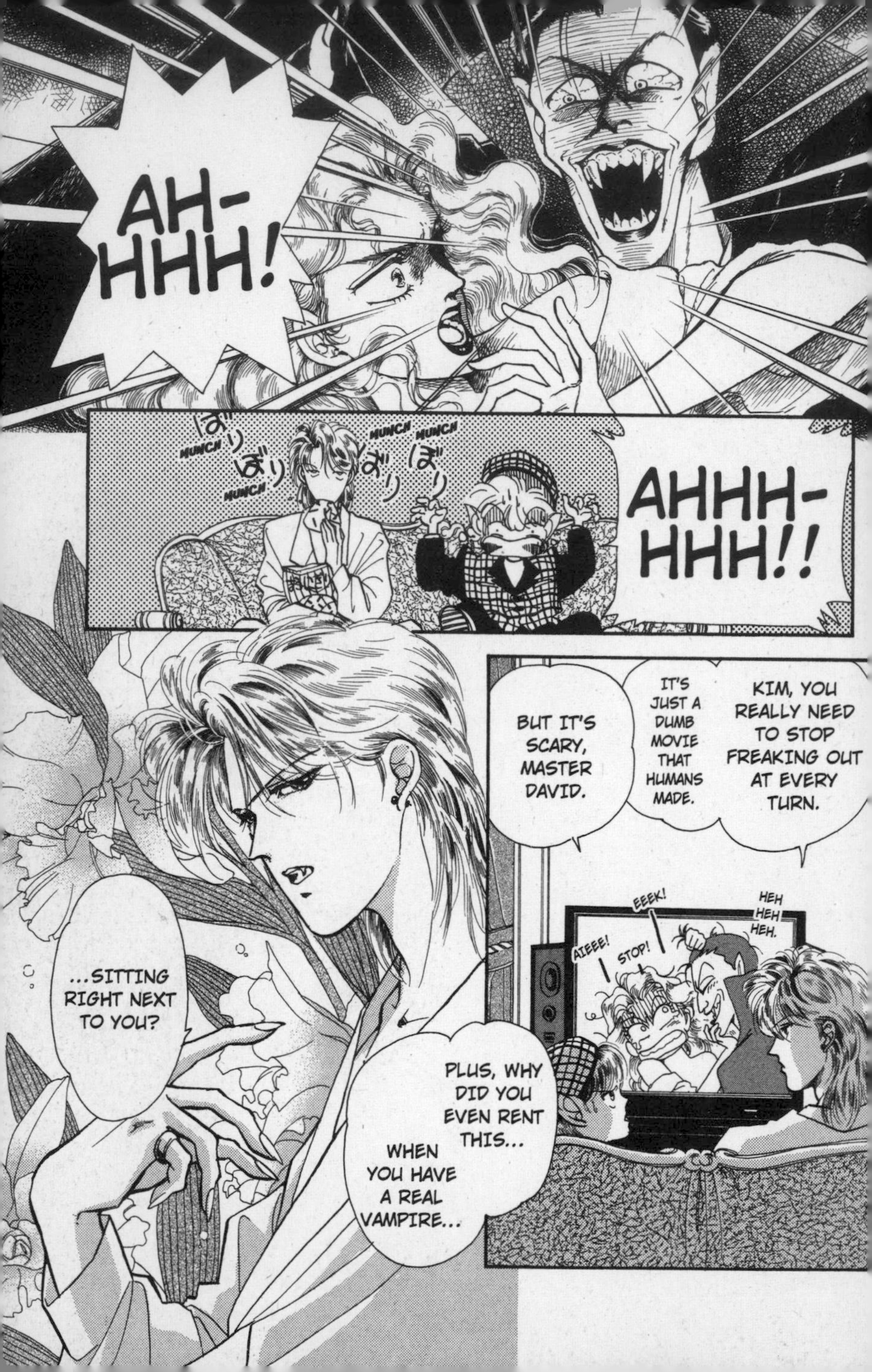
AH-HHH!
AHHHH-HHH!!
MUNCH
ぼりぼり
MUNCH
MUNCH
ぼりぼり
MUNCH
KIM, YOU REALLY NEED TO STOP FREAKING OUT AT EVERY TURN.
IT'S JUST A DUMB MOVIE THAT HUMANS MADE.
BUT IT'S SCARY, MASTER DAVID.
HEH HEH HEH.
EEEK!
STOP!
AIEEE!
PLUS, WHY DID YOU EVEN RENT THIS...
WHEN YOU HAVE A REAL VAMPIRE...
...SITTING RIGHT NEXT TO YOU?

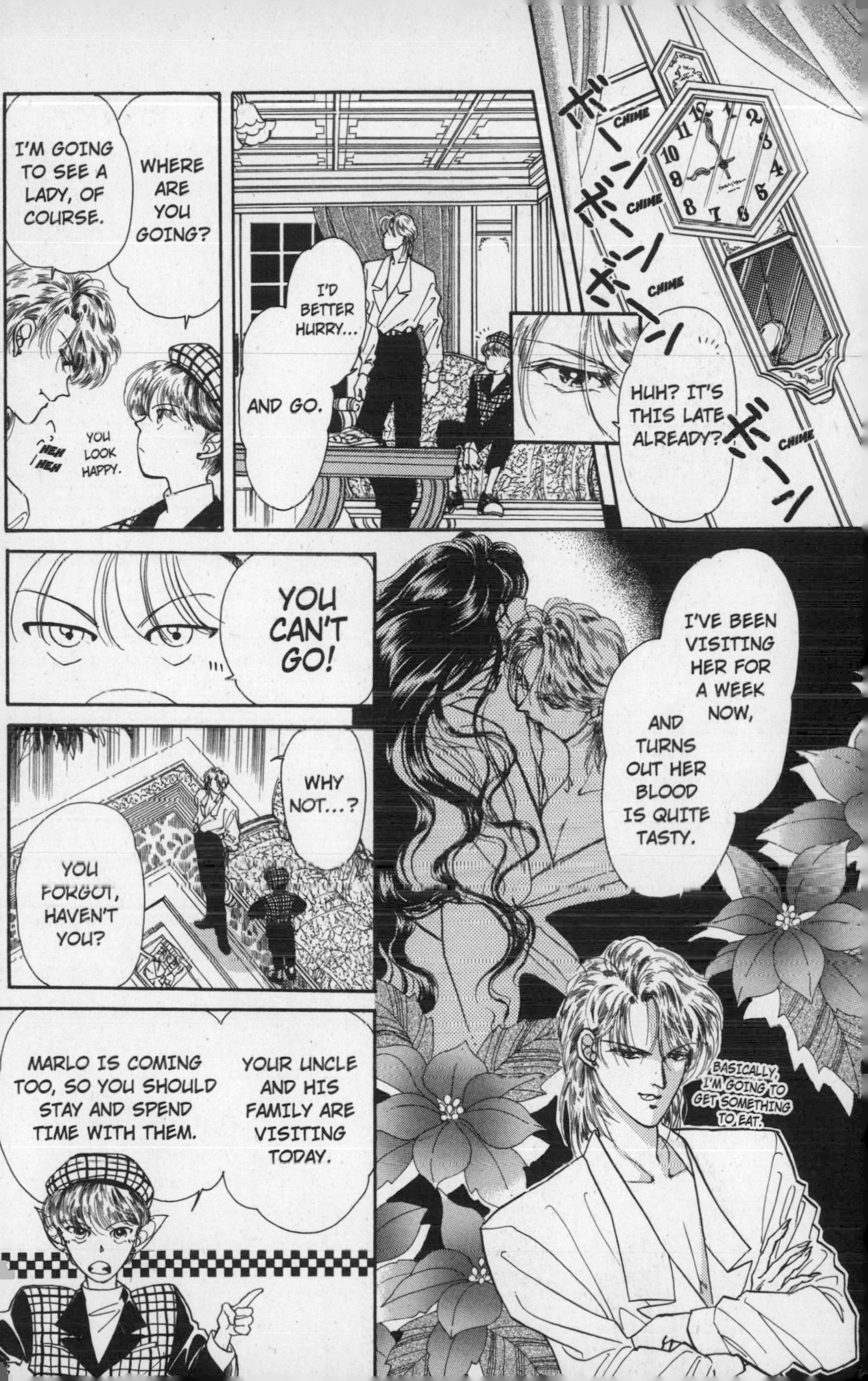
ボーン CHIME
ボーン CHIME
ボーン CHIME
ボーン CHIME
HUH? IT'S THIS LATE ALREADY?
I'D BETTER HURRY...
AND GO.
WHERE ARE YOU GOING?
I'M GOING TO SEE A LADY, OF COURSE.
HEH HEH
YOU LOOK HAPPY.
I'VE BEEN VISITING HER FOR A WEEK NOW,
AND TURNS OUT HER BLOOD IS QUITE TASTY.
BASICALLY, I'M GOING TO GET SOMETHING TO EAT.
YOU CAN'T GO!
WHY NOT...?
YOU FORGOT, HAVEN'T YOU?
YOUR UNCLE AND HIS FAMILY ARE VISITING TODAY.
MARLO IS COMING TOO, SO YOU SHOULD STAY AND SPEND TIME WITH THEM.

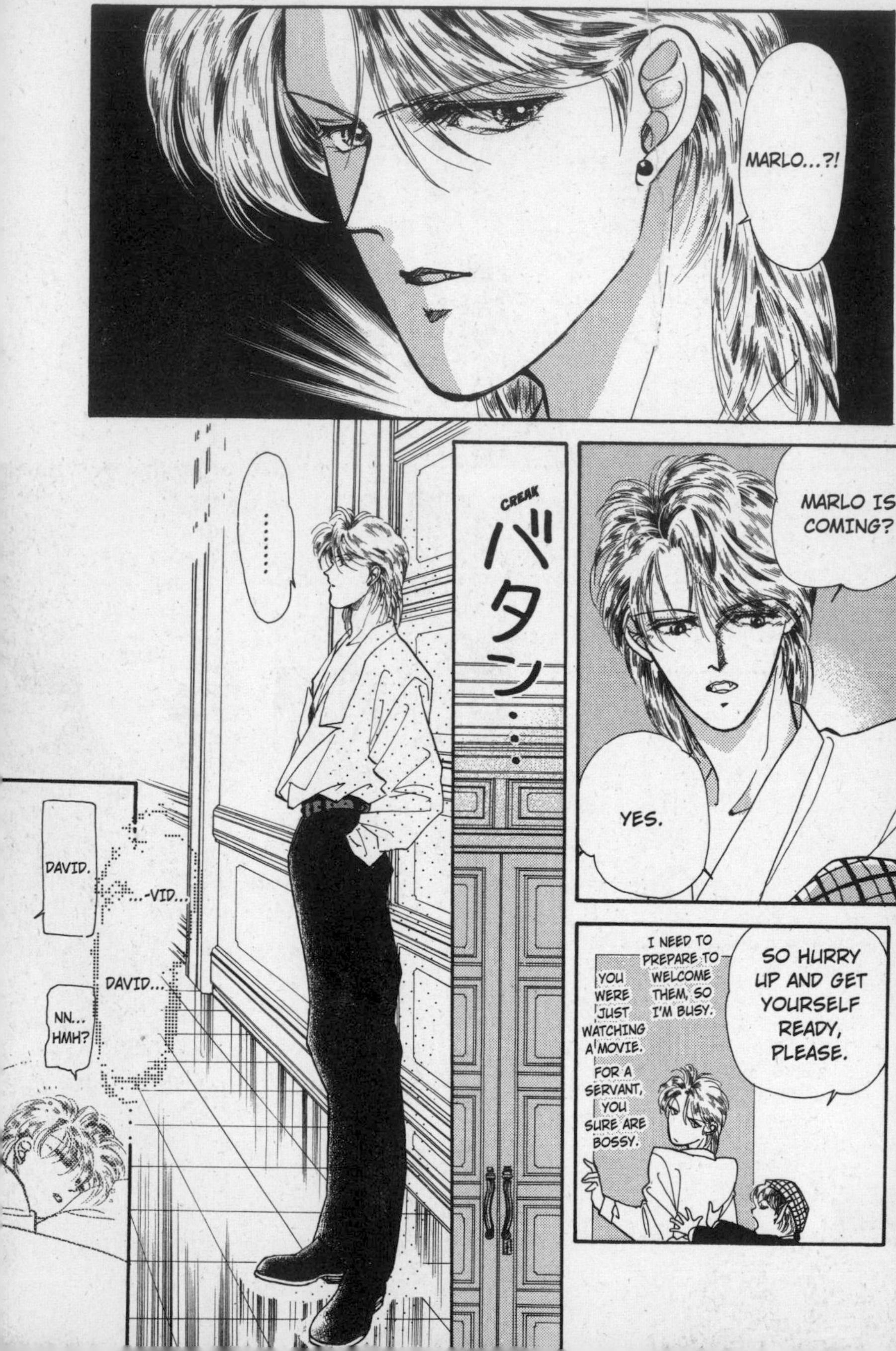
MARLO...?!
MARLO IS COMING?
YES.
SO HURRY UP AND GET YOURSELF READY, PLEASE.
I NEED TO PREPARE TO WELCOME THEM, SO I'M BUSY.
YOU WERE JUST WATCHING A MOVIE.
FOR A SERVANT, YOU SURE ARE BOSSY.
CREAK
バタン・・・
......
DAVID.
...-VID...
DAVID...
NN... HMH?

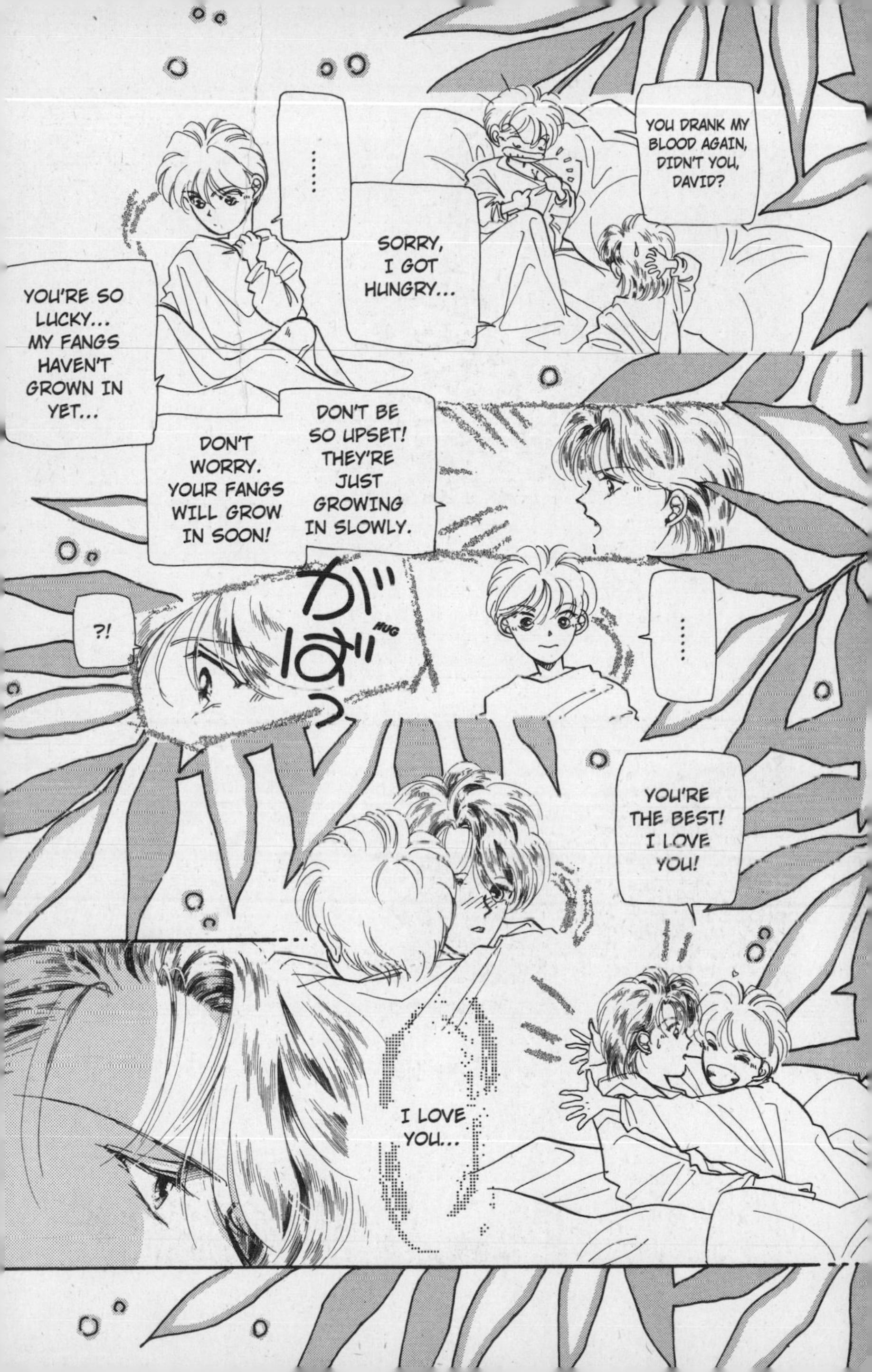
YOU DRANK MY BLOOD AGAIN, DIDN'T YOU, DAVID?
SORRY, I GOT HUNGRY...
......
YOU'RE SO LUCKY... MY FANGS HAVEN'T GROWN IN YET...
DON'T BE SO UPSET! THEY'RE JUST GROWING IN SLOWLY.
DON'T WORRY. YOUR FANGS WILL GROW IN SOON!
......
がばっ
HUG
?!
YOU'RE THE BEST! I LOVE YOU!
I LOVE YOU...

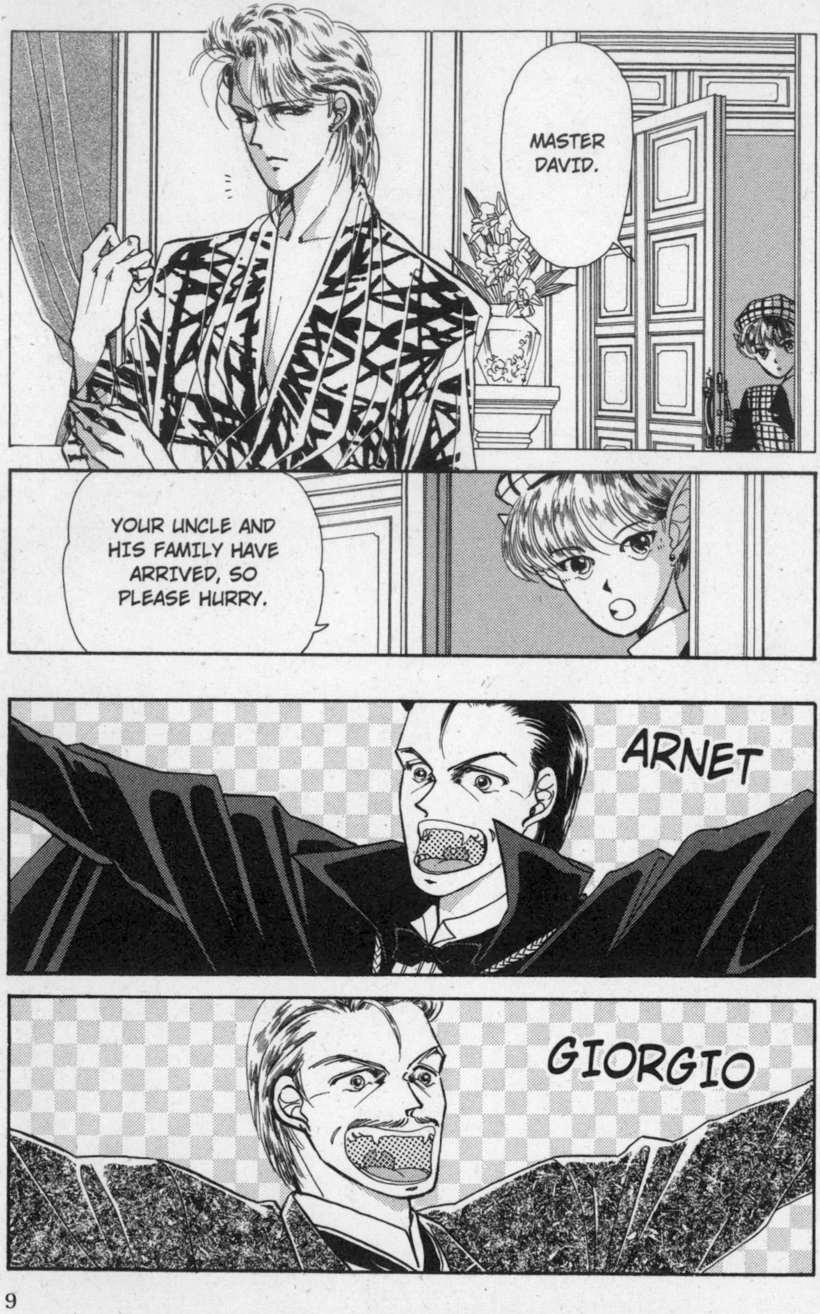
MASTER DAVID.
YOUR UNCLE AND HIS FAMILY HAVE ARRIVED, SO PLEASE HURRY.
ARNET
GIORGIO

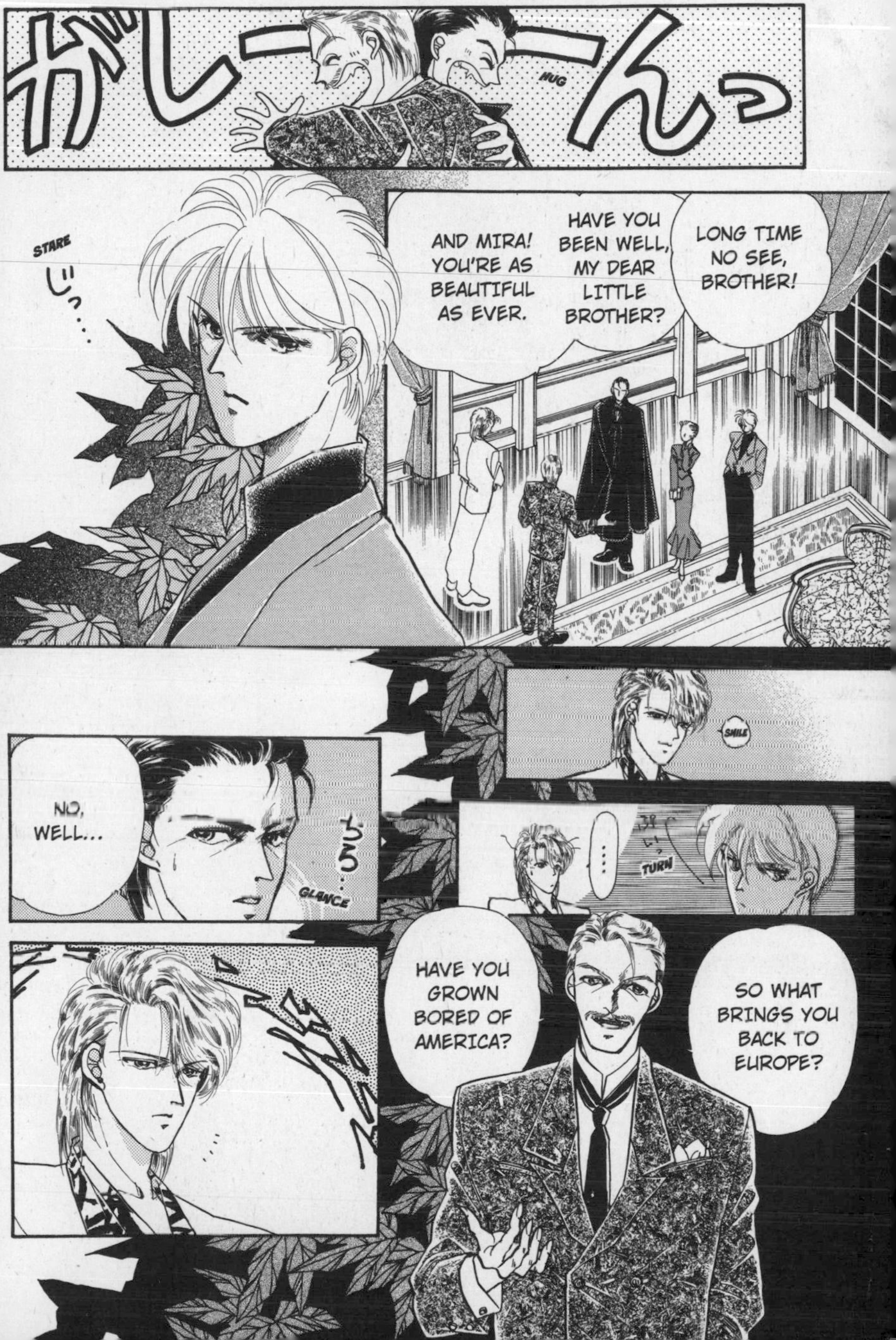
がしーーんっ
HUG
LONG TIME NO SEE, BROTHER!
HAVE YOU BEEN WELL, MY DEAR LITTLE BROTHER?
AND MIRA! YOU'RE AS BEAUTIFUL AS EVER.
STARE
SMILE
....
TURN
NO, WELL...
GLANCE
SO WHAT BRINGS YOU BACK TO EUROPE?
HAVE YOU GROWN BORED OF AMERICA?

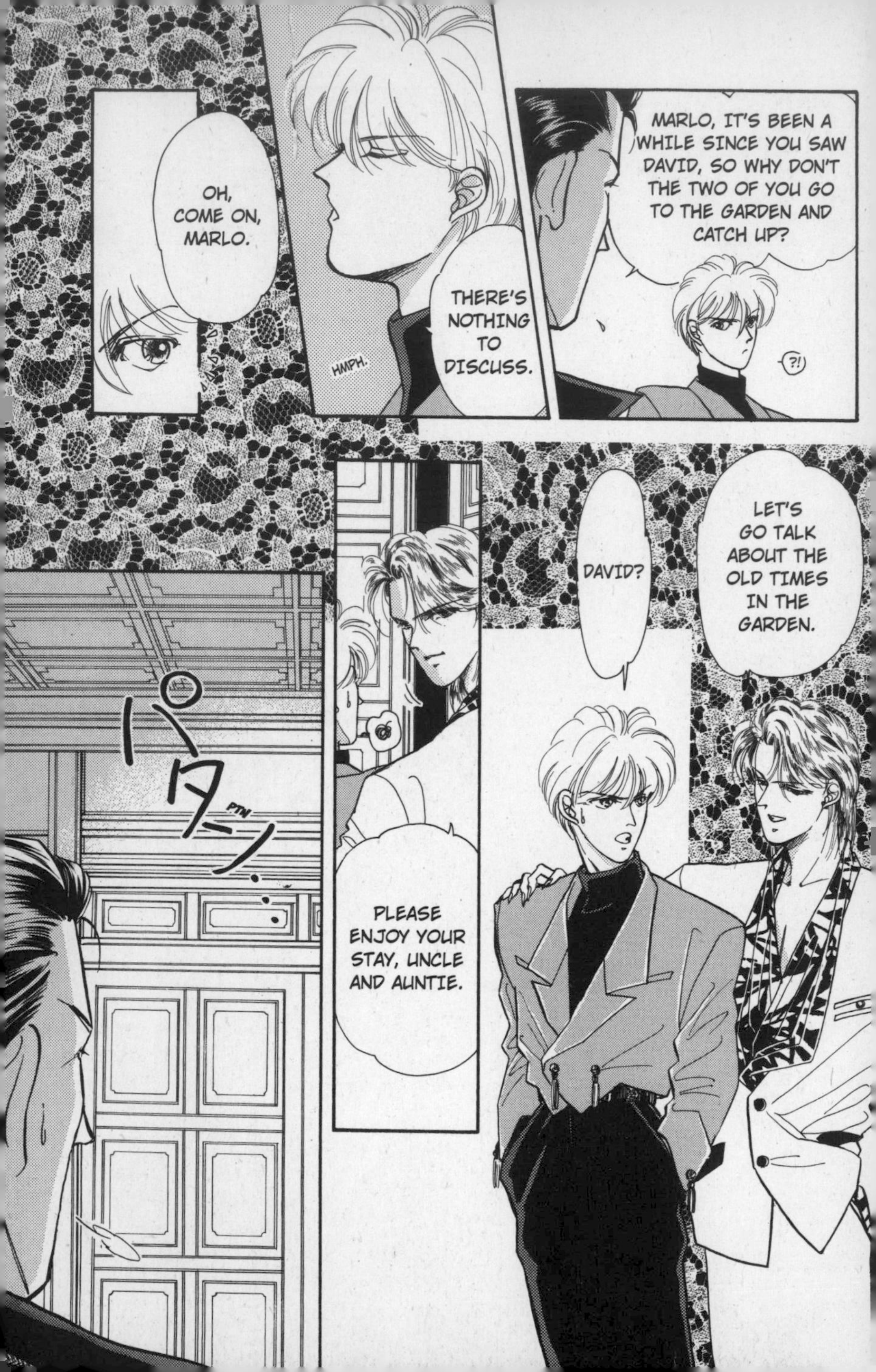
MARLO, IT'S BEEN A WHILE SINCE YOU SAW DAVID, SO WHY DON'T THE TWO OF YOU GO TO THE GARDEN AND CATCH UP?
?!
THERE'S NOTHING TO DISCUSS.
HMPH.
OH, COME ON, MARLO.
LET'S GO TALK ABOUT THE OLD TIMES IN THE GARDEN.
DAVID?
PLEASE ENJOY YOUR STAY, UNCLE AND AUNTIE.
PTN

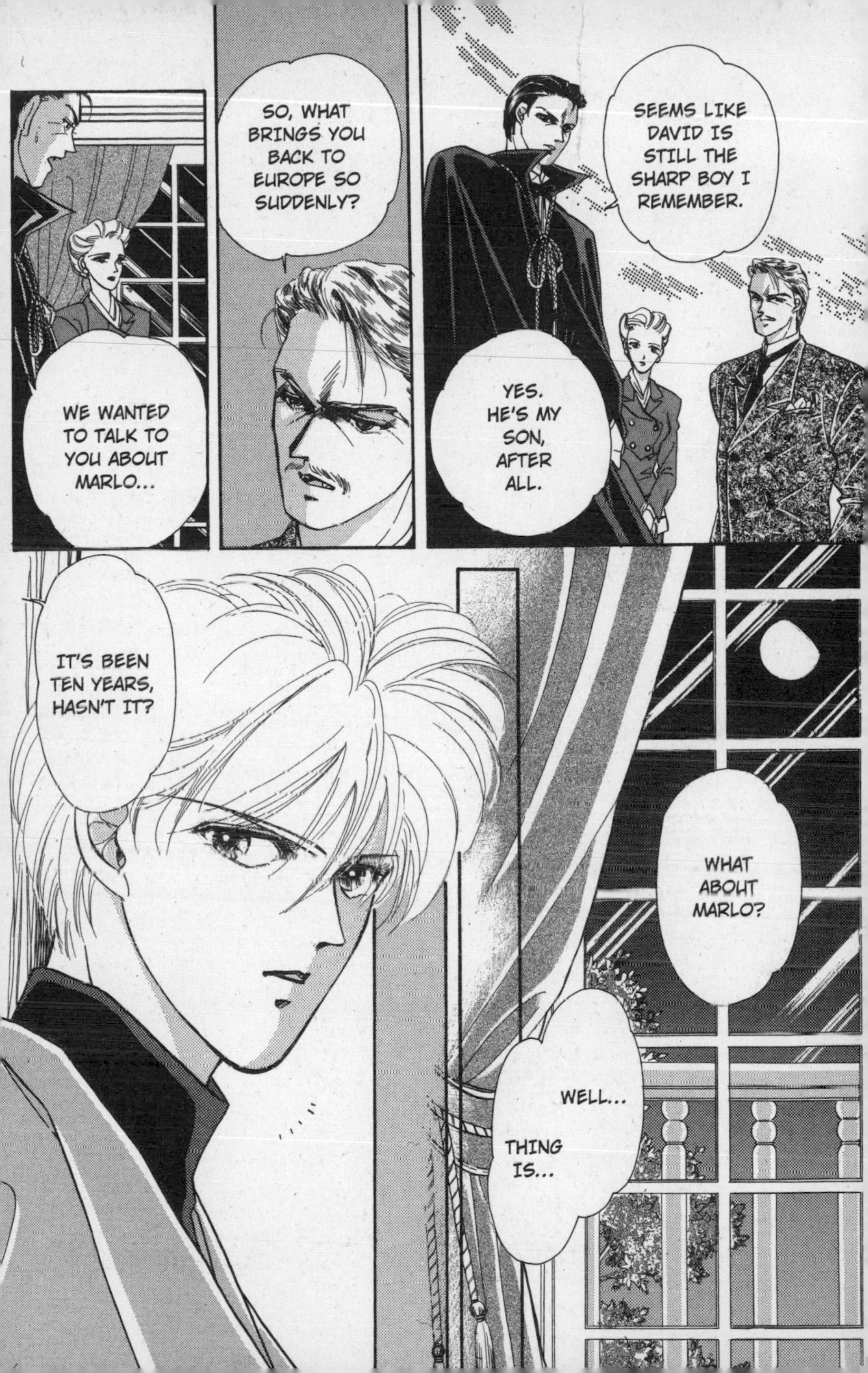
SEEMS LIKE DAVID IS STILL THE SHARP BOY I REMEMBER.
YES. HE'S MY SON, AFTER ALL.
SO, WHAT BRINGS YOU BACK TO EUROPE SO SUDDENLY?
WE WANTED TO TALK TO YOU ABOUT MARLO...
WHAT ABOUT MARLO?
WELL...
THING IS...
IT'S BEEN TEN YEARS, HASN'T IT?

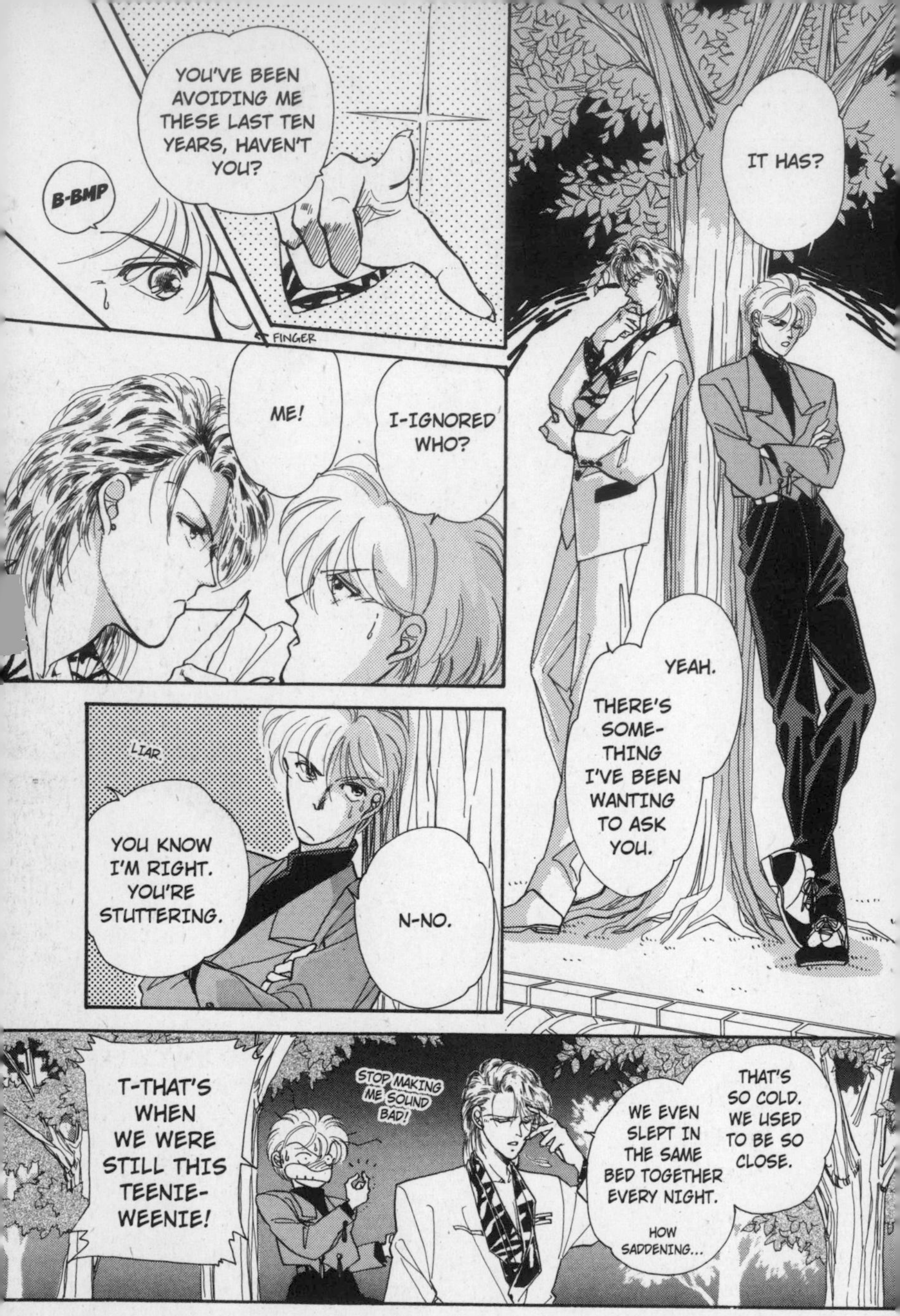
IT HAS?
YEAH. THERE'S SOME-THING I'VE BEEN WANTING TO ASK YOU.
YOU'VE BEEN AVOIDING ME THESE LAST TEN YEARS, HAVEN'T YOU?
B-BMP
FINGER
I-IGNORED WHO?
ME!
N-NO.
LIAR
YOU KNOW I'M RIGHT. YOU'RE STUTTERING.
THAT'S SO COLD. WE USED TO BE SO CLOSE.
WE EVEN SLEPT IN THE SAME BED TOGETHER EVERY NIGHT.
HOW SADDENING...
STOP MAKING ME SOUND BAD!
T-THAT'S WHEN WE WERE STILL THIS TEENIE-WEENIE!

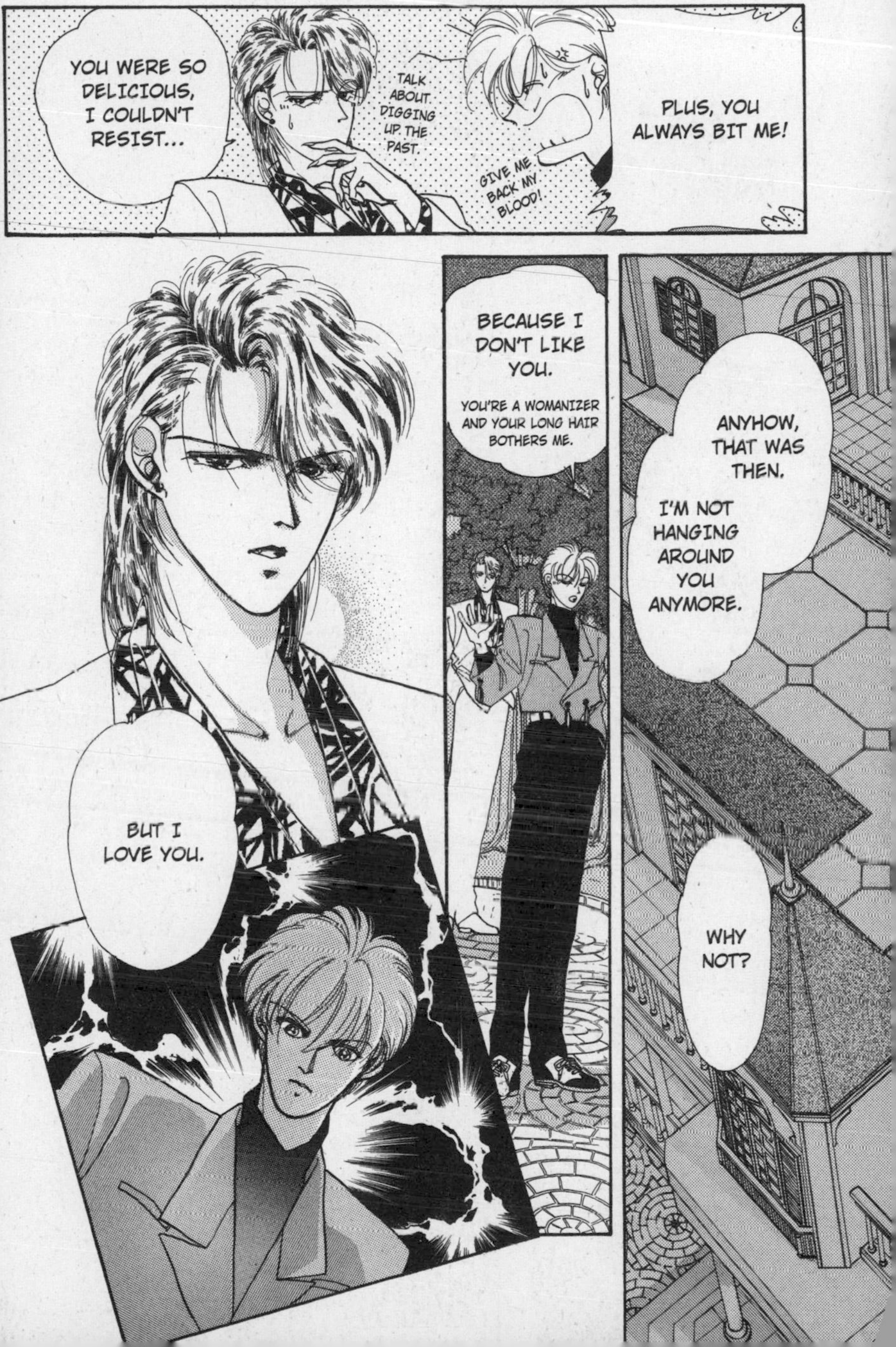
PLUS, YOU ALWAYS BIT ME!
GIVE ME BACK MY BLOOD!
TALK ABOUT DIGGING UP THE PAST.
YOU WERE SO DELICIOUS, I COULDN'T RESIST...
ANYHOW, THAT WAS THEN.
I'M NOT HANGING AROUND YOU ANYMORE.
WHY NOT?
BECAUSE I DON'T LIKE YOU.
YOU'RE A WOMANIZER AND YOUR LONG HAIR BOTHERS ME.
BUT I LOVE YOU.

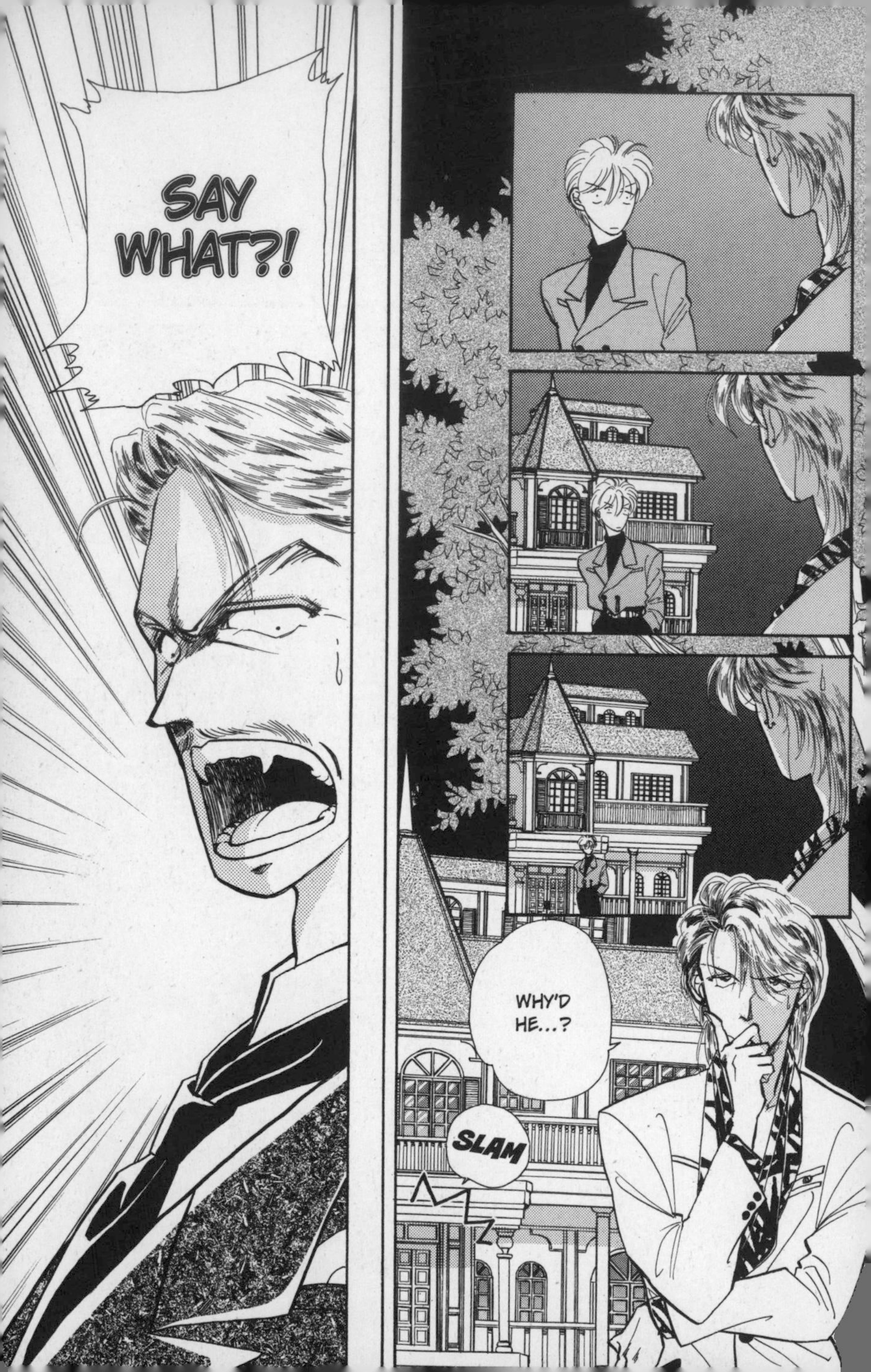
WHY'D HE...?
SLAM
SAY WHAT?!

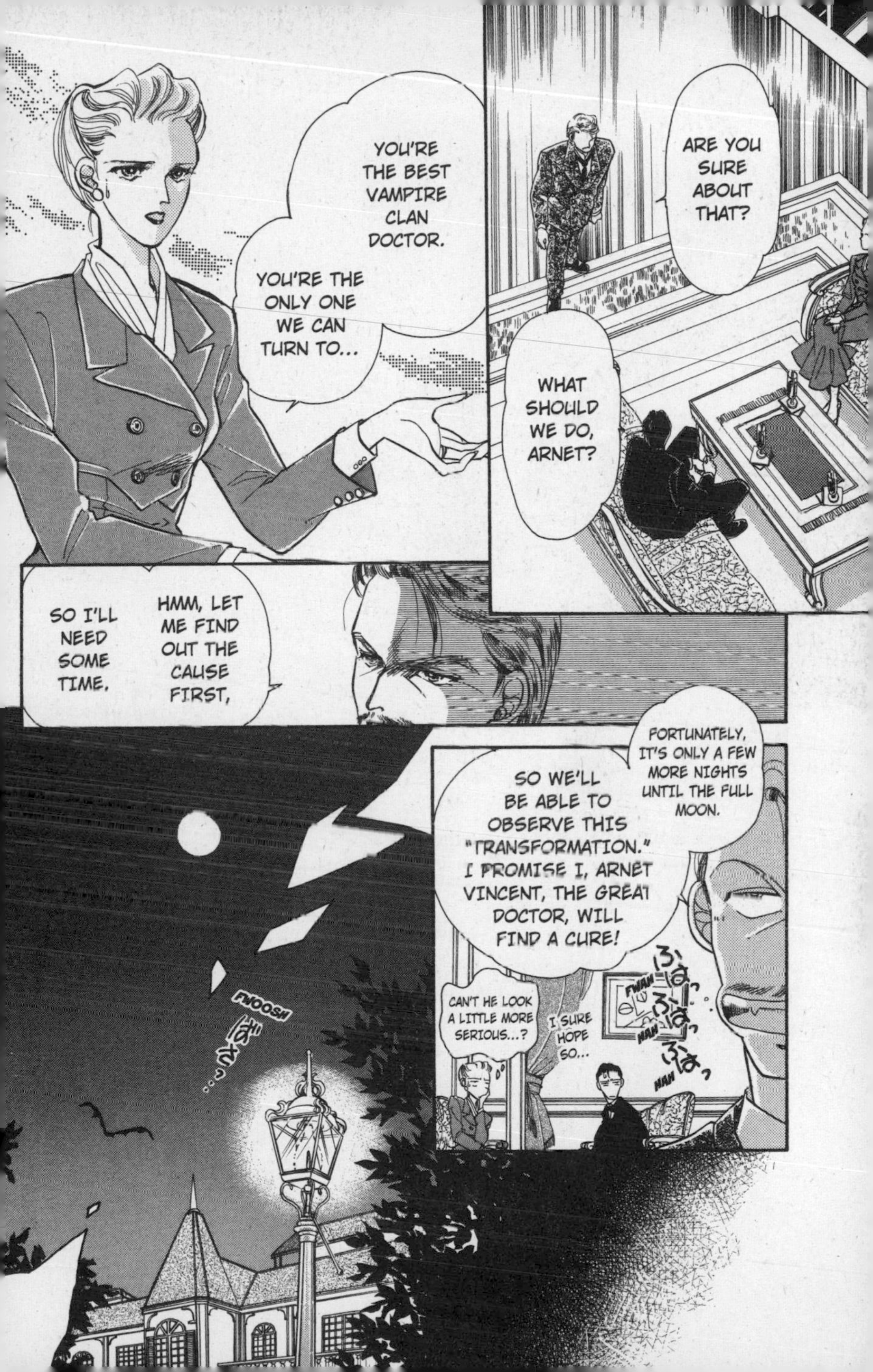

ARE YOU SURE ABOUT THAT?
WHAT SHOULD WE DO, ARNET?
YOU'RE THE BEST VAMPIRE CLAN DOCTOR.
YOU'RE THE ONLY ONE WE CAN TURN TO...
HMM, LET ME FIND OUT THE CAUSE FIRST,
SO I'LL NEED SOME TIME.
FORTUNATELY, IT'S ONLY A FEW MORE NIGHTS UNTIL THE FULL MOON.
SO WE'LL BE ABLE TO OBSERVE THIS "TRANSFORMATION." I PROMISE I, ARNET VINCENT, THE GREAT DOCTOR, WILL FIND A CURE!
ふはっ ふはっ ふはっ
FWAH HAH HAH
I SURE HOPE SO...
CAN'T HE LOOK A LITTLE MORE SERIOUS...?
ばさっ
FWOOSH

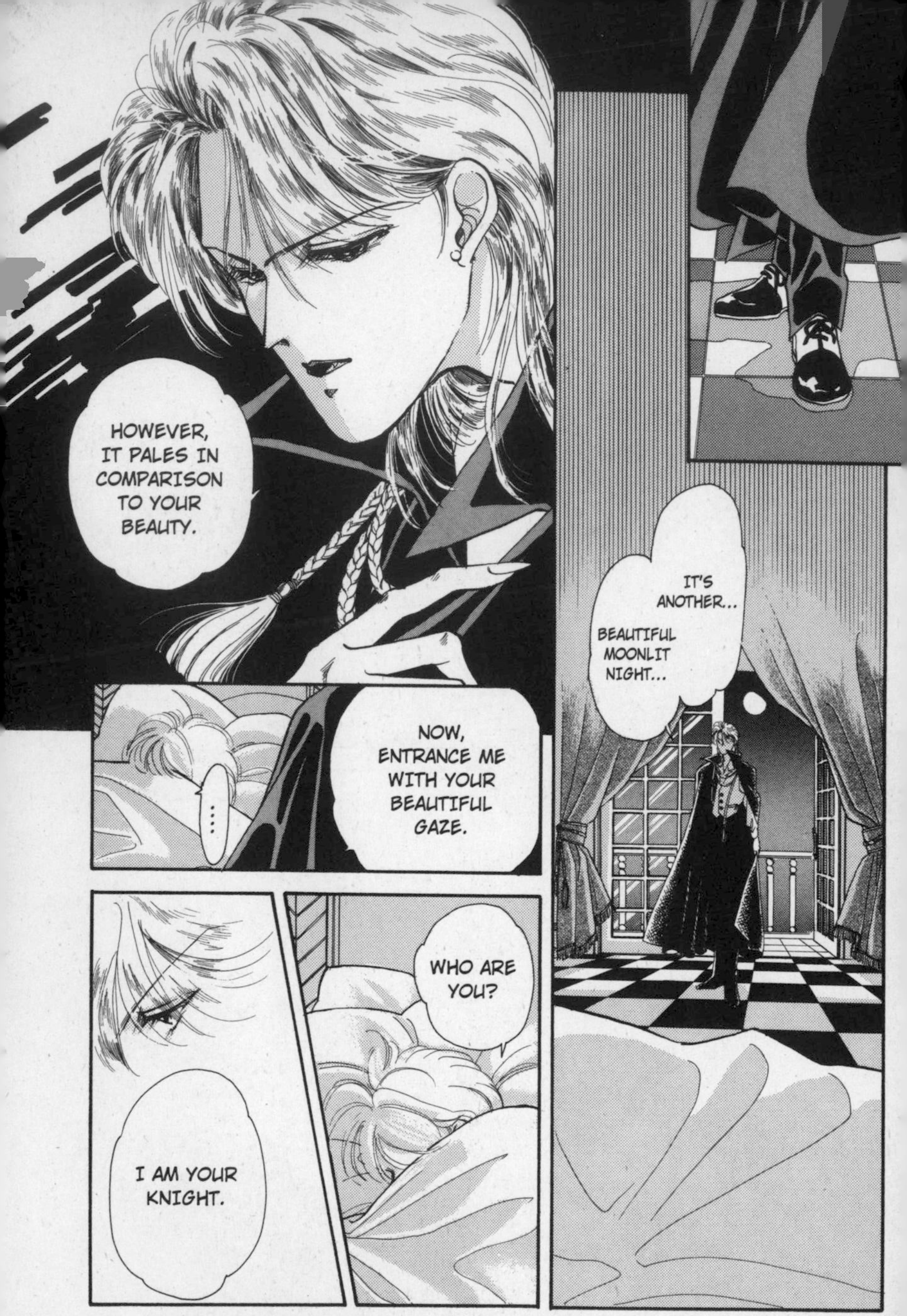
IT'S ANOTHER...
BEAUTIFUL MOONLIT NIGHT...
HOWEVER, IT PALES IN COMPARISON TO YOUR BEAUTY.
NOW, ENTRANCE ME WITH YOUR BEAUTIFUL GAZE.
....
WHO ARE YOU?
I AM YOUR KNIGHT.

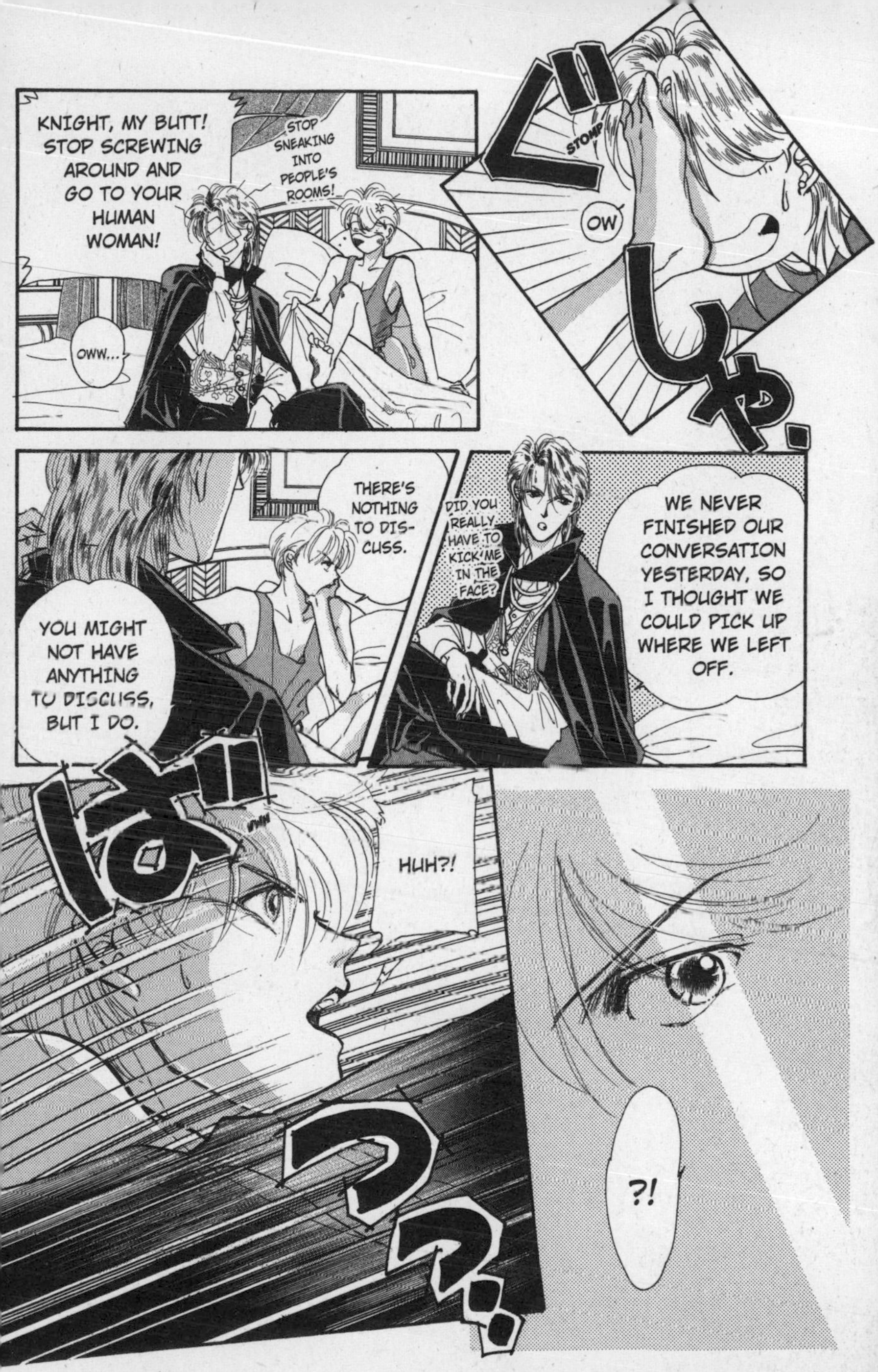
STOMP
OW
KNIGHT, MY BUTT! STOP SCREWING AROUND AND GO TO YOUR HUMAN WOMAN!
STOP SNEAKING INTO PEOPLE'S ROOMS!
OWW...
WE NEVER FINISHED OUR CONVERSATION YESTERDAY, SO I THOUGHT WE COULD PICK UP WHERE WE LEFT OFF.
DID YOU REALLY HAVE TO KICK ME IN THE FACE?
THERE'S NOTHING TO DISCUSS.
YOU MIGHT NOT HAVE ANYTHING TO DISCUSS, BUT I DO.
?!
HUH?!

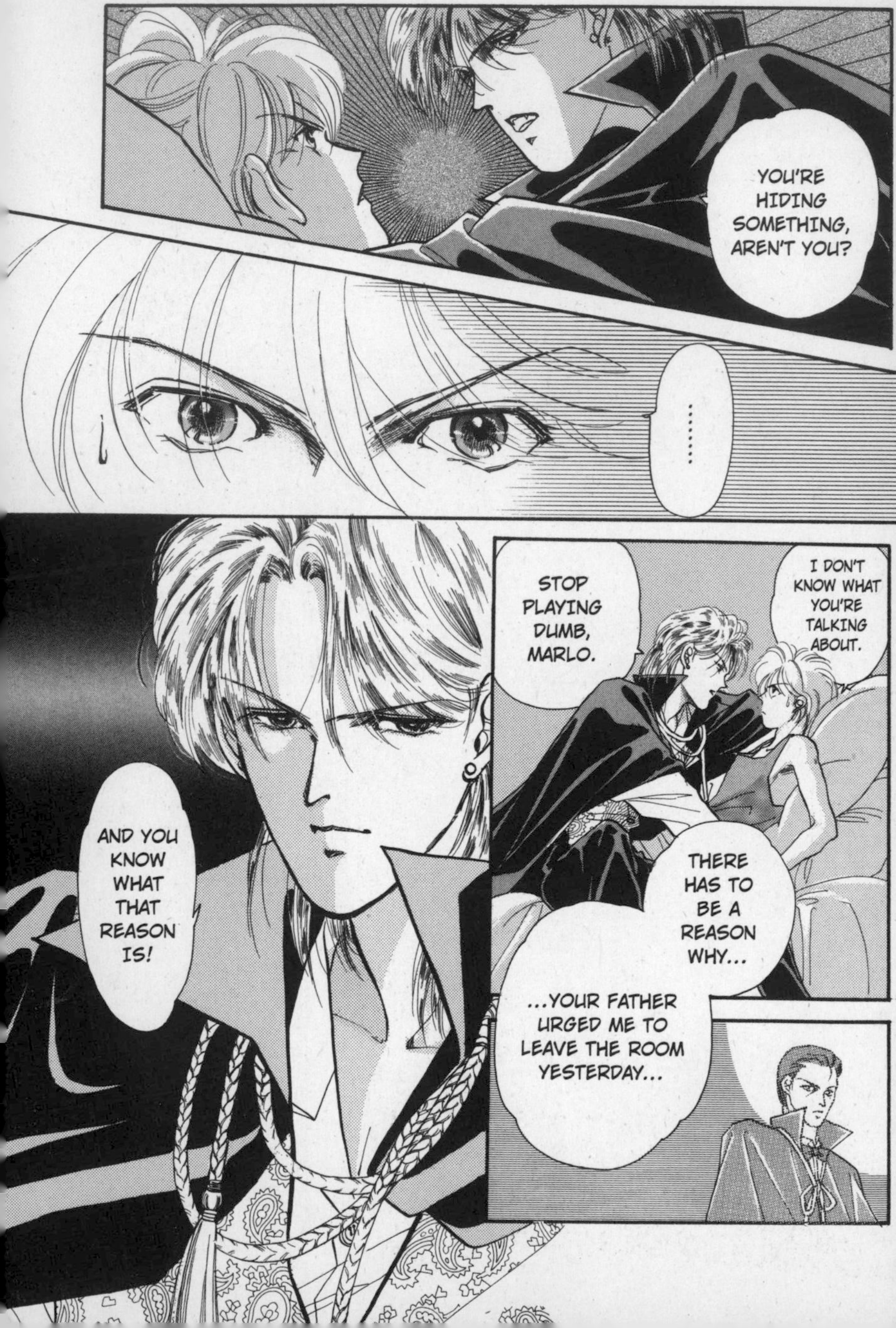
YOU'RE HIDING SOMETHING, AREN'T YOU?
......
I DON'T KNOW WHAT YOU'RE TALKING ABOUT.
STOP PLAYING DUMB, MARLO.
THERE HAS TO BE A REASON WHY...
...YOUR FATHER URGED ME TO LEAVE THE ROOM YESTERDAY...
AND YOU KNOW WHAT THAT REASON IS!

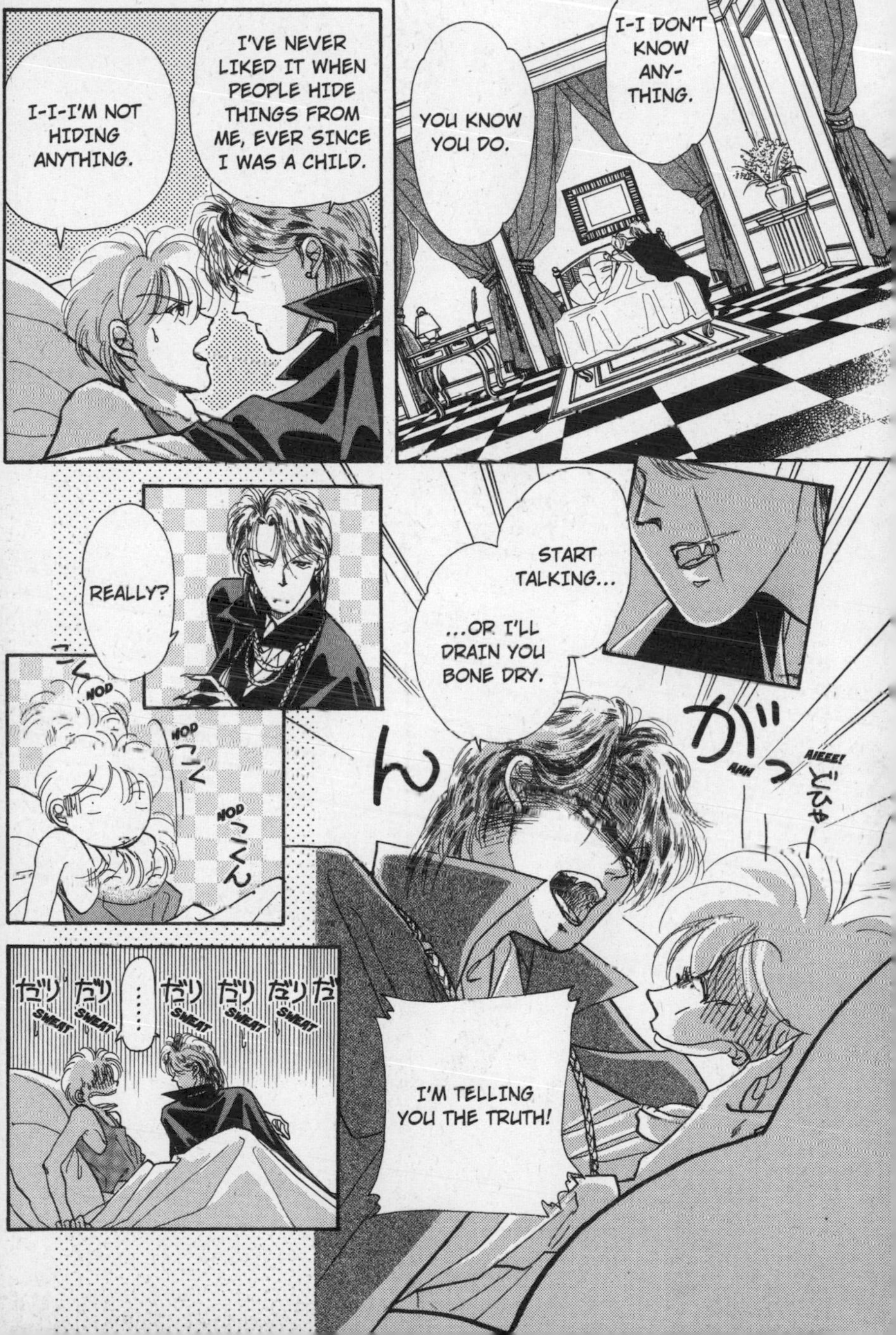
I-I DON'T KNOW ANY-THING.
YOU KNOW YOU DO.
I'VE NEVER LIKED IT WHEN PEOPLE HIDE THINGS FROM ME, EVER SINCE I WAS A CHILD.
I-I-I'M NOT HIDING ANYTHING.
START TALKING...
...OR I'LL DRAIN YOU BONE DRY.
ん
がっ AHH
どひゃー AIEEE!
I'M TELLING YOU THE TRUTH!
REALLY?
こく NOD
こく NOD
こくん NOD
だり だり ...... だり だり だりだ
SWEAT SWEAT SWEAT SWEAT

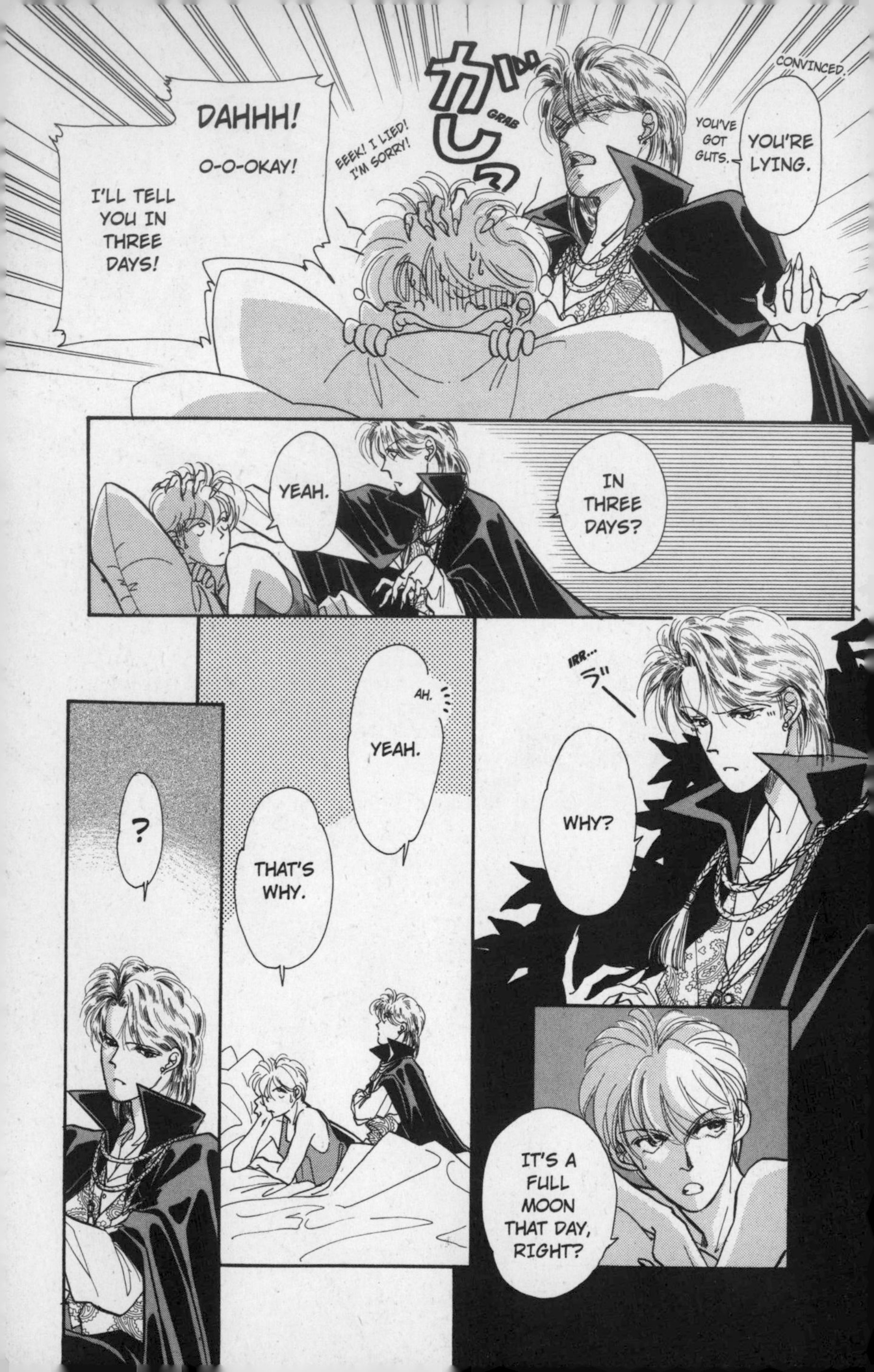

CONVINCED.
YOU'RE LYING.
YOU'VE GOT GUTS.
GRAB
EEEK! I LIED! I'M SORRY!
DAHHH!
O-O-OKAY!
I'LL TELL YOU IN THREE DAYS!
IN THREE DAYS?
YEAH.
IRR...
WHY?
IT'S A FULL MOON THAT DAY, RIGHT?
AH.
YEAH.
THAT'S WHY.
?

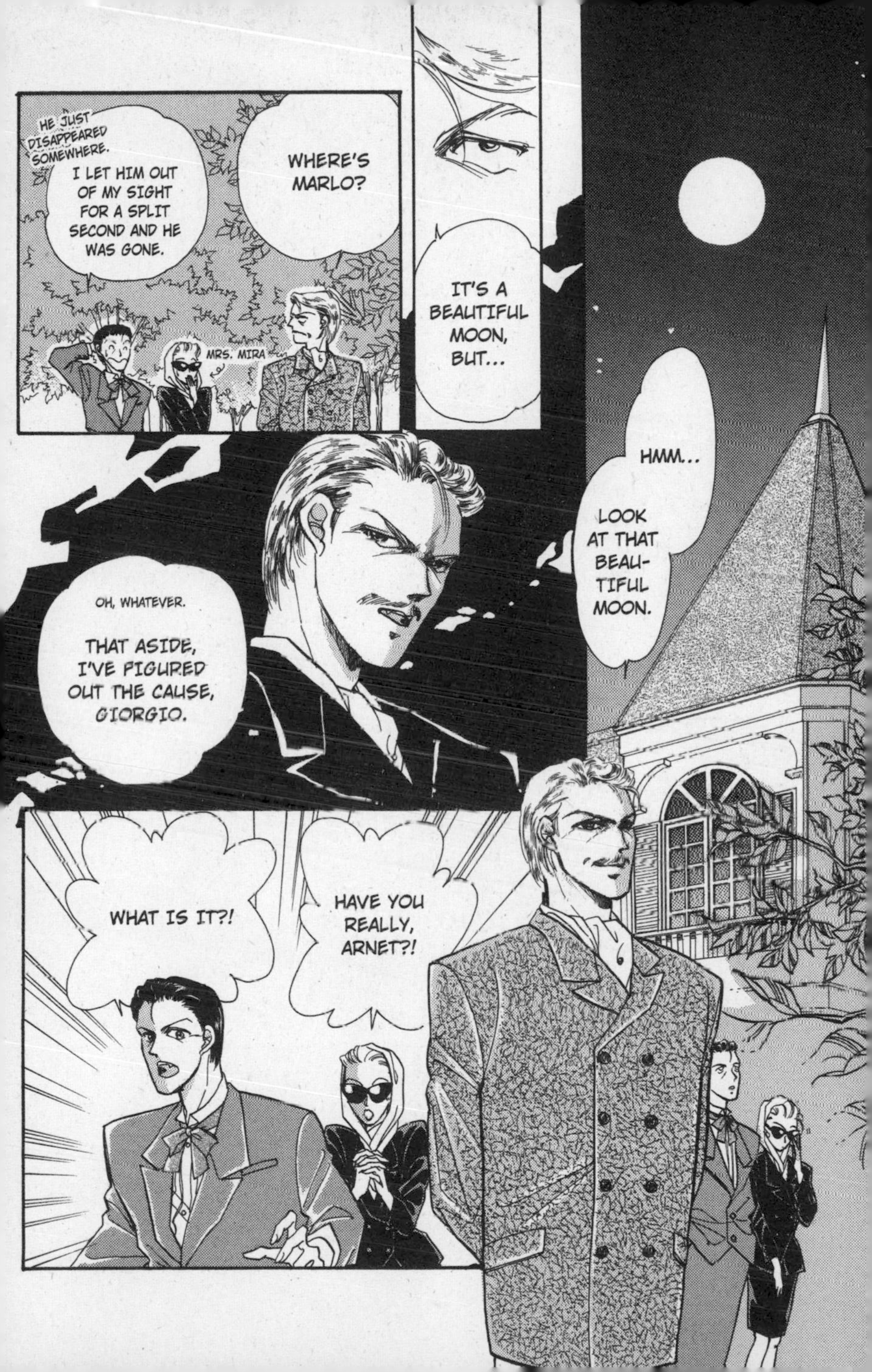
HMM...
LOOK AT THAT BEAUTIFUL MOON.
IT'S A BEAUTIFUL MOON, BUT...
WHERE'S MARLO?
I LET HIM OUT OF MY SIGHT FOR A SPLIT SECOND AND HE WAS GONE.
HE JUST DISAPPEARED SOMEWHERE.
MRS. MIRA
OH, WHATEVER.
THAT ASIDE, I'VE FIGURED OUT THE CAUSE, GIORGIO.
HAVE YOU REALLY, ARNET?!
WHAT IS IT?!

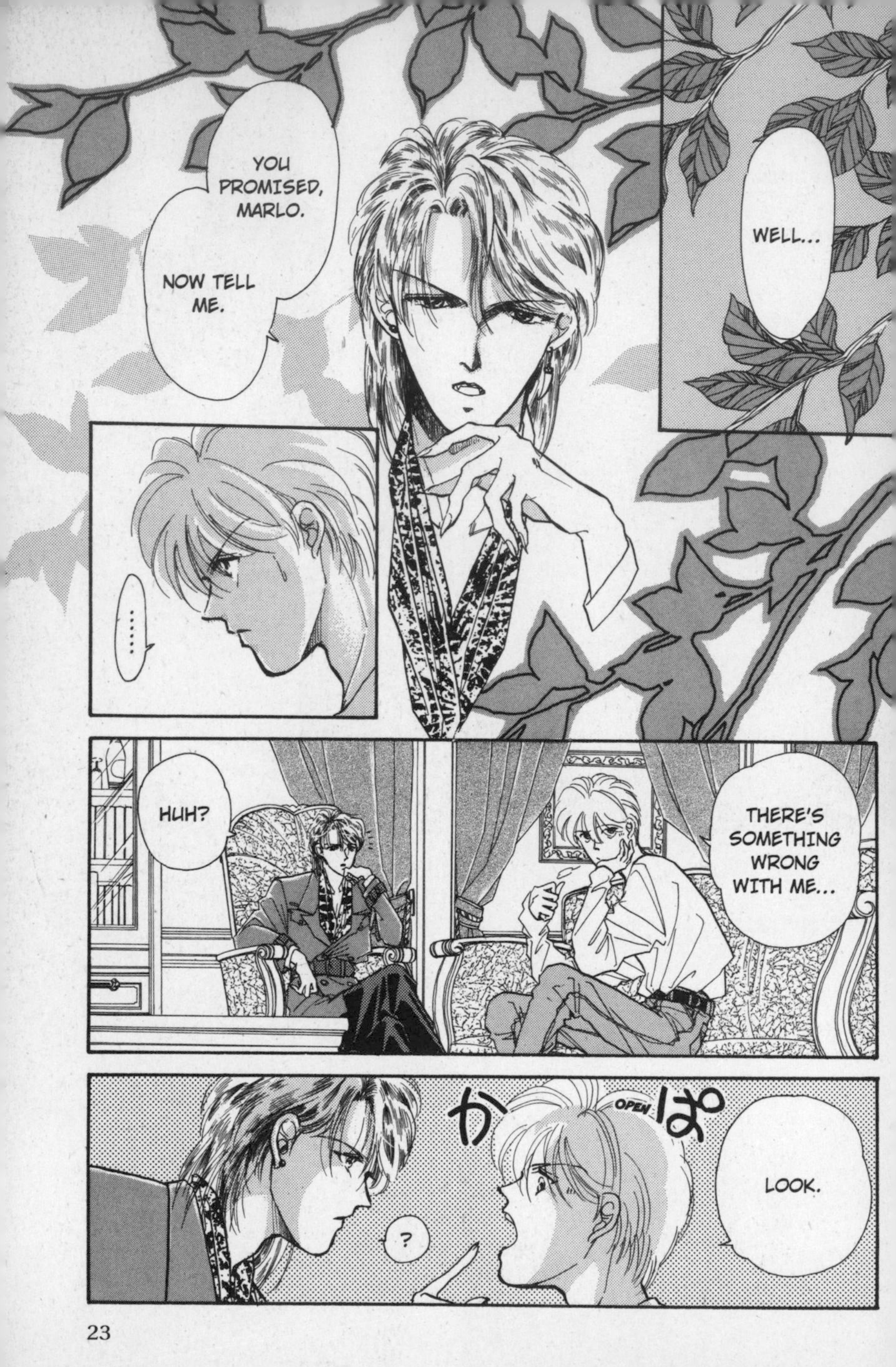
YOU PROMISED, MARLO.
NOW TELL ME.
WELL...
......
THERE'S SOMETHING WRONG WITH ME...
HUH?
LOOK.
かぱ
OPEN
?

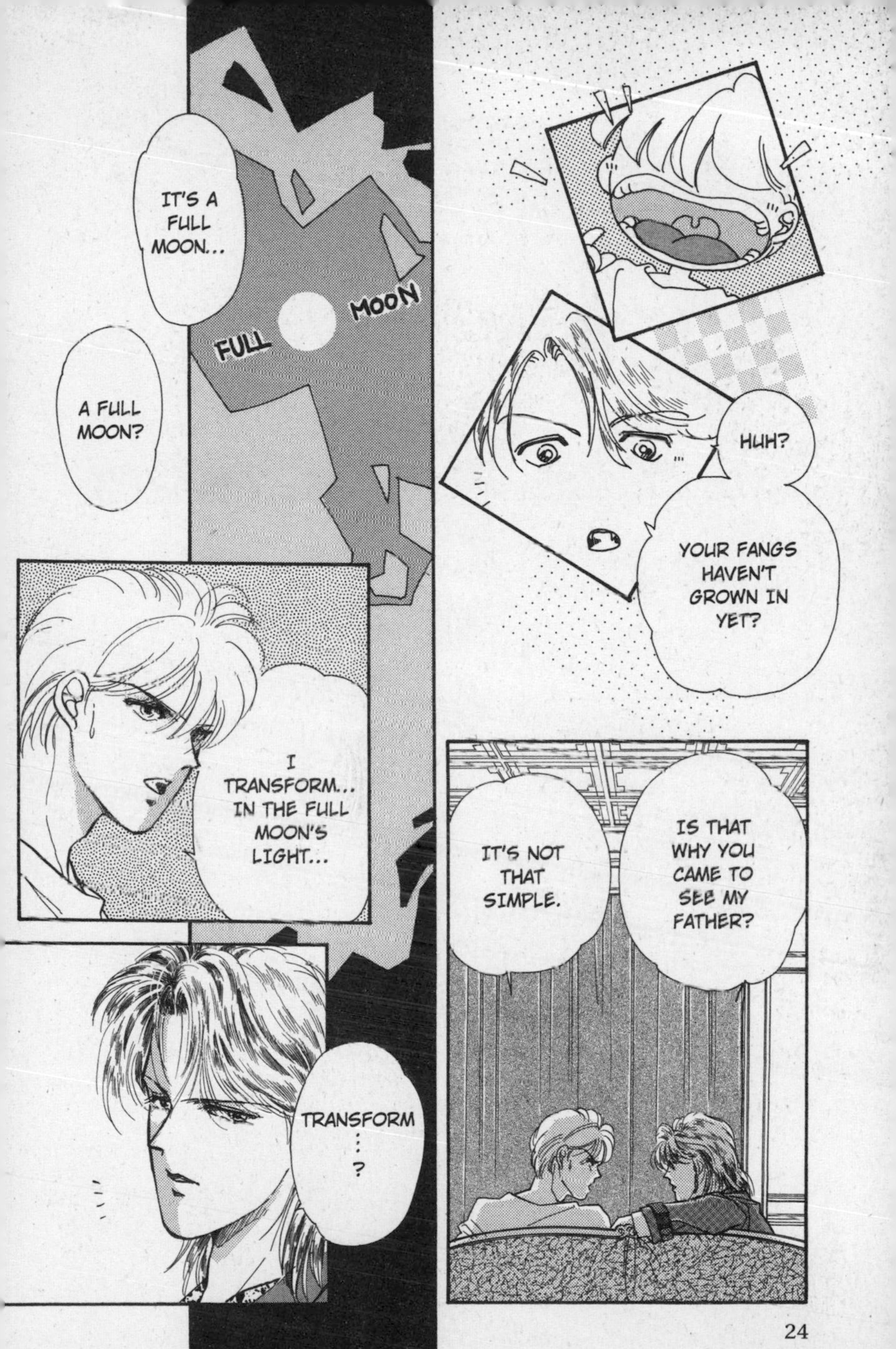

HUH?
YOUR FANGS HAVEN'T GROWN IN YET?
IS THAT WHY YOU CAME TO SEE MY FATHER?
IT'S NOT THAT SIMPLE.
IT'S A FULL MOON...
A FULL MOON?
FULL MOON
I TRANSFORM... IN THE FULL MOON'S LIGHT...
TRANSFORM ...?

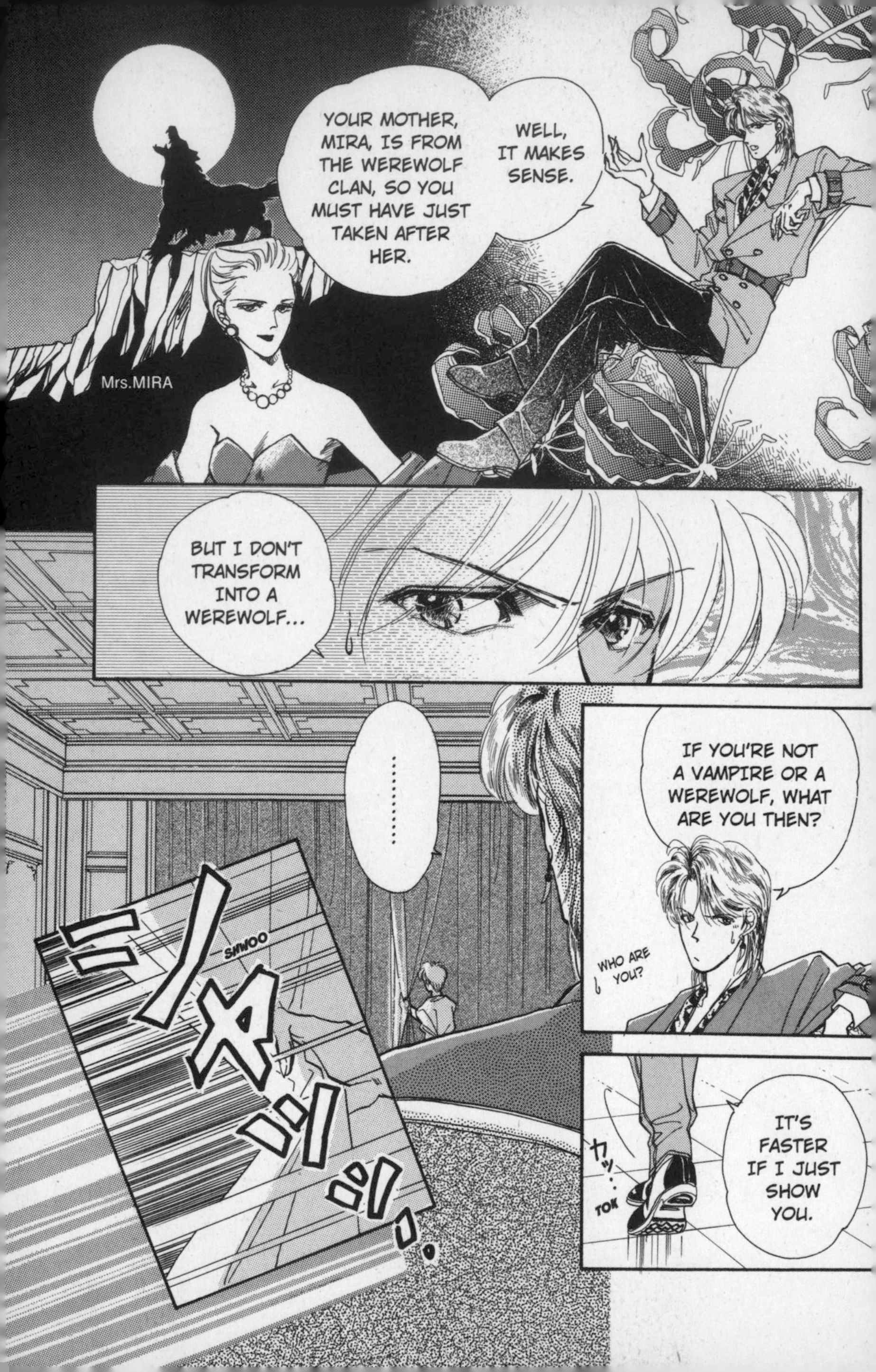
WELL, IT MAKES SENSE.
YOUR MOTHER, MIRA, IS FROM THE WEREWOLF CLAN, SO YOU MUST HAVE JUST TAKEN AFTER HER.
Mrs.MIRA
BUT I DON'T TRANSFORM INTO A WEREWOLF...
IF YOU'RE NOT A VAMPIRE OR A WEREWOLF, WHAT ARE YOU THEN?
WHO ARE YOU?
IT'S FASTER IF I JUST SHOW YOU.
TOK
......
SHWOO

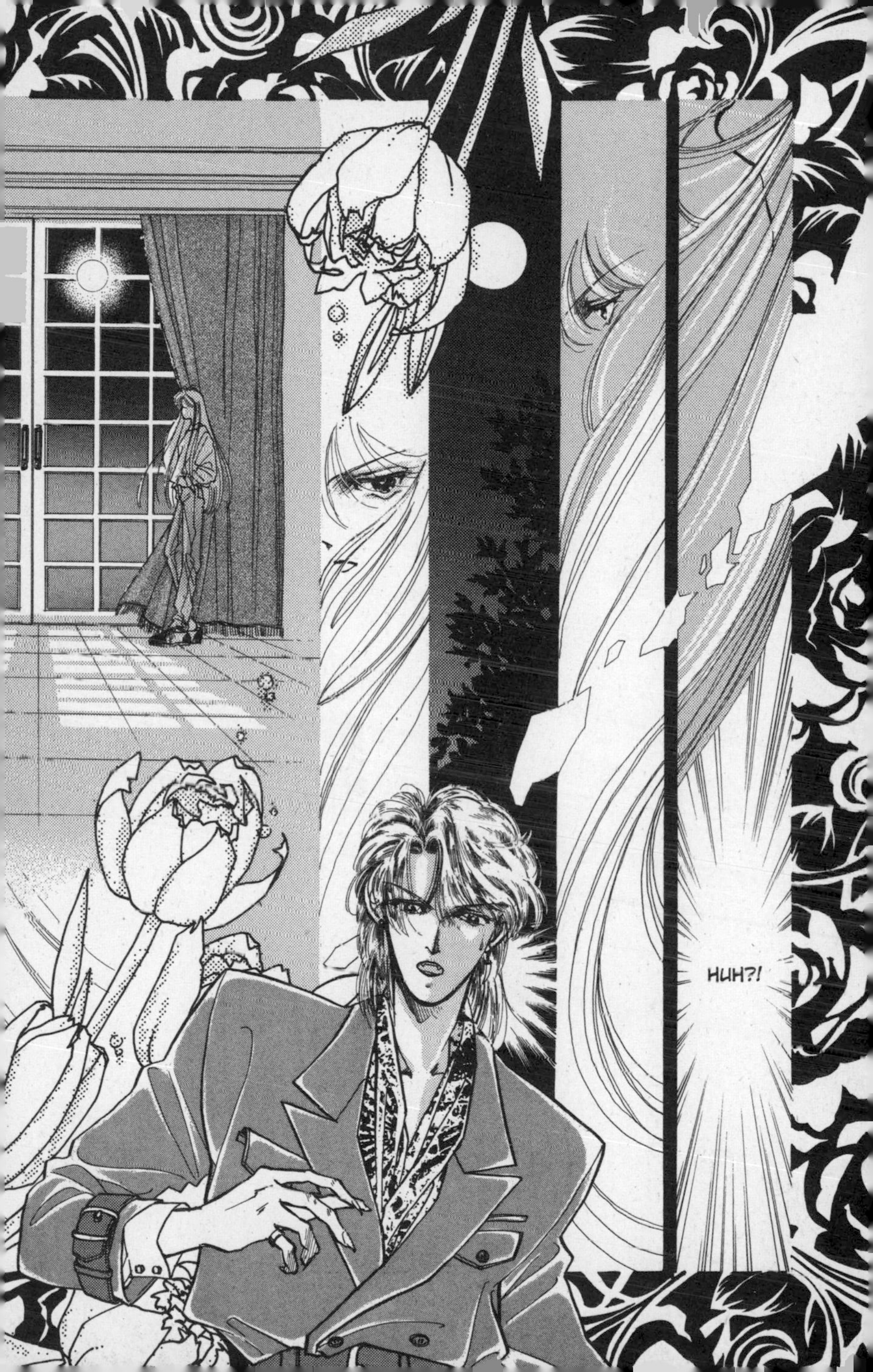
HUH?!

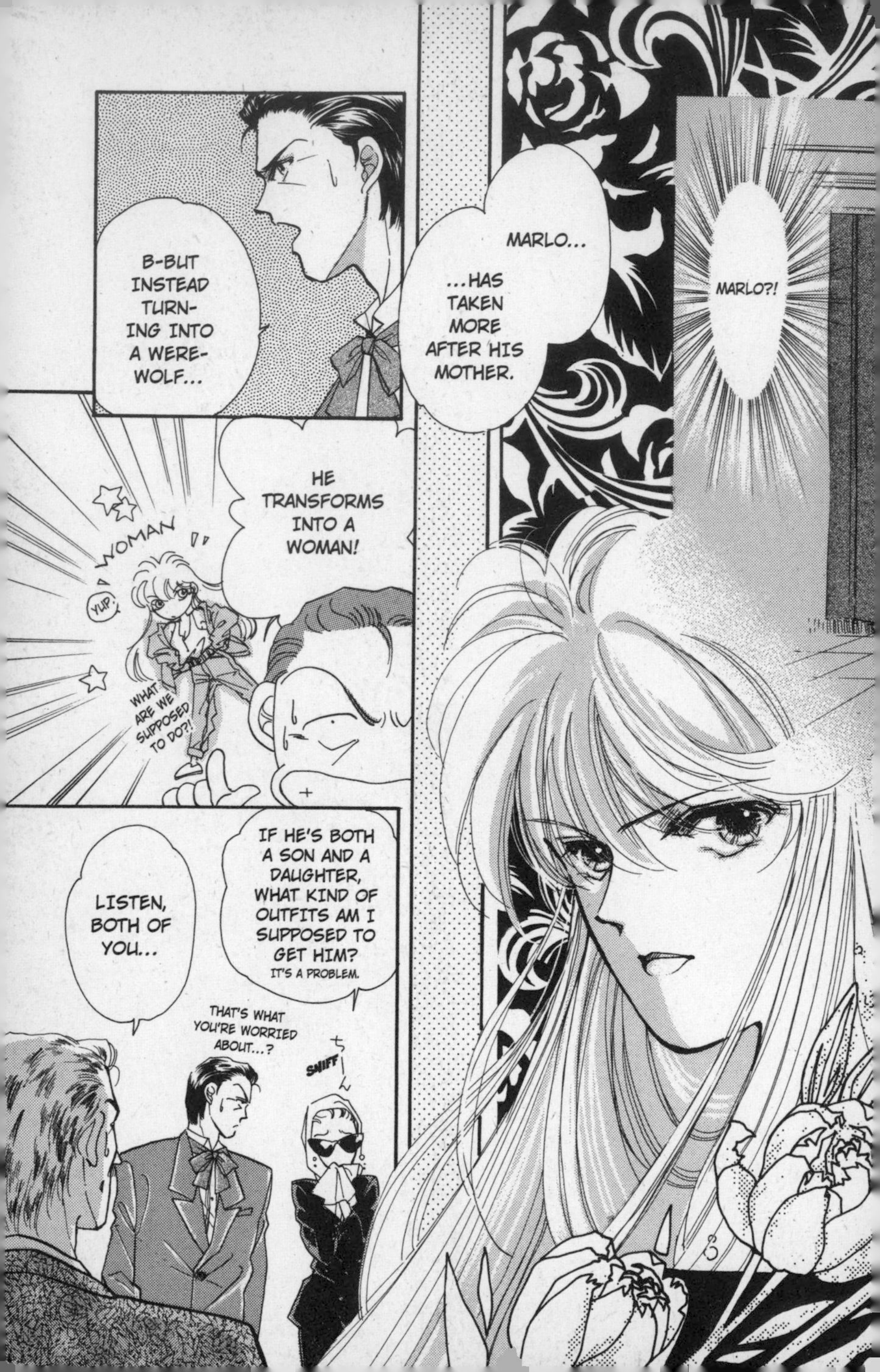
B-BUT INSTEAD TURNING INTO A WEREWOLF...
HE TRANSFORMS INTO A WOMAN!
WOMAN
YUP.
WHAT ARE WE SUPPOSED TO DO?!
LISTEN, BOTH OF YOU...
IF HE'S BOTH A SON AND A DAUGHTER, WHAT KIND OF OUTFITS AM I SUPPOSED TO GET HIM?
IT'S A PROBLEM.
THAT'S WHAT YOU'RE WORRIED ABOUT...?
SNIFF
MARLO...
...HAS TAKEN MORE AFTER HIS MOTHER.
MARLO?!

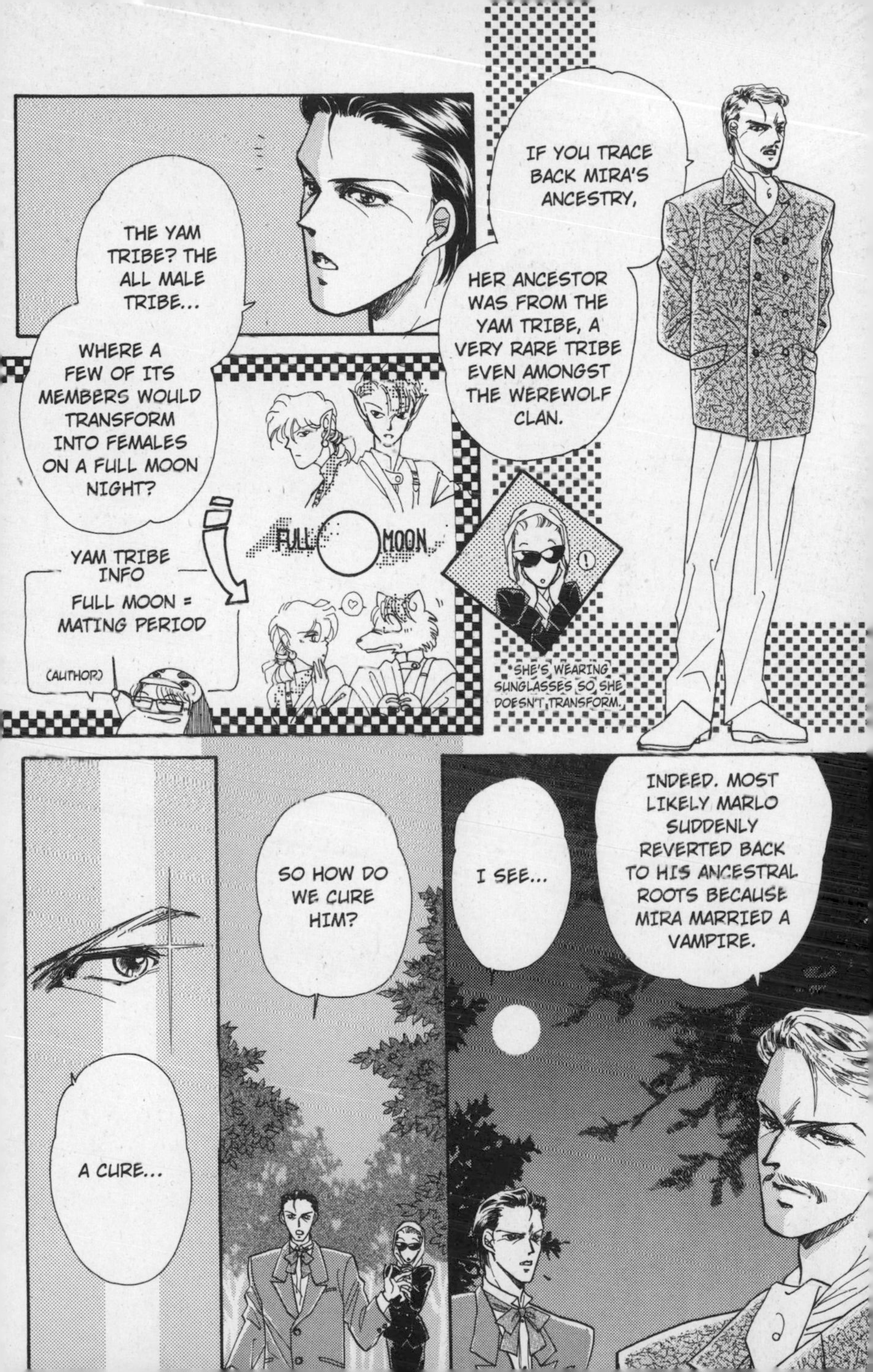
IF YOU TRACE BACK MIRA'S ANCESTRY,
HER ANCESTOR WAS FROM THE YAM TRIBE, A VERY RARE TRIBE EVEN AMONGST THE WEREWOLF CLAN.
!
*SHE'S WEARING SUNGLASSES SO SHE DOESN'T TRANSFORM.
THE YAM TRIBE? THE ALL MALE TRIBE...
WHERE A FEW OF ITS MEMBERS WOULD TRANSFORM INTO FEMALES ON A FULL MOON NIGHT?
FULL MOON
YAM TRIBE INFO
FULL MOON = MATING PERIOD
(AUTHOR)
INDEED. MOST LIKELY MARLO SUDDENLY REVERTED BACK TO HIS ANCESTRAL ROOTS BECAUSE MIRA MARRIED A VAMPIRE.
I SEE...
SO HOW DO WE CURE HIM?
A CURE...

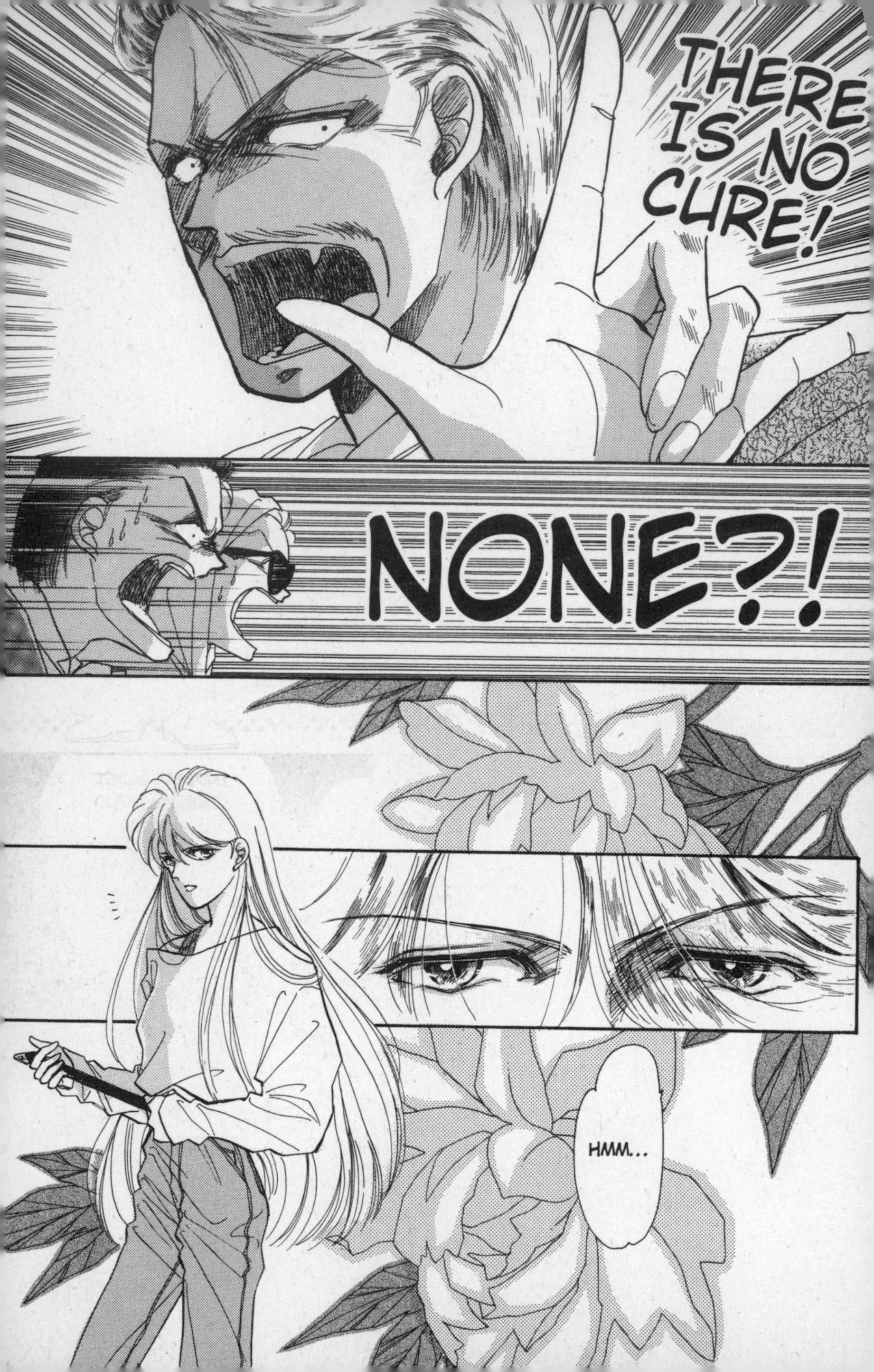
THERE IS NO CURE!
NONE?!
HMM...

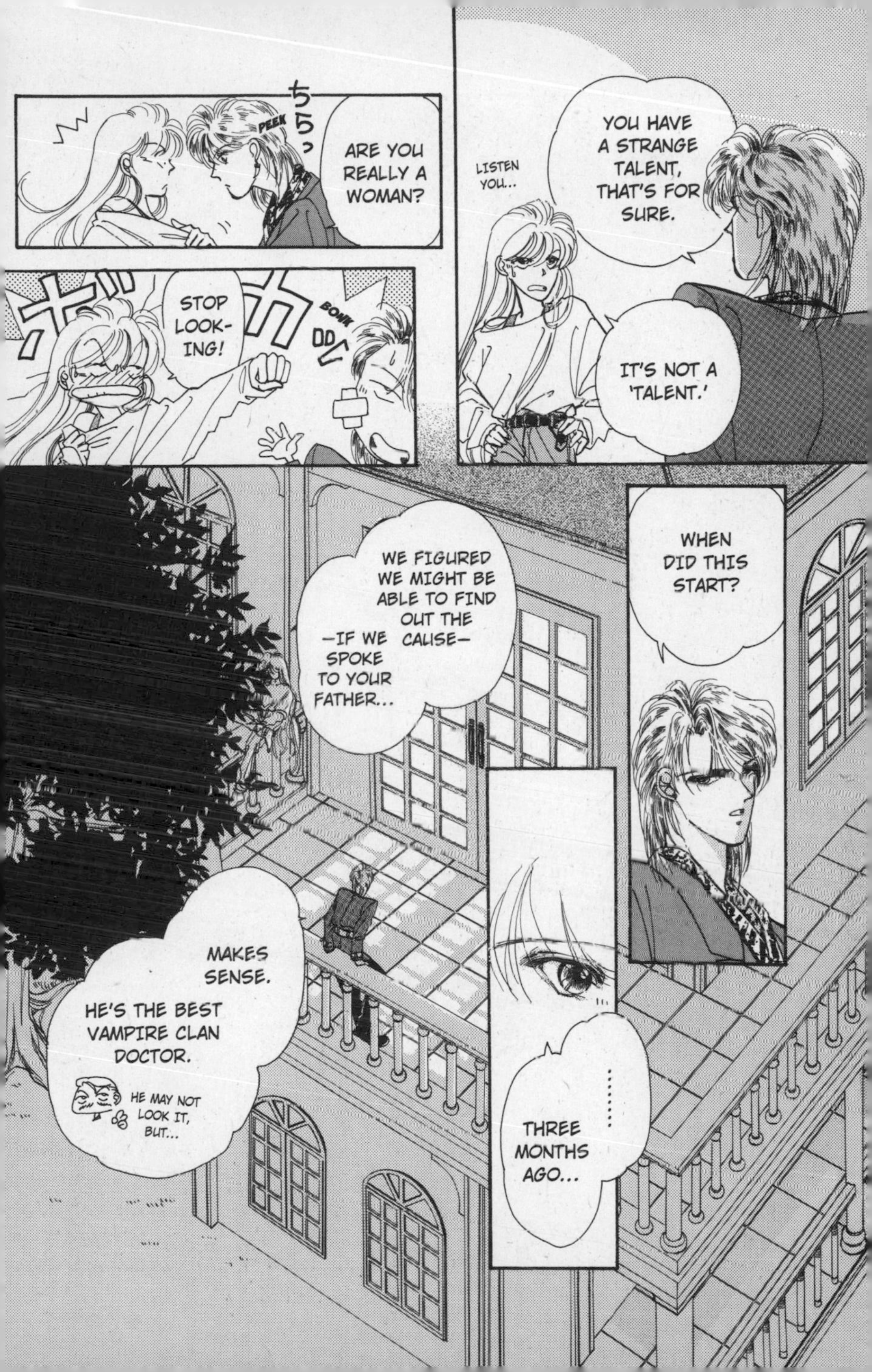
YOU HAVE A STRANGE TALENT, THAT'S FOR SURE.
LISTEN YOU...
IT'S NOT A 'TALENT.'
ちらっ
PEEK
ARE YOU REALLY A WOMAN?
BONK
STOP LOOKING!
WHEN DID THIS START?
......
THREE MONTHS AGO...
WE FIGURED WE MIGHT BE ABLE TO FIND OUT THE CAUSE—IF WE SPOKE TO YOUR FATHER...
MAKES SENSE.
HE'S THE BEST VAMPIRE CLAN DOCTOR.
HE MAY NOT LOOK IT, BUT...

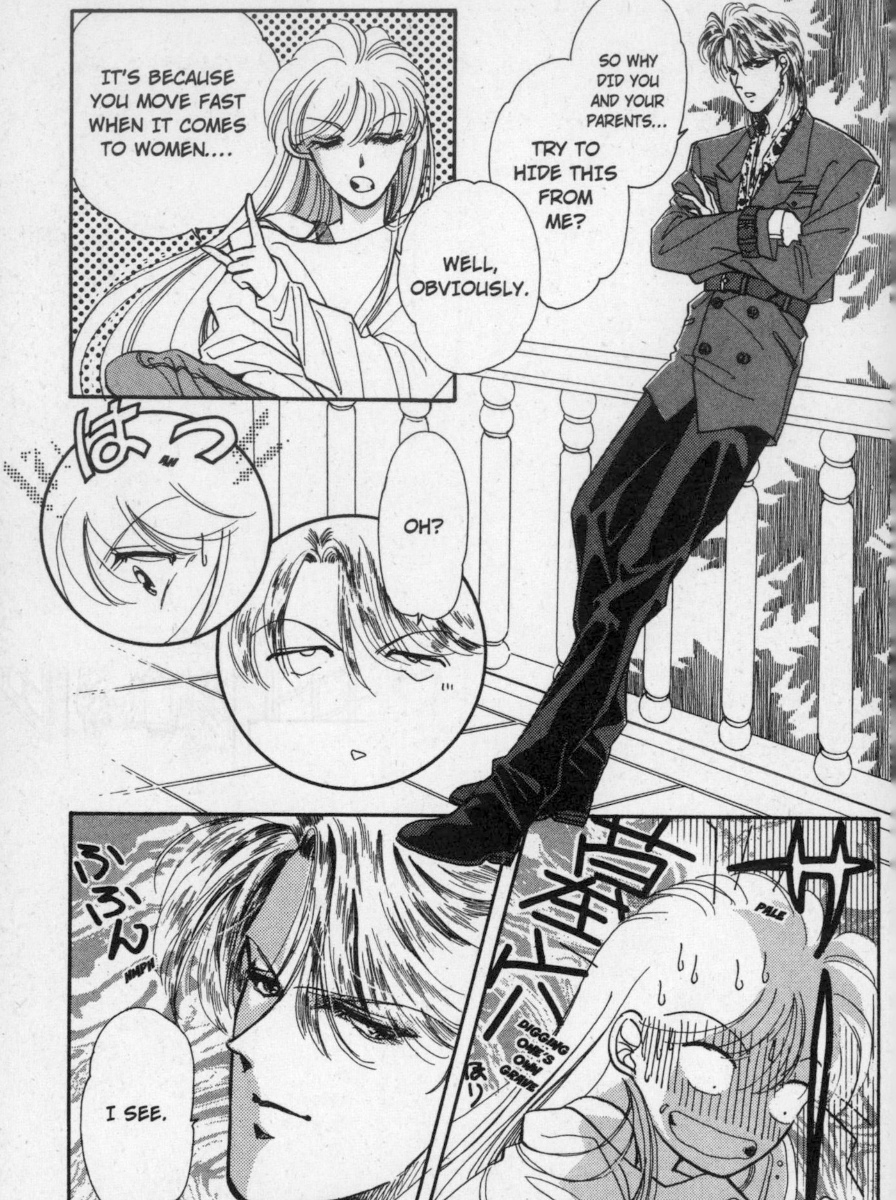

SO WHY DID YOU AND YOUR PARENTS...
TRY TO HIDE THIS FROM ME?
WELL, OBVIOUSLY.
IT'S BECAUSE YOU MOVE FAST WHEN IT COMES TO WOMEN....
OH?
はっ
AH
PALE
DIGGING ONE'S OWN GRAVE
ほり
ふふん
HMPH
I SEE.

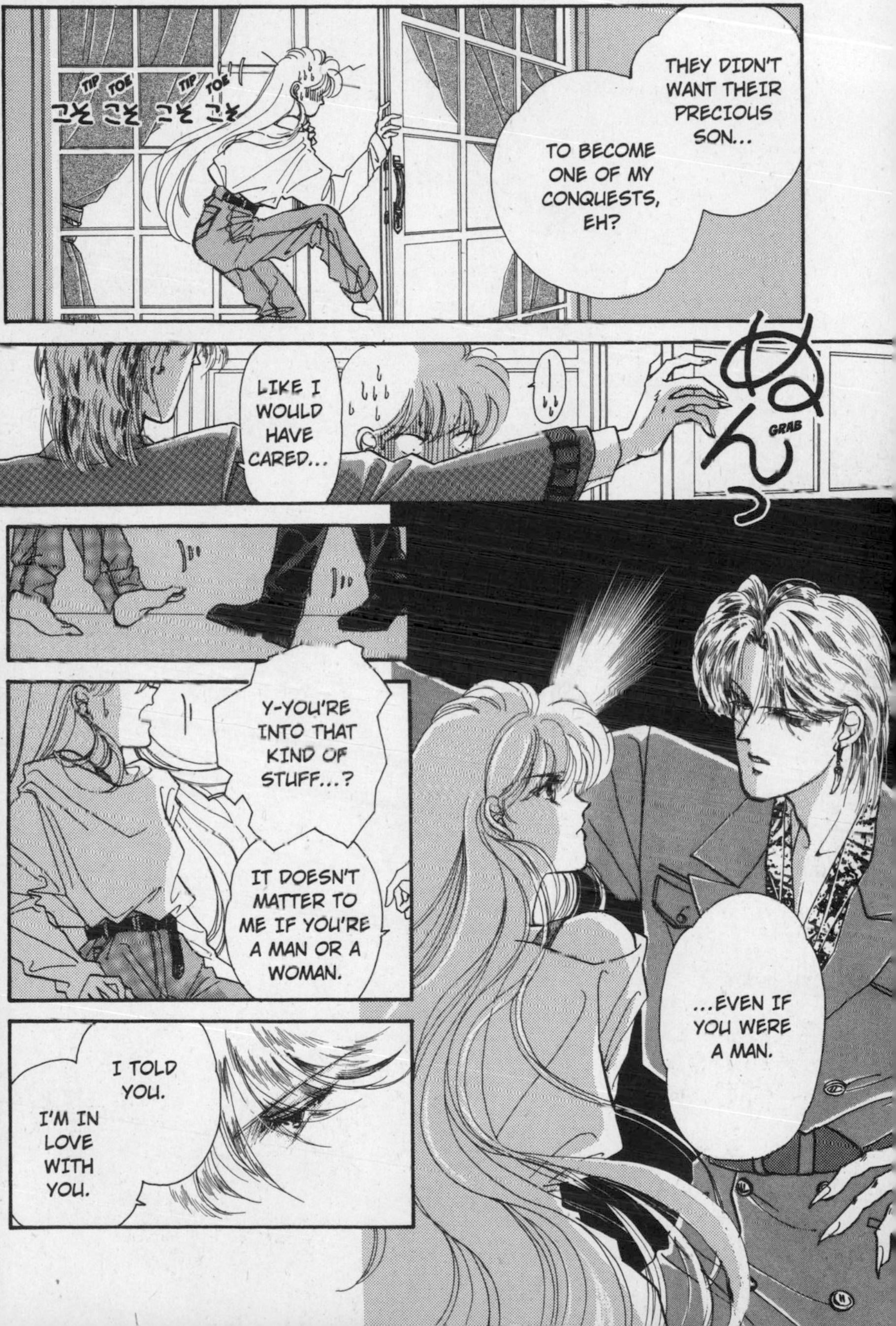
THEY DIDN'T WANT THEIR PRECIOUS SON...
TO BECOME ONE OF MY CONQUESTS, EH?
TIP TOE TIP TOE
こそこそこそこそ
ぬんっ
GRAB
!
LIKE I WOULD HAVE CARED...
...EVEN IF YOU WERE A MAN.
Y-YOU'RE INTO THAT KIND OF STUFF...?
IT DOESN'T MATTER TO ME IF YOU'RE A MAN OR A WOMAN.
I TOLD YOU.
I'M IN LOVE WITH YOU.

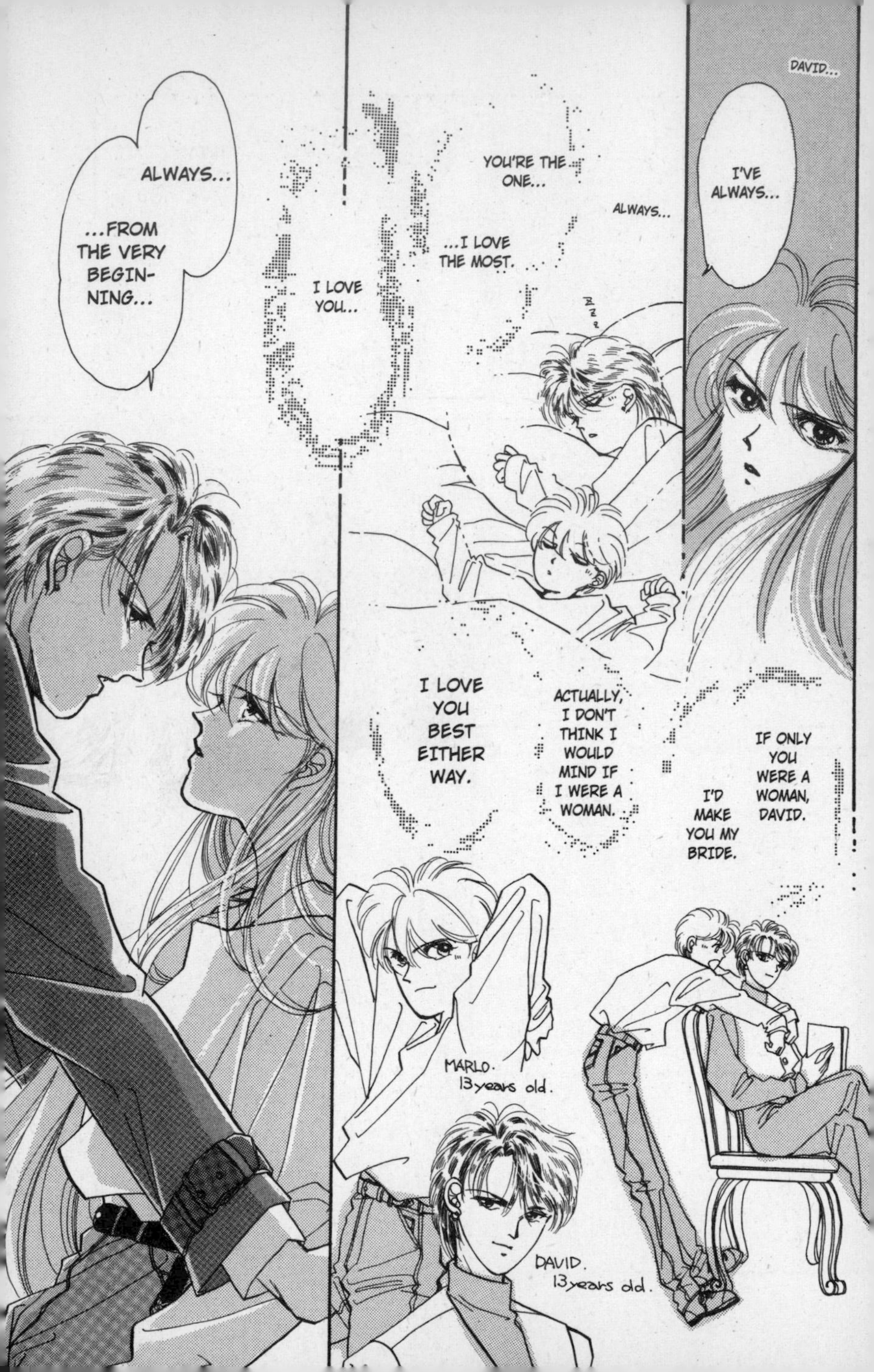
DAVID...
I'VE ALWAYS...
ALWAYS...
YOU'RE THE ONE...
...I LOVE THE MOST.
I LOVE YOU...
IF ONLY YOU WERE A WOMAN, DAVID.
I'D MAKE YOU MY BRIDE.
ACTUALLY, I DON'T THINK I WOULD MIND IF I WERE A WOMAN.
I LOVE YOU BEST EITHER WAY.
MARLO. 13 years old.
DAVID. 13 years old.
ALWAYS...
...FROM THE VERY BEGIN-NING...

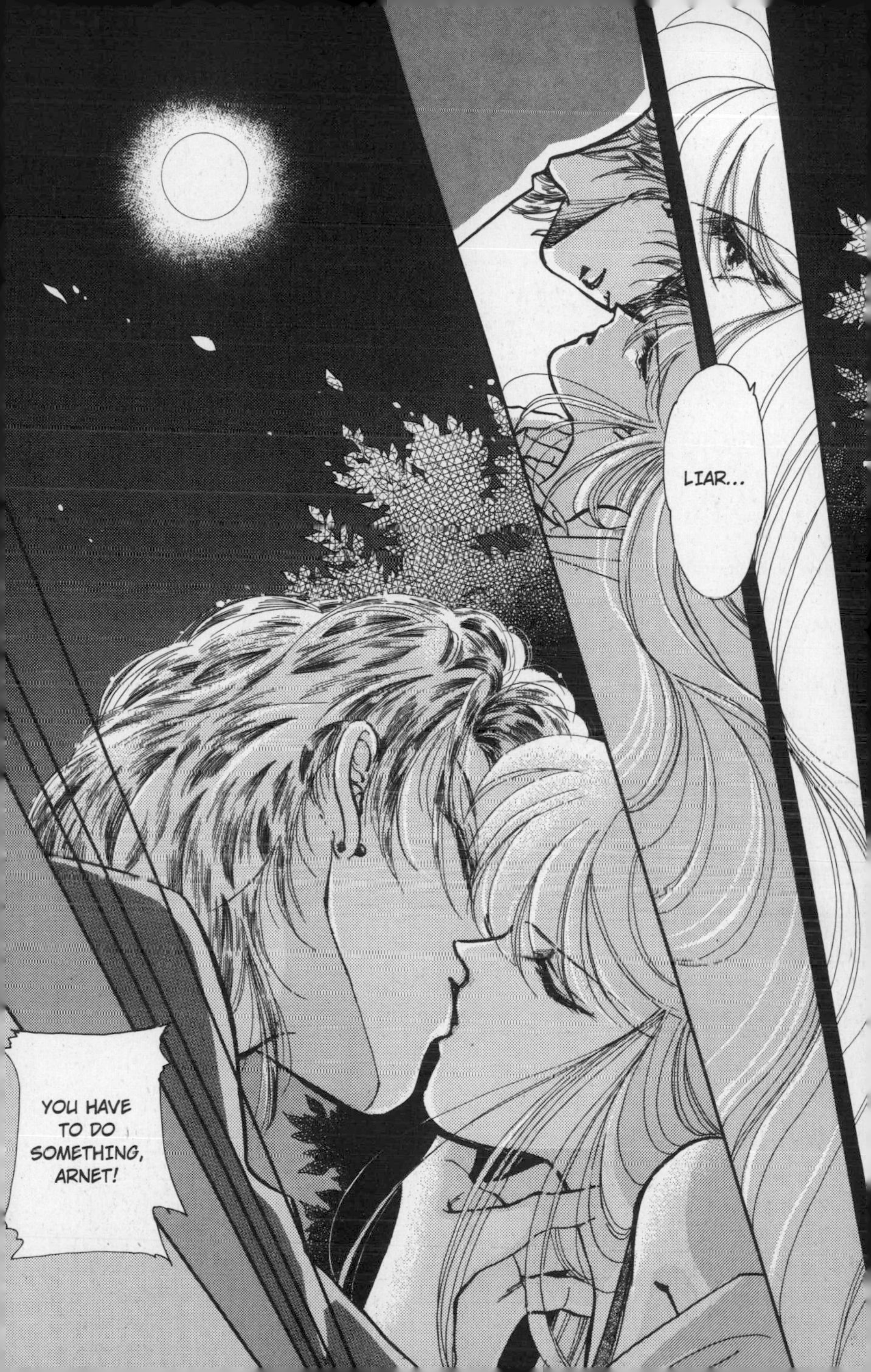
LIAR...
YOU HAVE TO DO SOMETHING, ARNET!

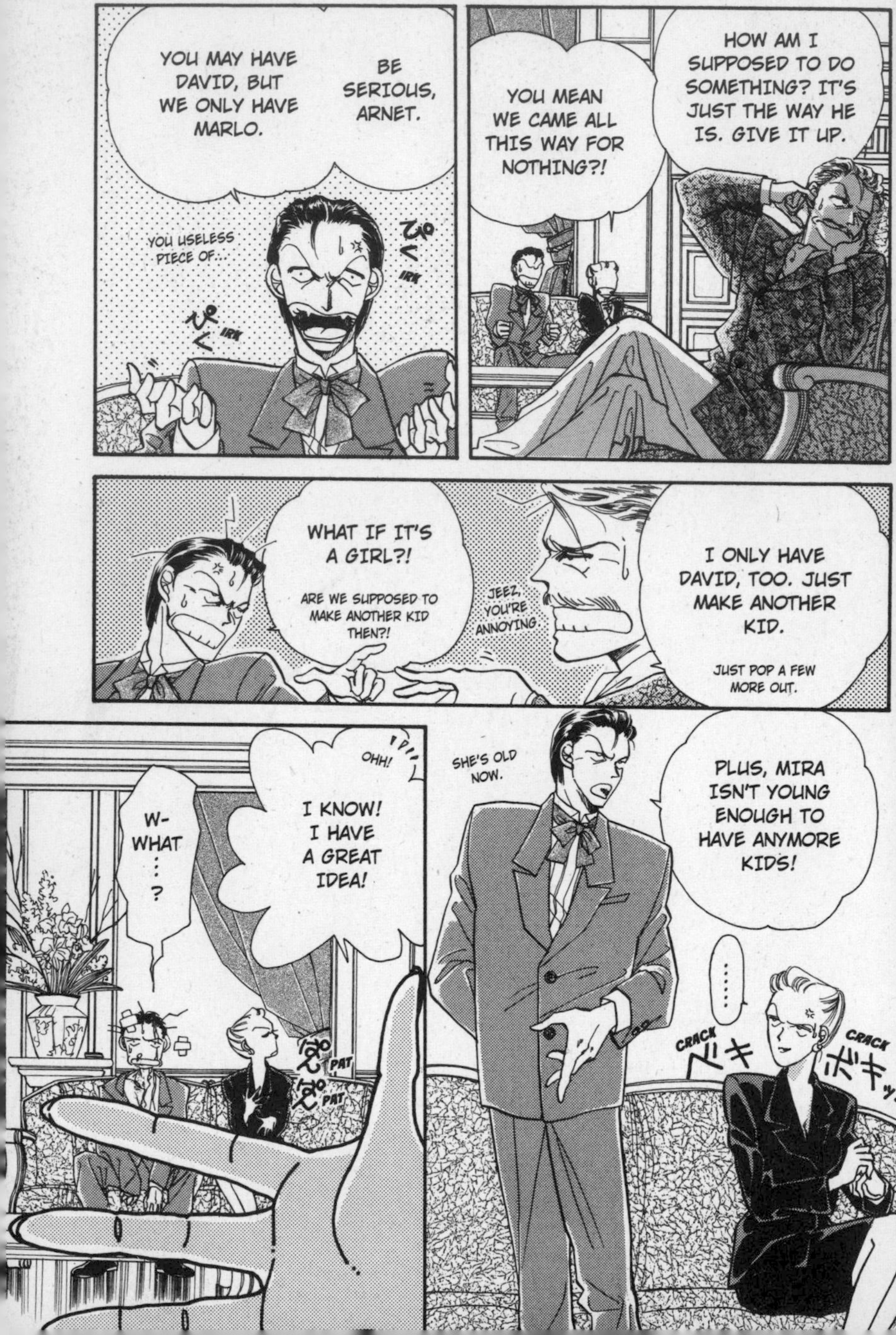
HOW AM I SUPPOSED TO DO SOMETHING? IT'S JUST THE WAY HE IS. GIVE IT UP.
YOU MEAN WE CAME ALL THIS WAY FOR NOTHING?!
BE SERIOUS, ARNET.
YOU MAY HAVE DAVID, BUT WE ONLY HAVE MARLO.
IRK
IRK
YOU USELESS PIECE OF...
I ONLY HAVE DAVID, TOO. JUST MAKE ANOTHER KID.
JUST POP A FEW MORE OUT.
JEEZ, YOU'RE ANNOYING.
WHAT IF IT'S A GIRL?!
ARE WE SUPPOSED TO MAKE ANOTHER KID THEN?!
PLUS, MIRA ISN'T YOUNG ENOUGH TO HAVE ANYMORE KIDS!
SHE'S OLD NOW.
......
CRACK
CRACK
OHH!
I KNOW! I HAVE A GREAT IDEA!
PAT
PAT
W-WHAT...?

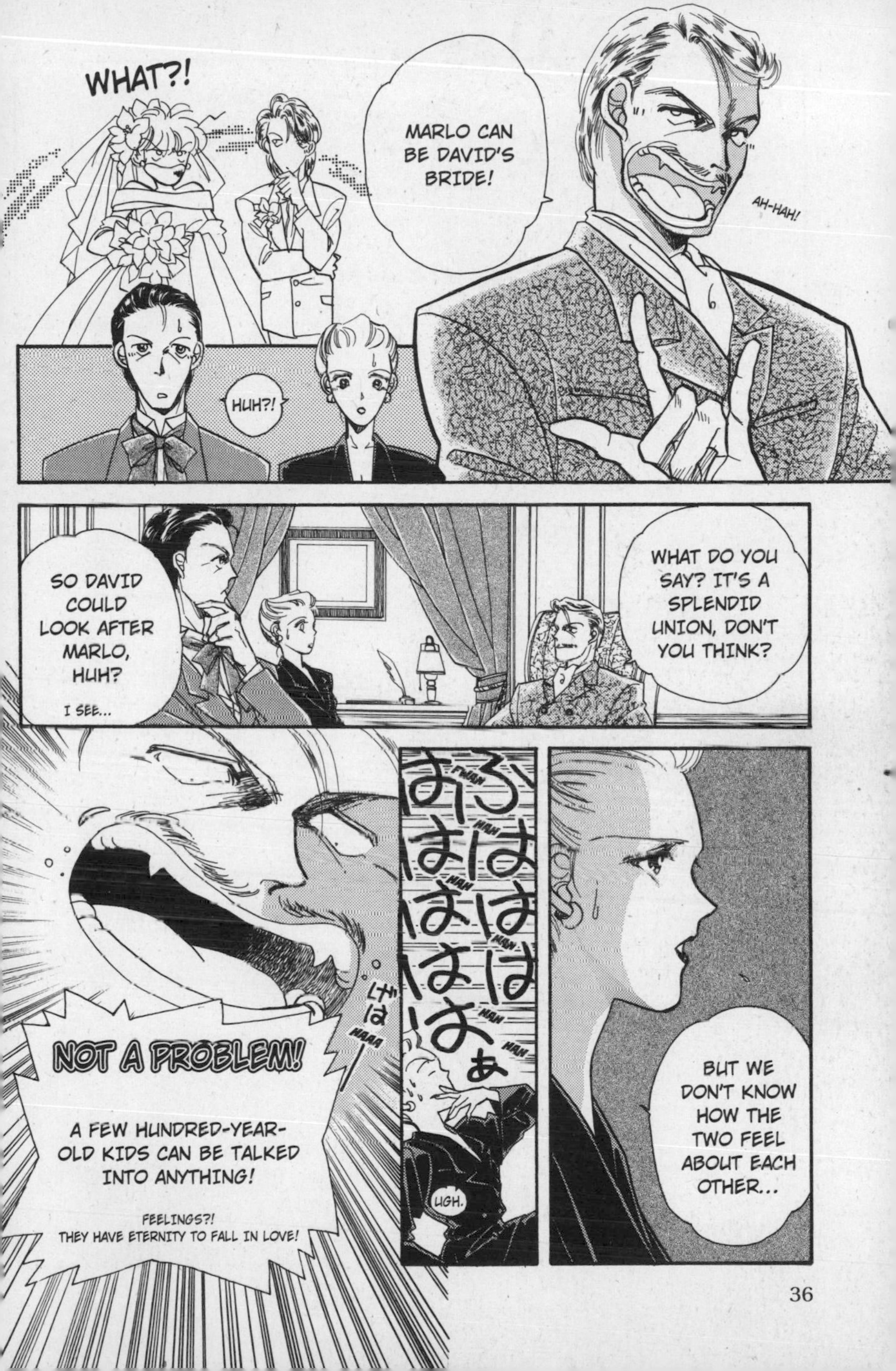
AH-HAH!
MARLO CAN BE DAVID'S BRIDE!
WHAT?!
HUH?!
WHAT DO YOU SAY? IT'S A SPLENDID UNION, DON'T YOU THINK?
SO DAVID COULD LOOK AFTER MARLO, HUH?
I SEE...
BUT WE DON'T KNOW HOW THE TWO FEEL ABOUT EACH OTHER...
ふははは
ははははぁ
FWAH HAH HAH HAH HAH HAH HAH
げは
HAAA
UGH.
NOT A PROBLEM!
A FEW HUNDRED-YEAR-OLD KIDS CAN BE TALKED INTO ANYTHING!
FEELINGS?! THEY HAVE ETERNITY TO FALL IN LOVE!

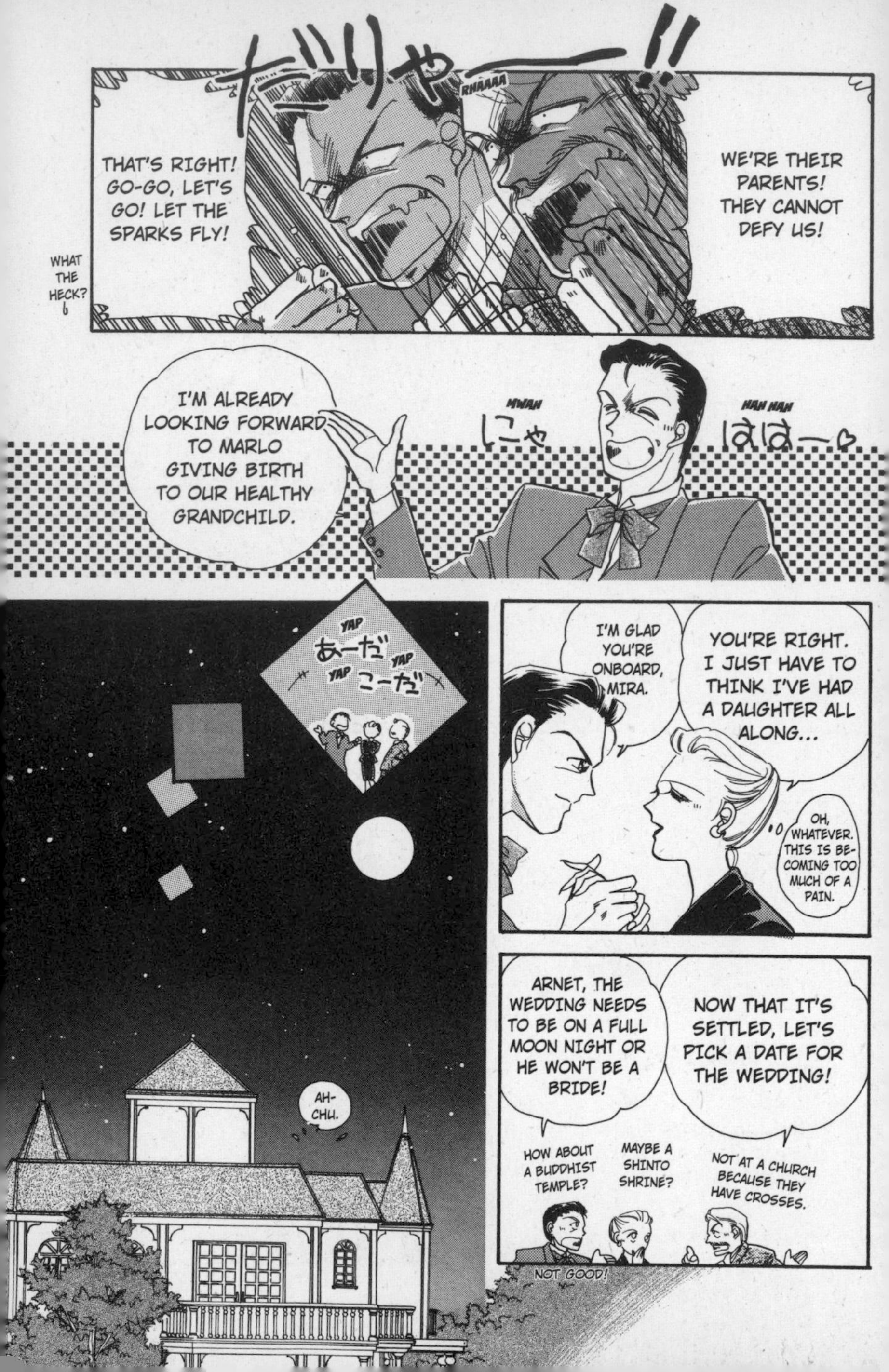
ダリャー!!
RHAAAA
WE'RE THEIR PARENTS! THEY CANNOT DEFY US!
THAT'S RIGHT! GO-GO, LET'S GO! LET THE SPARKS FLY!
WHAT THE HECK?
HAH HAH
はは—♥
MWAH
にゃ
I'M ALREADY LOOKING FORWARD TO MARLO GIVING BIRTH TO OUR HEALTHY GRANDCHILD.
YOU'RE RIGHT. I JUST HAVE TO THINK I'VE HAD A DAUGHTER ALL ALONG...
I'M GLAD YOU'RE ONBOARD, MIRA.
OH, WHATEVER. THIS IS BE-COMING TOO MUCH OF A PAIN.
NOW THAT IT'S SETTLED, LET'S PICK A DATE FOR THE WEDDING!
ARNET, THE WEDDING NEEDS TO BE ON A FULL MOON NIGHT OR HE WON'T BE A BRIDE!
NOT AT A CHURCH BECAUSE THEY HAVE CROSSES.
MAYBE A SHINTO SHRINE?
HOW ABOUT A BUDDHIST TEMPLE?
NOT GOOD!
YAP
あーだ
YAP
こーだ
YAP
AH-CHU.

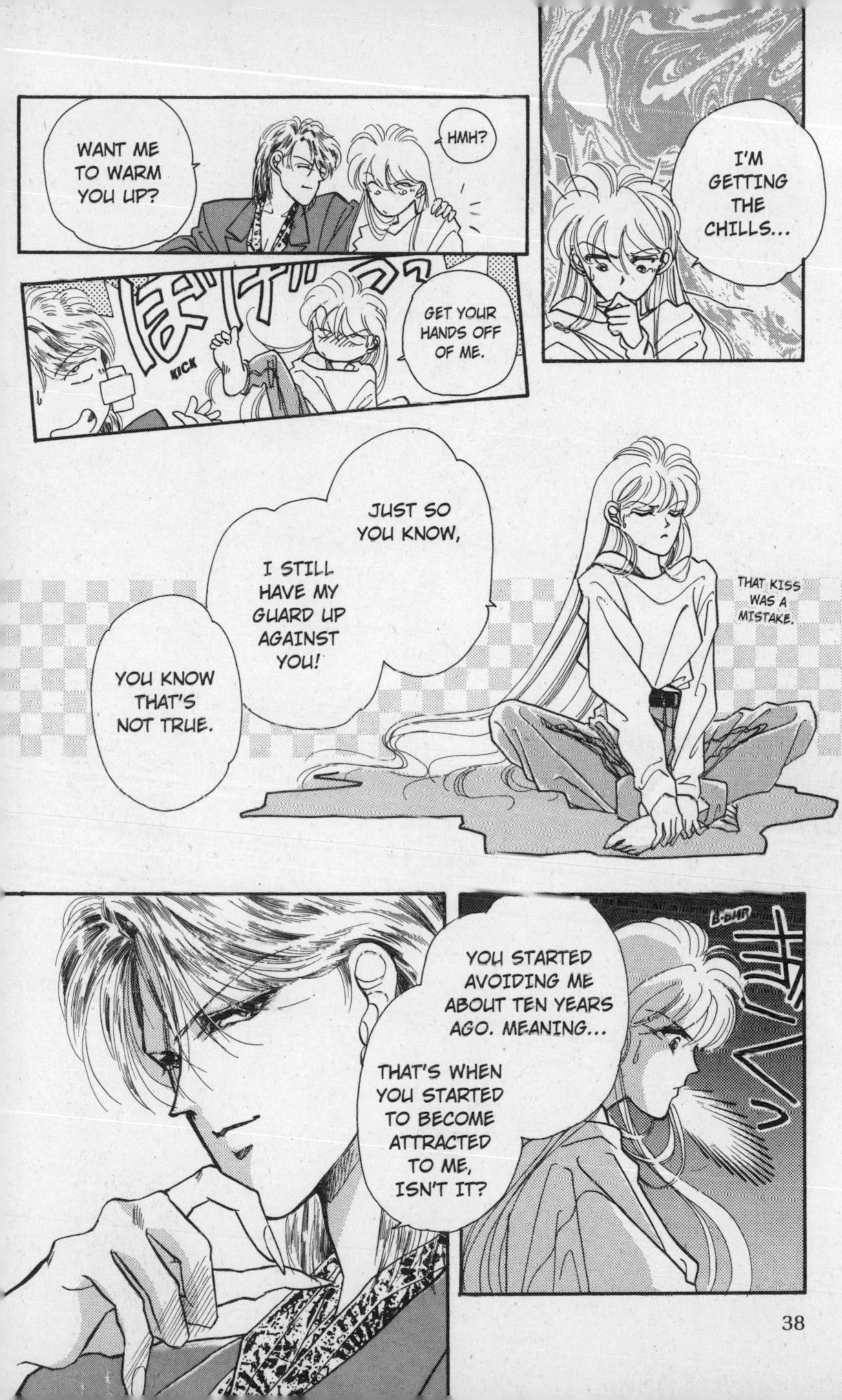
I'M GETTING THE CHILLS...
HMH?
WANT ME TO WARM YOU UP?
GET YOUR HANDS OFF OF ME.
KICK
THAT KISS WAS A MISTAKE.
JUST SO YOU KNOW, I STILL HAVE MY GUARD UP AGAINST YOU!
YOU KNOW THAT'S NOT TRUE.
B-BUMP
YOU STARTED AVOIDING ME ABOUT TEN YEARS AGO. MEANING...
THAT'S WHEN YOU STARTED TO BECOME ATTRACTED TO ME, ISN'T IT?

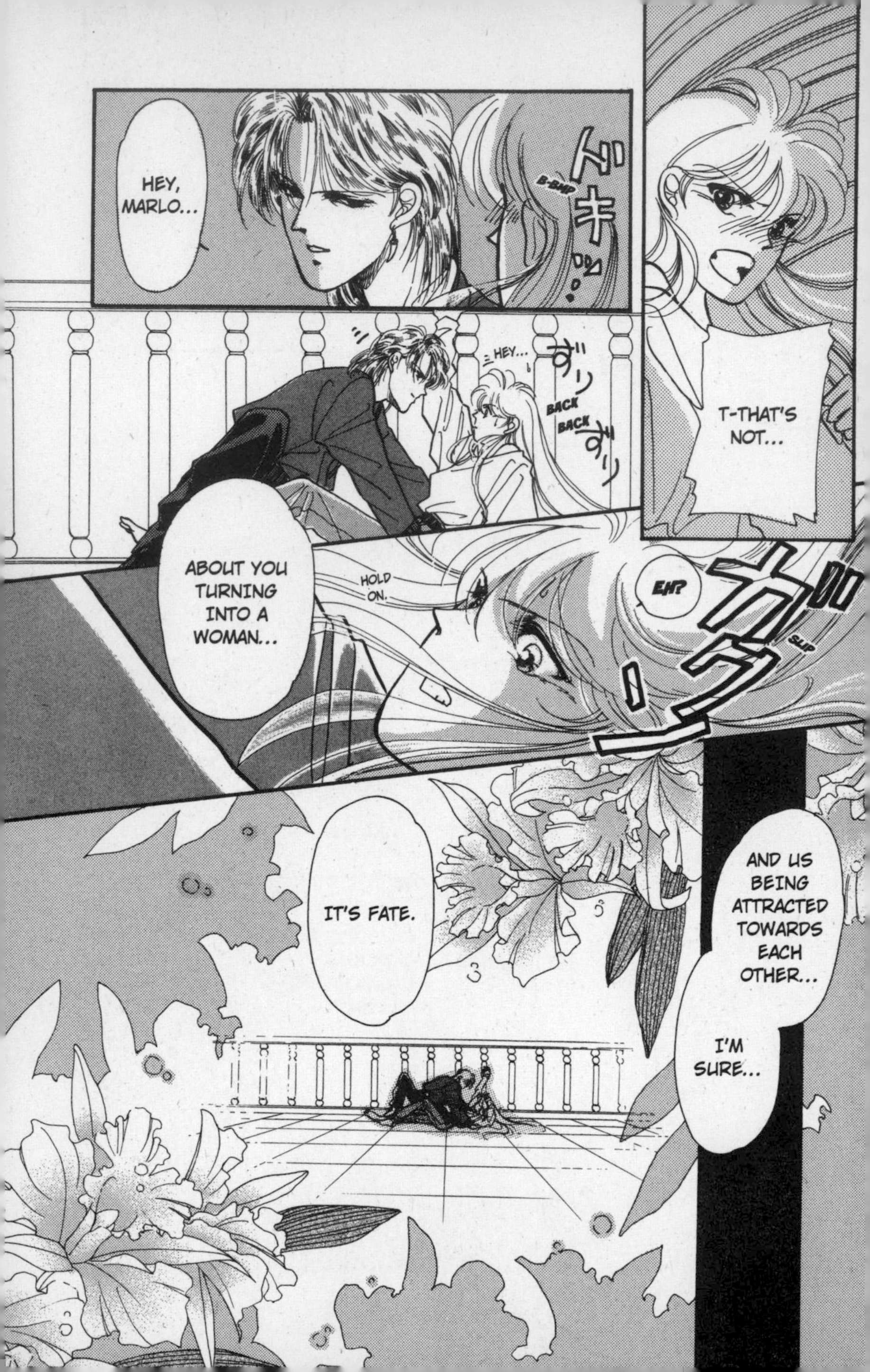
T-THAT'S NOT...
HEY, MARLO...
B-BMP
HEY...
BACK
BACK
EH?
SLIP
HOLD ON.
ABOUT YOU TURNING INTO A WOMAN...
AND US BEING ATTRACTED TOWARDS EACH OTHER...
I'M SURE...
IT'S FATE.

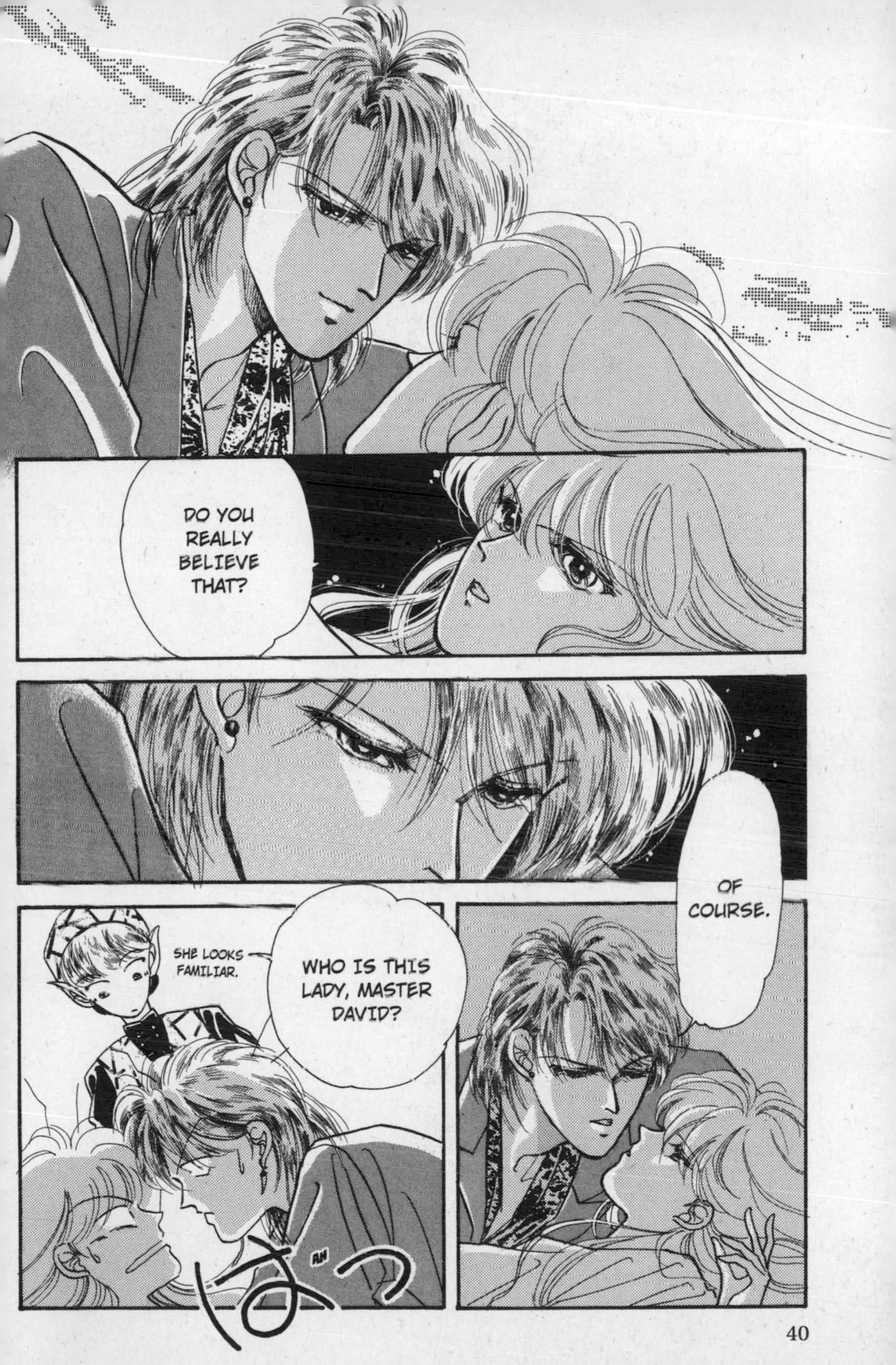
DO YOU REALLY BELIEVE THAT?
OF COURSE.
WHO IS THIS LADY, MASTER DAVID?
SHE LOOKS FAMILIAR.
AH
はっ

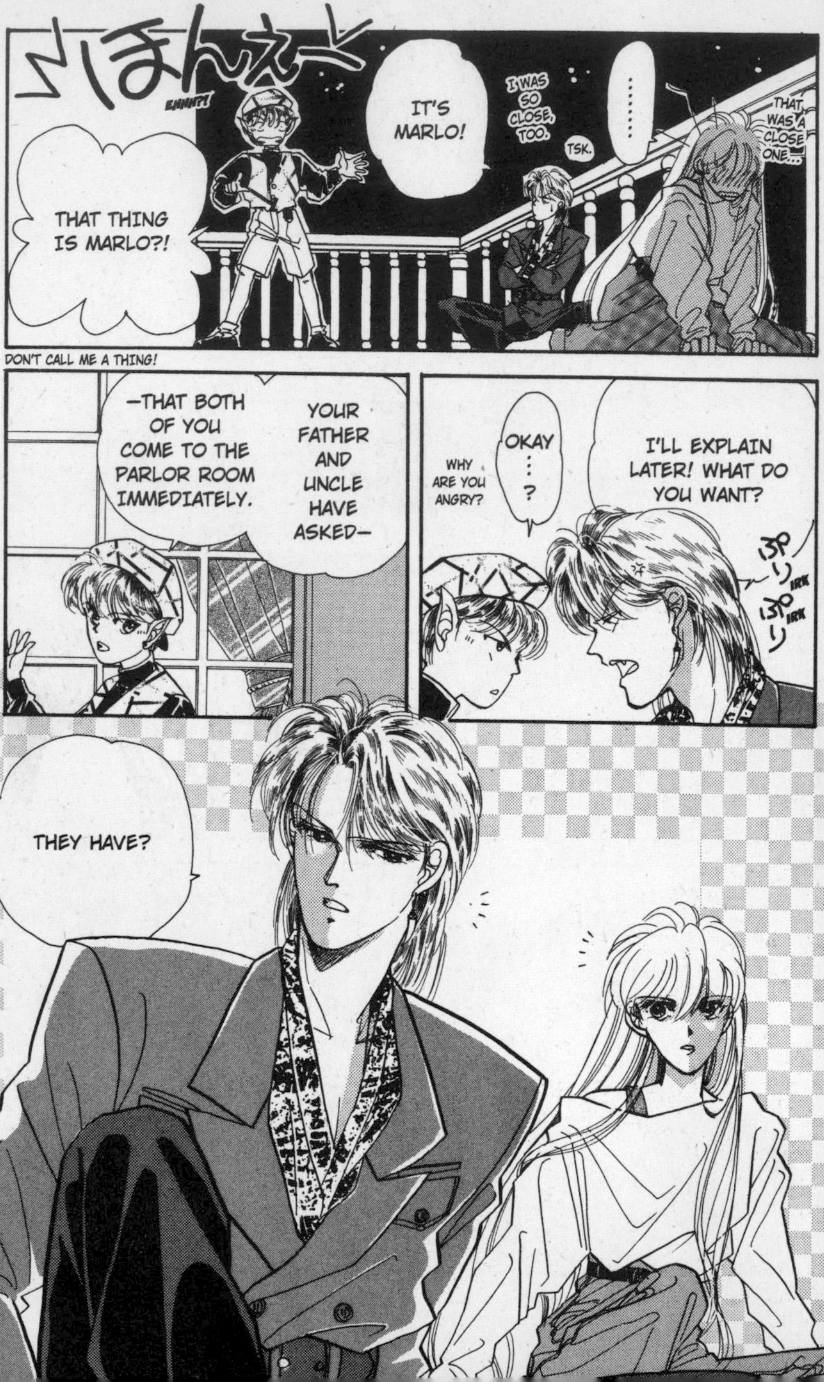
THAT WAS A CLOSE ONE...
......
I WAS SO CLOSE, TOO.
TSK.
IT'S MARLO!
EHHH?!
THAT THING IS MARLO?!
DON'T CALL ME A THING!
I'LL EXPLAIN LATER! WHAT DO YOU WANT?
IRK IRK
OKAY...?
WHY ARE YOU ANGRY?
YOUR FATHER AND UNCLE HAVE ASKED—
—THAT BOTH OF YOU COME TO THE PARLOR ROOM IMMEDIATELY.
THEY HAVE?

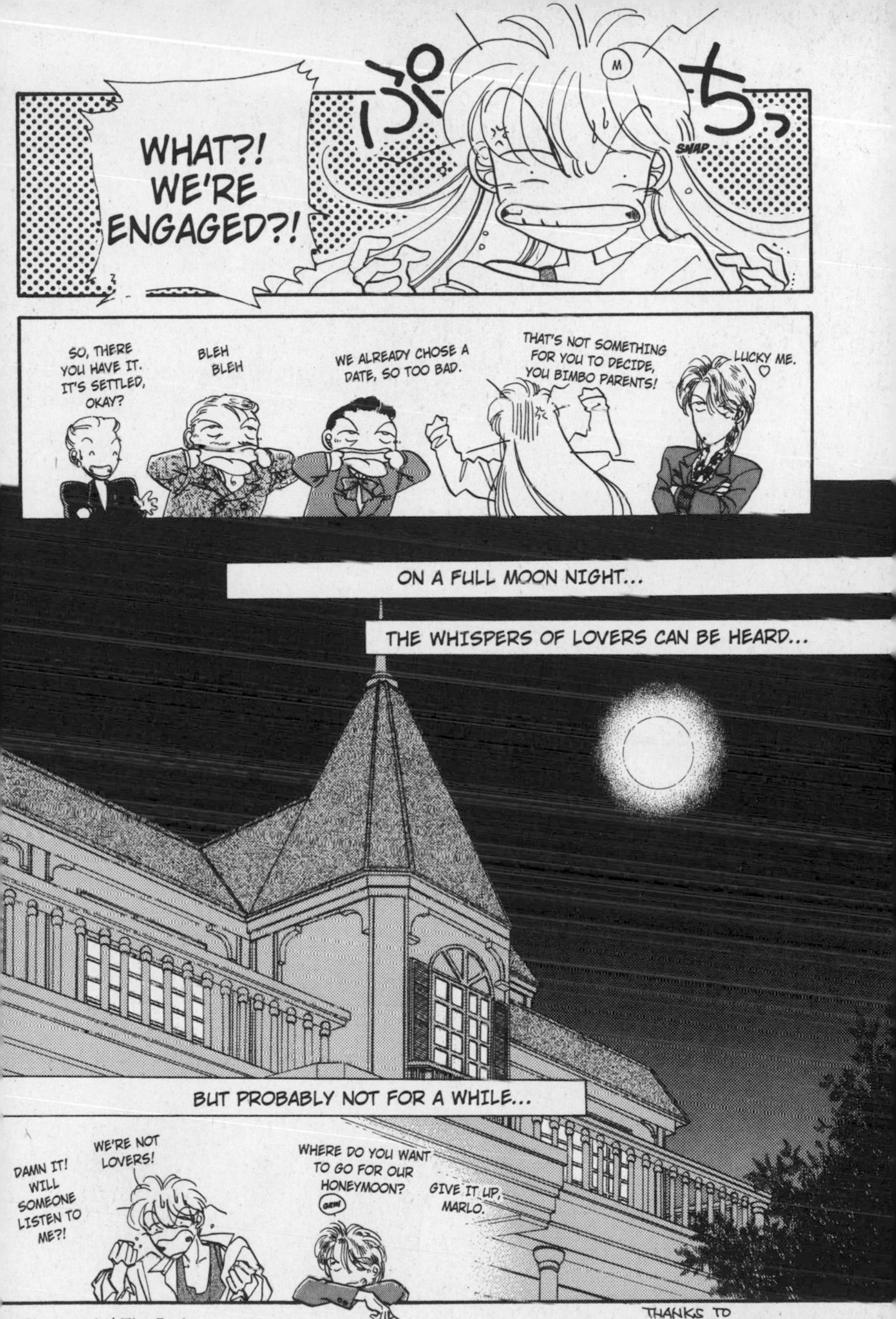
ぷーちっ
SNAP
WHAT?! WE'RE ENGAGED?!
LUCKY ME. ♡
THAT'S NOT SOMETHING FOR YOU TO DECIDE, YOU BIMBO PARENTS!
WE ALREADY CHOSE A DATE, SO TOO BAD.
BLEH BLEH
SO, THERE YOU HAVE IT. IT'S SETTLED, OKAY?
ON A FULL MOON NIGHT...
THE WHISPERS OF LOVERS CAN BE HEARD...
BUT PROBABLY NOT FOR A WHILE...
GIVE IT UP, MARLO.
WHERE DO YOU WANT TO GO FOR OUR HONEYMOON?
GRIN
WE'RE NOT LOVERS!
DAMN IT! WILL SOMEONE LISTEN TO ME?!

Chapter 1 / The End

THANKS TO MITSUKI-MAYA.

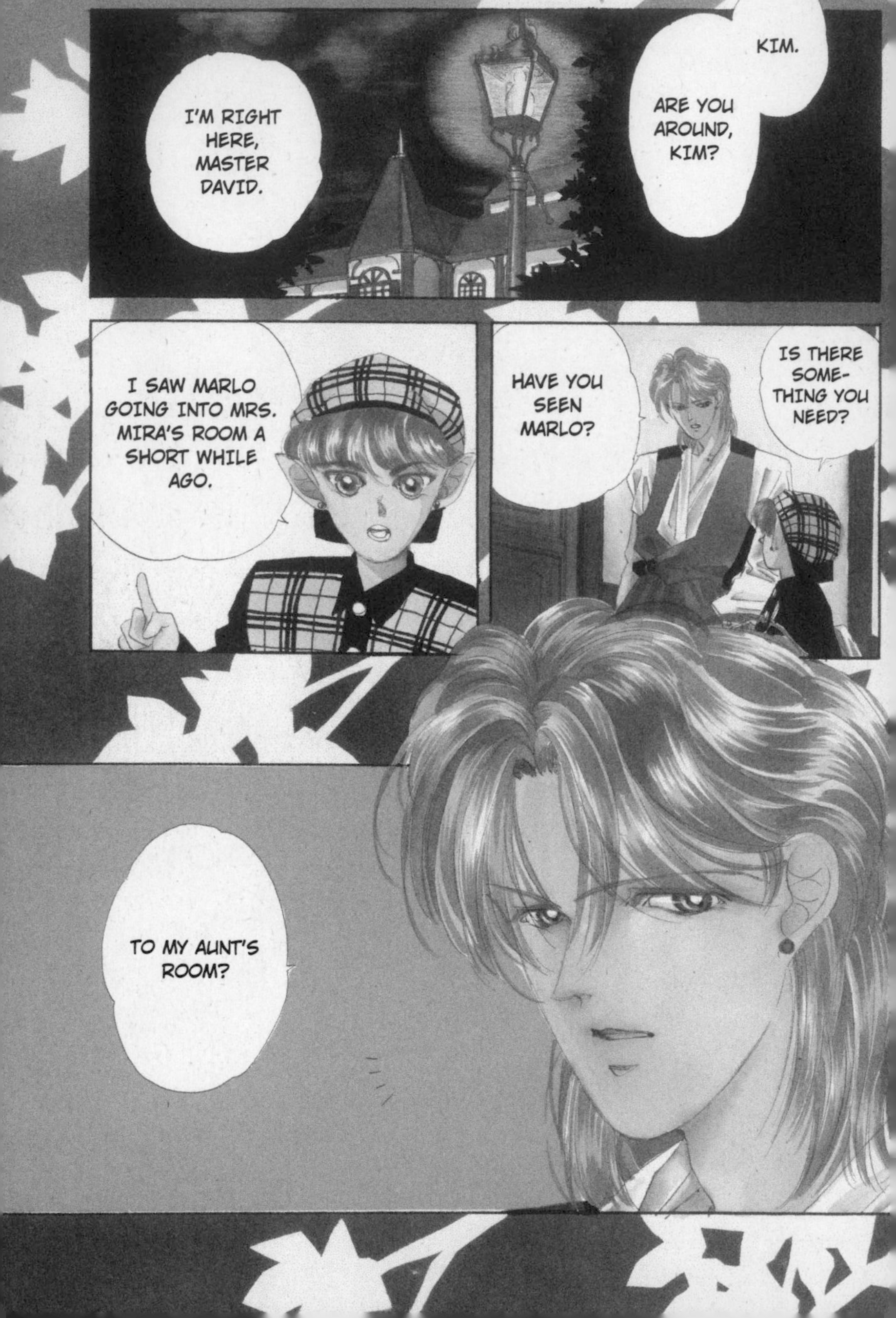
KIM.
ARE YOU AROUND, KIM?
I'M RIGHT HERE, MASTER DAVID.
IS THERE SOME-THING YOU NEED?
HAVE YOU SEEN MARLO?
I SAW MARLO GOING INTO MRS. MIRA'S ROOM A SHORT WHILE AGO.
TO MY AUNT'S ROOM?

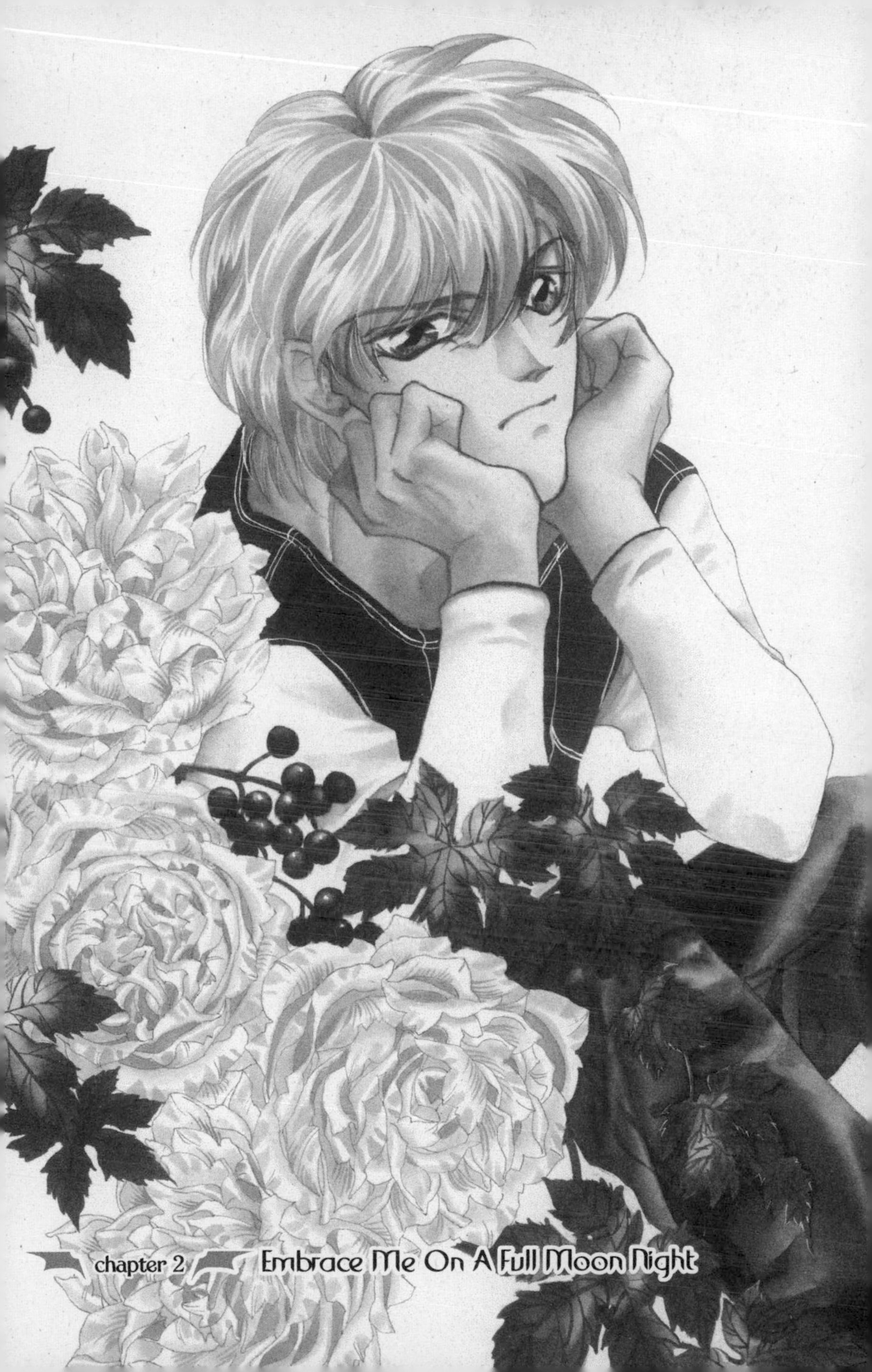
chapter 2
Embrace Me On A Full Moon Night

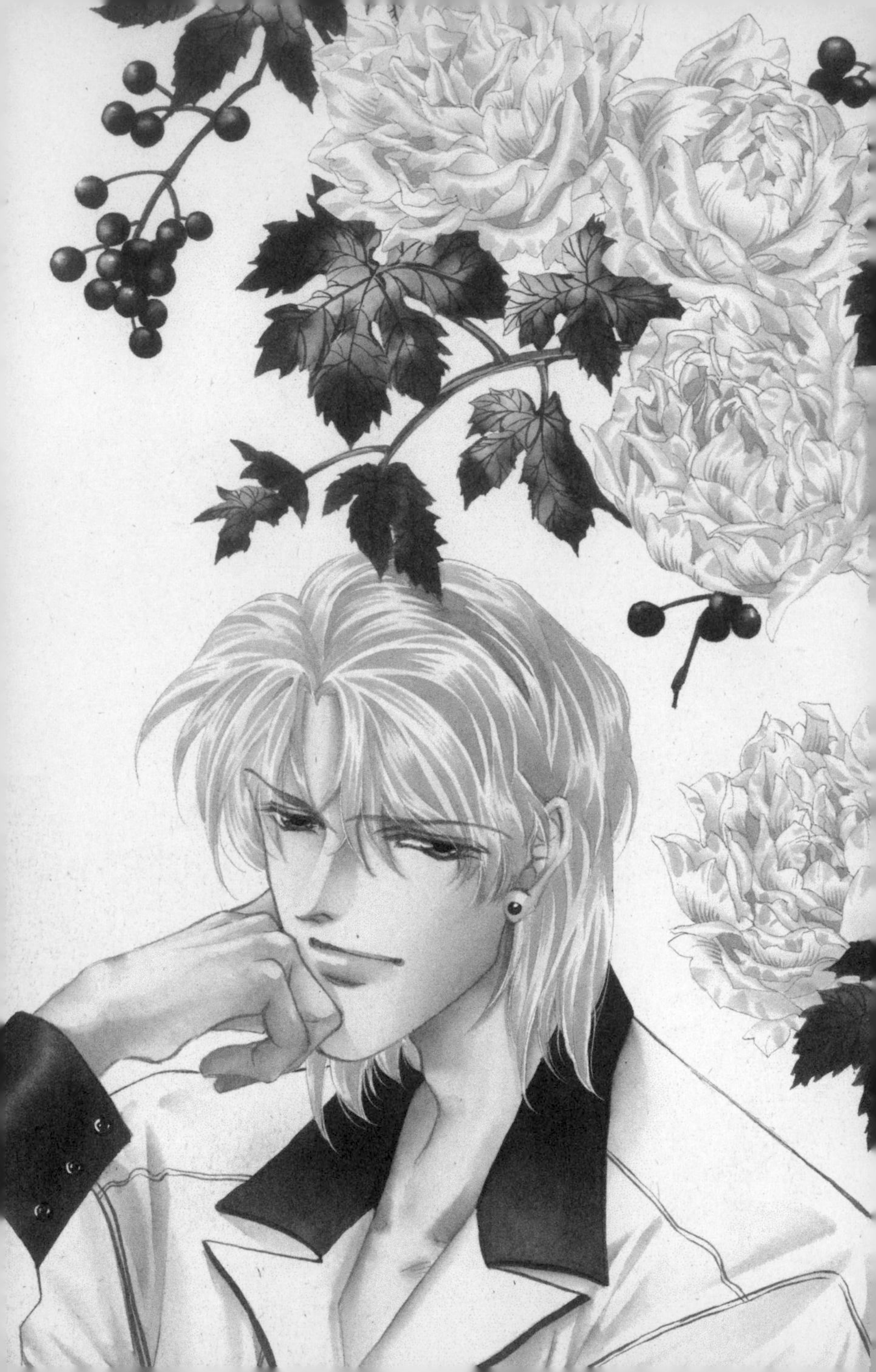

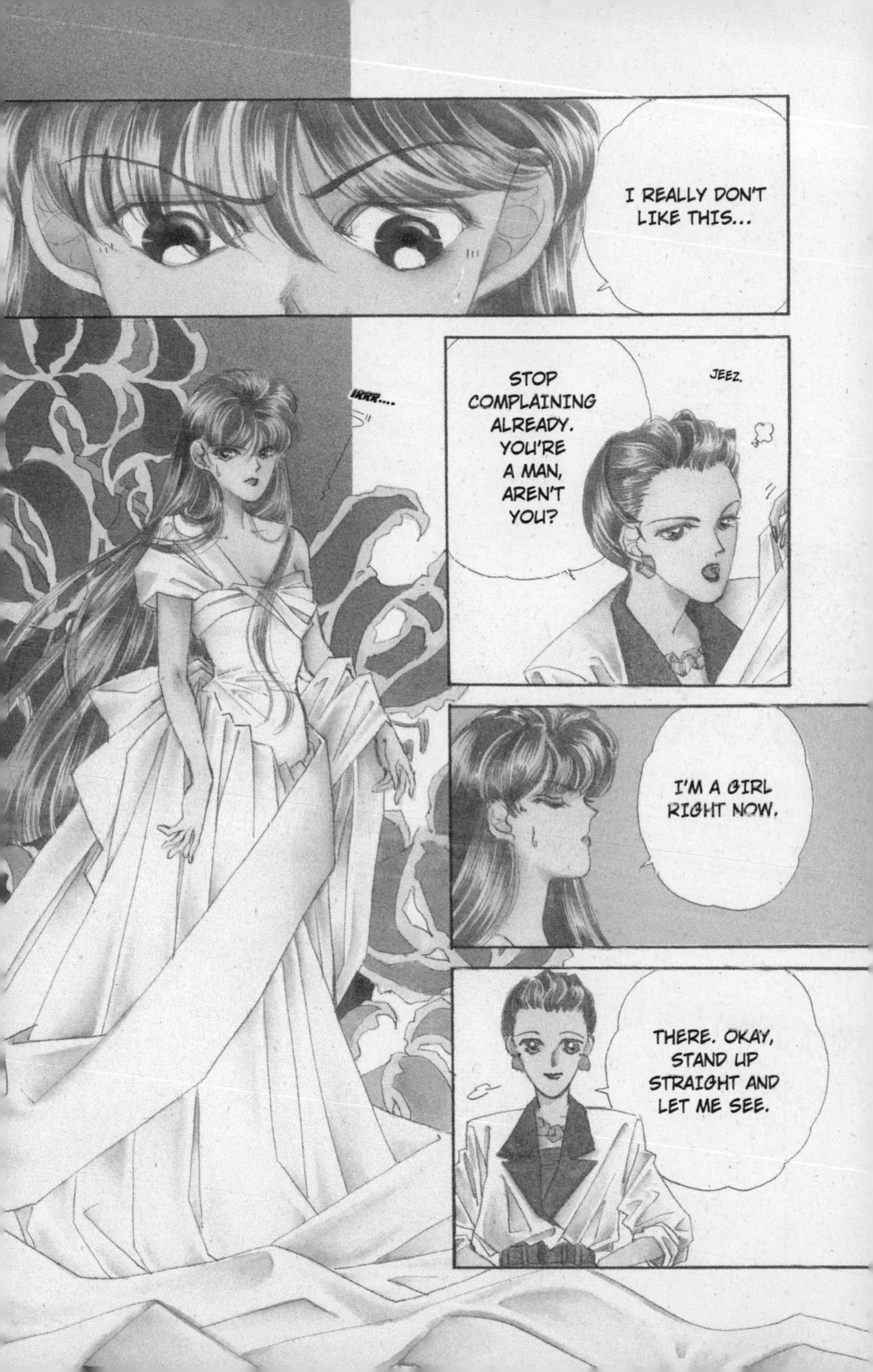
I REALLY DON'T LIKE THIS...
STOP COMPLAINING ALREADY. YOU'RE A MAN, AREN'T YOU?
JEEZ.
I'M A GIRL RIGHT NOW.
THERE. OKAY, STAND UP STRAIGHT AND LET ME SEE.
IRRR....

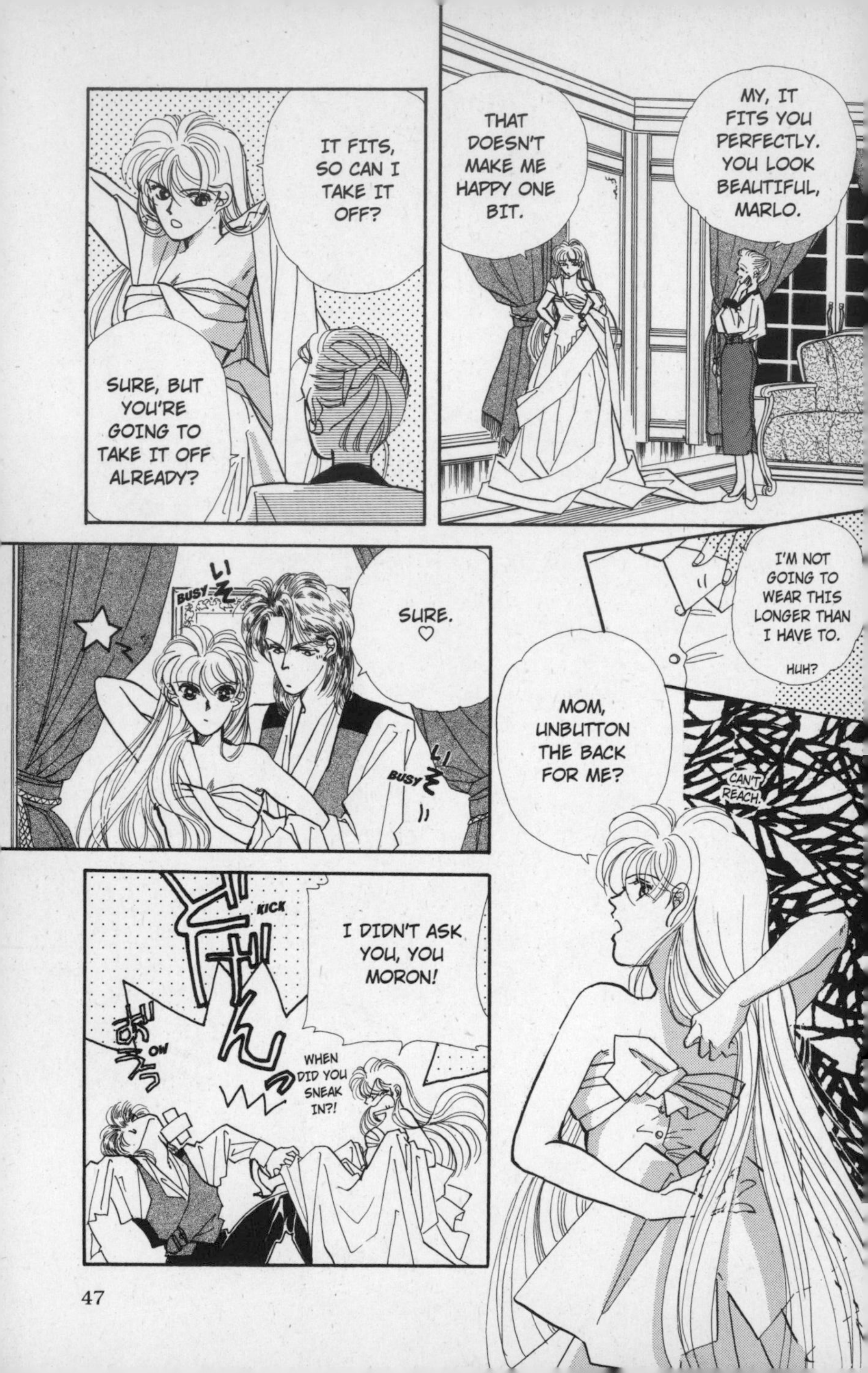
MY, IT FITS YOU PERFECTLY. YOU LOOK BEAUTIFUL, MARLO.
THAT DOESN'T MAKE ME HAPPY ONE BIT.
IT FITS, SO CAN I TAKE IT OFF?
SURE, BUT YOU'RE GOING TO TAKE IT OFF ALREADY?
I'M NOT GOING TO WEAR THIS LONGER THAN I HAVE TO.
HUH?
MOM, UNBUTTON THE BACK FOR ME?
CAN'T REACH.
SURE. ♡
BUSY
BUSY
KICK
I DIDN'T ASK YOU, YOU MORON!
OW
WHEN DID YOU SNEAK IN?!

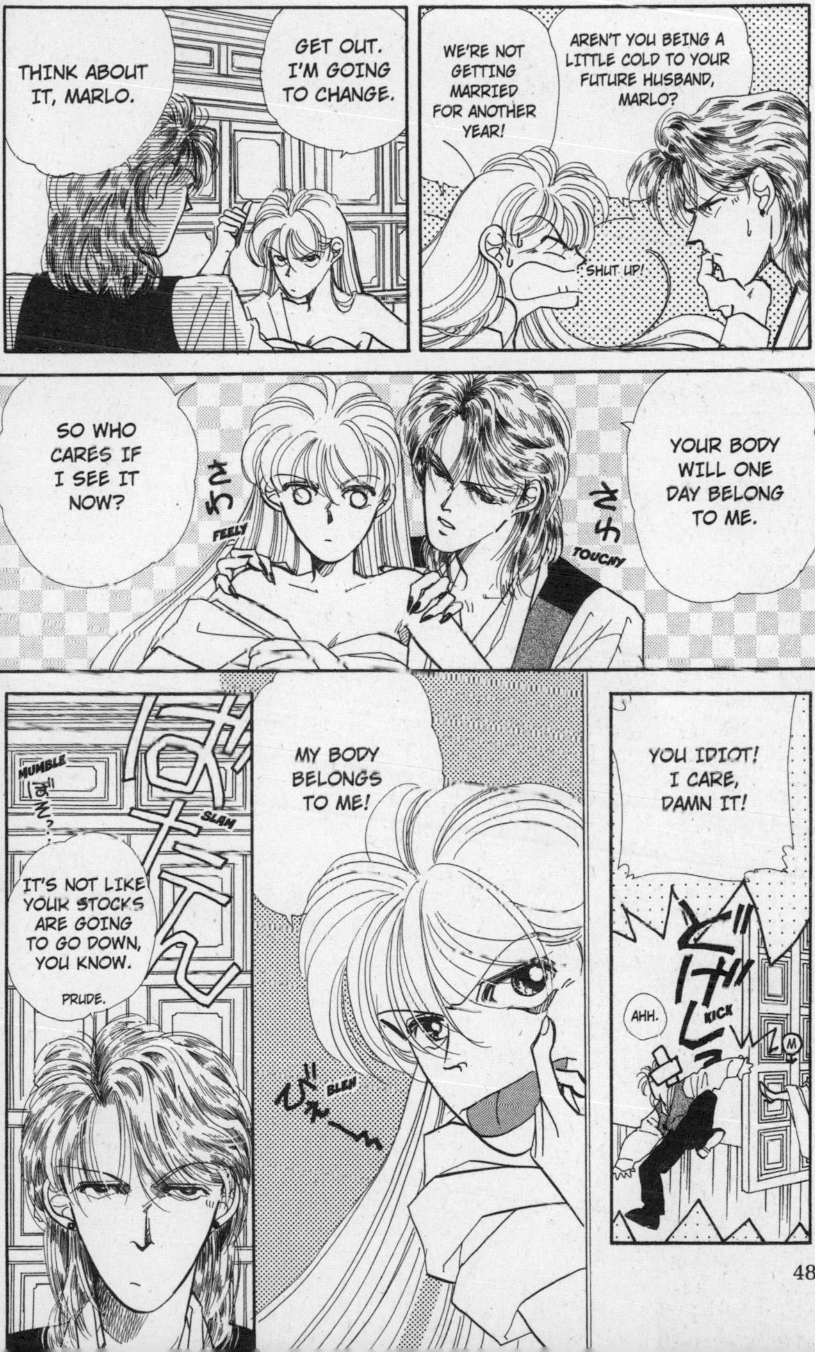
ARE'NT YOU BEING A LITTLE COLD TO YOUR FUTURE HUSBAND, MARLO?
WE'RE NOT GETTING MARRIED FOR ANOTHER YEAR!
SHUT UP!
GET OUT. I'M GOING TO CHANGE.
THINK ABOUT IT, MARLO.
YOUR BODY WILL ONE DAY BELONG TO ME.
TOUCHY
FEELY
SO WHO CARES IF I SEE IT NOW?
YOU IDIOT! I CARE, DAMN IT!
AHH.
KICK
M
MY BODY BELONGS TO ME!
BLEH
SLAM
HUMBLE
IT'S NOT LIKE YOUR STOCKS ARE GOING TO GO DOWN, YOU KNOW.
PRUDE.

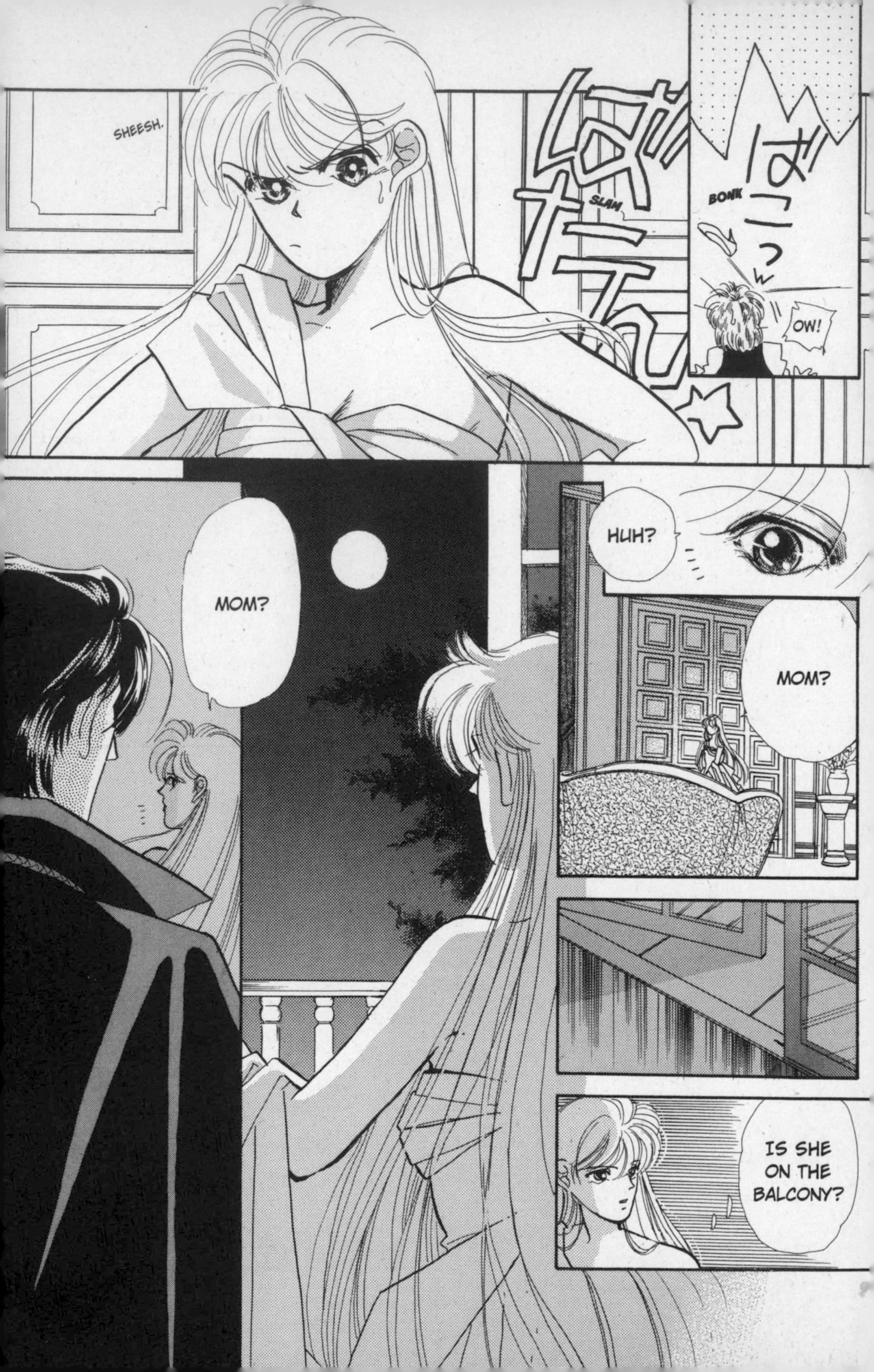

ばこっ
BONK
OW!
ばたん
SLAM
SHEESH.
HUH?
MOM?
IS SHE ON THE BALCONY?
MOM?

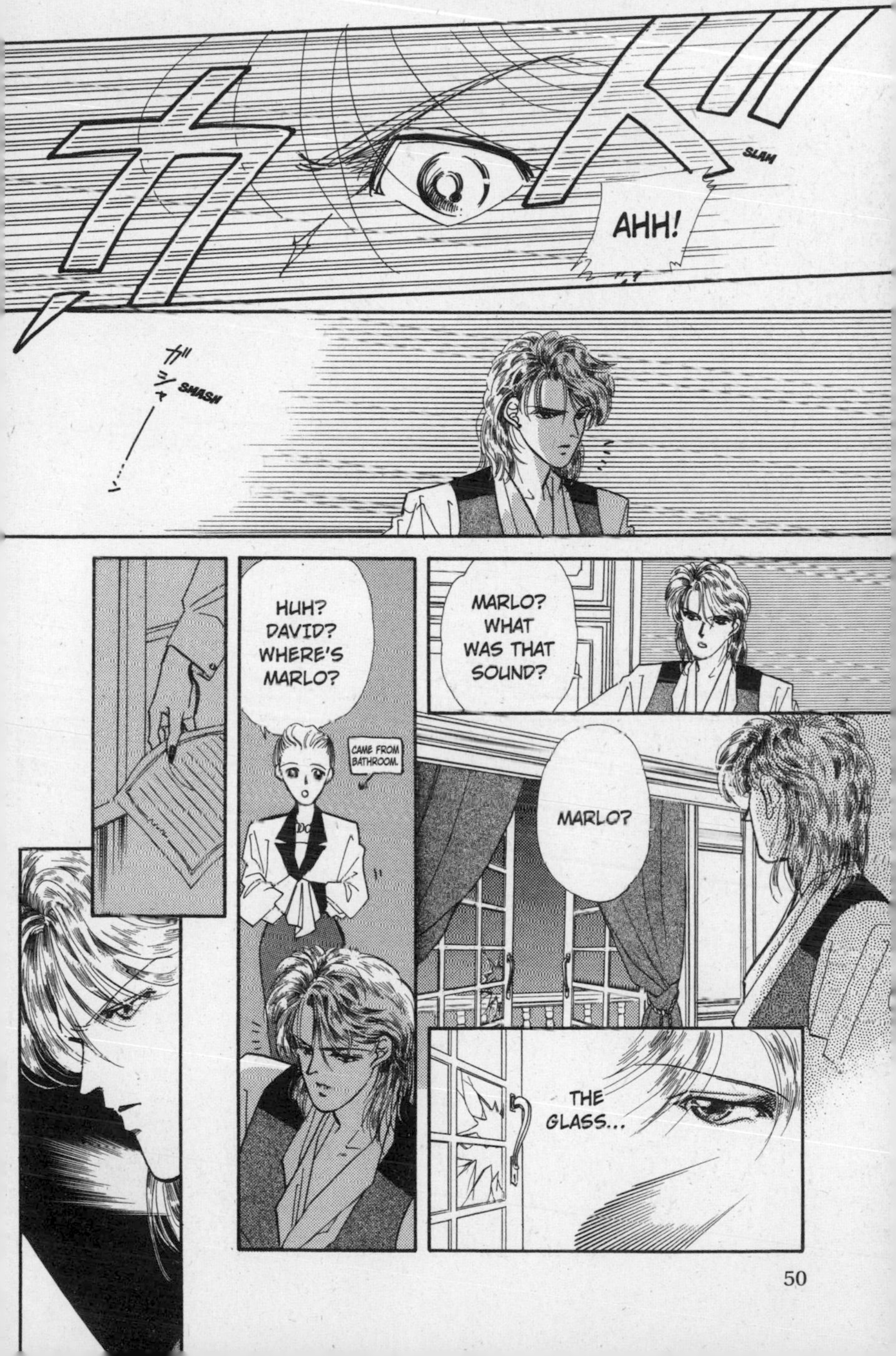
SLAM
AHH!
SMASH
MARLO? WHAT WAS THAT SOUND?
MARLO?
THE GLASS...
HUH? DAVID? WHERE'S MARLO?
CAME FROM BATHROOM.

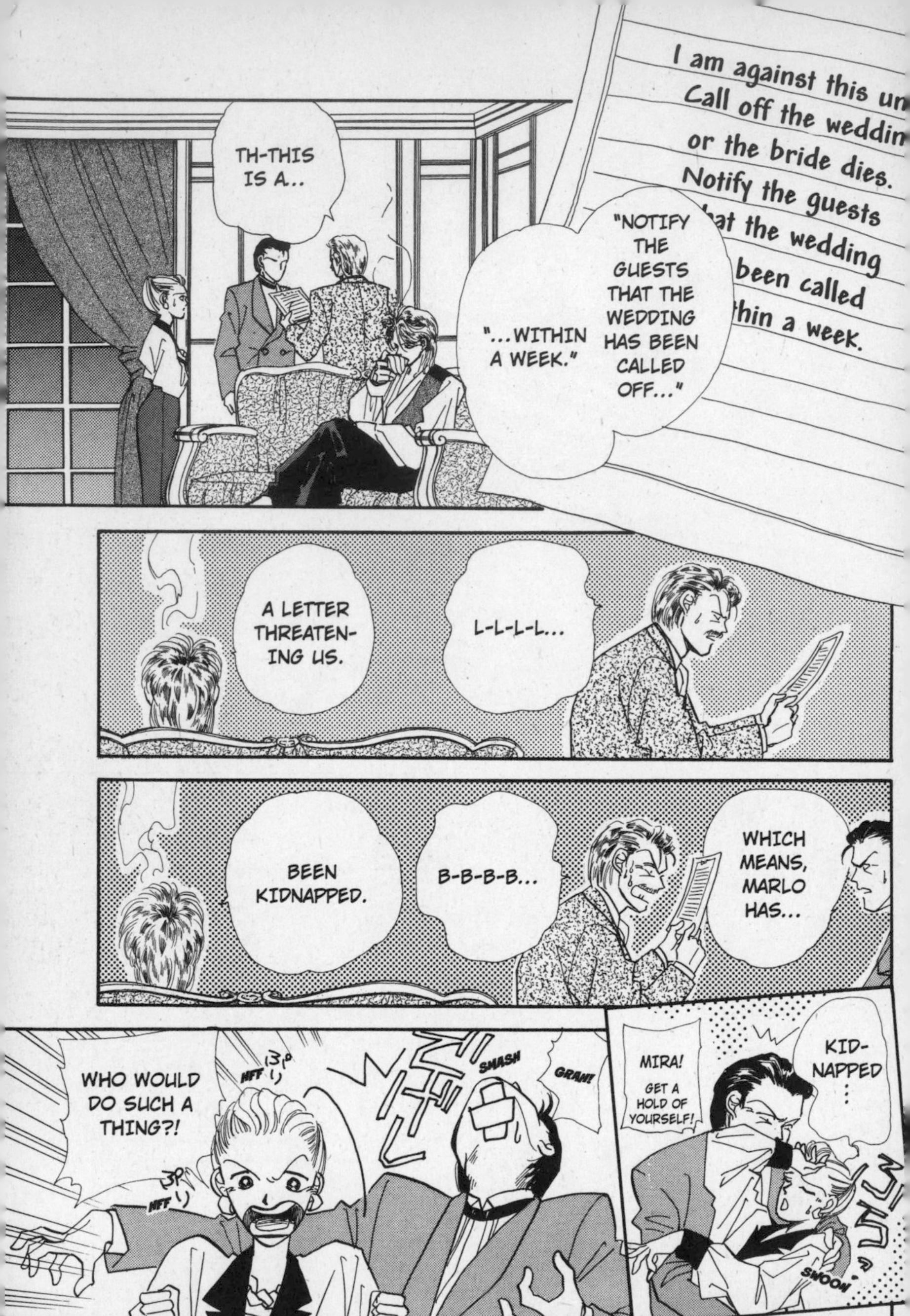
I am against this un
Call off the weddin
or the bride dies.
Notify the guests
hat the wedding
been called
thin a week.
"NOTIFY THE GUESTS THAT THE WEDDING HAS BEEN CALLED OFF..."
"...WITHIN A WEEK."
TH-THIS IS A...
L-L-L-L...
A LETTER THREATEN-ING US.
WHICH MEANS, MARLO HAS...
B-B-B-B...
BEEN KIDNAPPED.
KID-NAPPED...
SWOON
MIRA!
GET A HOLD OF YOURSELF!
GRAN!
SMASH
HFF
WHO WOULD DO SUCH A THING?!
HFF

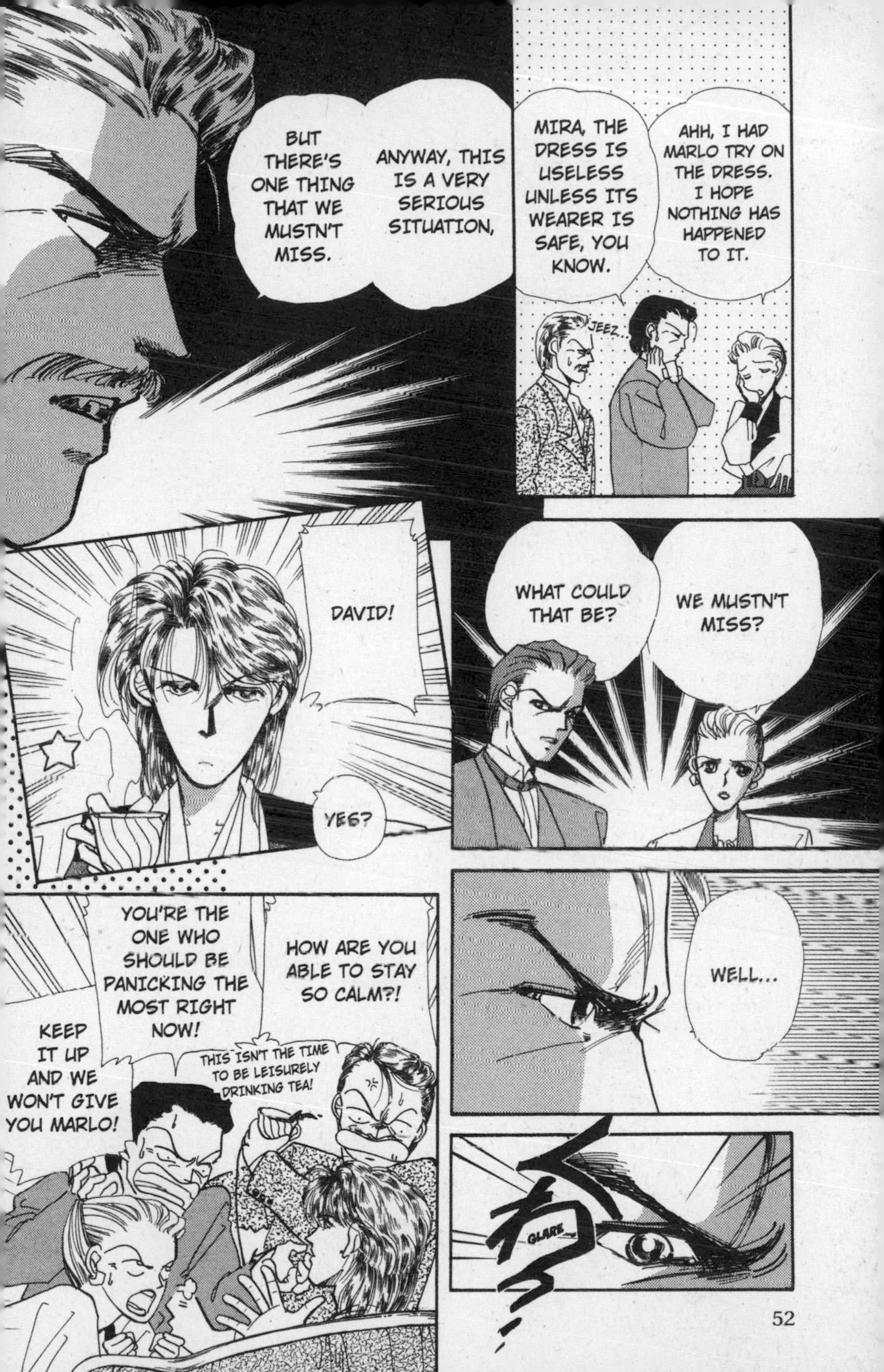
AHH, I HAD MARLO TRY ON THE DRESS. I HOPE NOTHING HAS HAPPENED TO IT.
MIRA, THE DRESS IS USELESS UNLESS ITS WEARER IS SAFE, YOU KNOW.
JEEZ...
ANYWAY, THIS IS A VERY SERIOUS SITUATION,
BUT THERE'S ONE THING THAT WE MUSTN'T MISS.
WE MUSTN'T MISS?
WHAT COULD THAT BE?
DAVID!
YES?
WELL...
GLARE
HOW ARE YOU ABLE TO STAY SO CALM?!
YOU'RE THE ONE WHO SHOULD BE PANICKING THE MOST RIGHT NOW!
THIS ISN'T THE TIME TO BE LEISURELY DRINKING TEA!
KEEP IT UP AND WE WON'T GIVE YOU MARLO!

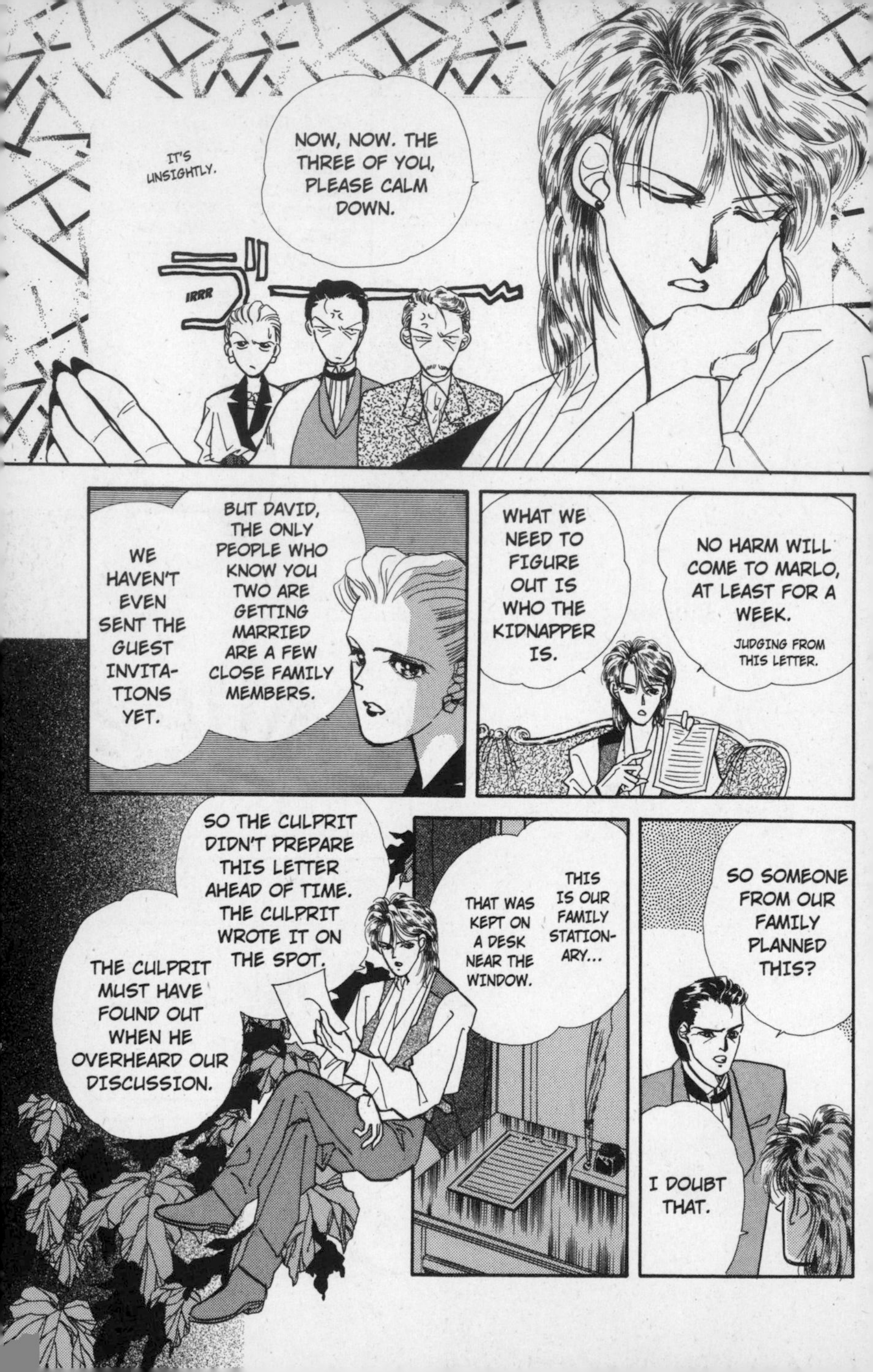
NOW, NOW. THE THREE OF YOU, PLEASE CALM DOWN.
IT'S UNSIGHTLY.
IRRR
NO HARM WILL COME TO MARLO, AT LEAST FOR A WEEK.
JUDGING FROM THIS LETTER.
WHAT WE NEED TO FIGURE OUT IS WHO THE KIDNAPPER IS.
BUT DAVID, THE ONLY PEOPLE WHO KNOW YOU TWO ARE GETTING MARRIED ARE A FEW CLOSE FAMILY MEMBERS.
WE HAVEN'T EVEN SENT THE GUEST INVITA-TIONS YET.
SO SOMEONE FROM OUR FAMILY PLANNED THIS?
I DOUBT THAT.
THIS IS OUR FAMILY STATION-ARY...
THAT WAS KEPT ON A DESK NEAR THE WINDOW.
SO THE CULPRIT DIDN'T PREPARE THIS LETTER AHEAD OF TIME. THE CULPRIT WROTE IT ON THE SPOT.
THE CULPRIT MUST HAVE FOUND OUT WHEN HE OVERHEARD OUR DISCUSSION.

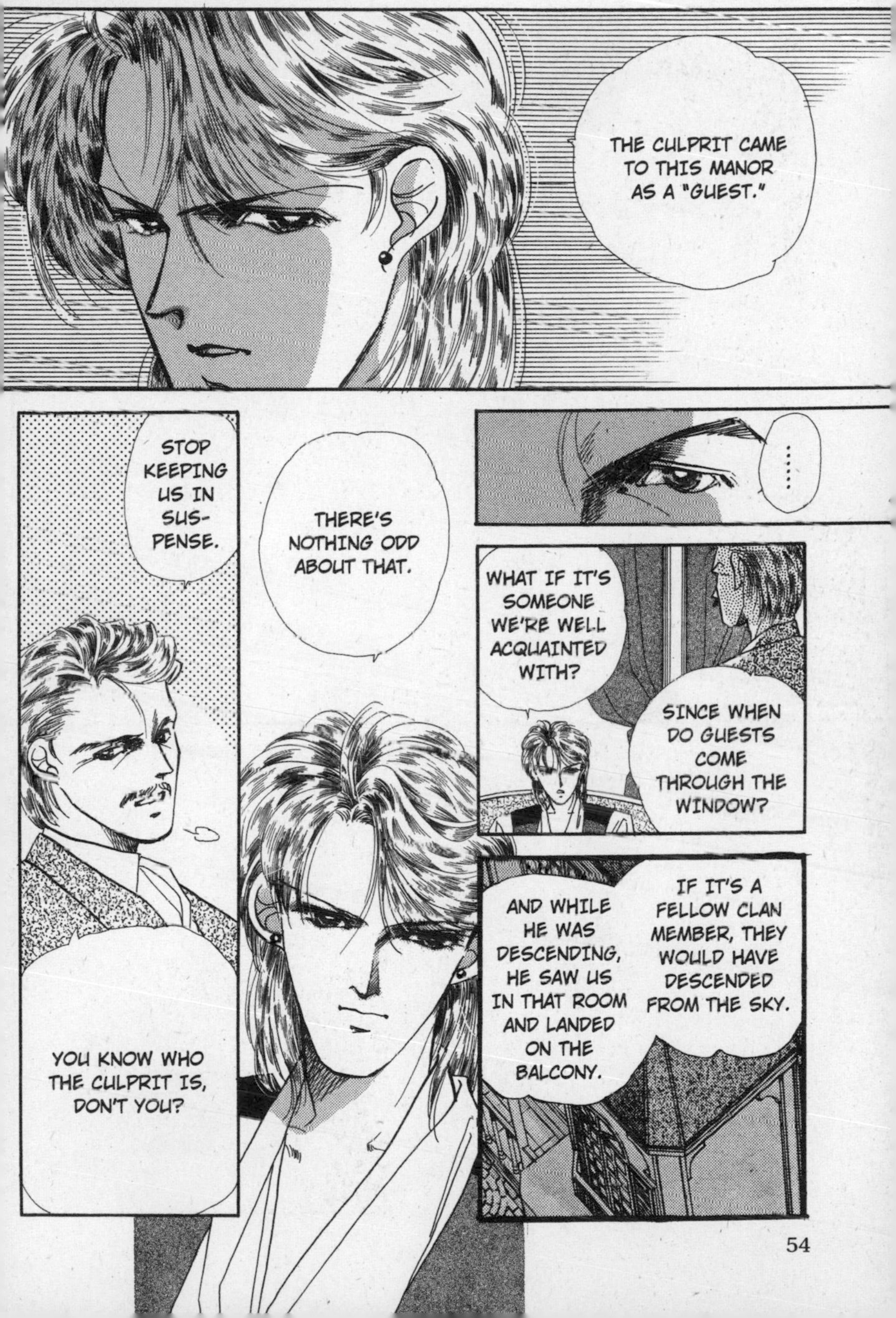
THE CULPRIT CAME TO THIS MANOR AS A "GUEST."
......
WHAT IF IT'S SOMEONE WE'RE WELL ACQUAINTED WITH?
SINCE WHEN DO GUESTS COME THROUGH THE WINDOW?
IF IT'S A FELLOW CLAN MEMBER, THEY WOULD HAVE DESCENDED FROM THE SKY.
AND WHILE HE WAS DESCENDING, HE SAW US IN THAT ROOM AND LANDED ON THE BALCONY.
THERE'S NOTHING ODD ABOUT THAT.
STOP KEEPING US IN SUS-PENSE.
YOU KNOW WHO THE CULPRIT IS, DON'T YOU?

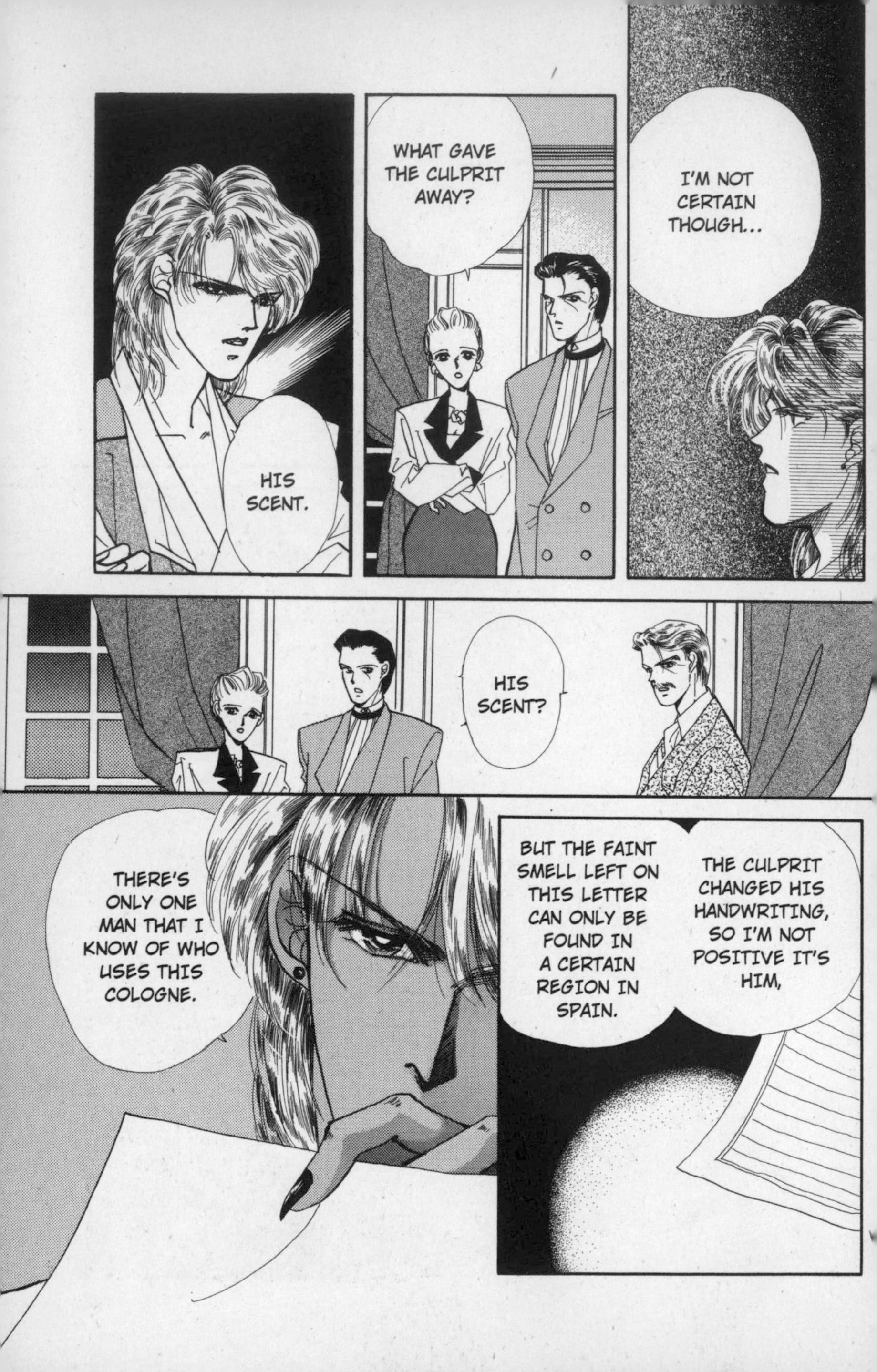
I'M NOT CERTAIN THOUGH...
WHAT GAVE THE CULPRIT AWAY?
HIS SCENT.
HIS SCENT?
THE CULPRIT CHANGED HIS HANDWRITING, SO I'M NOT POSITIVE IT'S HIM,
BUT THE FAINT SMELL LEFT ON THIS LETTER CAN ONLY BE FOUND IN A CERTAIN REGION IN SPAIN.
THERE'S ONLY ONE MAN THAT I KNOW OF WHO USES THIS COLOGNE.

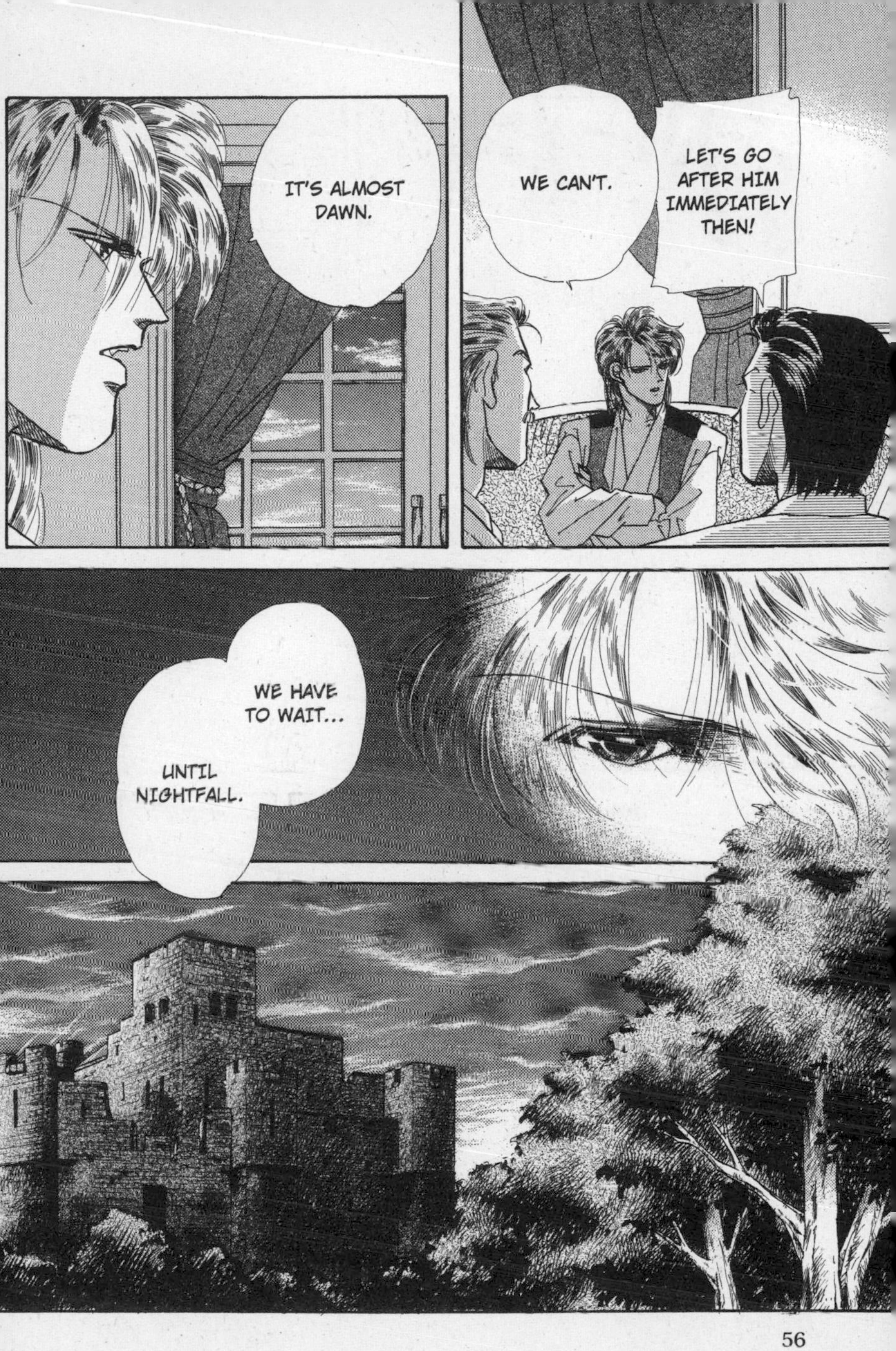
LET'S GO AFTER HIM IMMEDIATELY THEN!
WE CAN'T.
IT'S ALMOST DAWN.
WE HAVE TO WAIT...
UNTIL NIGHTFALL.

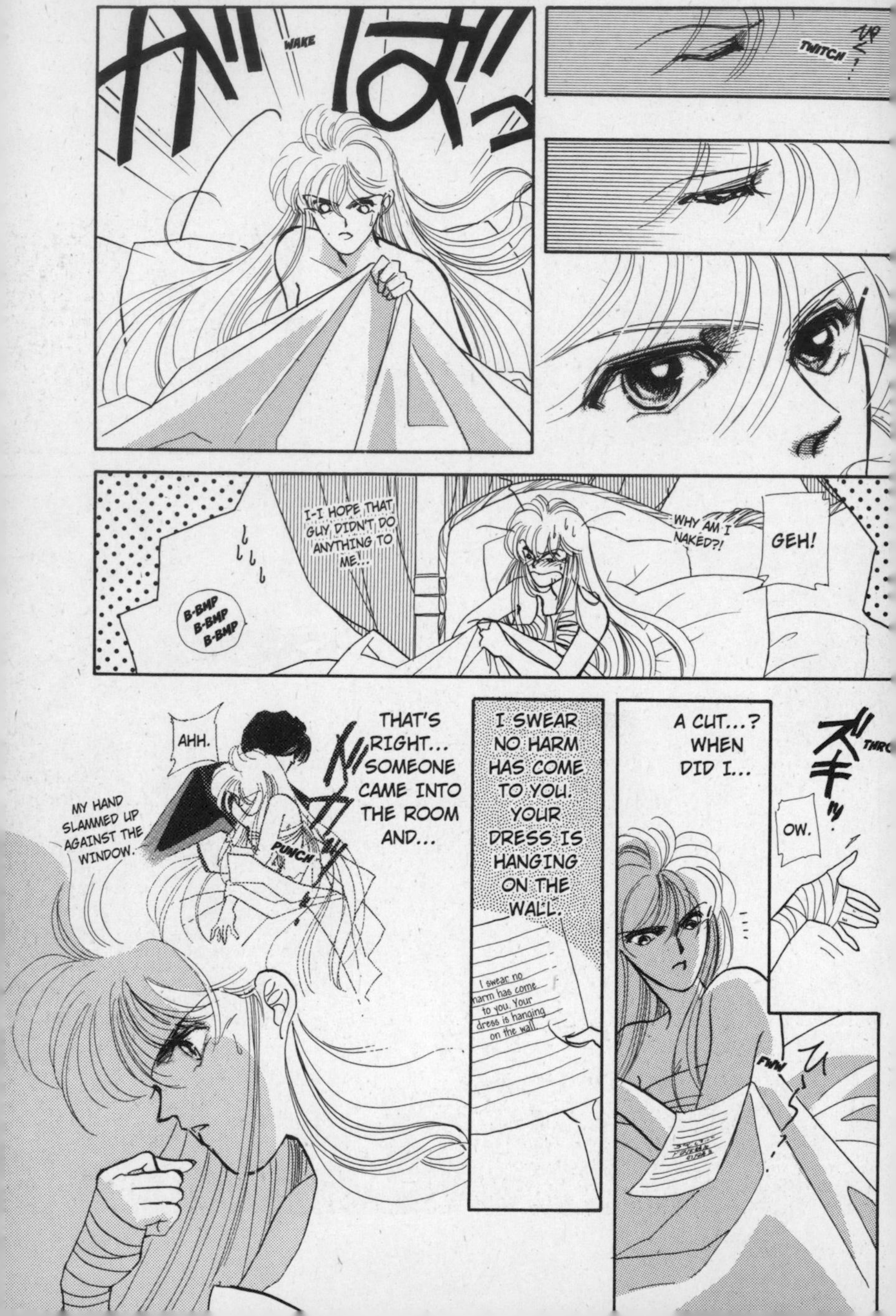
TWITCH
がばっ
WAKE
GEH!
WHY AM I NAKED?!
I-I HOPE THAT GUY DIDN'T DO ANYTHING TO ME...
B-BMP B-BMP B-BMP
ズキッ
THRO
OW.
A CUT...? WHEN DID I...
FWW
I SWEAR NO HARM HAS COME TO YOU. YOUR DRESS IS HANGING ON THE WALL.
I swear no harm has come to you. Your dress is hanging on the wall
THAT'S RIGHT... SOMEONE CAME INTO THE ROOM AND...
AHH.
PUNCH
MY HAND SLAMMED UP AGAINST THE WINDOW.

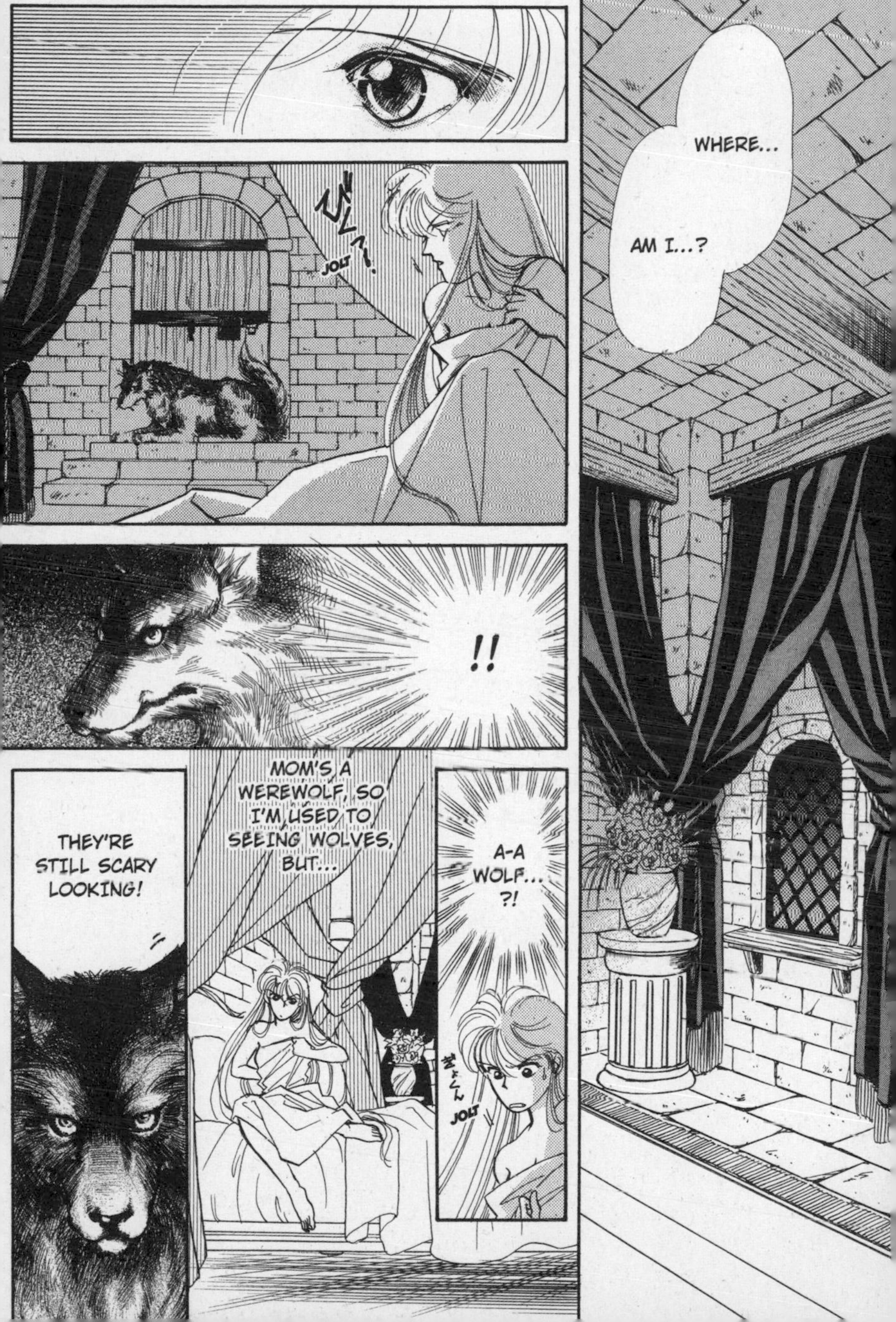
WHERE...
AM I...?
JOLT
!!
A-A WOLF...?!
JOLT
MOM'S A WEREWOLF, SO I'M USED TO SEEING WOLVES, BUT...
THEY'RE STILL SCARY LOOKING!

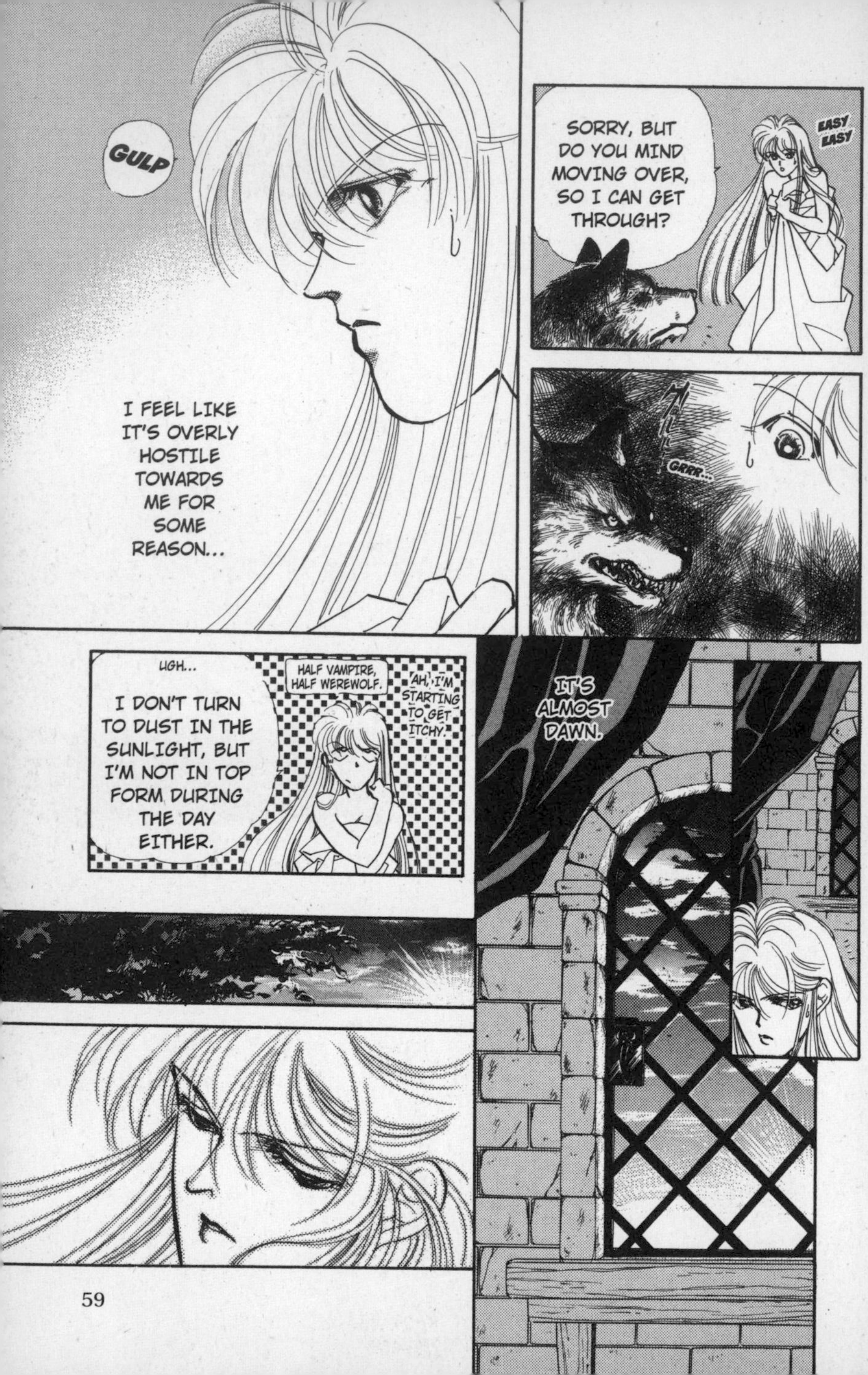
SORRY, BUT DO YOU MIND MOVING OVER, SO I CAN GET THROUGH?
EASY EASY
GRRR...
GULP
I FEEL LIKE IT'S OVERLY HOSTILE TOWARDS ME FOR SOME REASON...
IT'S ALMOST DAWN.
UGH...
I DON'T TURN TO DUST IN THE SUNLIGHT, BUT I'M NOT IN TOP FORM DURING THE DAY EITHER.
HALF VAMPIRE, HALF WEREWOLF.
AH, I'M STARTING TO GET ITCHY.

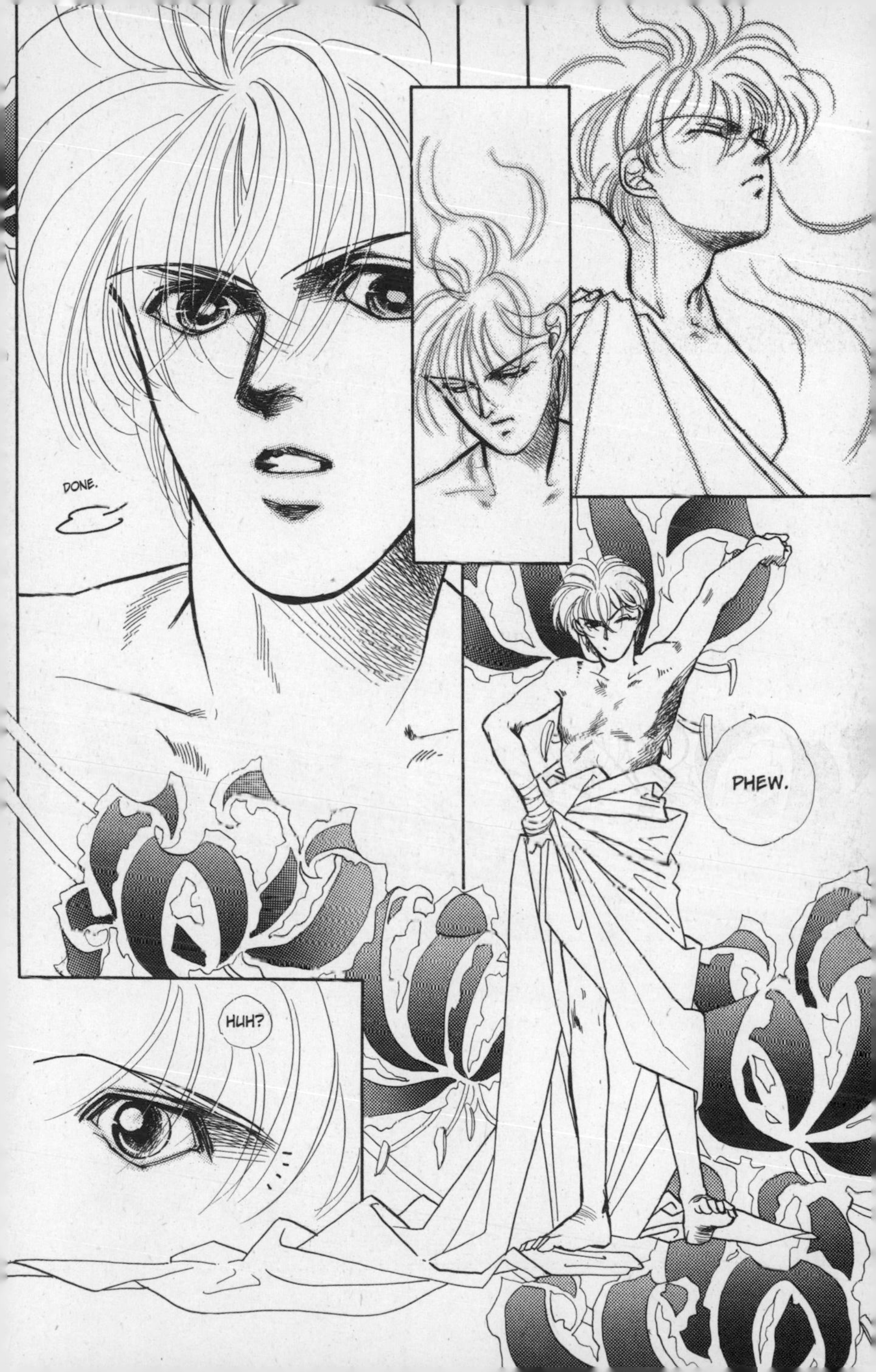
DONE.
PHEW.
HUH?

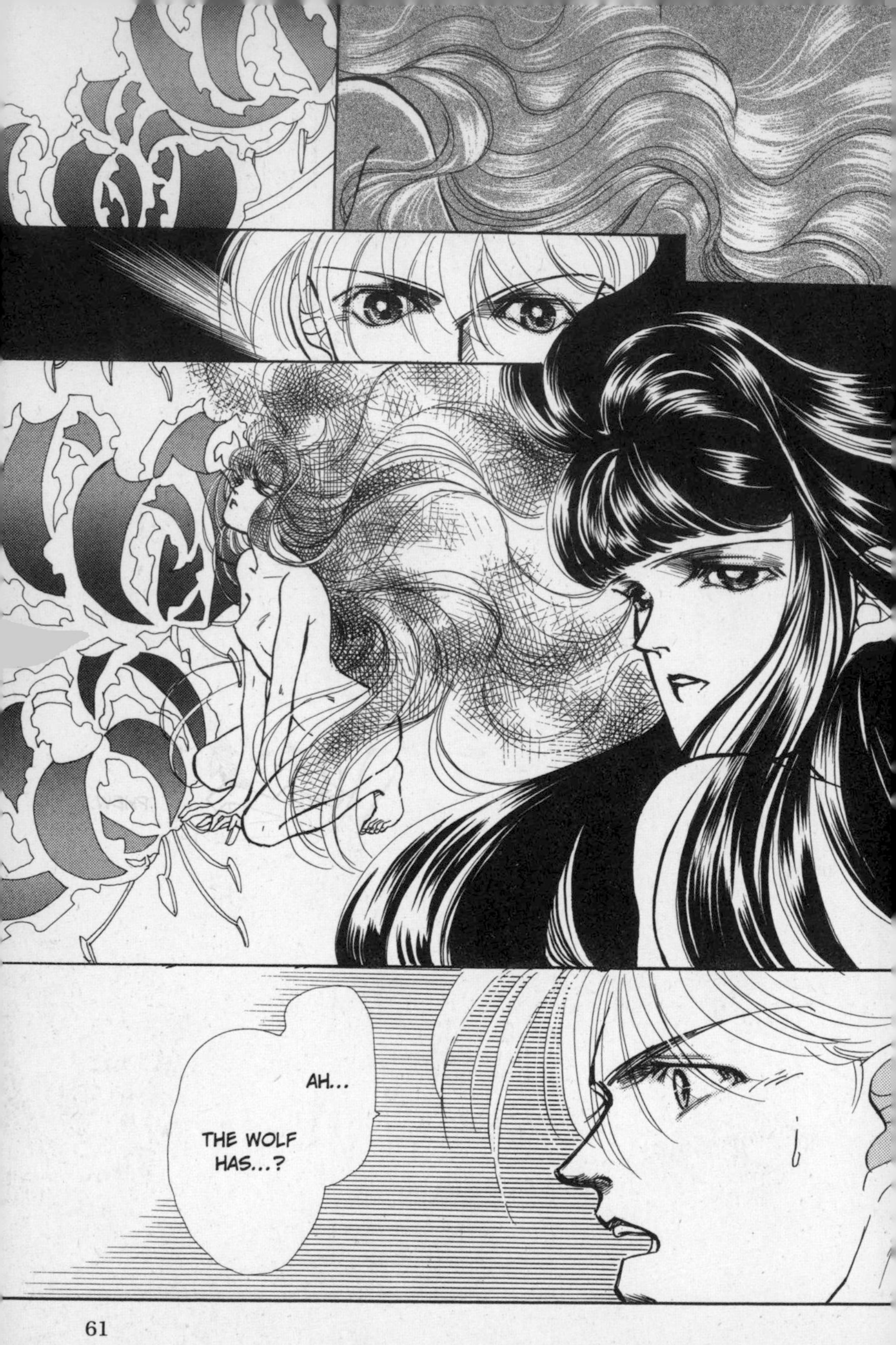
AH...
THE WOLF HAS...?

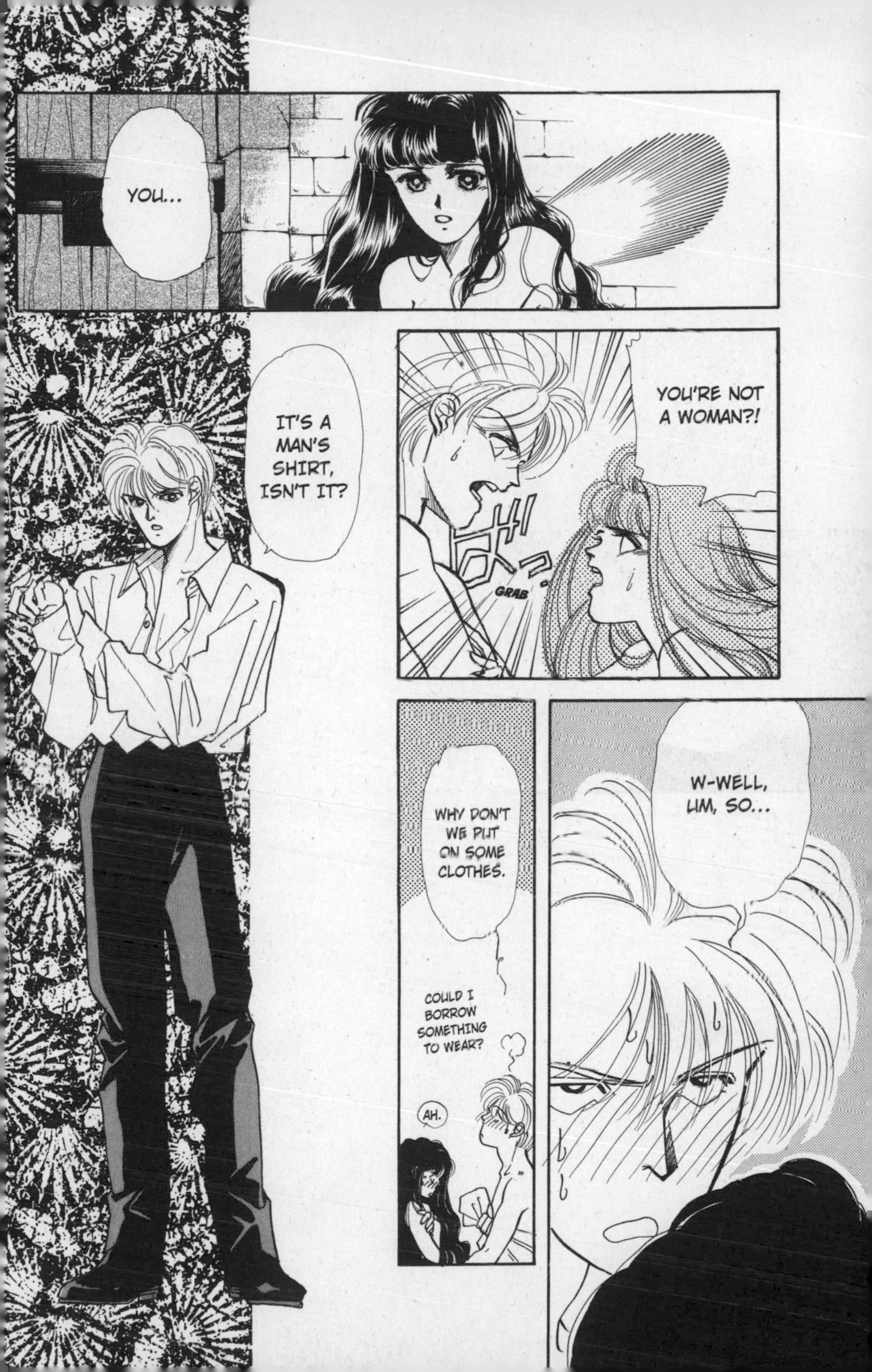
YOU...
YOU'RE NOT A WOMAN?!
GRAB
W-WELL, UM, SO...
WHY DON'T WE PUT ON SOME CLOTHES.
COULD I BORROW SOMETHING TO WEAR?
AH.
IT'S A MAN'S SHIRT, ISN'T IT?

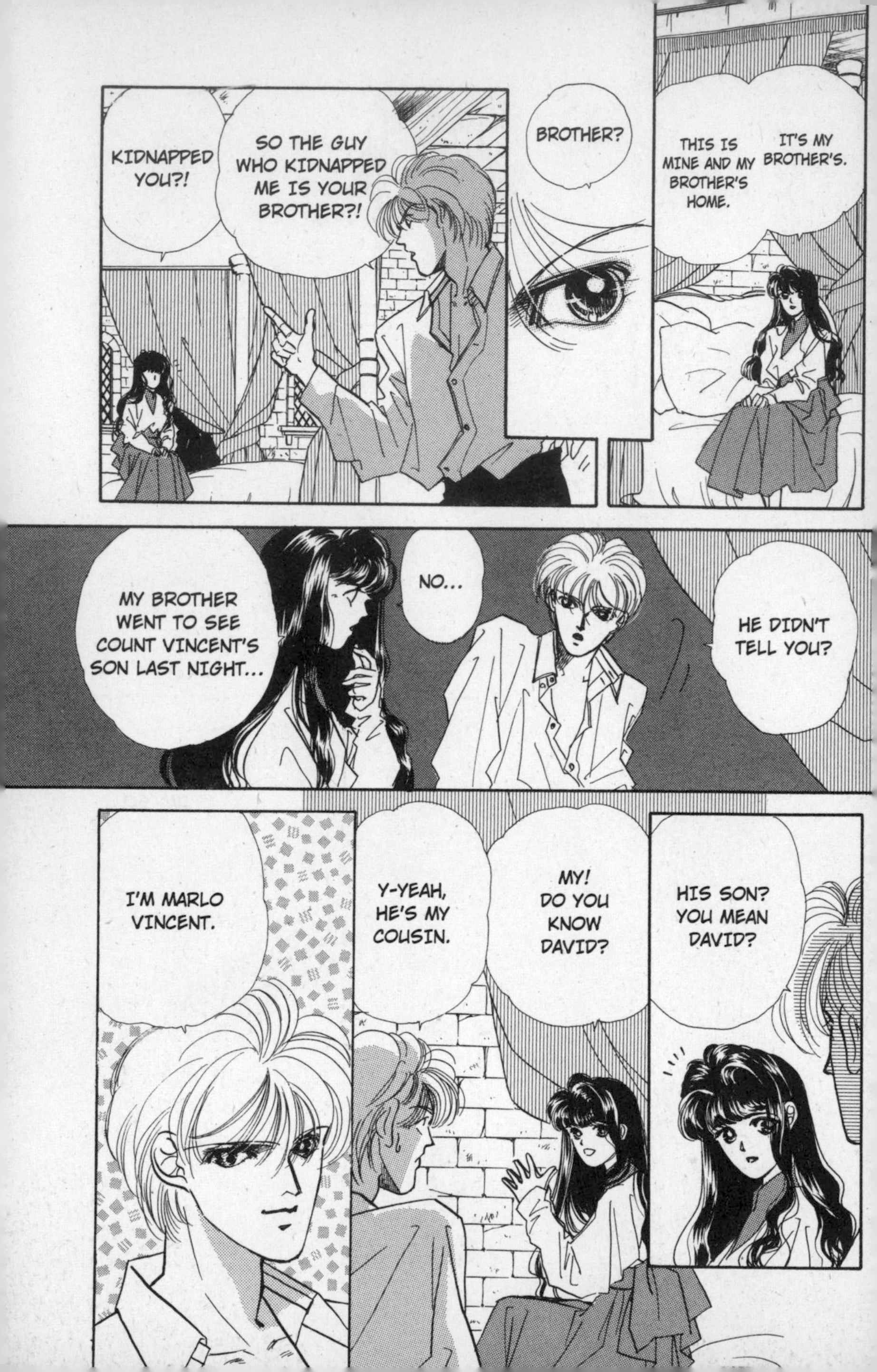

IT'S MY BROTHER'S.
THIS IS MINE AND MY BROTHER'S HOME.
BROTHER?
SO THE GUY WHO KIDNAPPED ME IS YOUR BROTHER?!
KIDNAPPED YOU?!
HE DIDN'T TELL YOU?
NO...
MY BROTHER WENT TO SEE COUNT VINCENT'S SON LAST NIGHT...
HIS SON? YOU MEAN DAVID?
MY! DO YOU KNOW DAVID?
Y-YEAH, HE'S MY COUSIN.
I'M MARLO VINCENT.

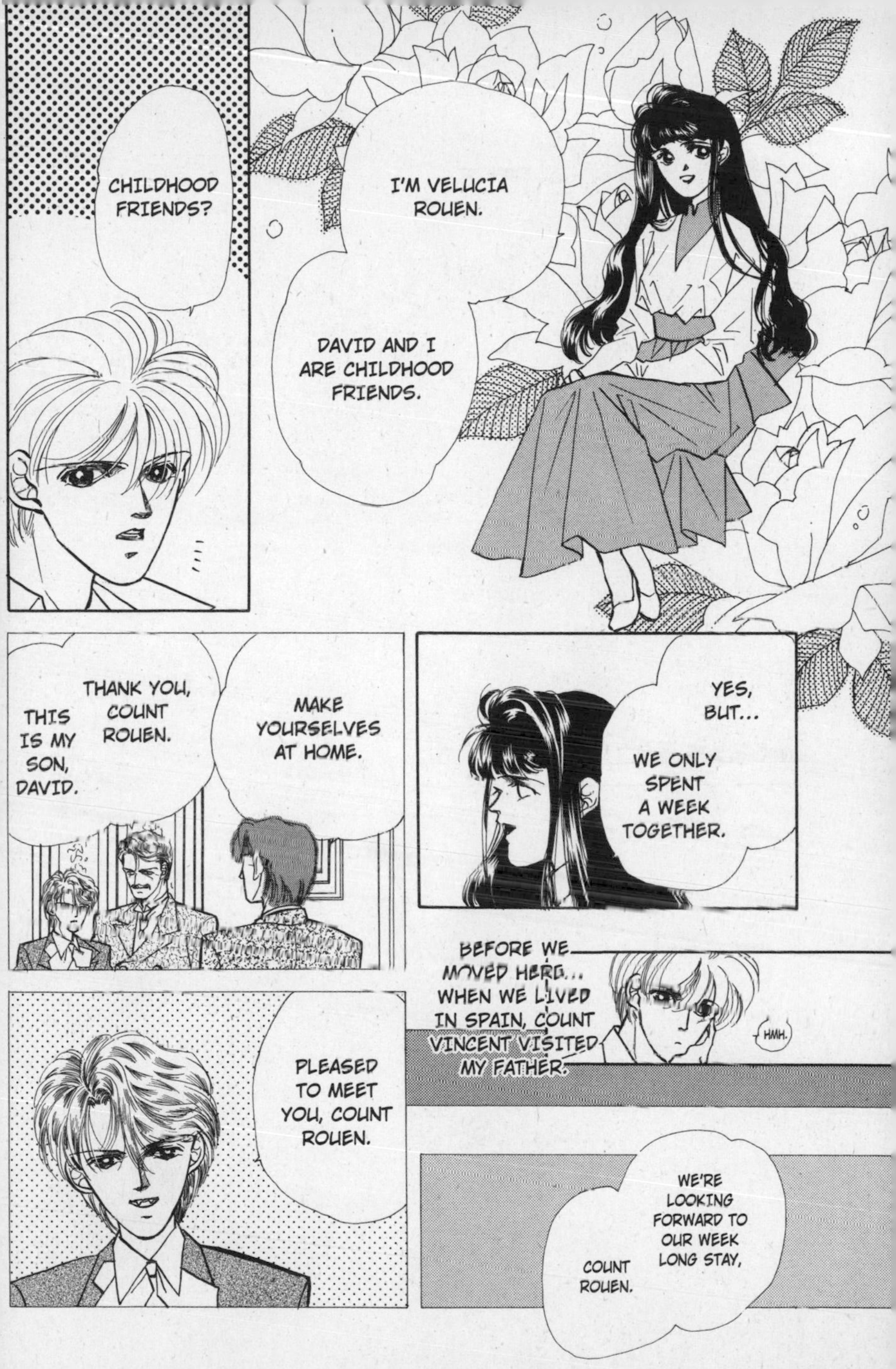
I'M VELUCIA ROUEN.
DAVID AND I ARE CHILDHOOD FRIENDS.
CHILDHOOD FRIENDS?
YES, BUT...
WE ONLY SPENT A WEEK TOGETHER.
MAKE YOURSELVES AT HOME.
THANK YOU, COUNT ROUEN.
THIS IS MY SON, DAVID.
BEFORE WE MOVED HERE... WHEN WE LIVED IN SPAIN, COUNT VINCENT VISITED MY FATHER.
HMH.
WE'RE LOOKING FORWARD TO OUR WEEK LONG STAY,
COUNT ROUEN.
PLEASED TO MEET YOU, COUNT ROUEN.

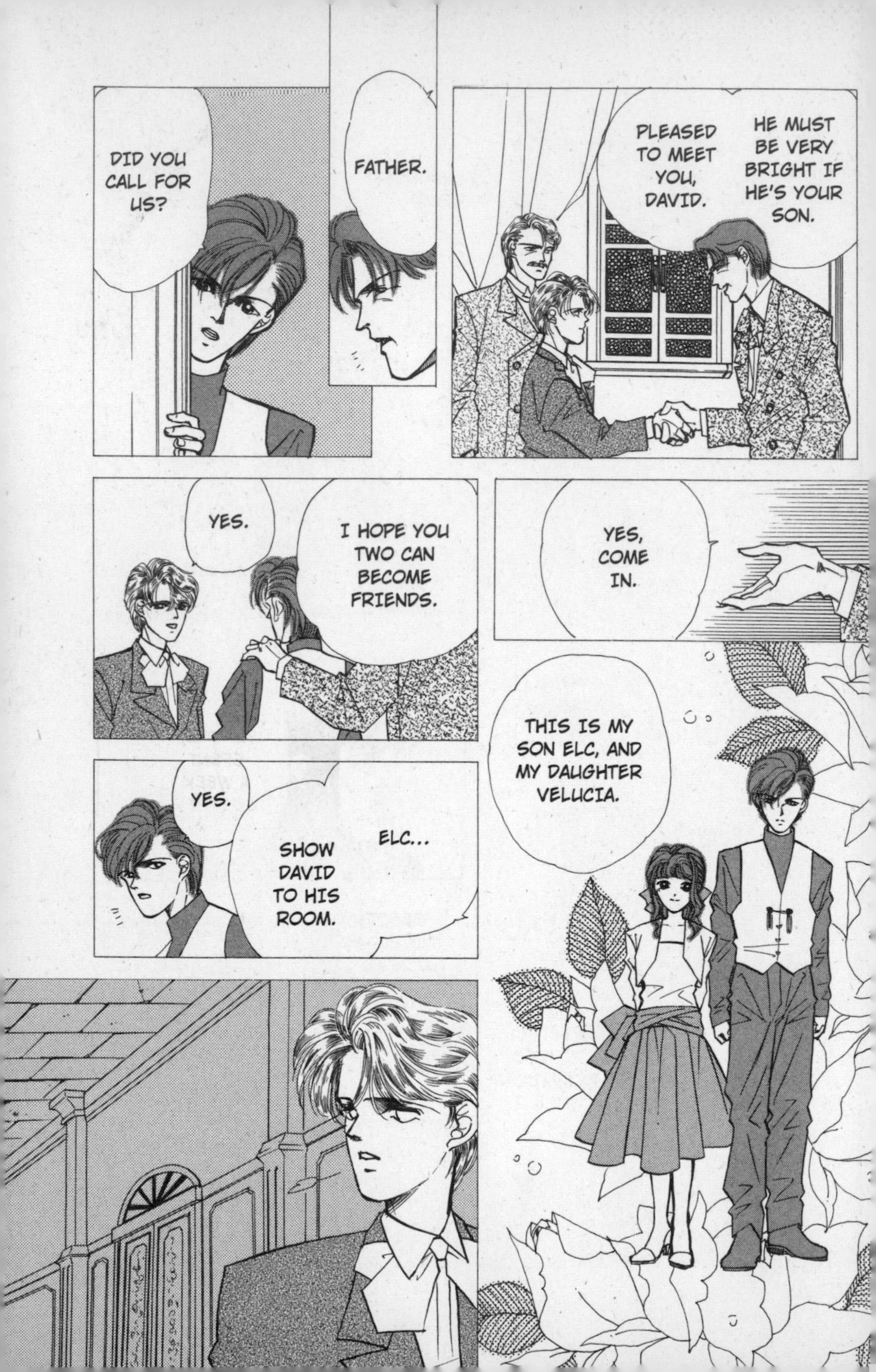
HE MUST BE VERY BRIGHT IF HE'S YOUR SON.
PLEASED TO MEET YOU, DAVID.
FATHER.
DID YOU CALL FOR US?
YES, COME IN.
I HOPE YOU TWO CAN BECOME FRIENDS.
YES.
THIS IS MY SON ELC, AND MY DAUGHTER VELUCIA.
ELC...
SHOW DAVID TO HIS ROOM.
YES.

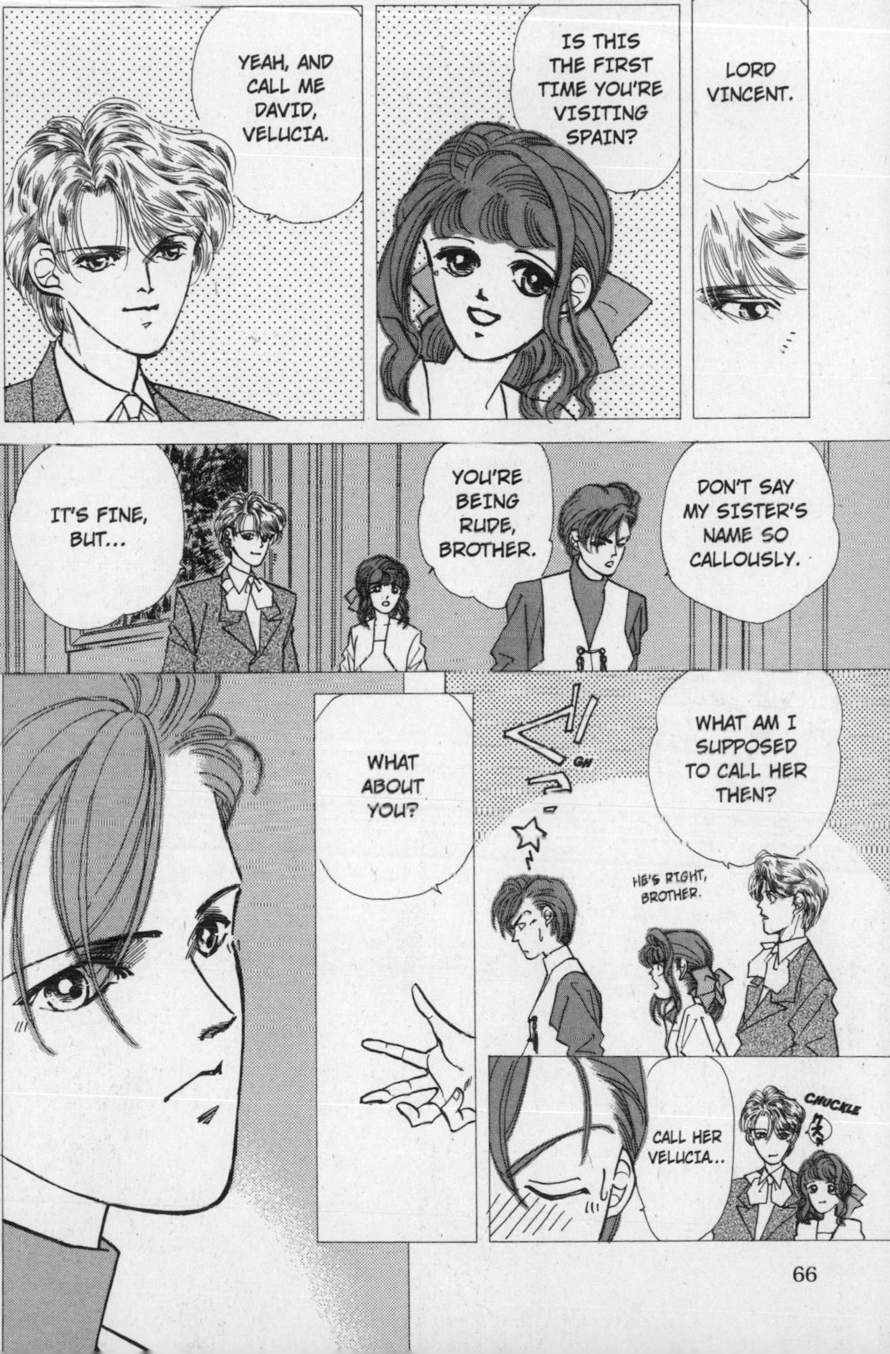
LORD VINCENT.
IS THIS THE FIRST TIME YOU'RE VISITING SPAIN?
YEAH, AND CALL ME DAVID, VELUCIA.
DON'T SAY MY SISTER'S NAME SO CALLOUSLY.
YOU'RE BEING RUDE, BROTHER.
IT'S FINE, BUT...
WHAT AM I SUPPOSED TO CALL HER THEN?
GH
HE'S RIGHT, BROTHER.
CHUCKLE
CALL HER VELUCIA...
WHAT ABOUT YOU?

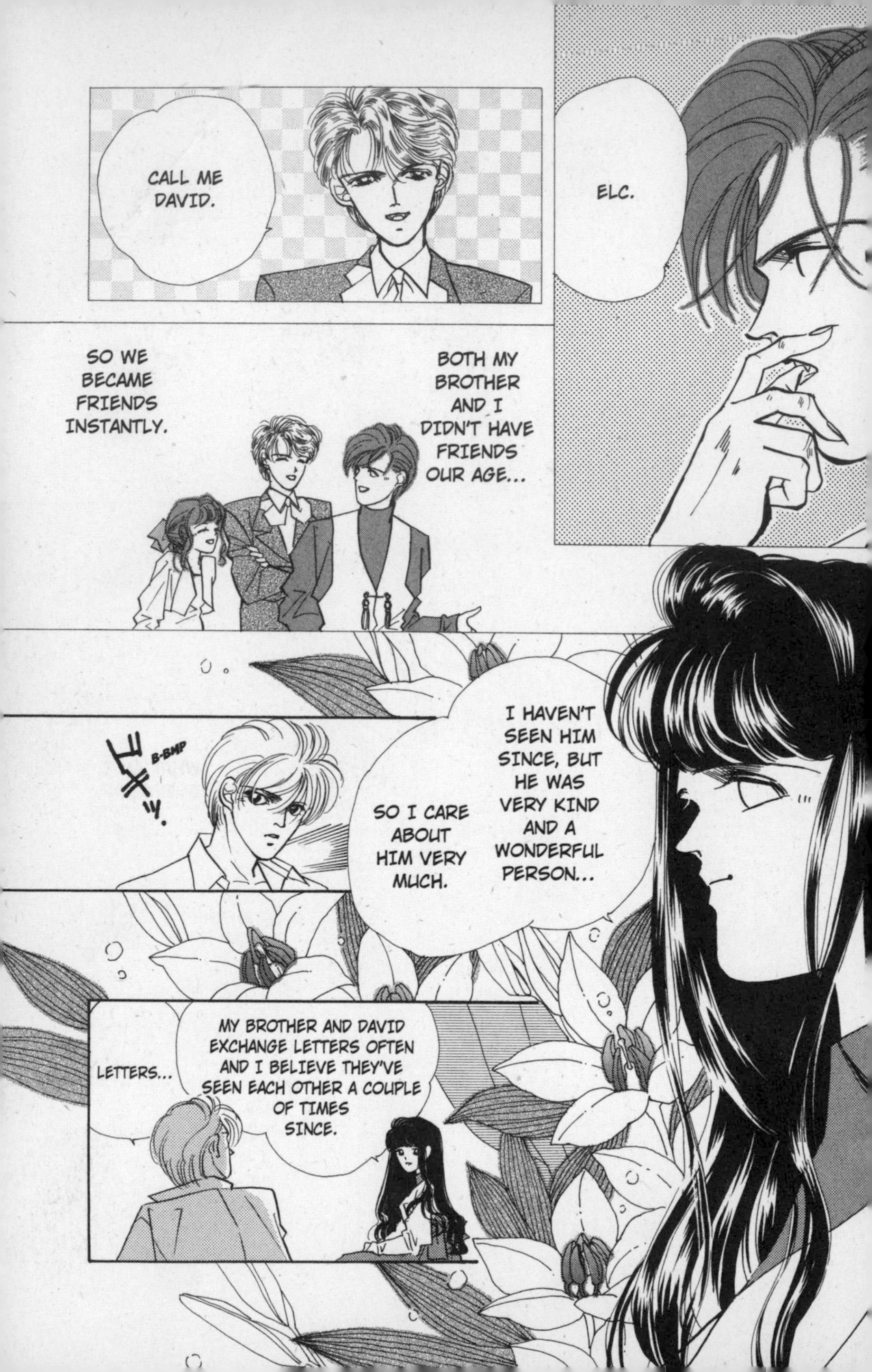
ELC.
CALL ME DAVID.
BOTH MY BROTHER AND I DIDN'T HAVE FRIENDS OUR AGE...
SO WE BECAME FRIENDS INSTANTLY.
I HAVEN'T SEEN HIM SINCE, BUT HE WAS VERY KIND AND A WONDERFUL PERSON...
SO I CARE ABOUT HIM VERY MUCH.
B-BMP
MY BROTHER AND DAVID EXCHANGE LETTERS OFTEN AND I BELIEVE THEY'VE SEEN EACH OTHER A COUPLE OF TIMES SINCE.
LETTERS...

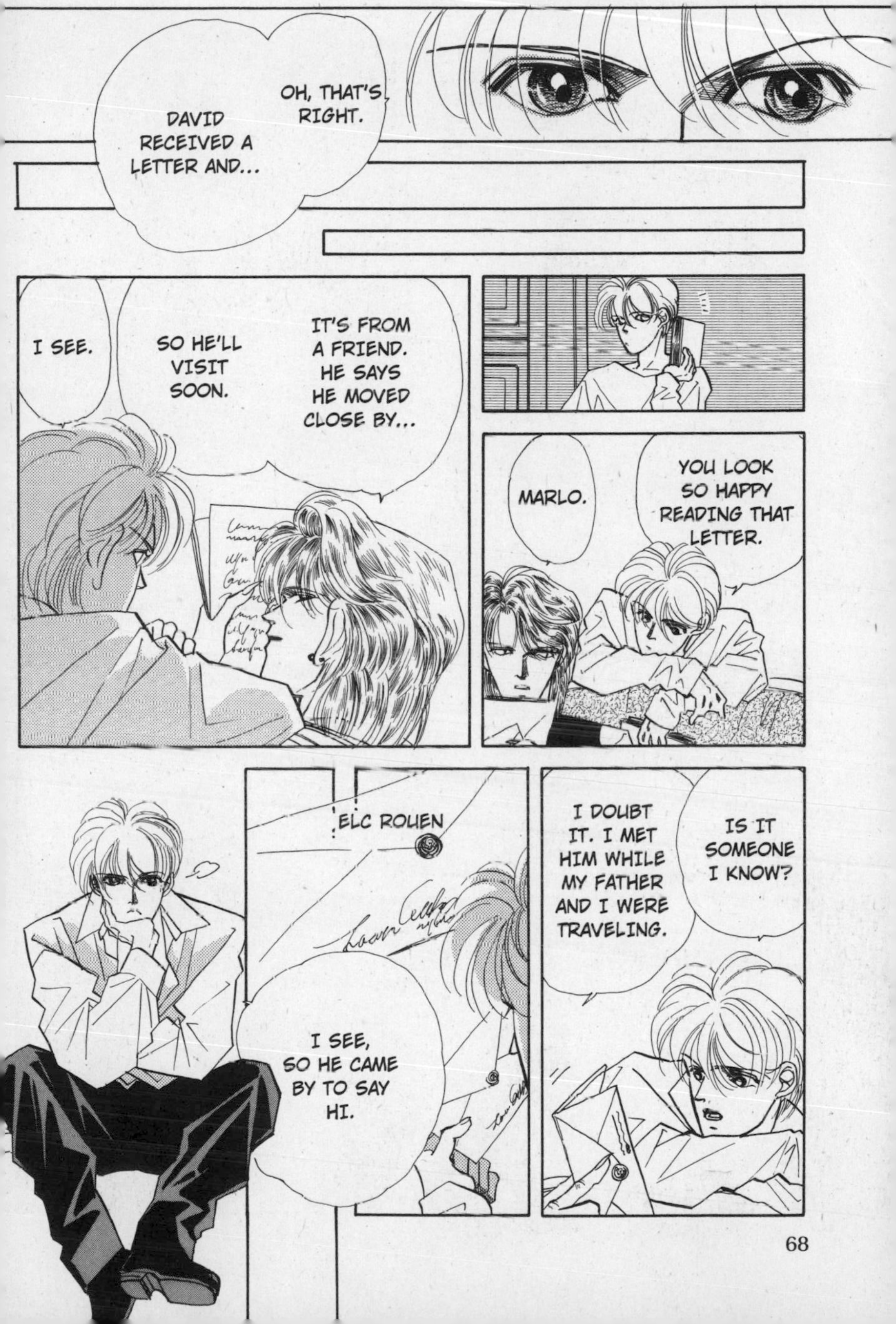
OH, THAT'S RIGHT.
DAVID RECEIVED A LETTER AND...
YOU LOOK SO HAPPY READING THAT LETTER.
MARLO.
IT'S FROM A FRIEND. HE SAYS HE MOVED CLOSE BY...
SO HE'LL VISIT SOON.
I SEE.
IS IT SOMEONE I KNOW?
I DOUBT IT. I MET HIM WHILE MY FATHER AND I WERE TRAVELING.
ELC ROUEN
I SEE, SO HE CAME BY TO SAY HI.

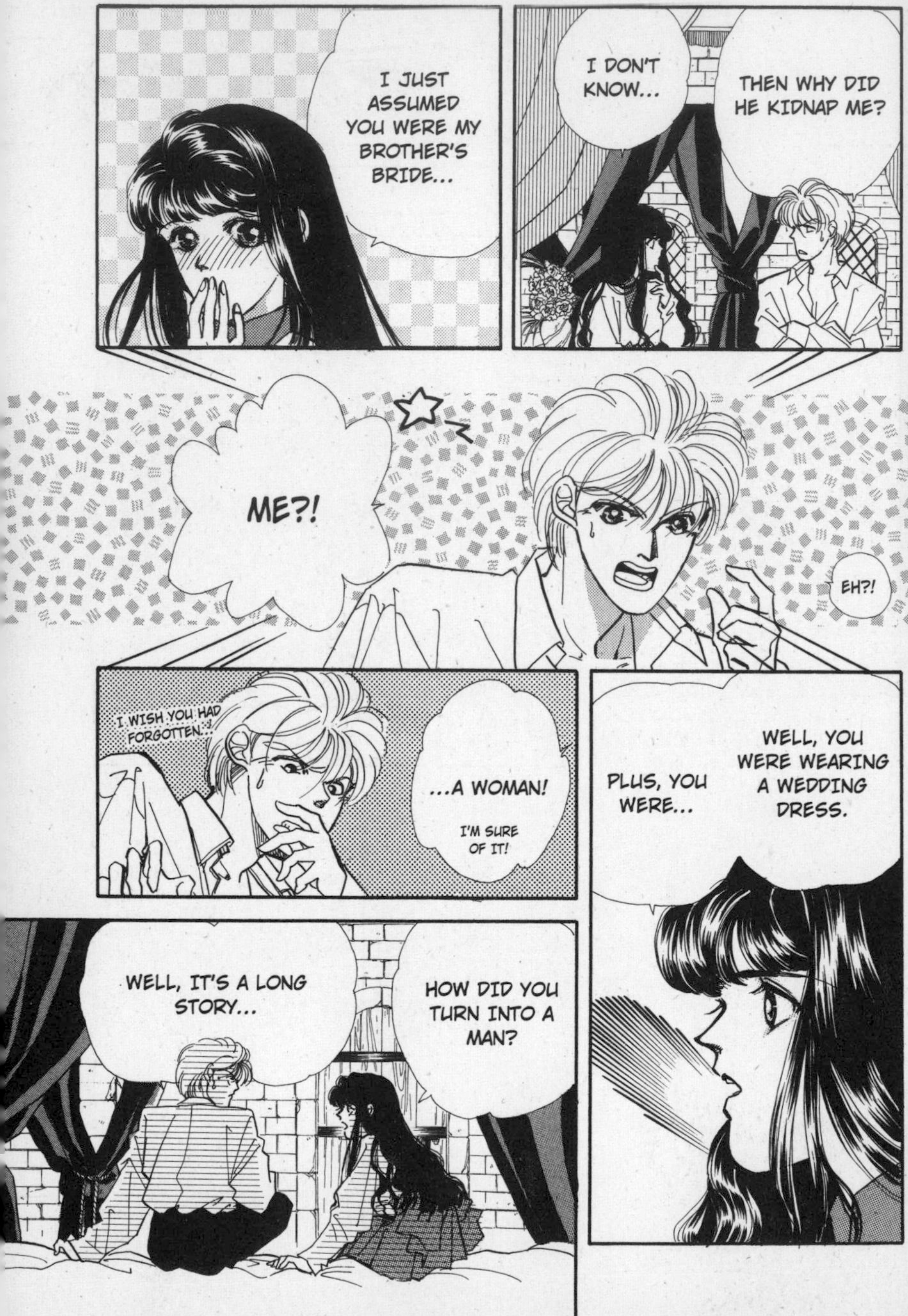
THEN WHY DID HE KIDNAP ME?
I DON'T KNOW...
I JUST ASSUMED YOU WERE MY BROTHER'S BRIDE...
EH?!
ME?!
WELL, YOU WERE WEARING A WEDDING DRESS.
PLUS, YOU WERE...
...A WOMAN!
I'M SURE OF IT!
I WISH YOU HAD FORGOTTEN...
HOW DID YOU TURN INTO A MAN?
WELL, IT'S A LONG STORY...

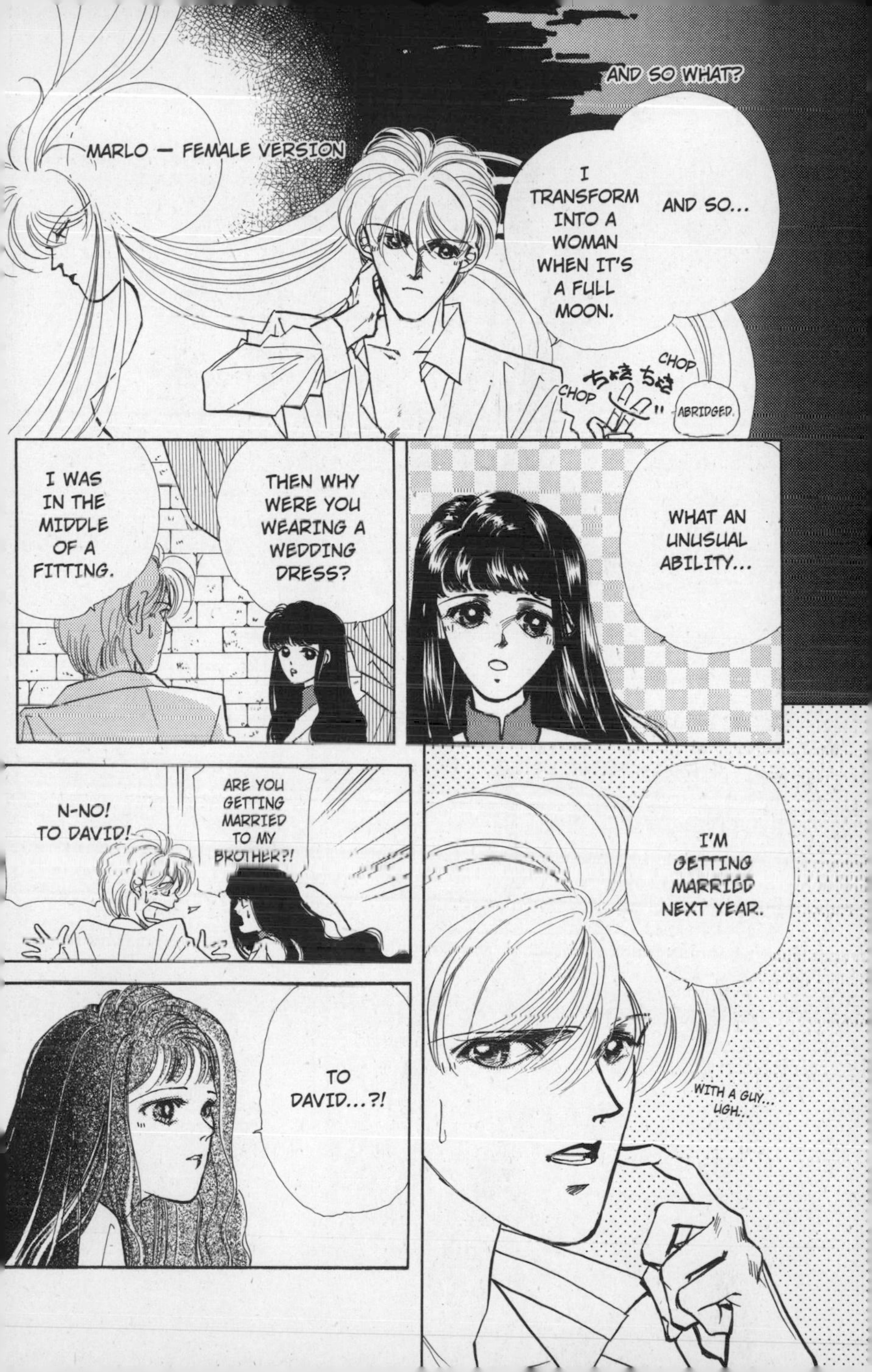
AND SO WHAT?
AND SO...
I TRANSFORM INTO A WOMAN WHEN IT'S A FULL MOON.
CHOP
ちょきちょき
CHOP
ABRIDGED.
MARLO — FEMALE VERSION
WHAT AN UNUSUAL ABILITY...
THEN WHY WERE YOU WEARING A WEDDING DRESS?
I WAS IN THE MIDDLE OF A FITTING.
I'M GETTING MARRIED NEXT YEAR.
WITH A GUY... UGH...
ARE YOU GETTING MARRIED TO MY BROTHER?!
N-NO! TO DAVID!
TO DAVID...?!

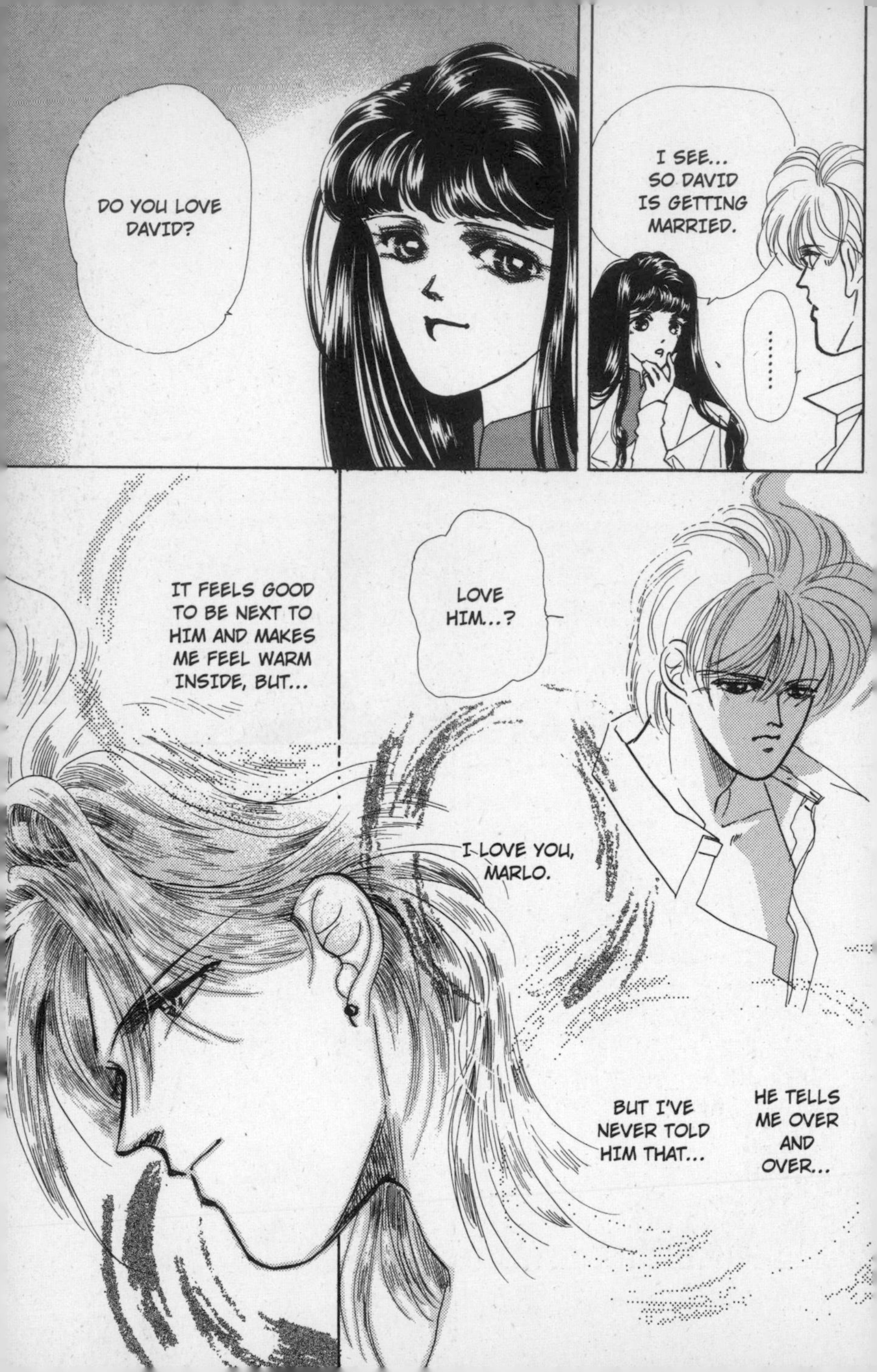
I SEE... SO DAVID IS GETTING MARRIED.
......
DO YOU LOVE DAVID?
LOVE HIM...?
I LOVE YOU, MARLO.
HE TELLS ME OVER AND OVER...
BUT I'VE NEVER TOLD HIM THAT...
IT FEELS GOOD TO BE NEXT TO HIM AND MAKES ME FEEL WARM INSIDE, BUT...

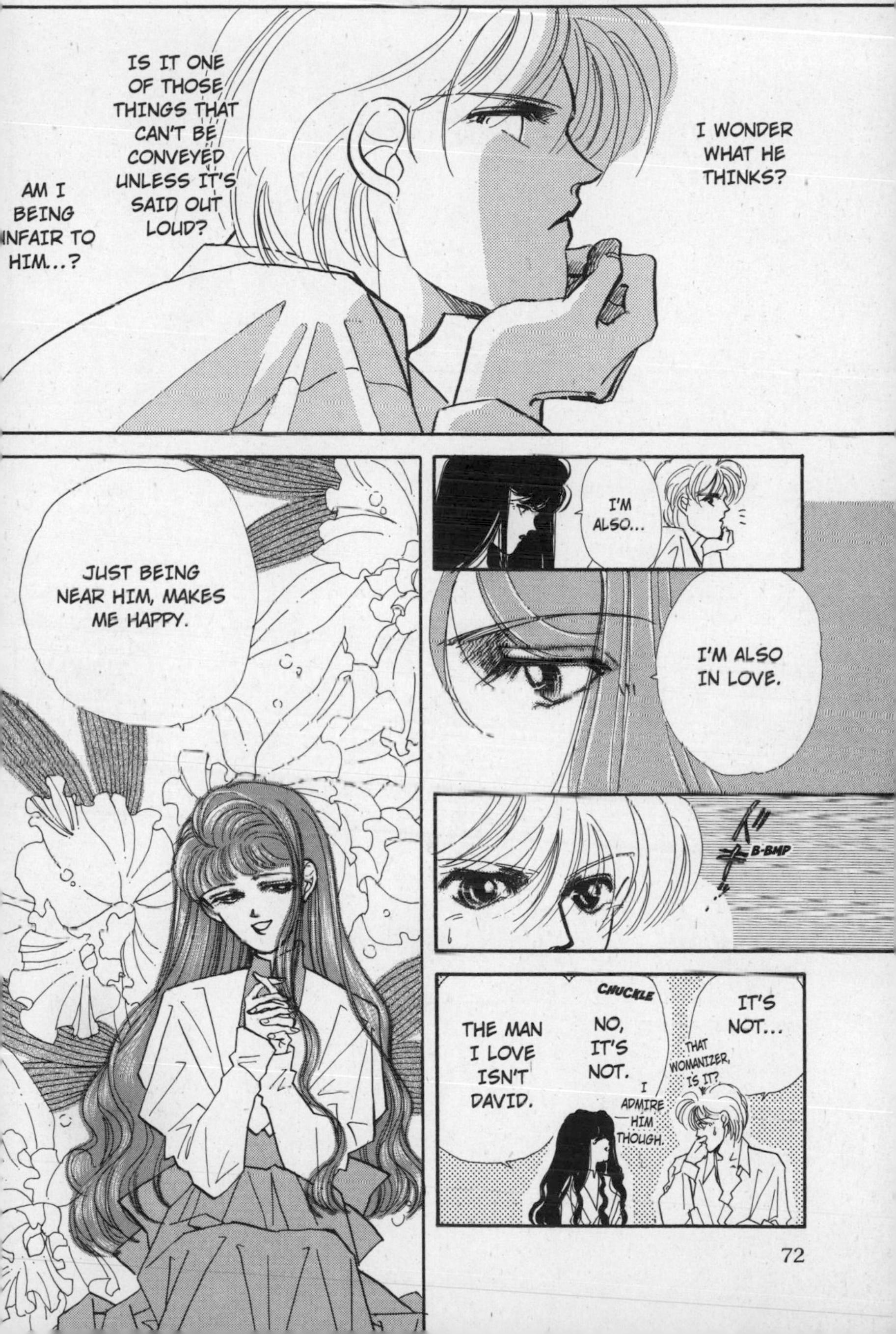
I WONDER WHAT HE THINKS?
IS IT ONE OF THOSE THINGS THAT CAN'T BE CONVEYED UNLESS IT'S SAID OUT LOUD?
AM I BEING INFAIR TO HIM...?
I'M ALSO...
I'M ALSO IN LOVE.
B-BMP
IT'S NOT...
THAT WOMANIZER, IS IT?
CHUCKLE
NO, IT'S NOT.
I ADMIRE HIM THOUGH.
THE MAN I LOVE ISN'T DAVID.
JUST BEING NEAR HIM, MAKES ME HAPPY.

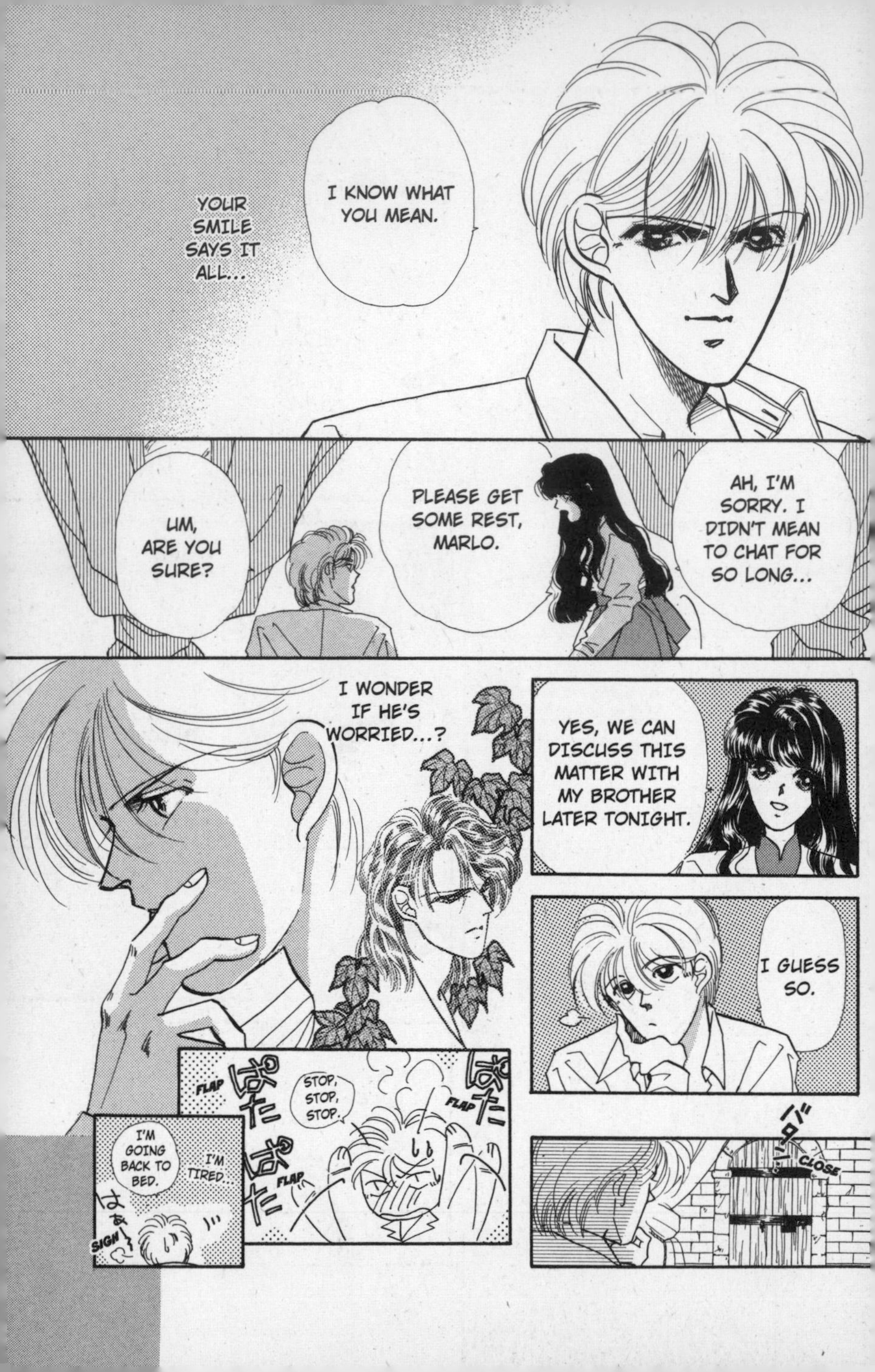
I KNOW WHAT YOU MEAN.
YOUR SMILE SAYS IT ALL...
AH, I'M SORRY. I DIDN'T MEAN TO CHAT FOR SO LONG...
PLEASE GET SOME REST, MARLO.
UM, ARE YOU SURE?
YES, WE CAN DISCUSS THIS MATTER WITH MY BROTHER LATER TONIGHT.
I GUESS SO.
バタン
CLOSE
I WONDER IF HE'S WORRIED...?
ぱたー
FLAP
ぱた
FLAP
ぱたー
FLAP
STOP, STOP, STOP.
I'M TIRED.
I'M GOING BACK TO BED.
はぁ~
SIGH

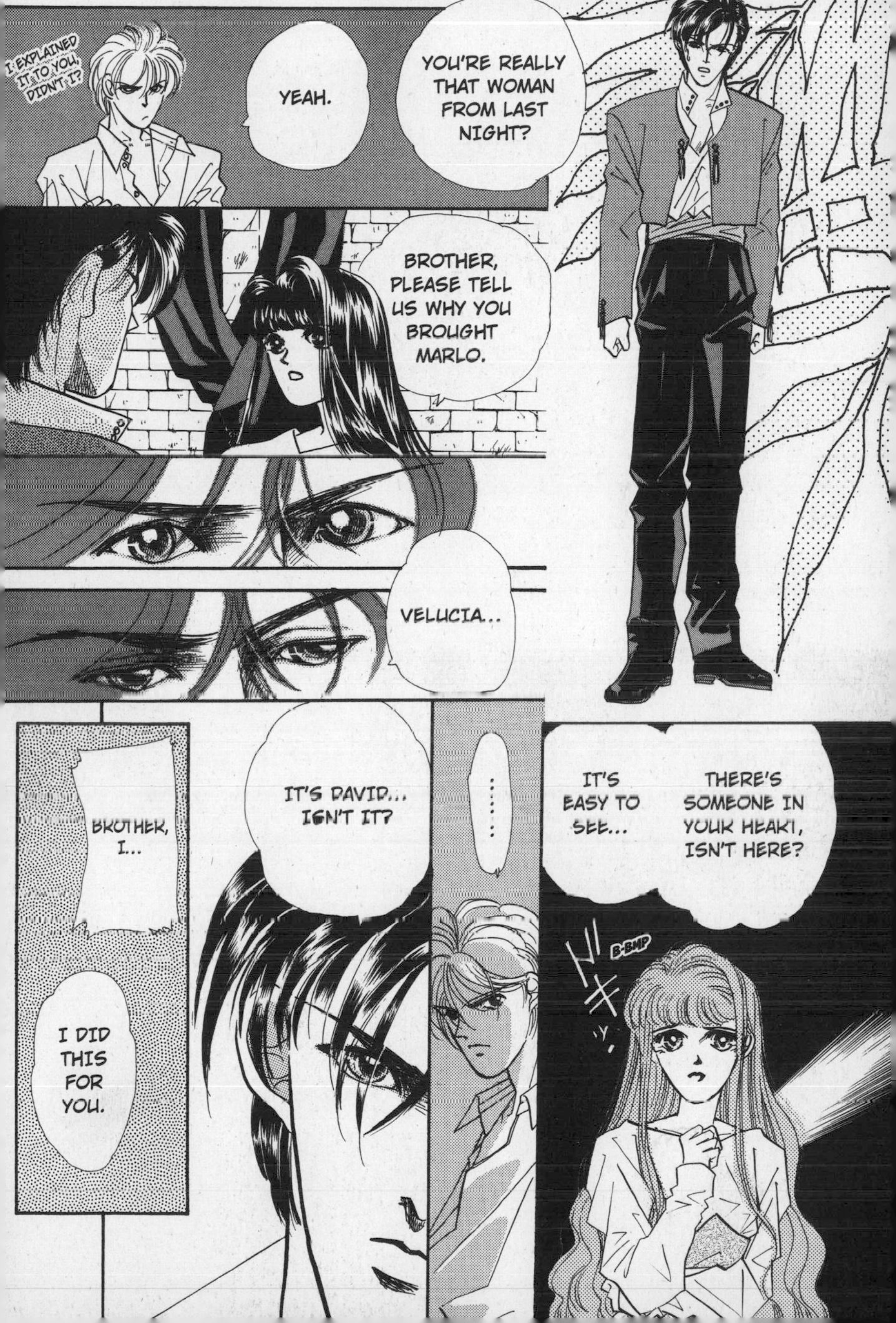

YOU'RE REALLY THAT WOMAN FROM LAST NIGHT?
YEAH.
I EXPLAINED IT TO YOU, DIDN'T I?
BROTHER, PLEASE TELL US WHY YOU BROUGHT MARLO.
VELUCIA...
THERE'S SOMEONE IN YOUR HEART, ISN'T HERE?
IT'S EASY TO SEE...
B-BMP
......
IT'S DAVID... ISN'T IT?
BROTHER, I...
I DID THIS FOR YOU.

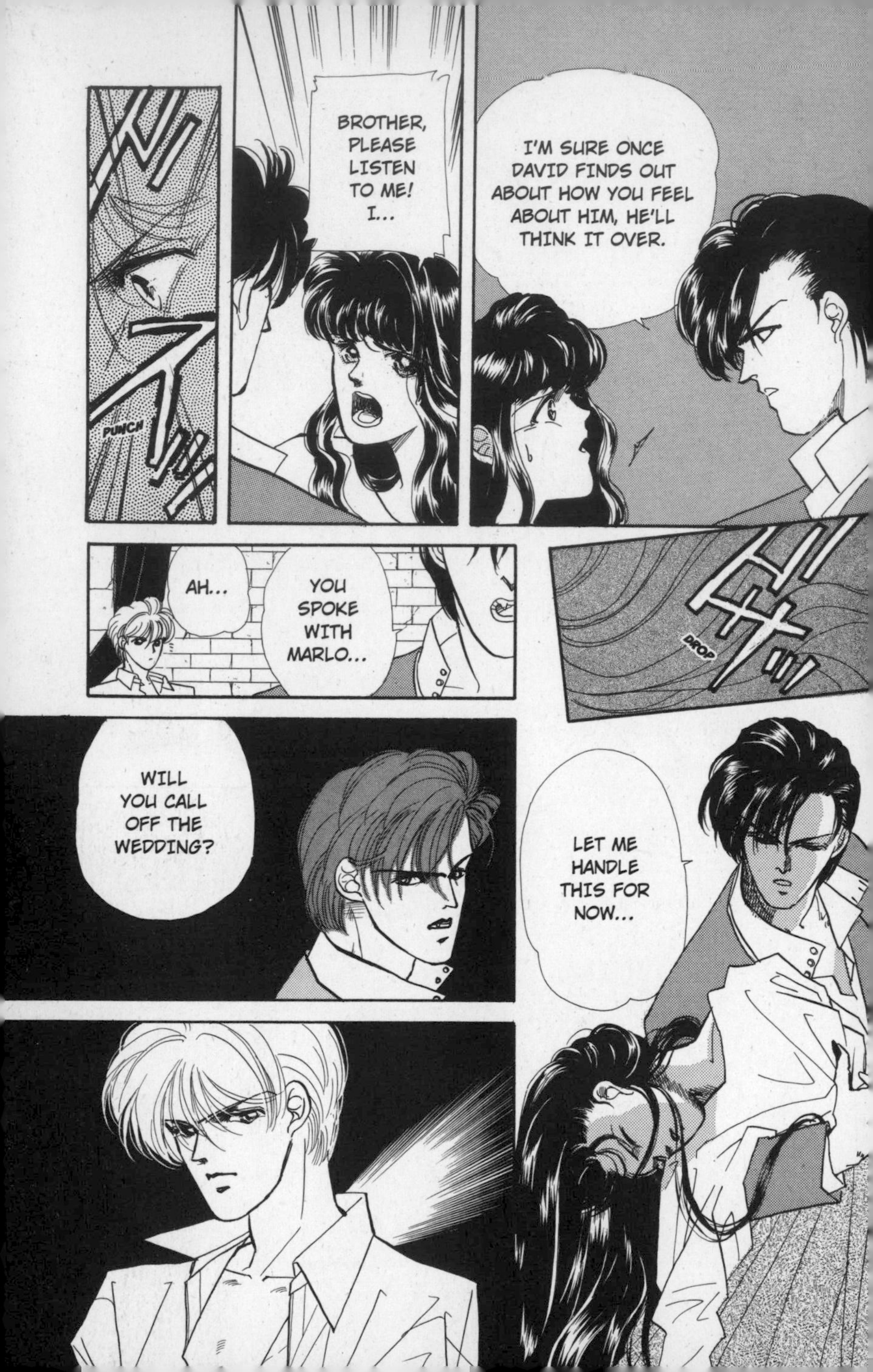
I'M SURE ONCE DAVID FINDS OUT ABOUT HOW YOU FEEL ABOUT HIM, HE'LL THINK IT OVER.
BROTHER, PLEASE LISTEN TO ME! I...
PUNCH
DROP
YOU SPOKE WITH MARLO...
AH...
LET ME HANDLE THIS FOR NOW...
WILL YOU CALL OFF THE WEDDING?

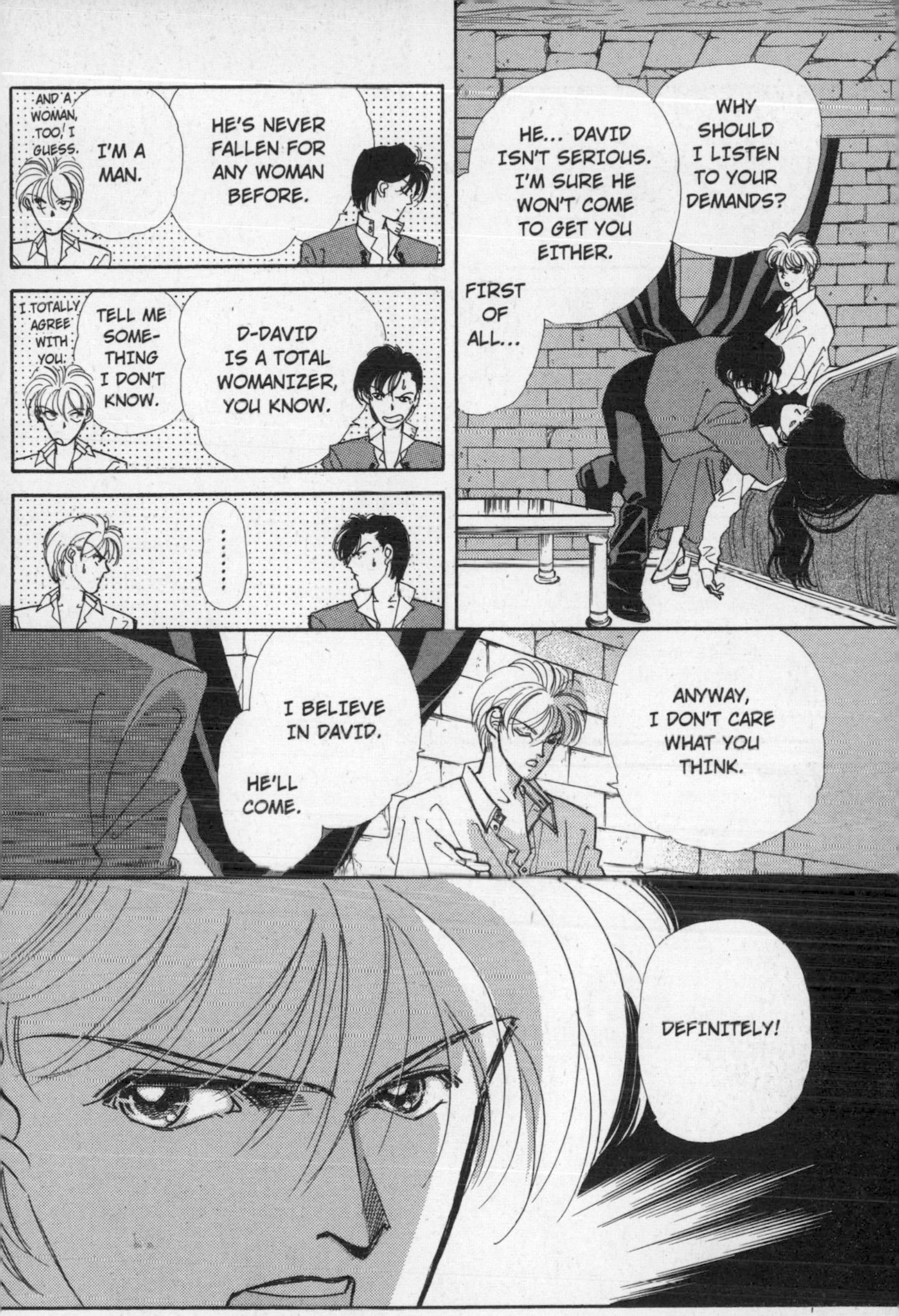
WHY SHOULD I LISTEN TO YOUR DEMANDS?
HE... DAVID ISN'T SERIOUS. I'M SURE HE WON'T COME TO GET YOU EITHER.
FIRST OF ALL...
HE'S NEVER FALLEN FOR ANY WOMAN BEFORE.
I'M A MAN.
AND A WOMAN, TOO, I GUESS.
D-DAVID IS A TOTAL WOMANIZER, YOU KNOW.
TELL ME SOME-THING I DON'T KNOW.
I TOTALLY AGREE WITH YOU.
......
ANYWAY, I DON'T CARE WHAT YOU THINK.
I BELIEVE IN DAVID.
HE'LL COME.
DEFINITELY!

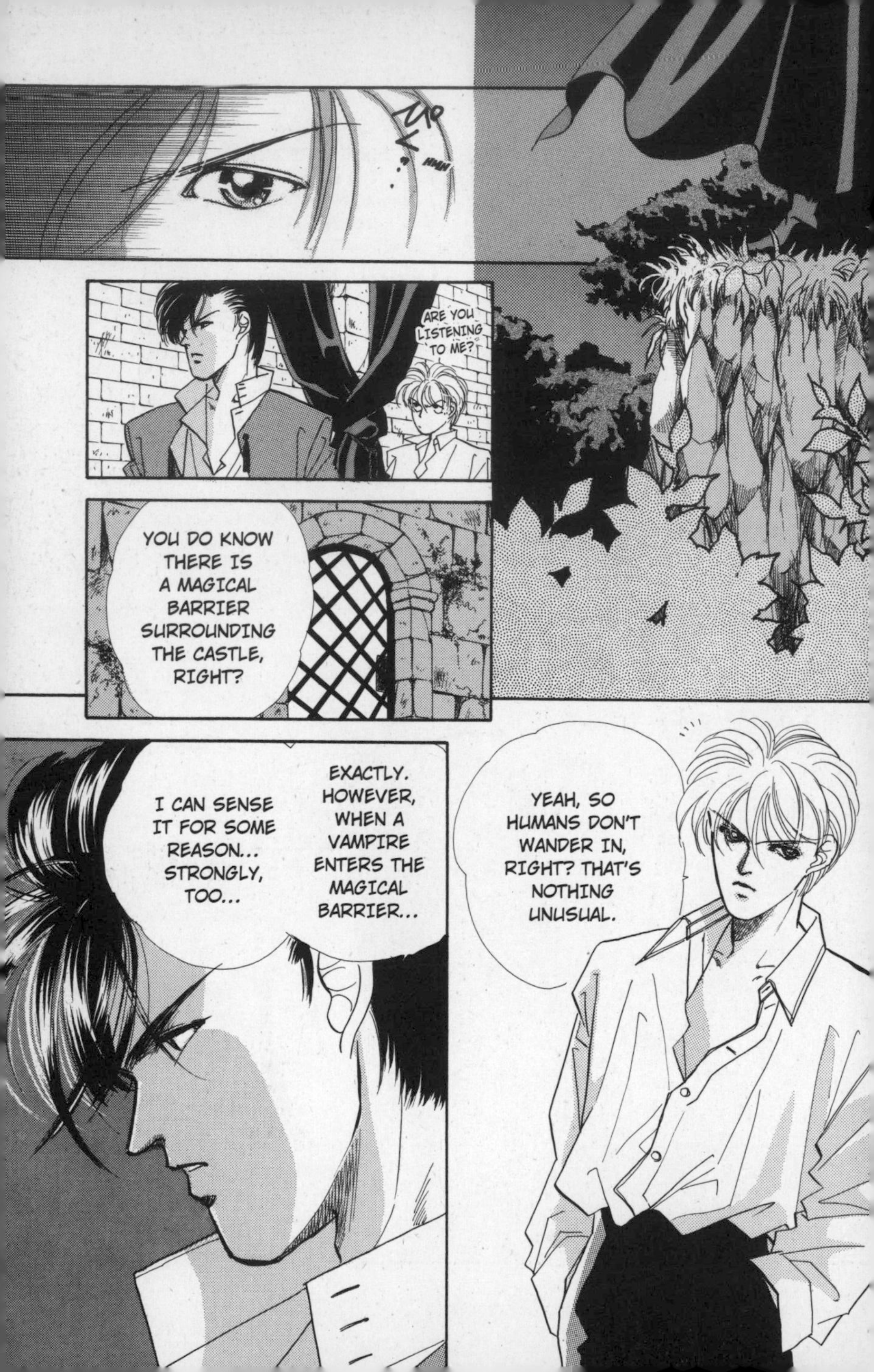
ARE YOU LISTENING TO ME?
YOU DO KNOW THERE IS A MAGICAL BARRIER SURROUNDING THE CASTLE, RIGHT?
YEAH, SO HUMANS DON'T WANDER IN, RIGHT? THAT'S NOTHING UNUSUAL.
EXACTLY. HOWEVER, WHEN A VAMPIRE ENTERS THE MAGICAL BARRIER...
I CAN SENSE IT FOR SOME REASON... STRONGLY, TOO...

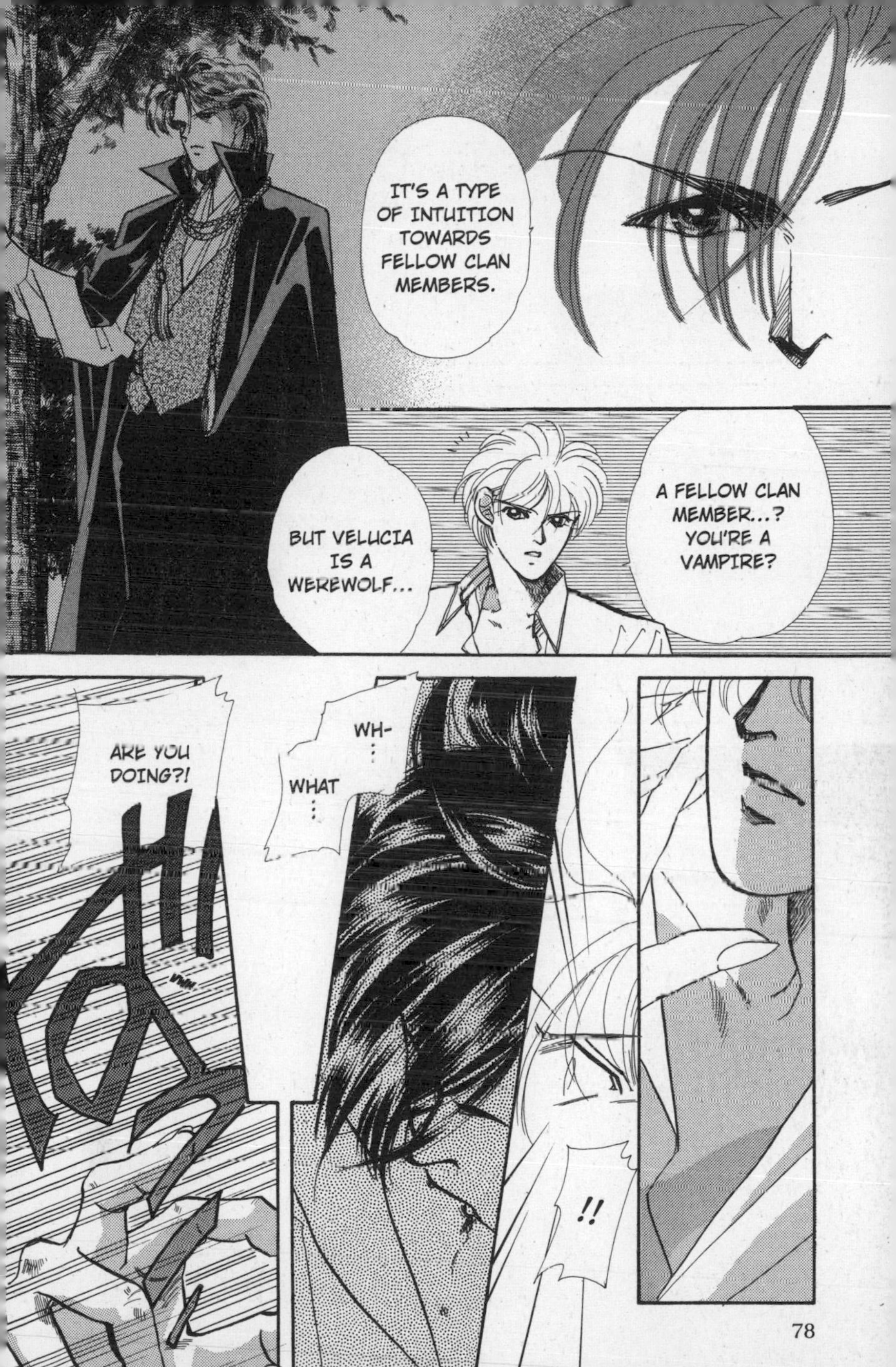
IT'S A TYPE OF INTUITION TOWARDS FELLOW CLAN MEMBERS.
A FELLOW CLAN MEMBER...? YOU'RE A VAMPIRE?
BUT VELUCIA IS A WEREWOLF...
WH- …
WHAT …
!!
ARE YOU DOING?!

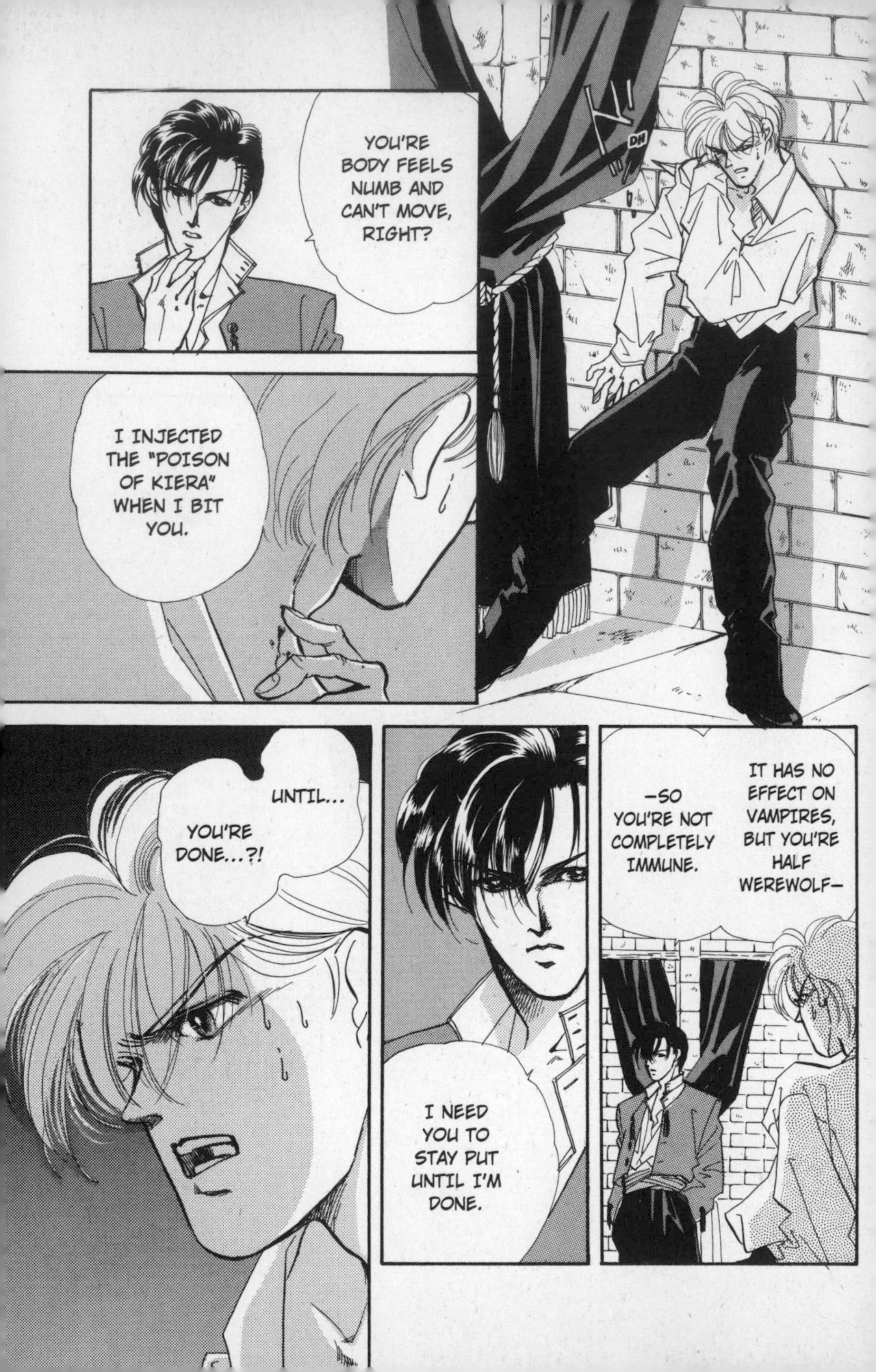
DH
YOU'RE BODY FEELS NUMB AND CAN'T MOVE, RIGHT?
I INJECTED THE "POISON OF KIERA" WHEN I BIT YOU.
IT HAS NO EFFECT ON VAMPIRES, BUT YOU'RE HALF WEREWOLF—
—SO YOU'RE NOT COMPLETELY IMMUNE.
I NEED YOU TO STAY PUT UNTIL I'M DONE.
UNTIL...
YOU'RE DONE...?!

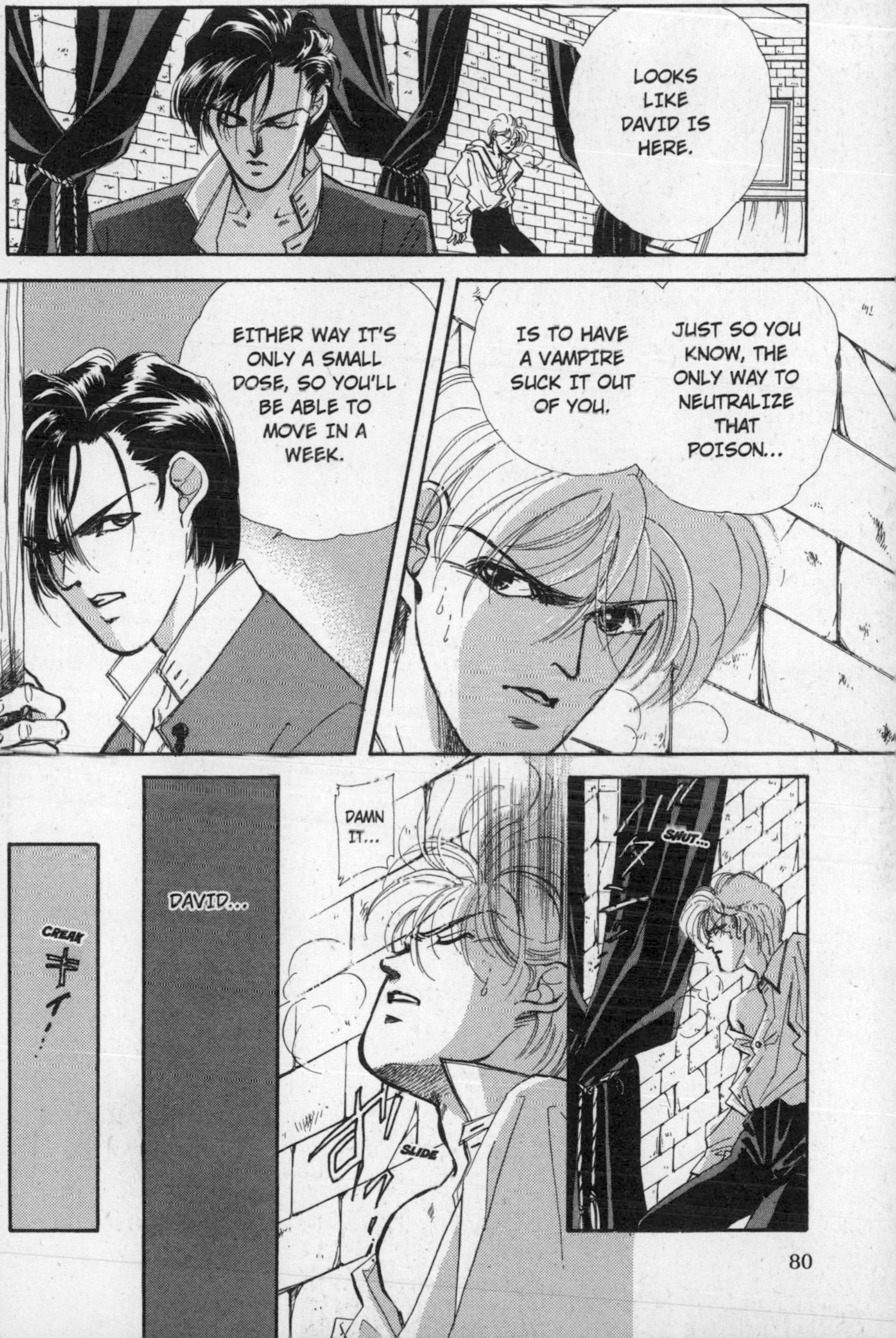
LOOKS LIKE DAVID IS HERE.
JUST SO YOU KNOW, THE ONLY WAY TO NEUTRALIZE THAT POISON...
IS TO HAVE A VAMPIRE SUCK IT OUT OF YOU.
EITHER WAY IT'S ONLY A SMALL DOSE, SO YOU'LL BE ABLE TO MOVE IN A WEEK.
SHUT...
DAMN IT...
SLIDE
DAVID...
CREAK
キイ

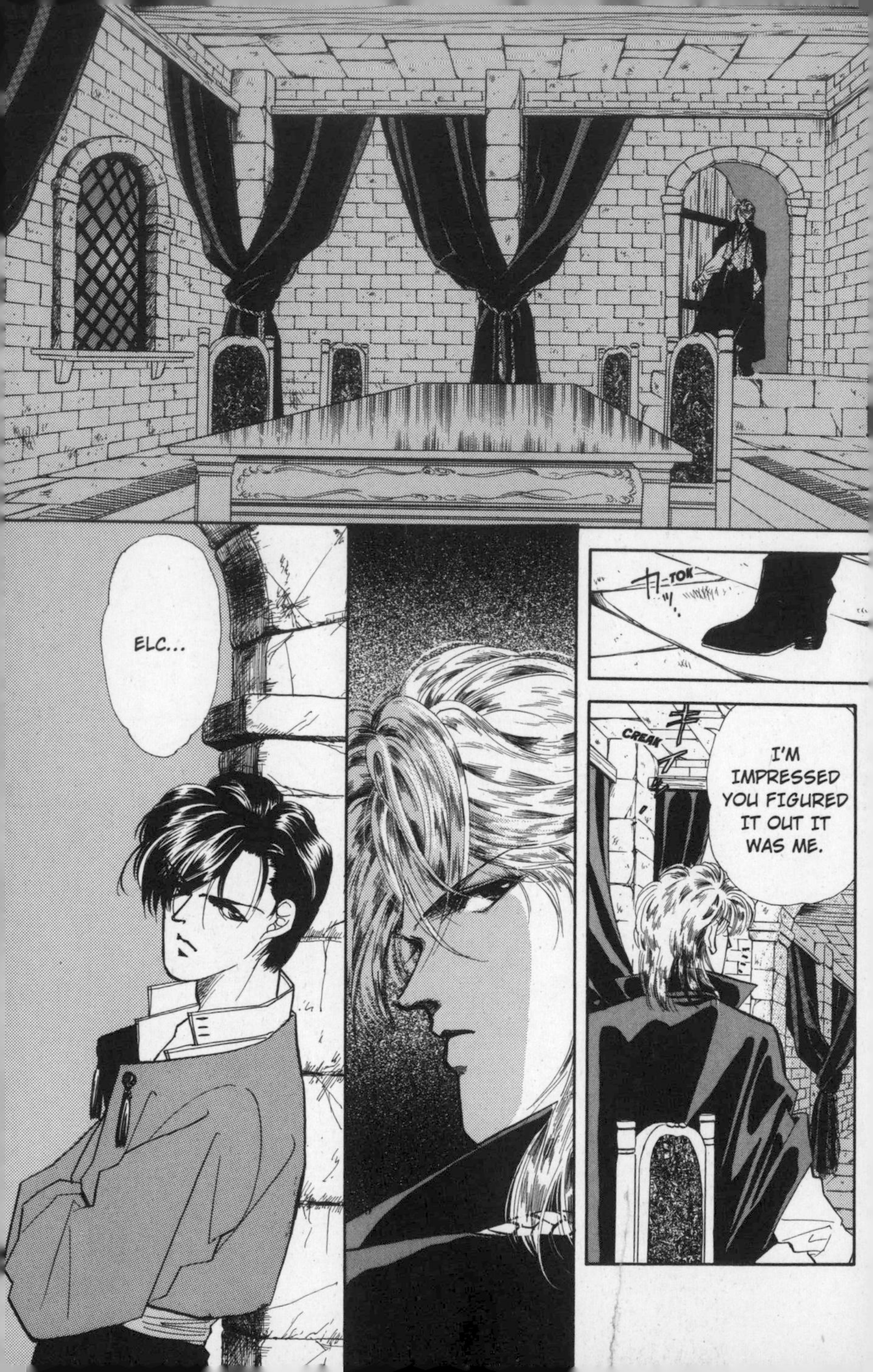
TOK
CREAK
I'M IMPRESSED YOU FIGURED IT OUT IT WAS ME.
ELC...

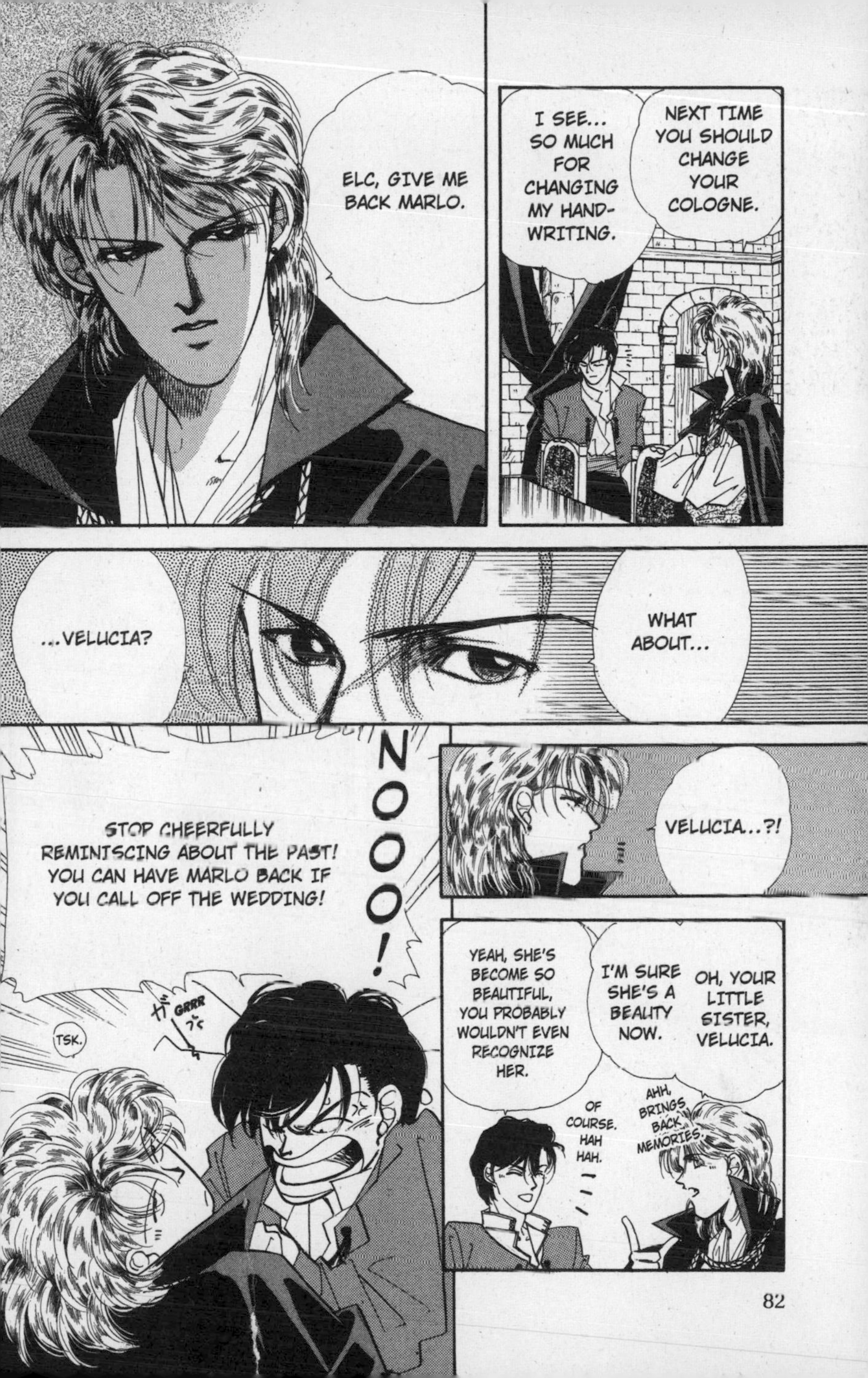
NEXT TIME YOU SHOULD CHANGE YOUR COLOGNE.
I SEE... SO MUCH FOR CHANGING MY HAND-WRITING.
ELC, GIVE ME BACK MARLO.
WHAT ABOUT...
...VELUCIA?
VELUCIA...?!
OH, YOUR LITTLE SISTER, VELUCIA.
I'M SURE SHE'S A BEAUTY NOW.
YEAH, SHE'S BECOME SO BEAUTIFUL, YOU PROBABLY WOULDN'T EVEN RECOGNIZE HER.
AHH, BRINGS BACK MEMORIES.
OF COURSE. HAH HAH.
NOOO!
STOP CHEERFULLY REMINISCING ABOUT THE PAST! YOU CAN HAVE MARLO BACK IF YOU CALL OFF THE WEDDING!
GRRR
TSK.

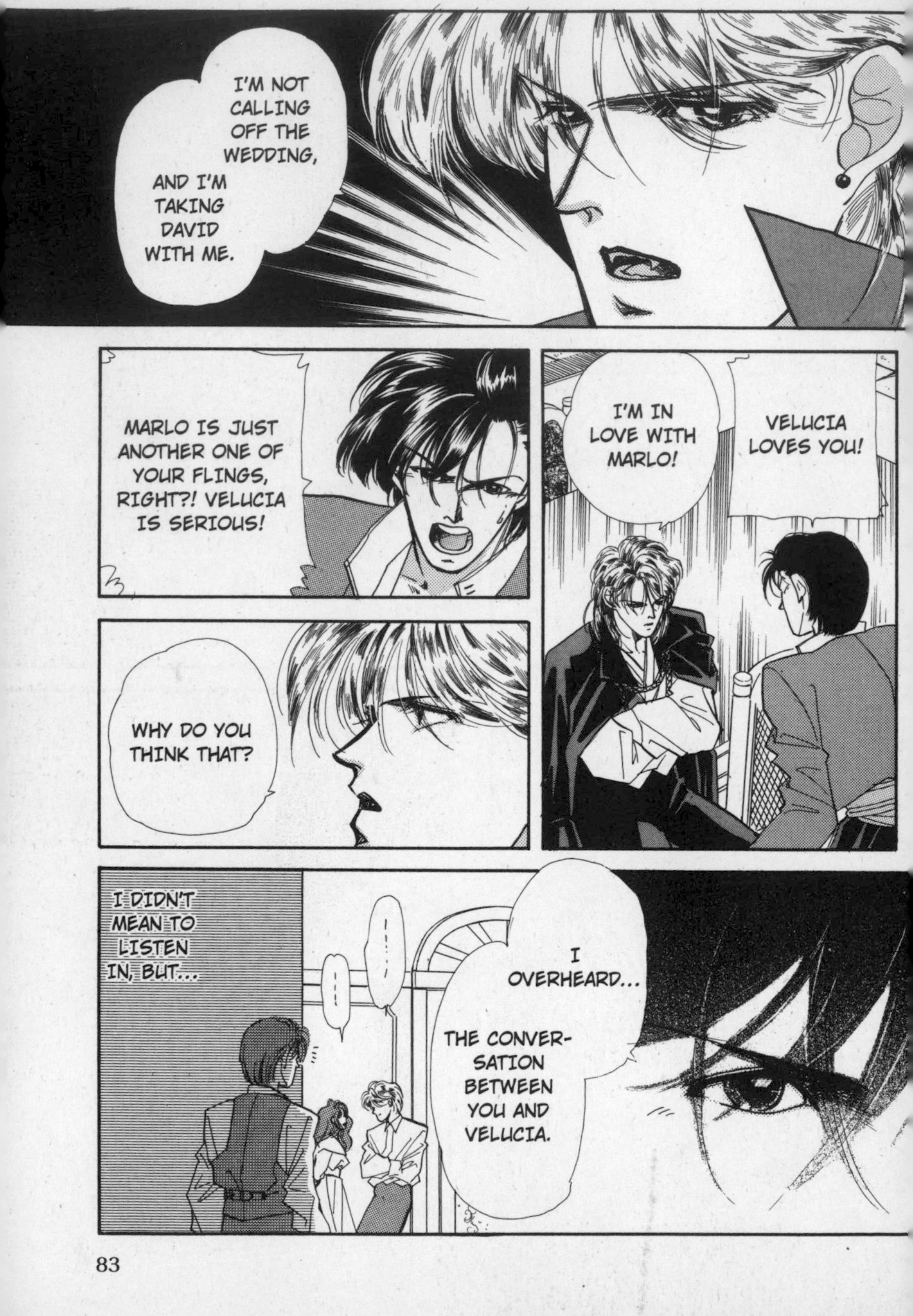
I'M NOT CALLING OFF THE WEDDING,
AND I'M TAKING DAVID WITH ME.
VELUCIA LOVES YOU!
I'M IN LOVE WITH MARLO!
MARLO IS JUST ANOTHER ONE OF YOUR FLINGS, RIGHT?! VELUCIA IS SERIOUS!
WHY DO YOU THINK THAT?
I OVERHEARD...
THE CONVER-SATION BETWEEN YOU AND VELUCIA.
!...
!...
I DIDN'T MEAN TO LISTEN IN, BUT...

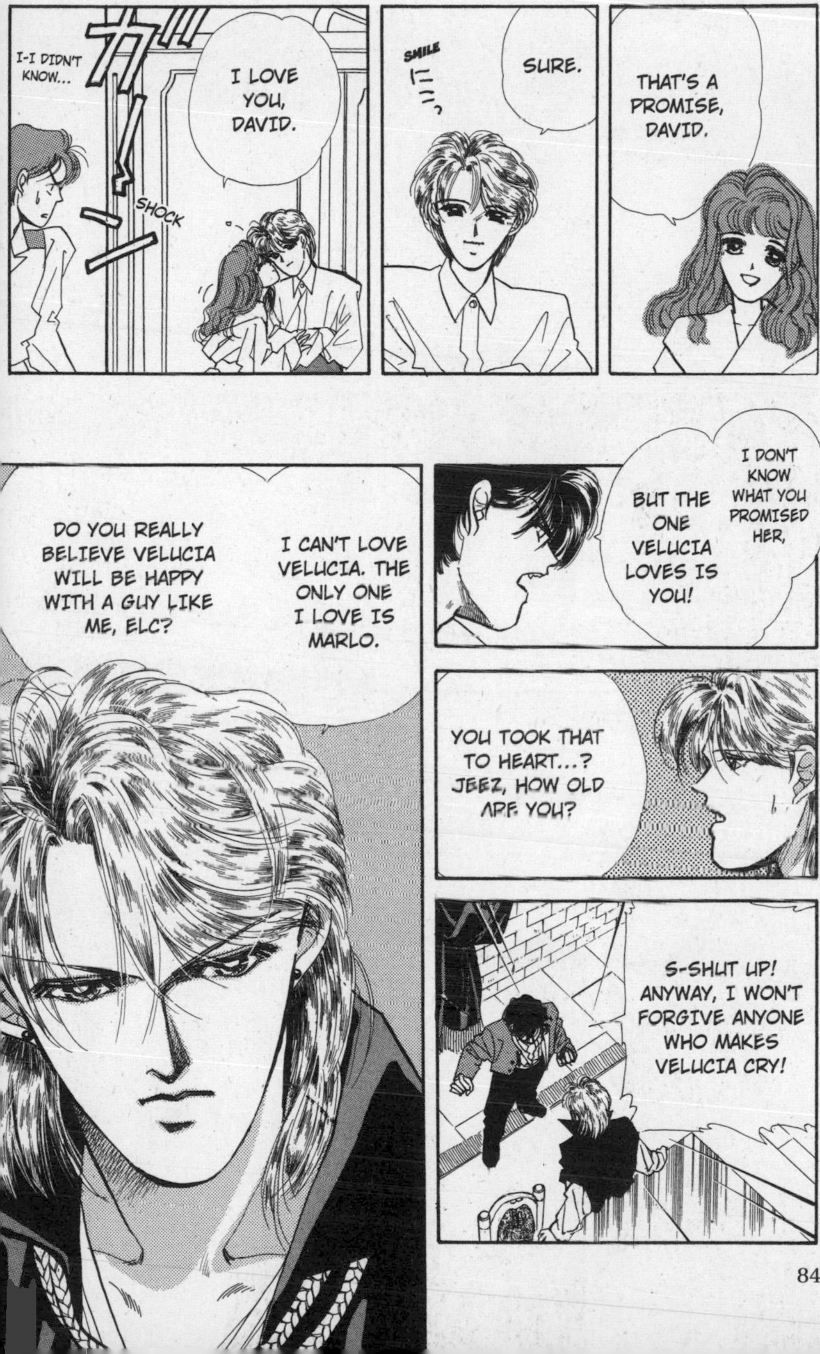
THAT'S A PROMISE, DAVID.
SMILE
SURE.
I LOVE YOU, DAVID.
SHOCK
I-I DIDN'T KNOW...
I DON'T KNOW WHAT YOU PROMISED HER,
BUT THE ONE VELUCIA LOVES IS YOU!
YOU TOOK THAT TO HEART...? JEEZ, HOW OLD ARE YOU?
S-SHUT UP! ANYWAY, I WON'T FORGIVE ANYONE WHO MAKES VELUCIA CRY!
I CAN'T LOVE VELUCIA. THE ONLY ONE I LOVE IS MARLO.
DO YOU REALLY BELIEVE VELUCIA WILL BE HAPPY WITH A GUY LIKE ME, ELC?

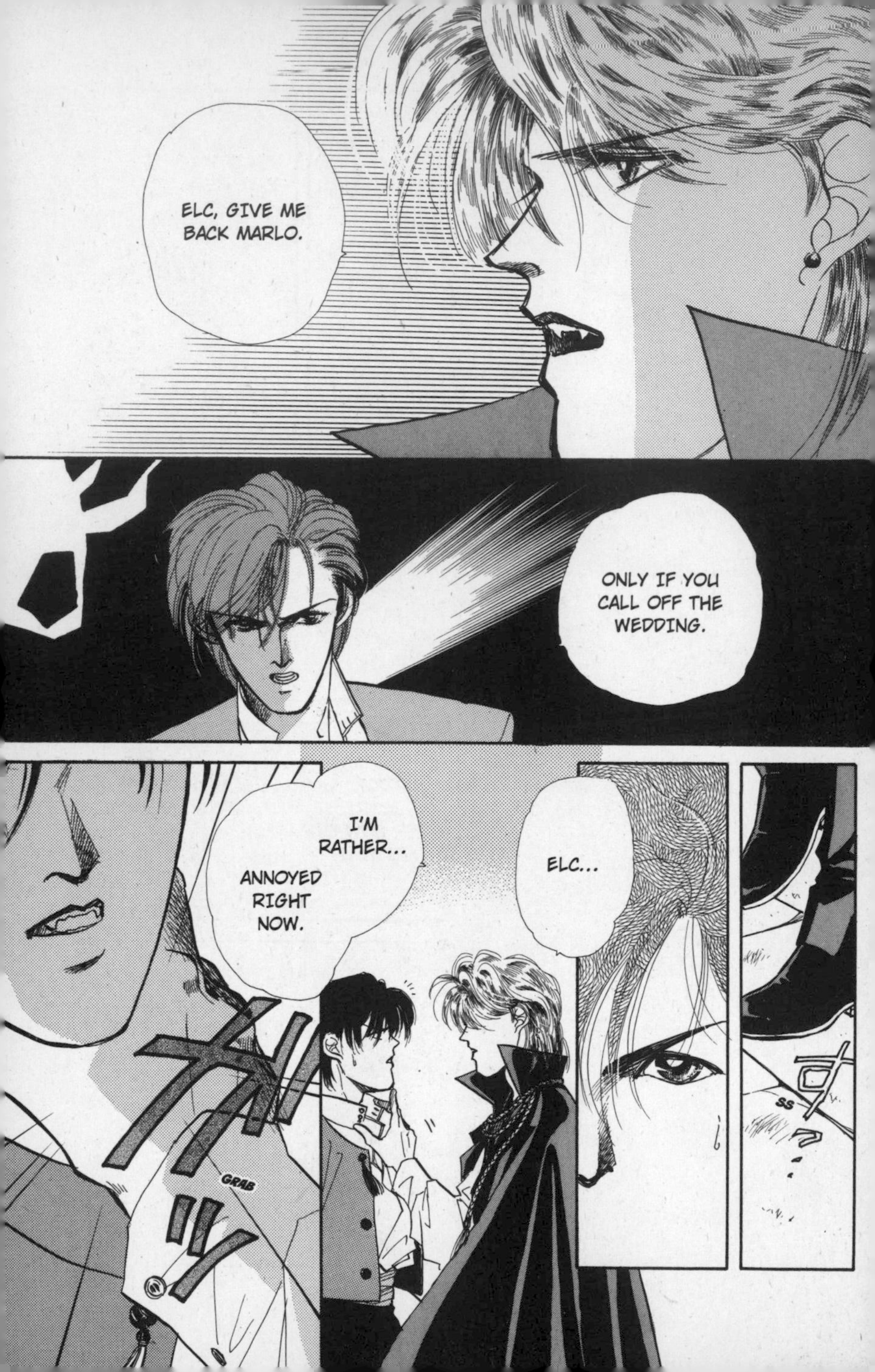
ELC, GIVE ME BACK MARLO.
ONLY IF YOU CALL OFF THE WEDDING.
SS
ELC...
I'M RATHER...
ANNOYED RIGHT NOW.
GRAB

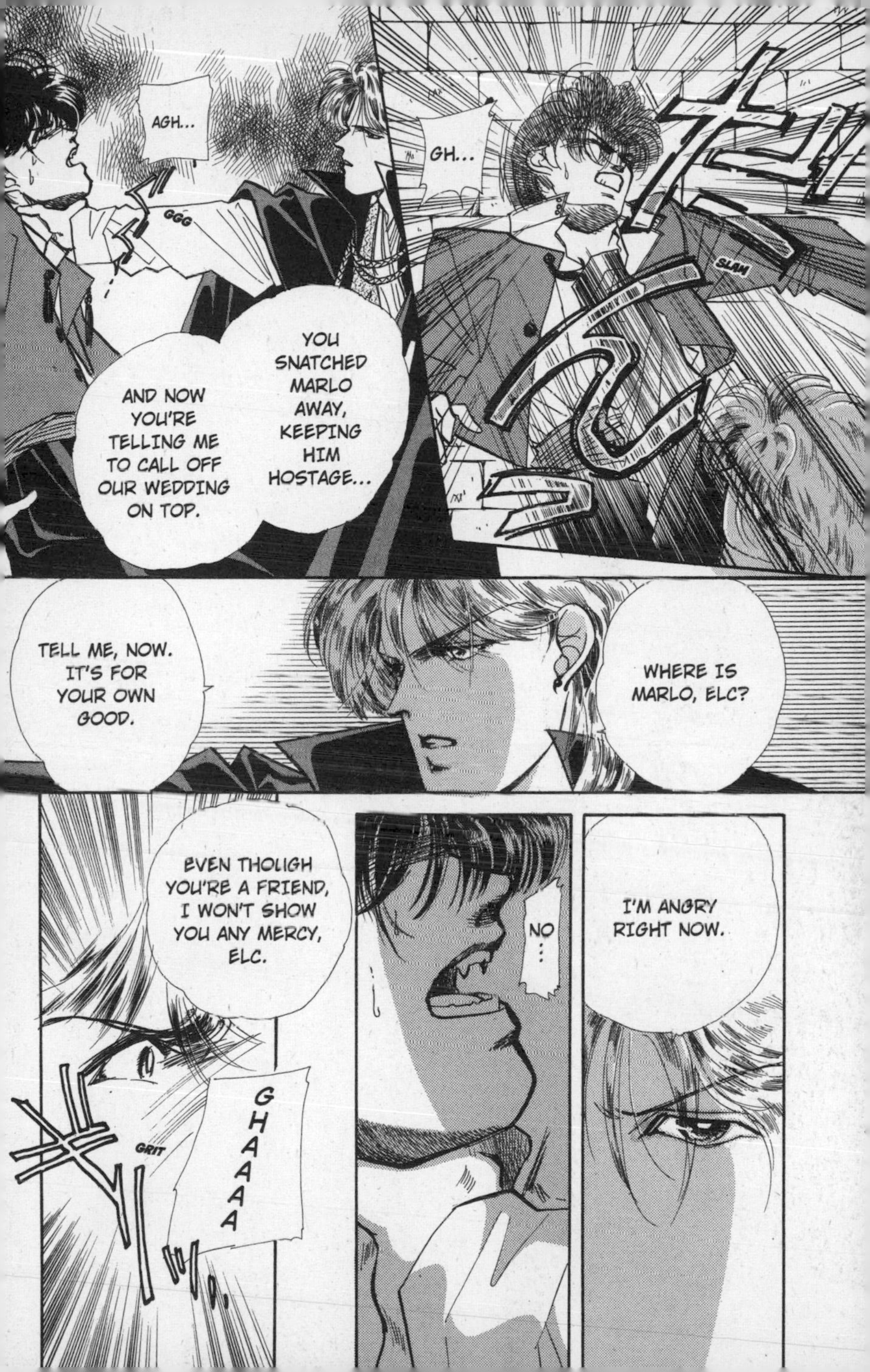

GH...
SLAM
AGH...
GGG
YOU SNATCHED MARLO AWAY, KEEPING HIM HOSTAGE...
AND NOW YOU'RE TELLING ME TO CALL OFF OUR WEDDING ON TOP.
WHERE IS MARLO, ELC?
TELL ME, NOW. IT'S FOR YOUR OWN GOOD.
I'M ANGRY RIGHT NOW.
NO...
EVEN THOUGH YOU'RE A FRIEND, I WON'T SHOW YOU ANY MERCY, ELC.
GHAAAAA
GRIT

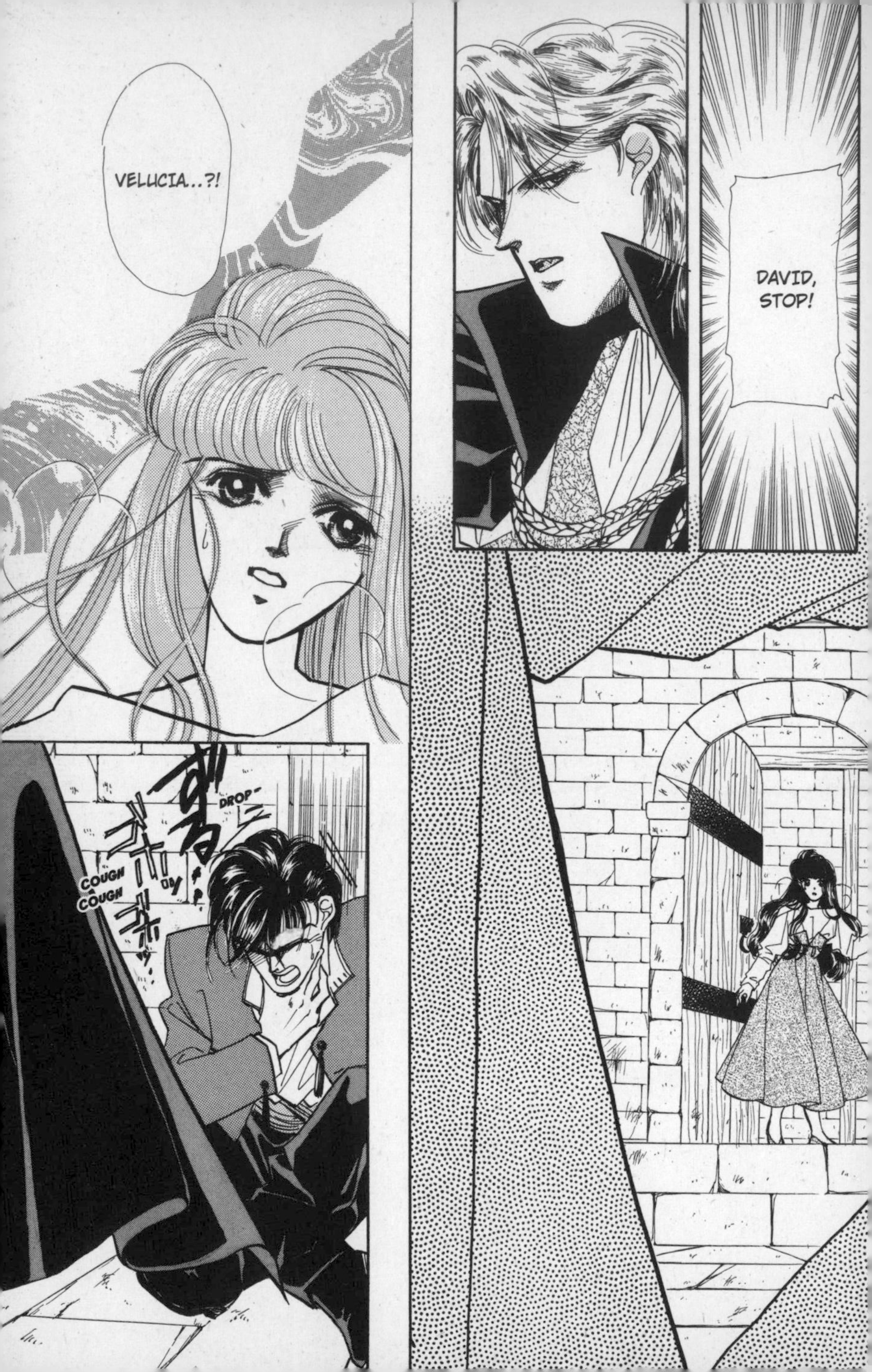
DAVID, STOP!
VELUCIA..?!
DROP
COUGH
COUGH

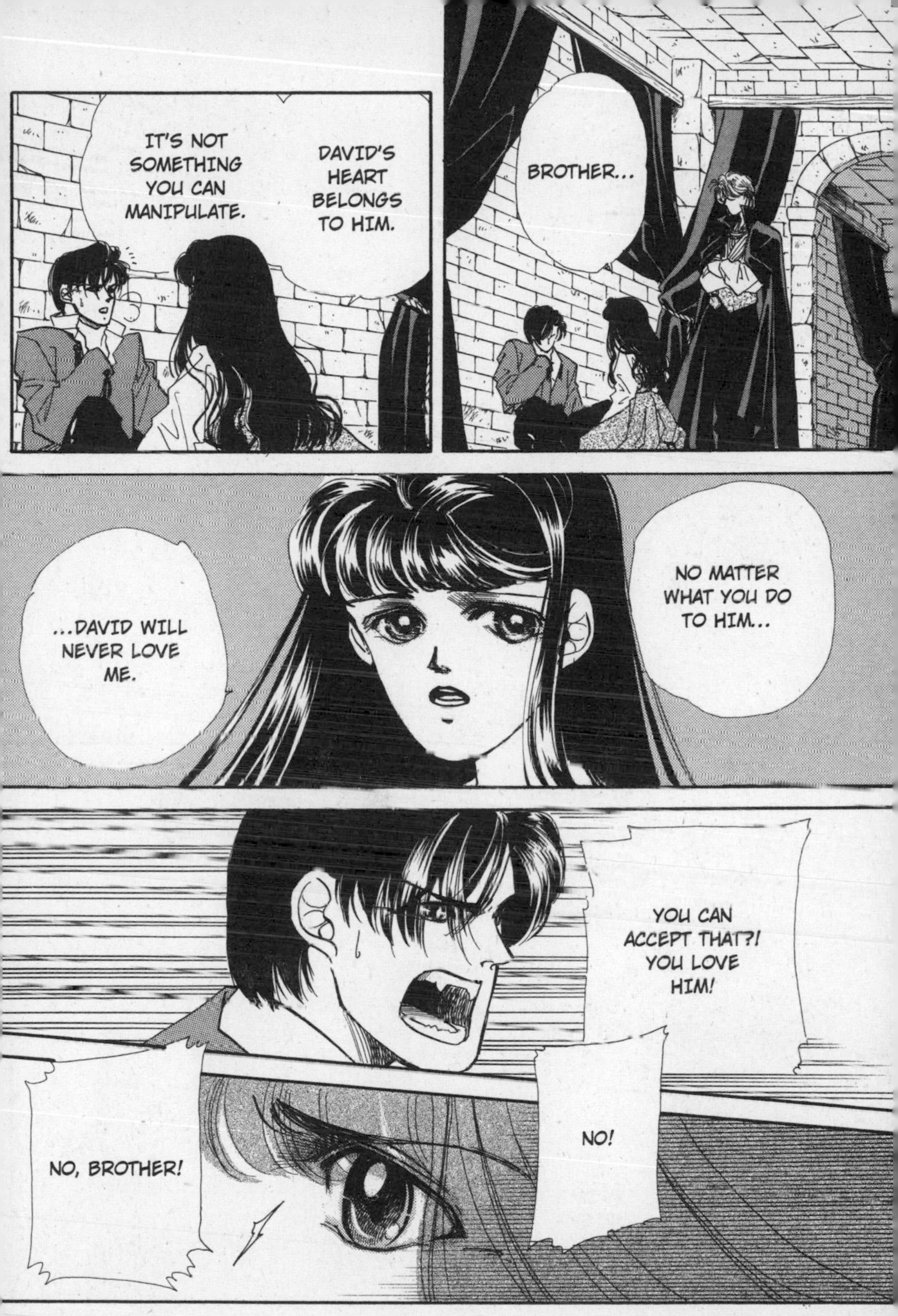
BROTHER...
DAVID'S HEART BELONGS TO HIM.
IT'S NOT SOMETHING YOU CAN MANIPULATE.
NO MATTER WHAT YOU DO TO HIM...
...DAVID WILL NEVER LOVE ME.
YOU CAN ACCEPT THAT?! YOU LOVE HIM!
NO!
NO, BROTHER!

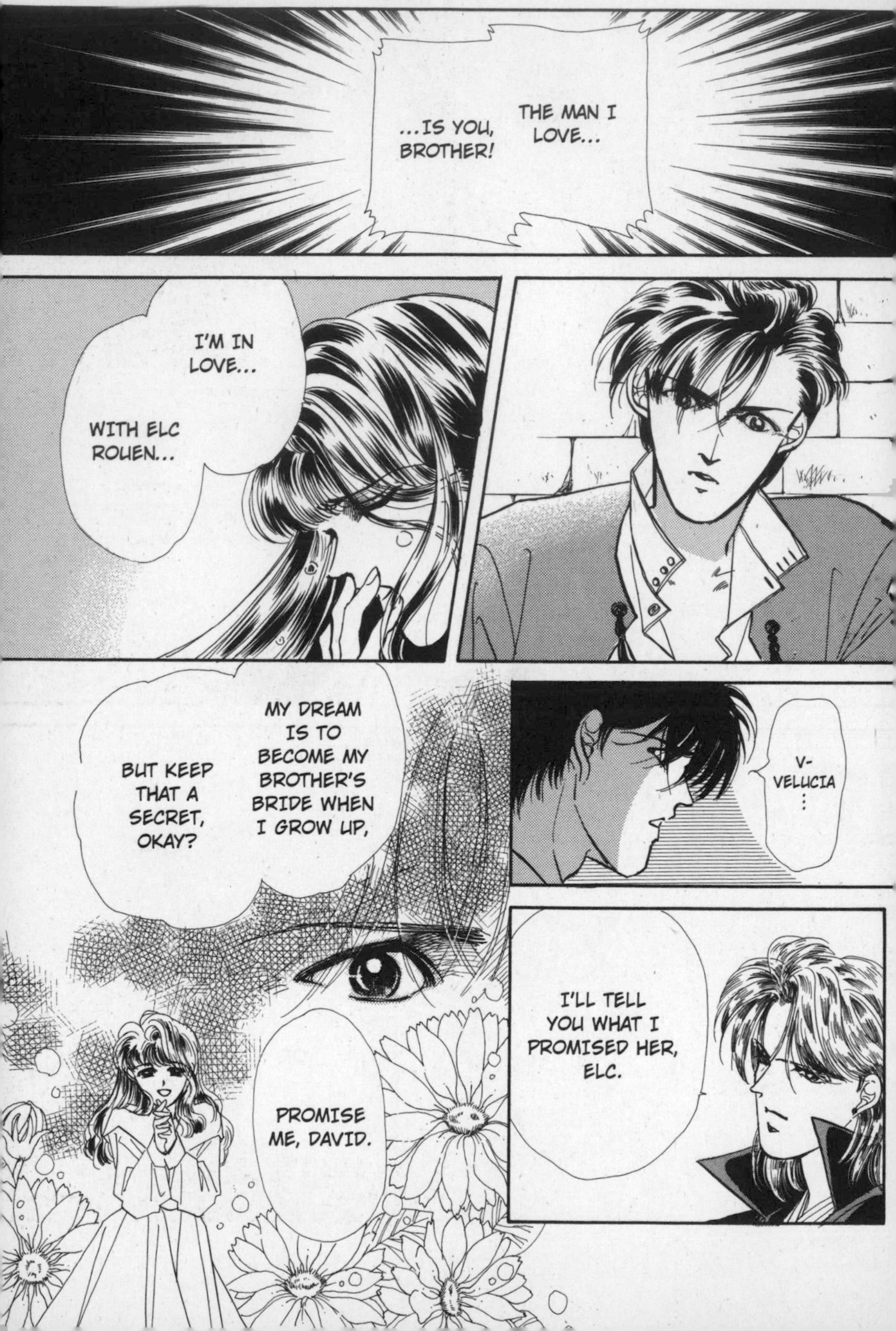
THE MAN I LOVE...
...IS YOU, BROTHER!
I'M IN LOVE...
WITH ELC ROUEN...
V-VELUCIA...
I'LL TELL YOU WHAT I PROMISED HER, ELC.
MY DREAM IS TO BECOME MY BROTHER'S BRIDE WHEN I GROW UP,
BUT KEEP THAT A SECRET, OKAY?
PROMISE ME, DAVID.

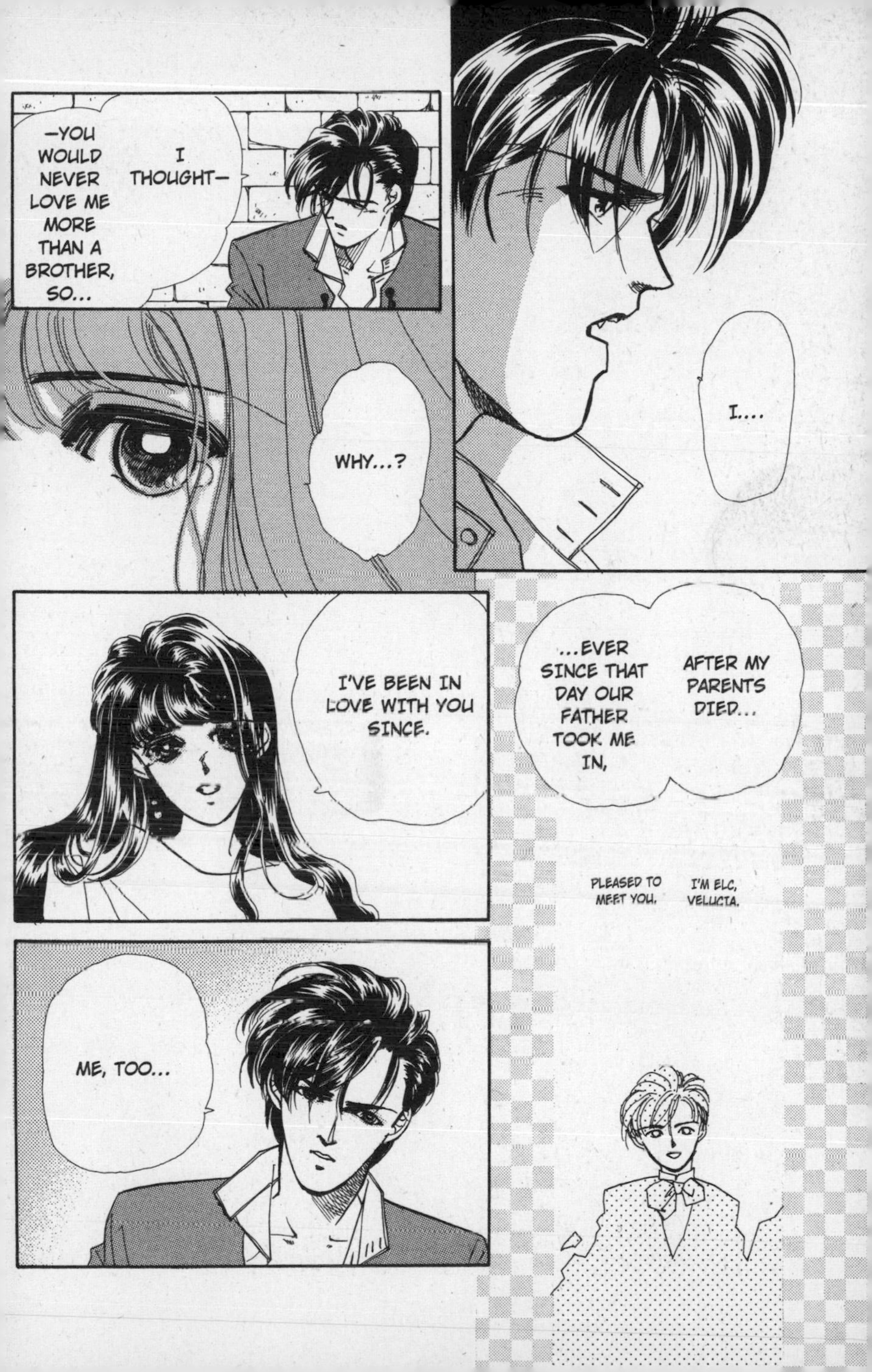
I...
I THOUGHT—
—YOU WOULD NEVER LOVE ME MORE THAN A BROTHER, SO...
WHY...?
AFTER MY PARENTS DIED...
...EVER SINCE THAT DAY OUR FATHER TOOK ME IN,
I'M ELC, VELUCTA.
PLEASED TO MEET YOU.
I'VE BEEN IN LOVE WITH YOU SINCE.
ME, TOO...

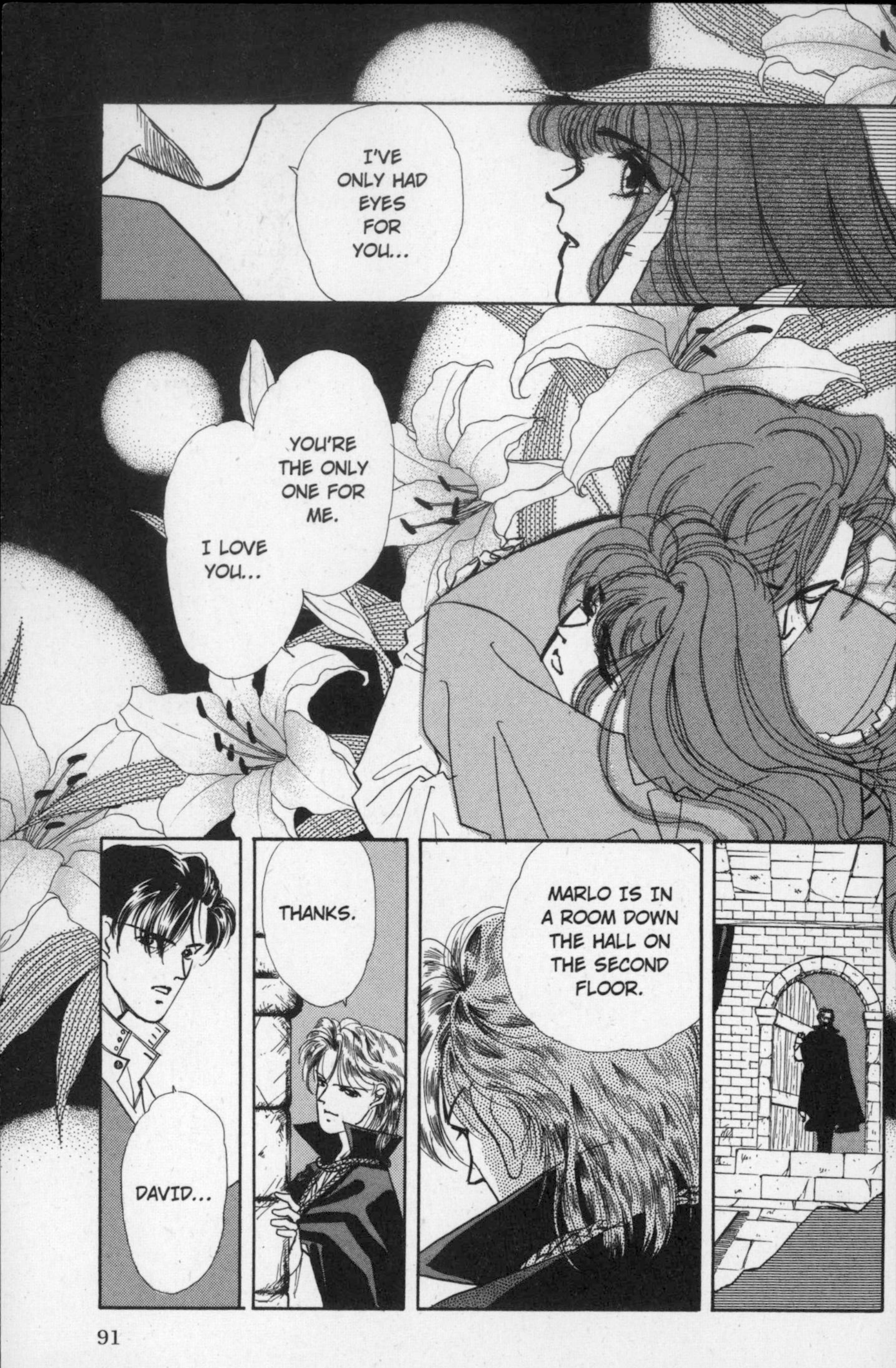
I'VE ONLY HAD EYES FOR YOU...
YOU'RE THE ONLY ONE FOR ME.
I LOVE YOU...
MARLO IS IN A ROOM DOWN THE HALL ON THE SECOND FLOOR.
THANKS.
DAVID...

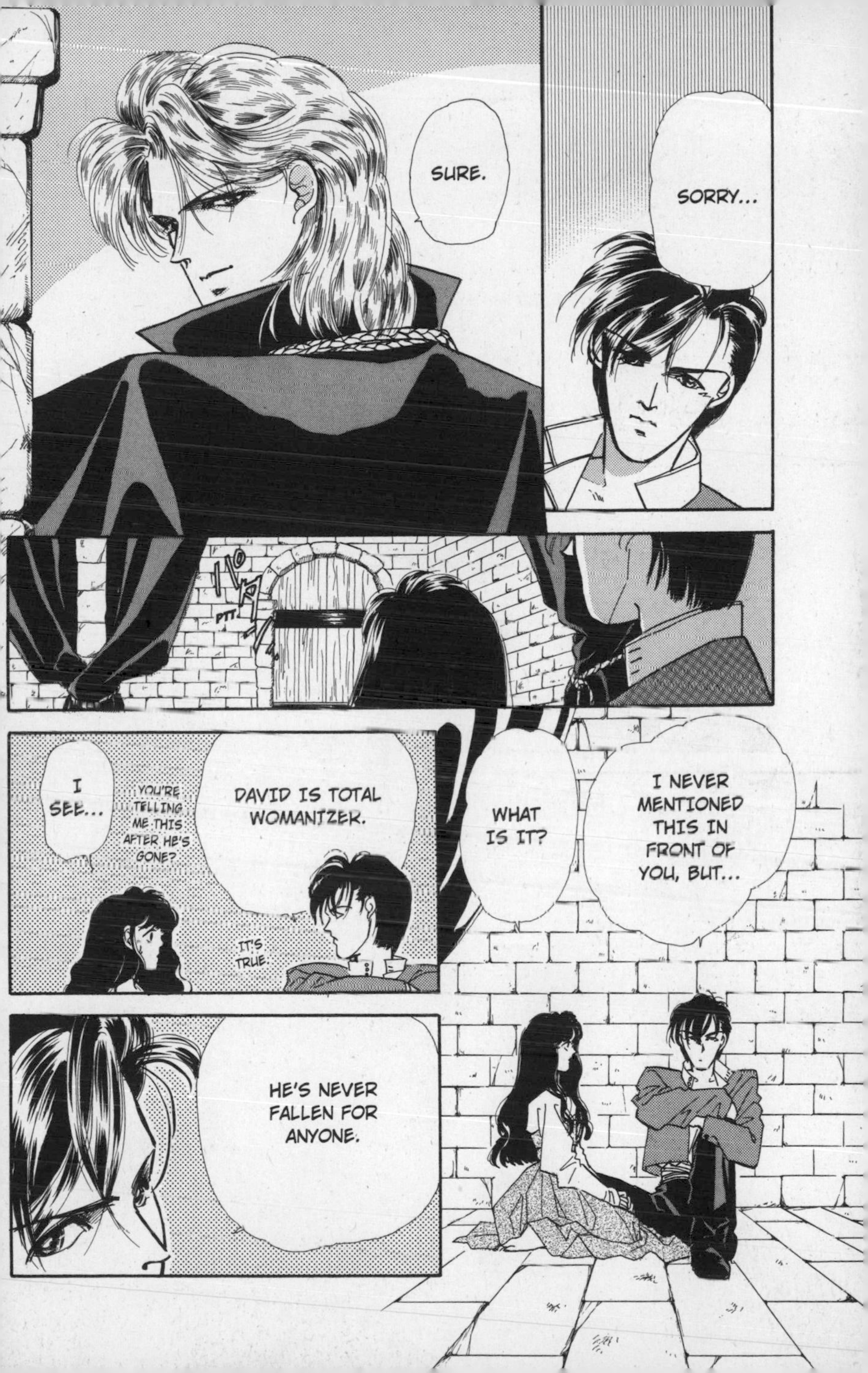
SORRY...
SURE.
PTT
I NEVER MENTIONED THIS IN FRONT OF YOU, BUT...
WHAT IS IT?
DAVID IS TOTAL WOMANIZER.
IT'S TRUE.
YOU'RE TELLING ME THIS AFTER HE'S GONE?
I SEE...
HE'S NEVER FALLEN FOR ANYONE.

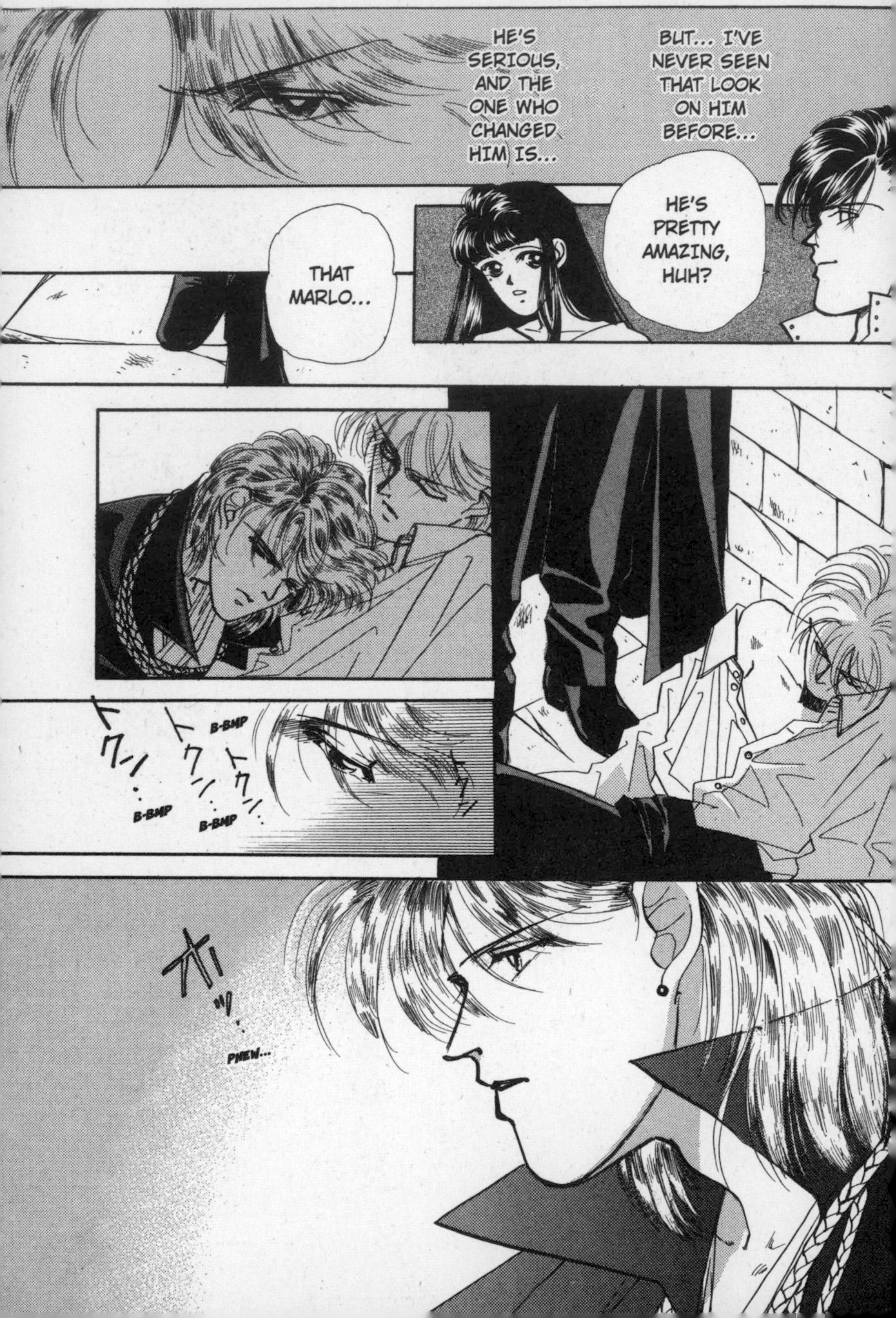
BUT... I'VE NEVER SEEN THAT LOOK ON HIM BEFORE...
HE'S SERIOUS, AND THE ONE WHO CHANGED HIM IS...
HE'S PRETTY AMAZING, HUH?
THAT MARLO...
B-BMP
B-BMP
B-BMP
PHEW...

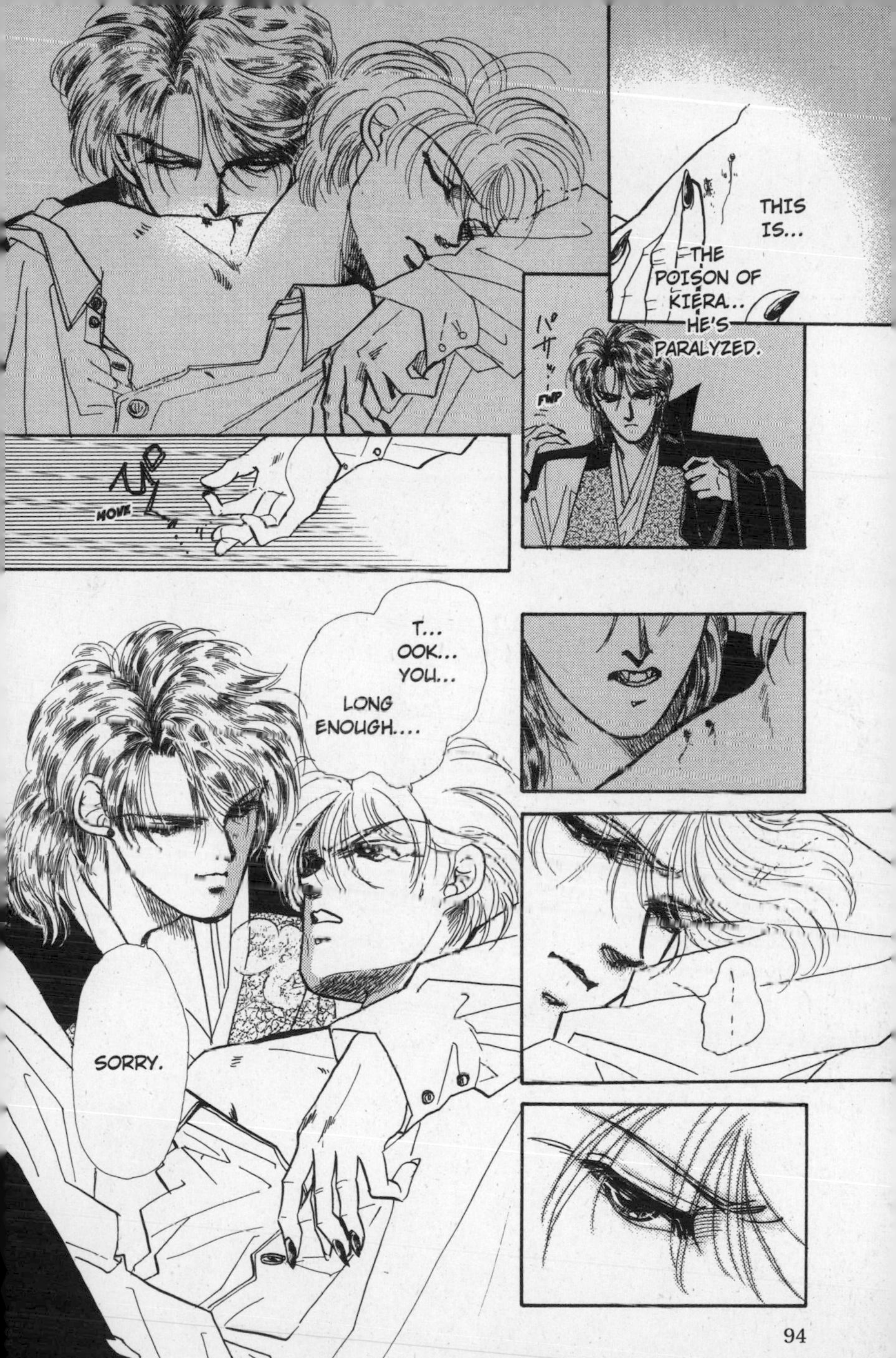
THIS IS... THE POISON OF KIERA... HE'S PARALYZED.
FWP
MOVE
T... OOK... YOU... LONG ENOUGH....
SORRY.

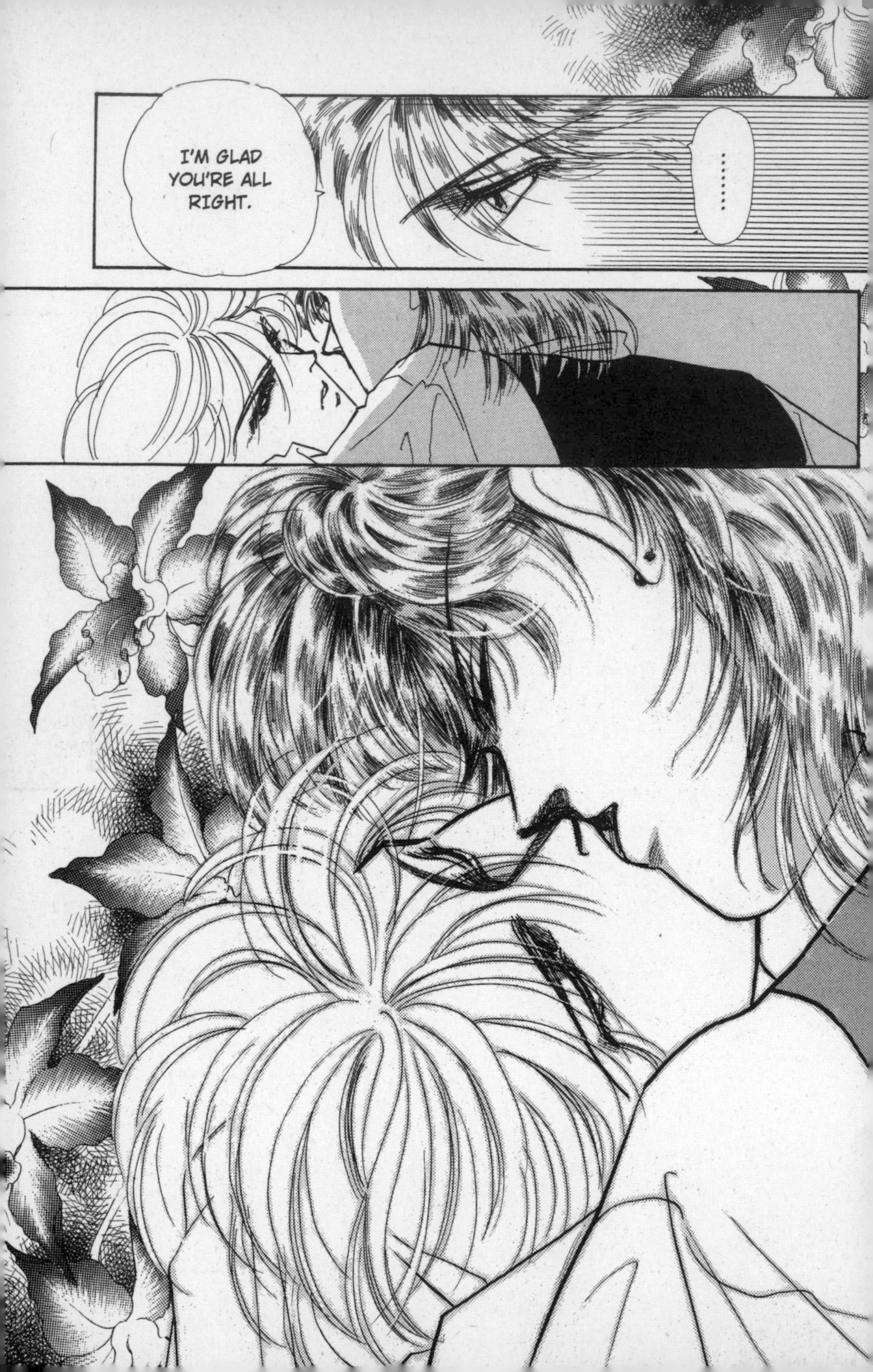
......
I'M GLAD YOU'RE ALL RIGHT.

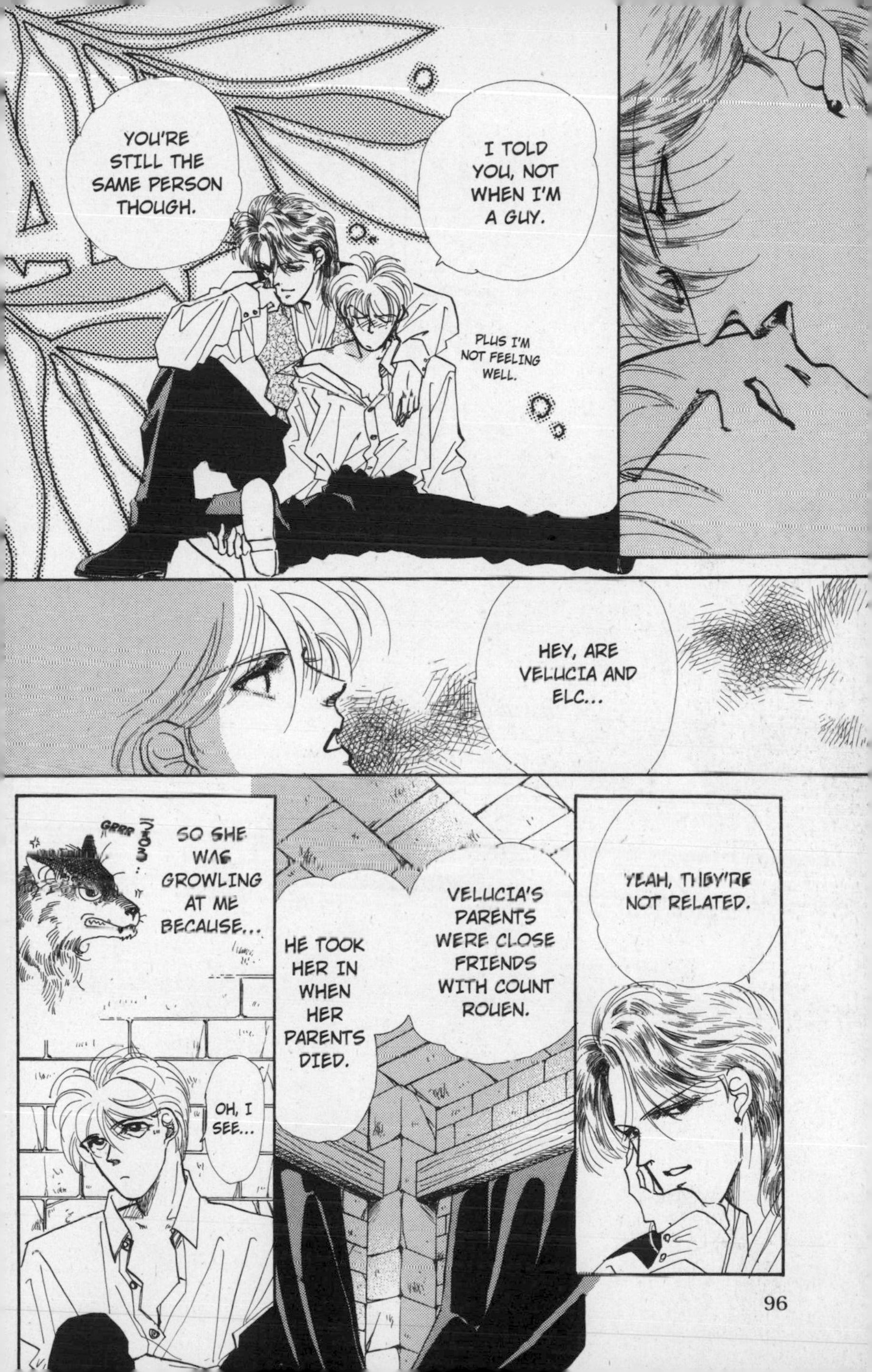
I TOLD YOU, NOT WHEN I'M A GUY.
YOU'RE STILL THE SAME PERSON THOUGH.
PLUS I'M NOT FEELING WELL.
HEY, ARE VELUCIA AND ELC...
YEAH, THEY'RE NOT RELATED.
VELUCIA'S PARENTS WERE CLOSE FRIENDS WITH COUNT ROUEN.
HE TOOK HER IN WHEN HER PARENTS DIED.
SO SHE WAS GROWLING AT ME BECAUSE...
GRRR
OH, I SEE...

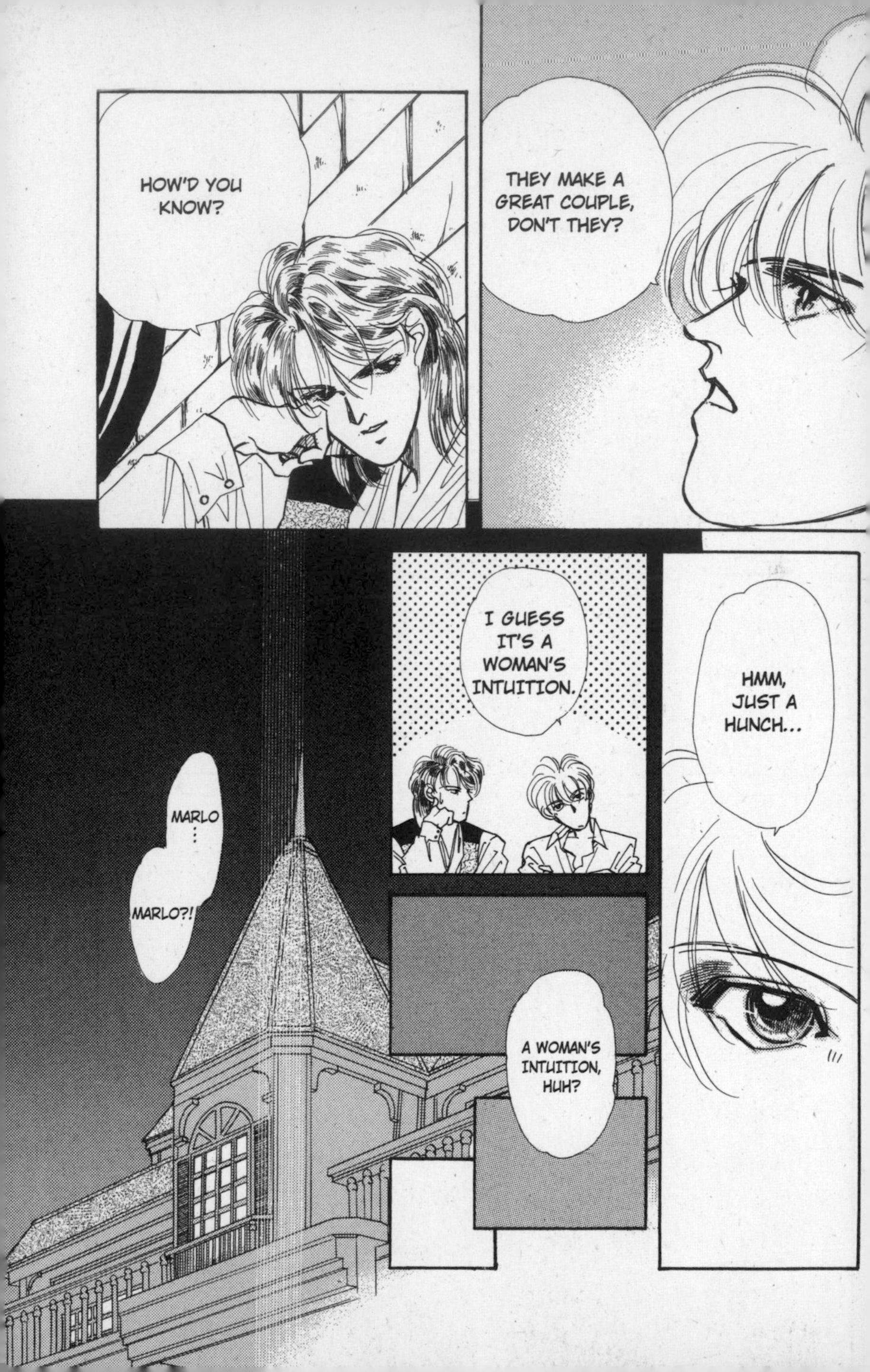
THEY MAKE A GREAT COUPLE, DON'T THEY?
HOW'D YOU KNOW?
HMM, JUST A HUNCH...
I GUESS IT'S A WOMAN'S INTUITION.
A WOMAN'S INTUITION, HUH?
MARLO ...
MARLO?!

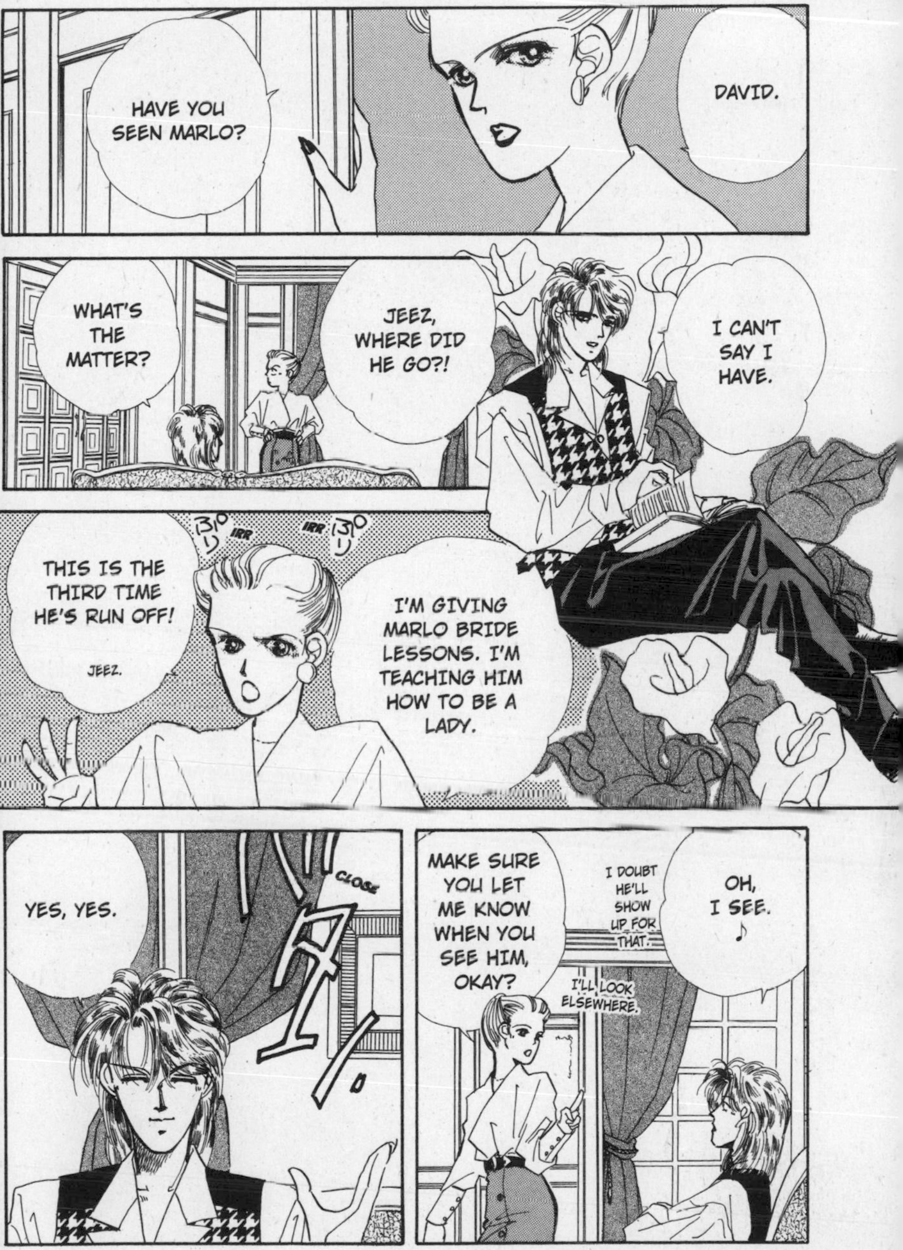
DAVID.
HAVE YOU SEEN MARLO?
I CAN'T SAY I HAVE.
JEEZ, WHERE DID HE GO?!
WHAT'S THE MATTER?
IRR
IRR
I'M GIVING MARLO BRIDE LESSONS. I'M TEACHING HIM HOW TO BE A LADY.
THIS IS THE THIRD TIME HE'S RUN OFF!
JEEZ.
OH, I SEE. ♪
I DOUBT HE'LL SHOW UP FOR THAT.
MAKE SURE YOU LET ME KNOW WHEN YOU SEE HIM, OKAY?
I'LL LOOK ELSEWHERE.
CLOSE
YES, YES.

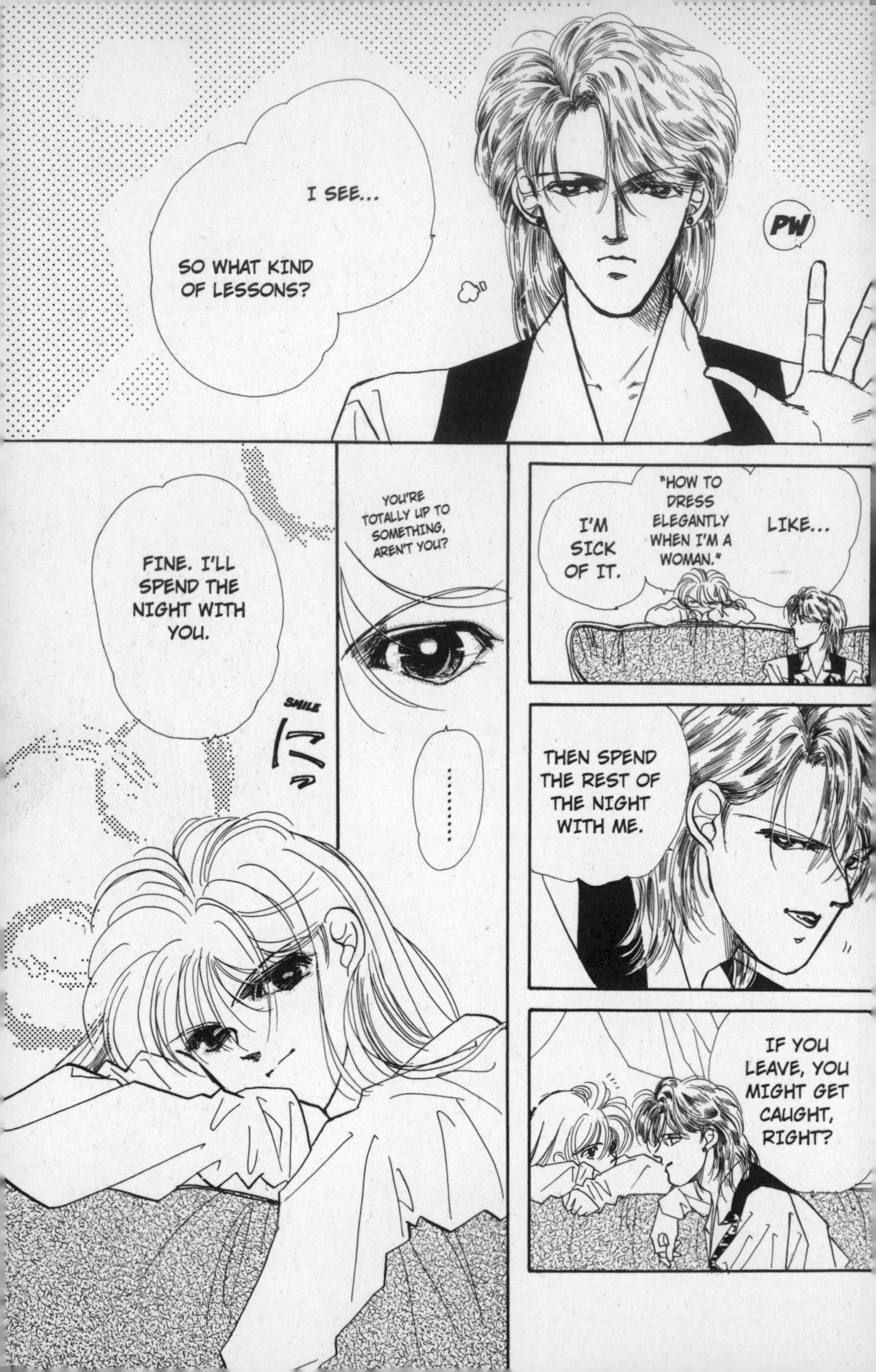
PW
I SEE...
SO WHAT KIND OF LESSONS?
LIKE...
"HOW TO DRESS ELEGANTLY WHEN I'M A WOMAN."
I'M SICK OF IT.
THEN SPEND THE REST OF THE NIGHT WITH ME.
IF YOU LEAVE, YOU MIGHT GET CAUGHT, RIGHT?
YOU'RE TOTALLY UP TO SOMETHING, AREN'T YOU?
......
SMILE
FINE. I'LL SPEND THE NIGHT WITH YOU.

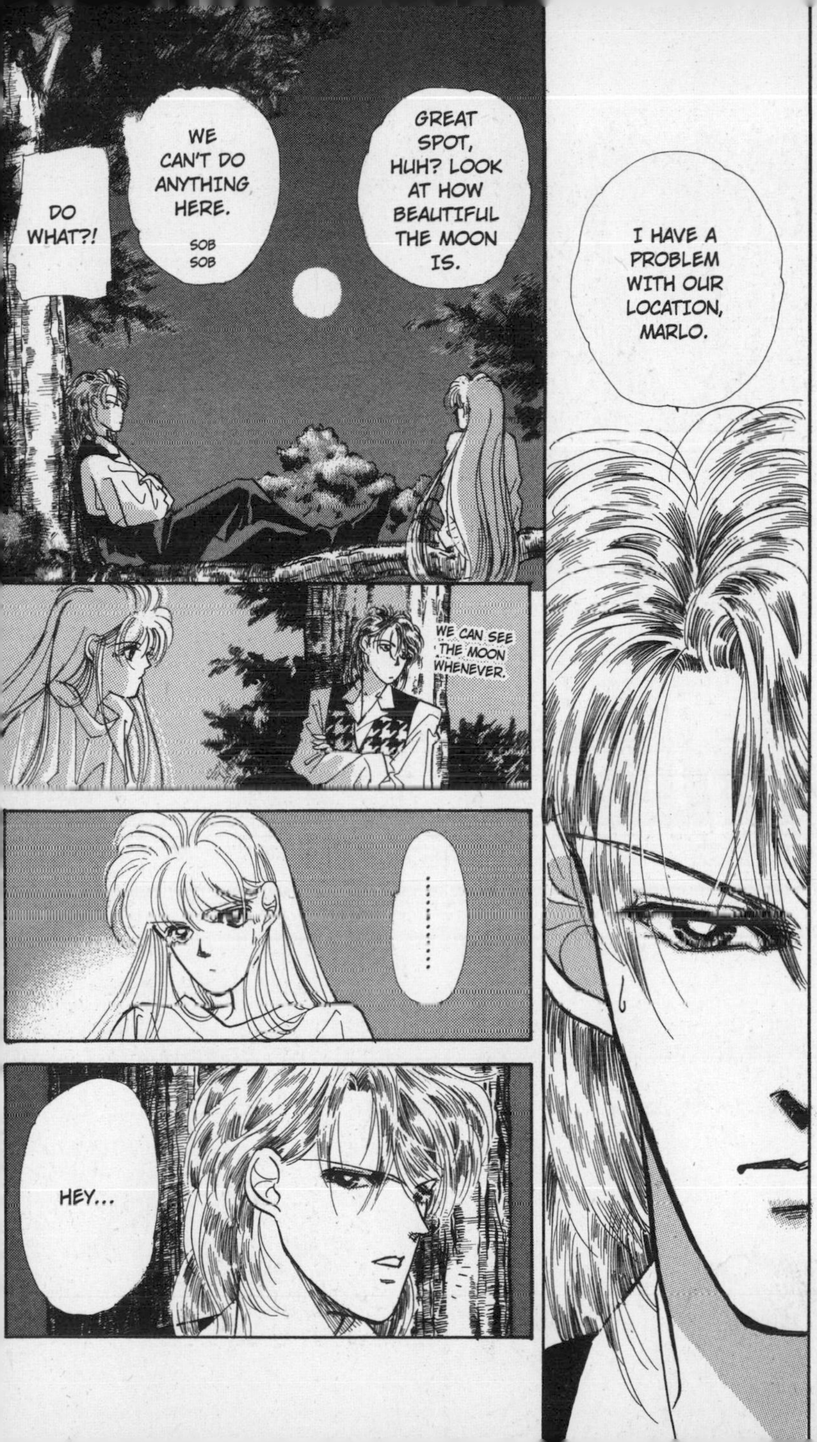
I HAVE A PROBLEM WITH OUR LOCATION, MARLO.
GREAT SPOT, HUH? LOOK AT HOW BEAUTIFUL THE MOON IS.
WE CAN'T DO ANYTHING HERE.
SOB SOB
DO WHAT?!
WE CAN SEE THE MOON WHENEVER.
......
HEY...

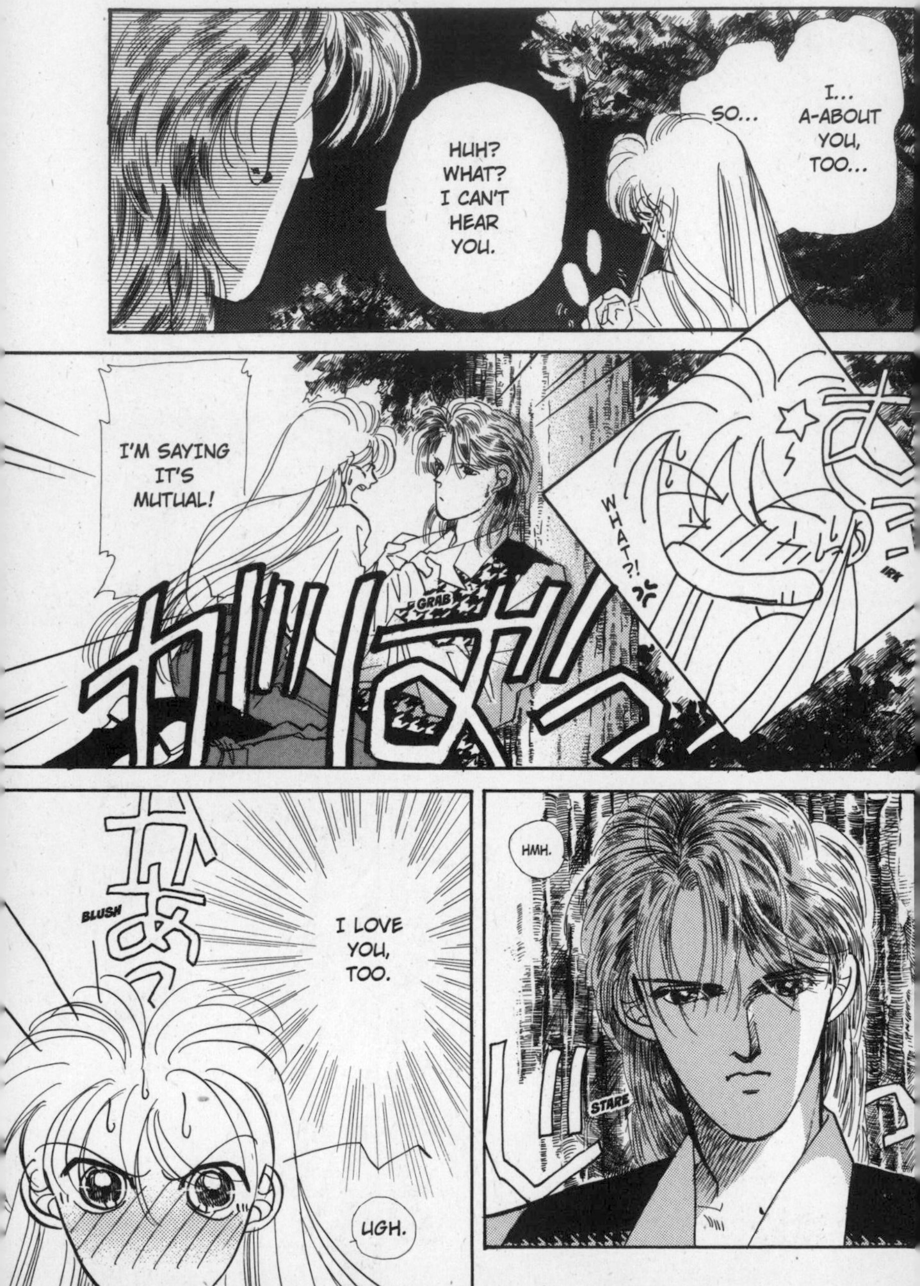
I...
A-ABOUT
YOU,
TOO...
SO...
HUH?
WHAT?
I CAN'T
HEAR
YOU.
WHAT?!
IRK
I'M SAYING
IT'S
MUTUAL!
GRAB
HMH.
STARE
I LOVE
YOU,
TOO.
BLUSH
UGH.

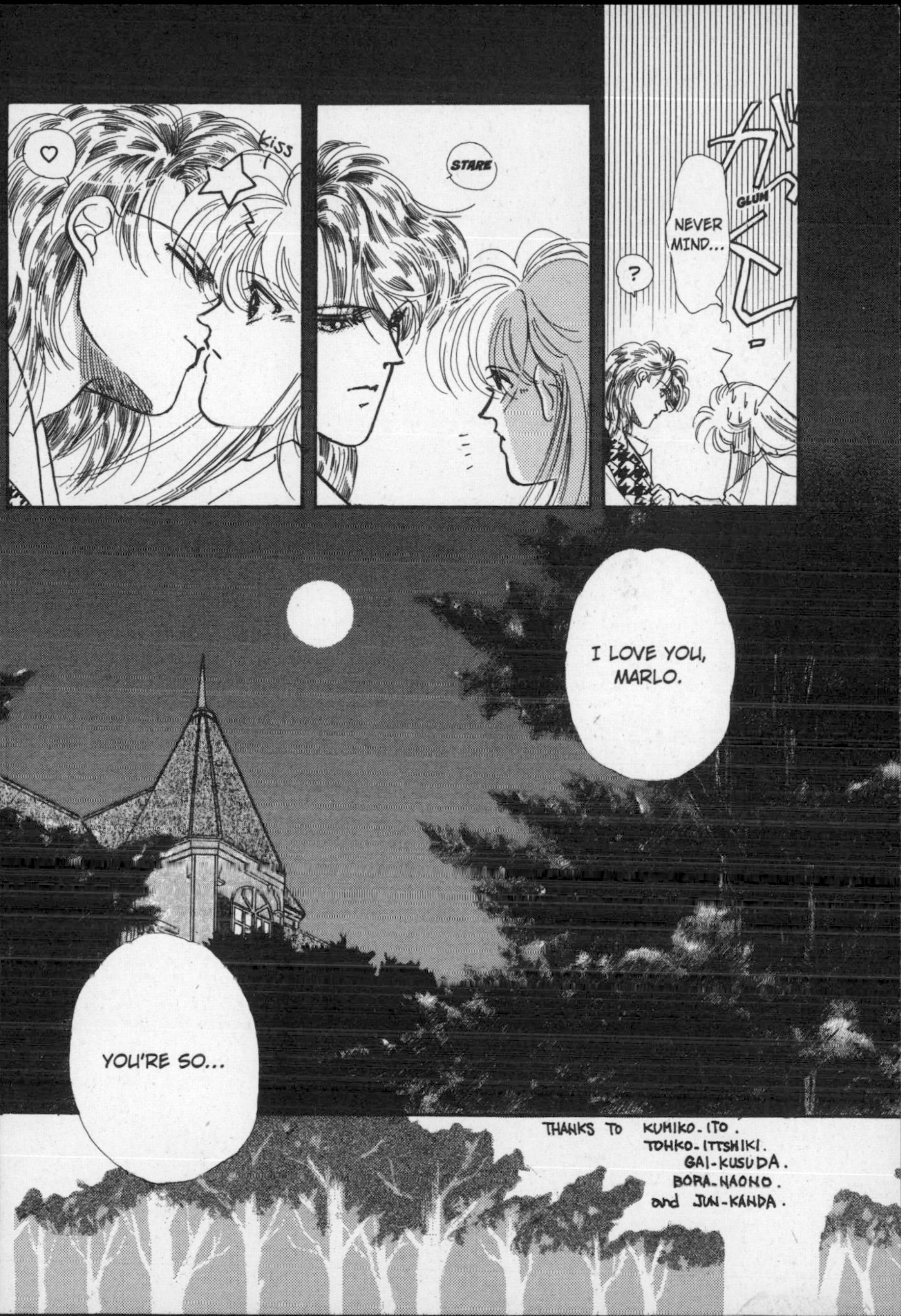
GLUM
NEVER MIND...
?
STARE
♡
kiss
I LOVE YOU, MARLO.
YOU'RE SO...
THANKS TO KUMIKO-ITO.
TOHKO-ITTSHIKI.
GAI-KUSUDA.
BORA-NAONO.
and JUN-KANDA.

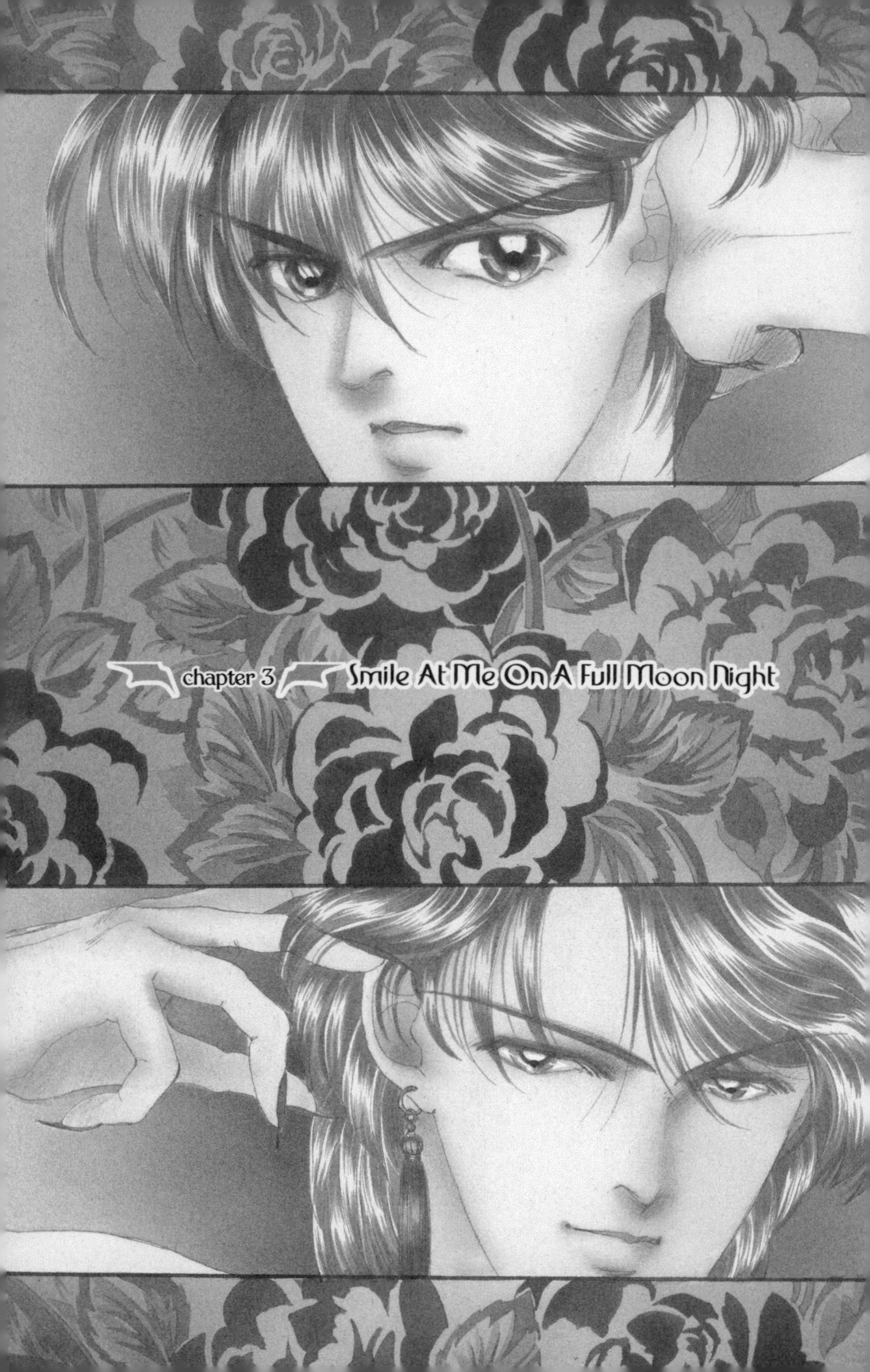
chapter 3
Smile At Me On A Full Moon Night

Whisper to Me
at
Full Moon Night

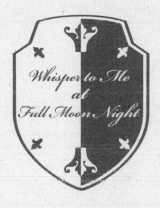

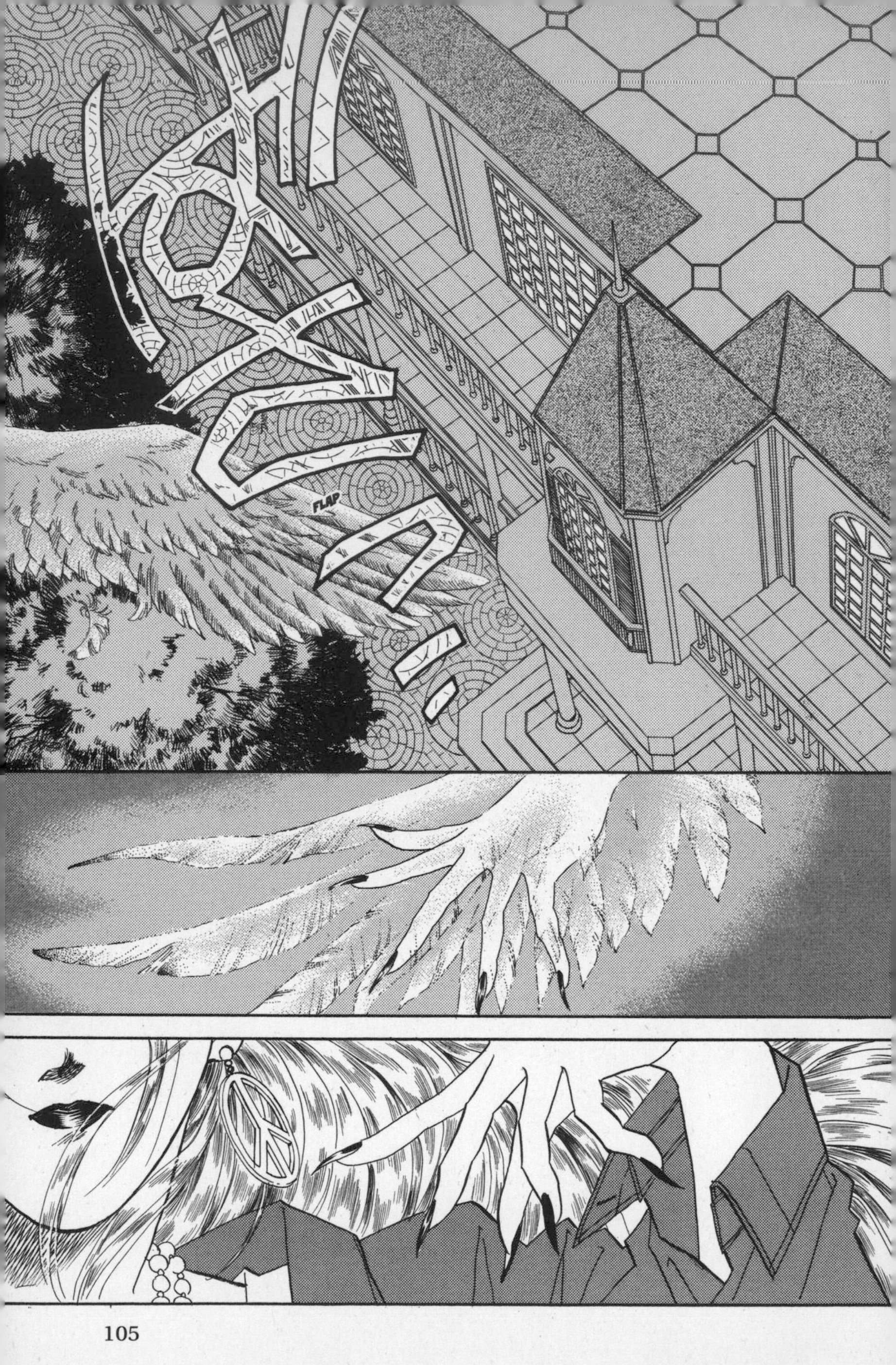
FLAP

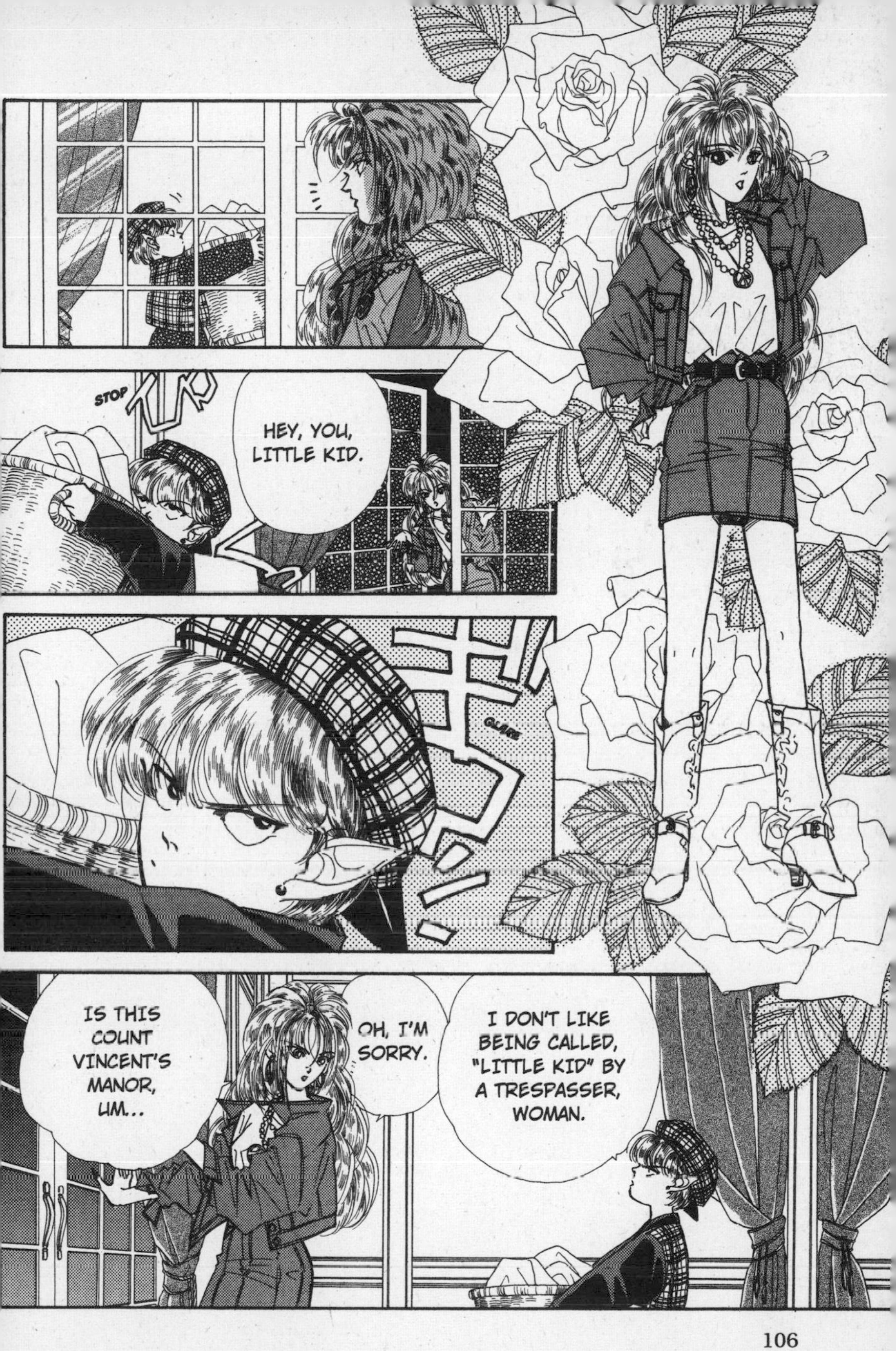
STOP
HEY, YOU, LITTLE KID.
GLARE
I DON'T LIKE BEING CALLED, "LITTLE KID" BY A TRESPASSER, WOMAN.
OH, I'M SORRY.
IS THIS COUNT VINCENT'S MANOR, UM...

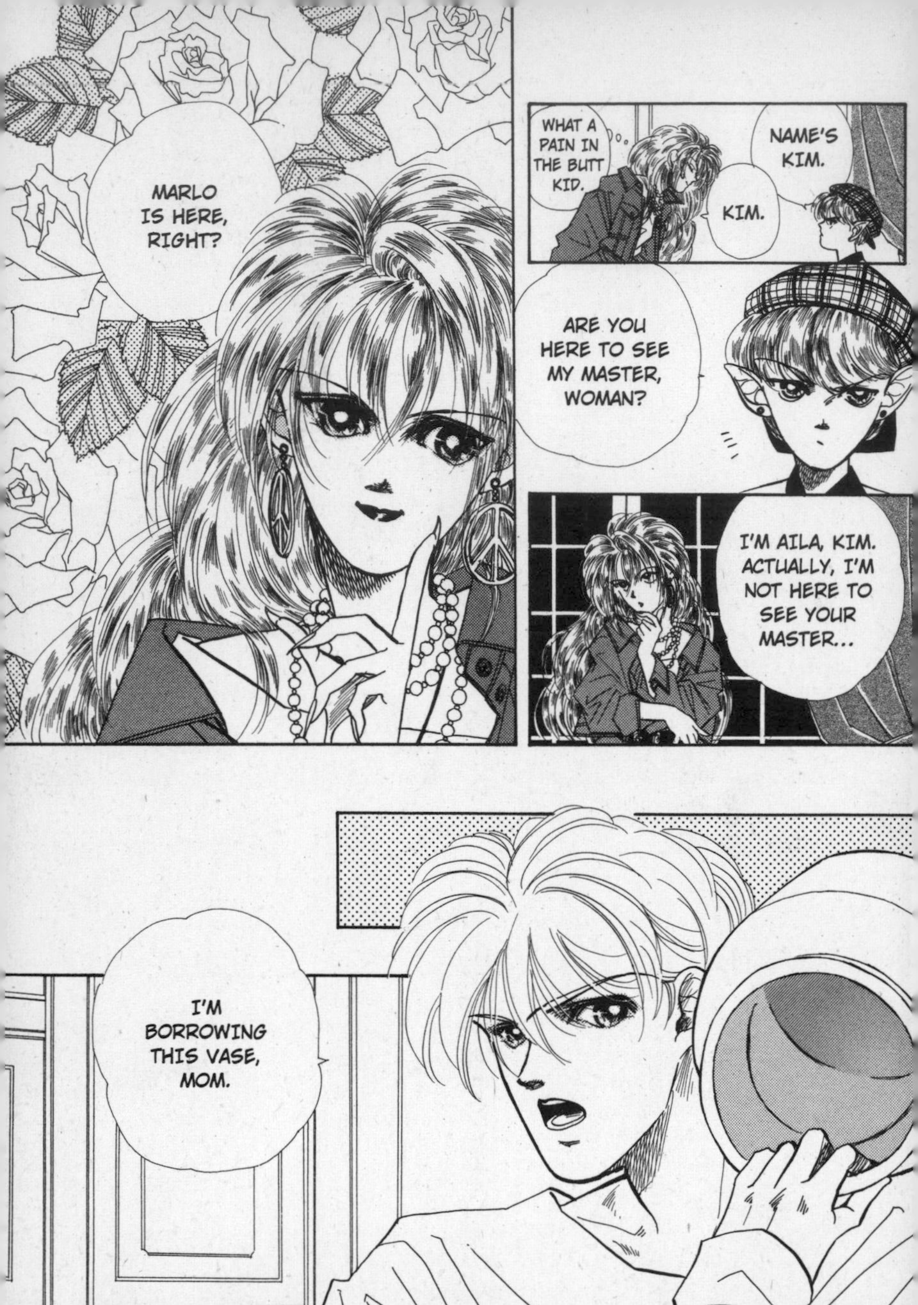
NAME'S KIM.
WHAT A PAIN IN THE BUTT KID.
KIM.
ARE YOU HERE TO SEE MY MASTER, WOMAN?
I'M AILA, KIM. ACTUALLY, I'M NOT HERE TO SEE YOUR MASTER...
MARLO IS HERE, RIGHT?
I'M BORROWING THIS VASE, MOM.

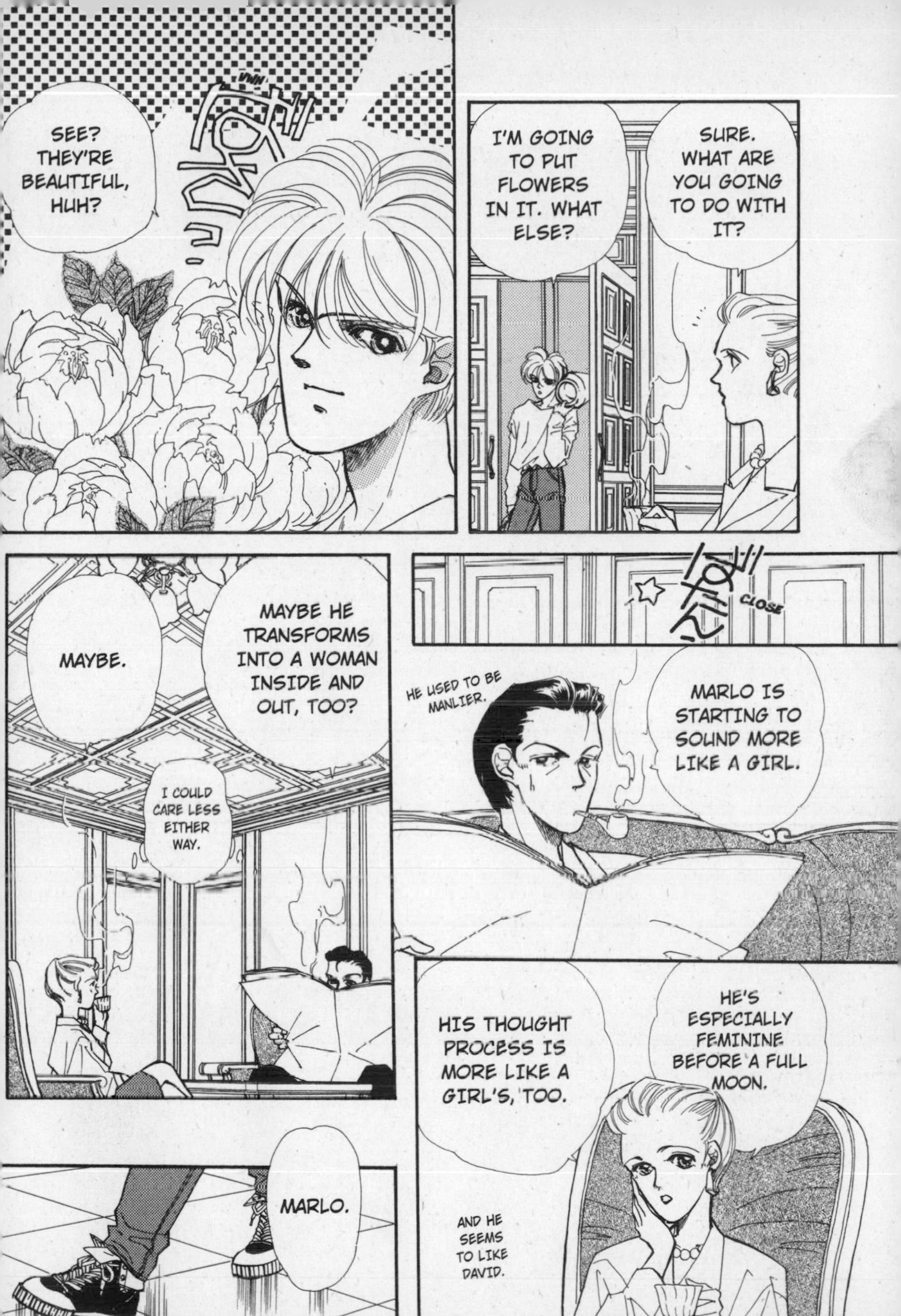
SURE. WHAT ARE YOU GOING TO DO WITH IT?
I'M GOING TO PUT FLOWERS IN IT. WHAT ELSE?
VWH
SEE? THEY'RE BEAUTIFUL, HUH?
CLOSE
MARLO IS STARTING TO SOUND MORE LIKE A GIRL.
HE USED TO BE MANLIER.
HE'S ESPECIALLY FEMININE BEFORE A FULL MOON.
HIS THOUGHT PROCESS IS MORE LIKE A GIRL'S, TOO.
AND HE SEEMS TO LIKE DAVID.
MAYBE HE TRANSFORMS INTO A WOMAN INSIDE AND OUT, TOO?
MAYBE.
I COULD CARE LESS EITHER WAY.
MARLO.

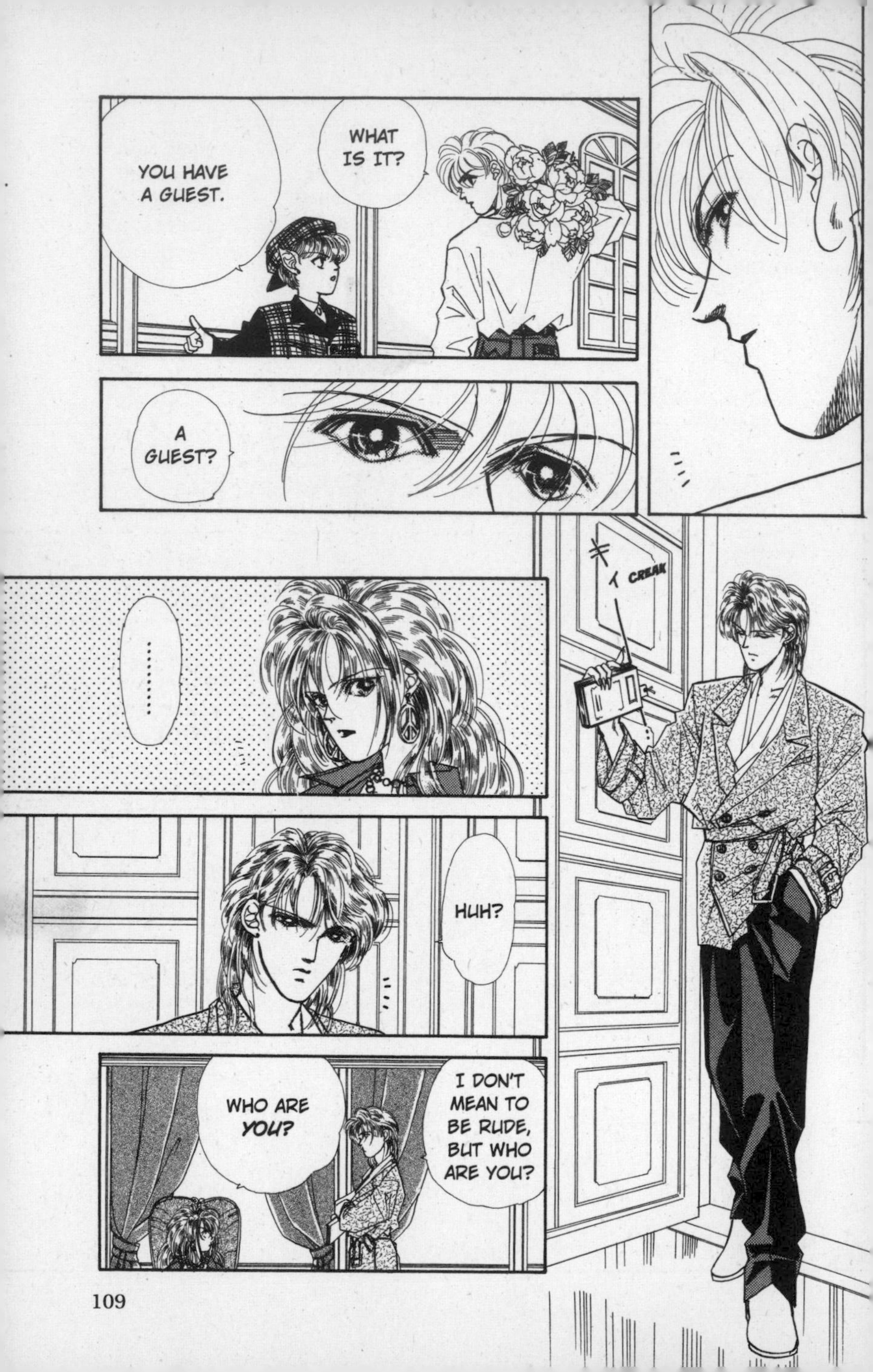
WHAT IS IT?
YOU HAVE A GUEST.
A GUEST?
CREAK
......
HUH?
I DON'T MEAN TO BE RUDE, BUT WHO ARE YOU?
WHO ARE *YOU*?

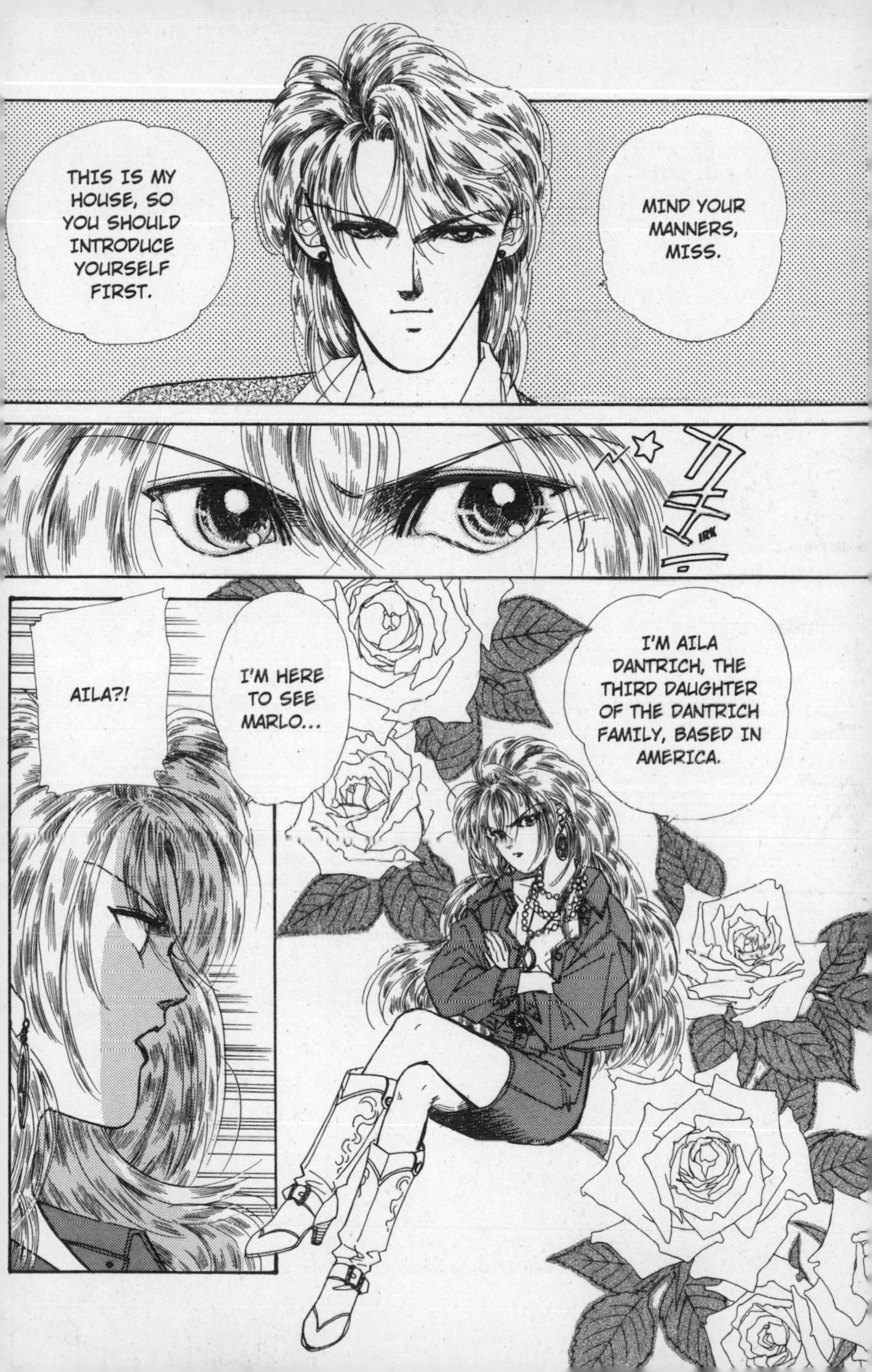
MIND YOUR MANNERS, MISS.
THIS IS MY HOUSE, SO YOU SHOULD INTRODUCE YOURSELF FIRST.
IRK
I'M AILA DANTRICH, THE THIRD DAUGHTER OF THE DANTRICH FAMILY, BASED IN AMERICA.
I'M HERE TO SEE MARLO...
AILA?!

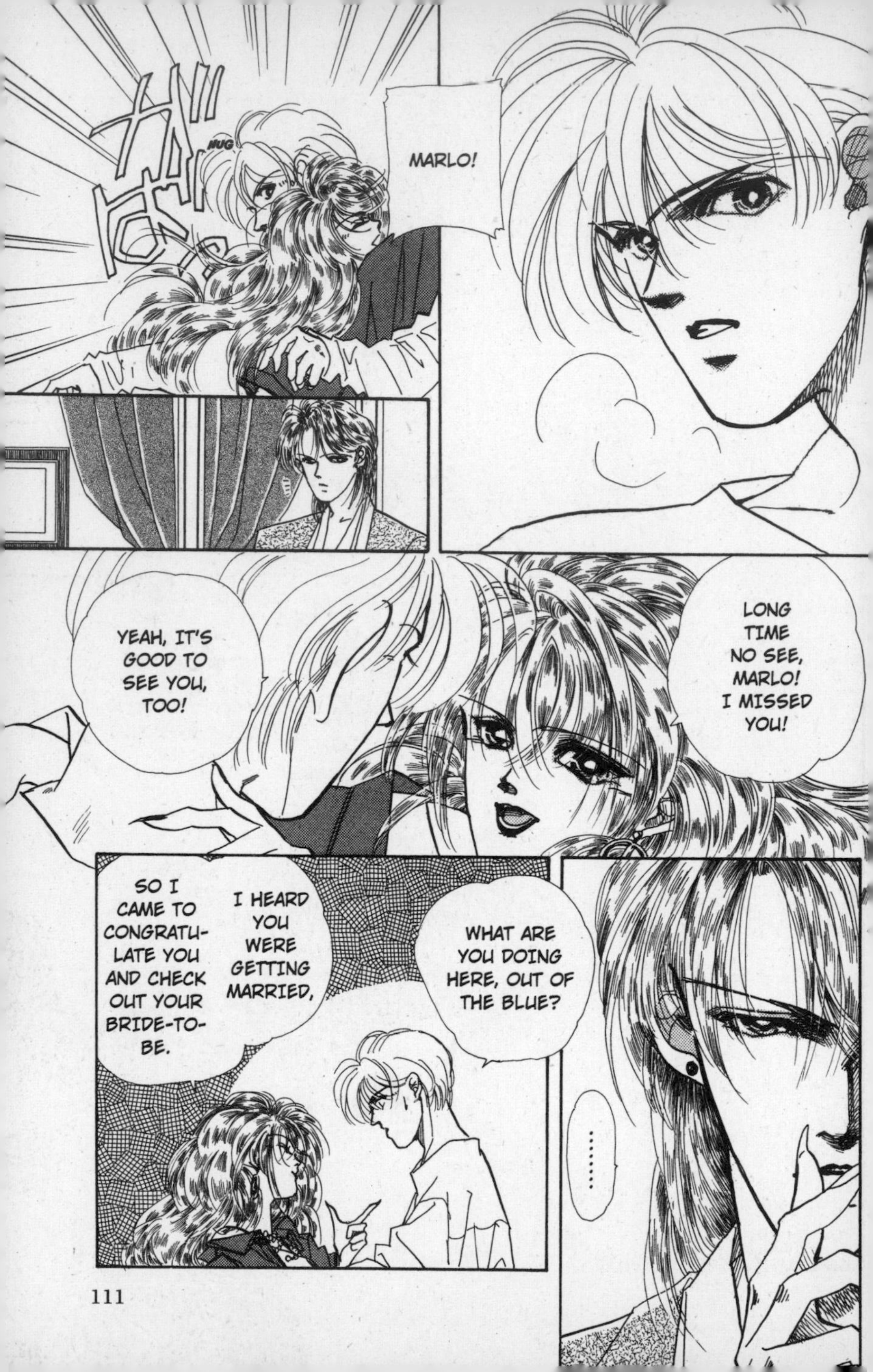
MARLO!
HUG
LONG TIME NO SEE, MARLO! I MISSED YOU!
YEAH, IT'S GOOD TO SEE YOU, TOO!
……
WHAT ARE YOU DOING HERE, OUT OF THE BLUE?
I HEARD YOU WERE GETTING MARRIED,
SO I CAME TO CONGRATULATE YOU AND CHECK OUT YOUR BRIDE-TO-BE.

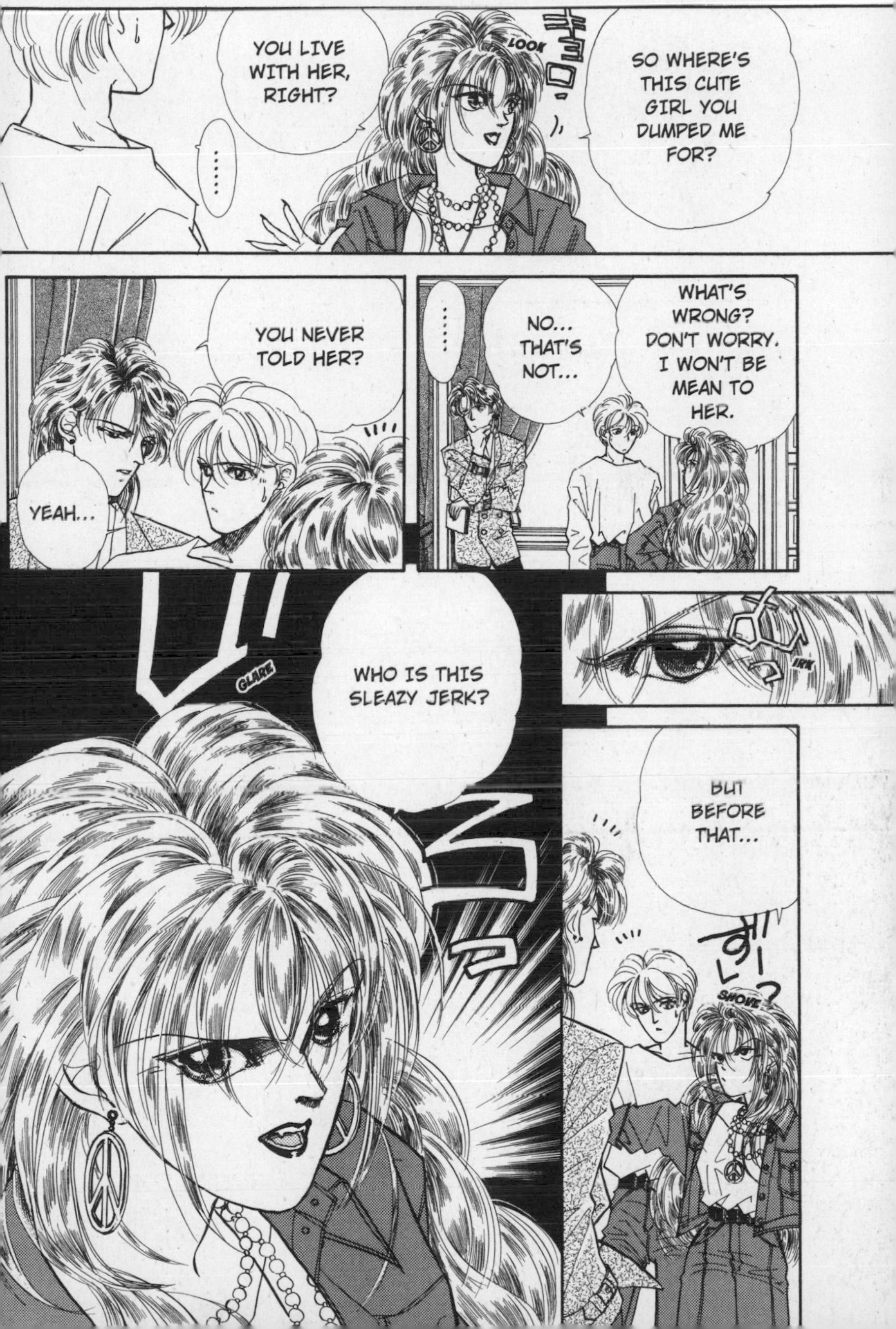
SO WHERE'S THIS CUTE GIRL YOU DUMPED ME FOR?
LOOK
YOU LIVE WITH HER, RIGHT?
……
WHAT'S WRONG? DON'T WORRY. I WON'T BE MEAN TO HER.
NO... THAT'S NOT...
……
YOU NEVER TOLD HER?
YEAH...
JERK
BUT BEFORE THAT...
SHOVE
WHO IS THIS SLEAZY JERK?
GLARE

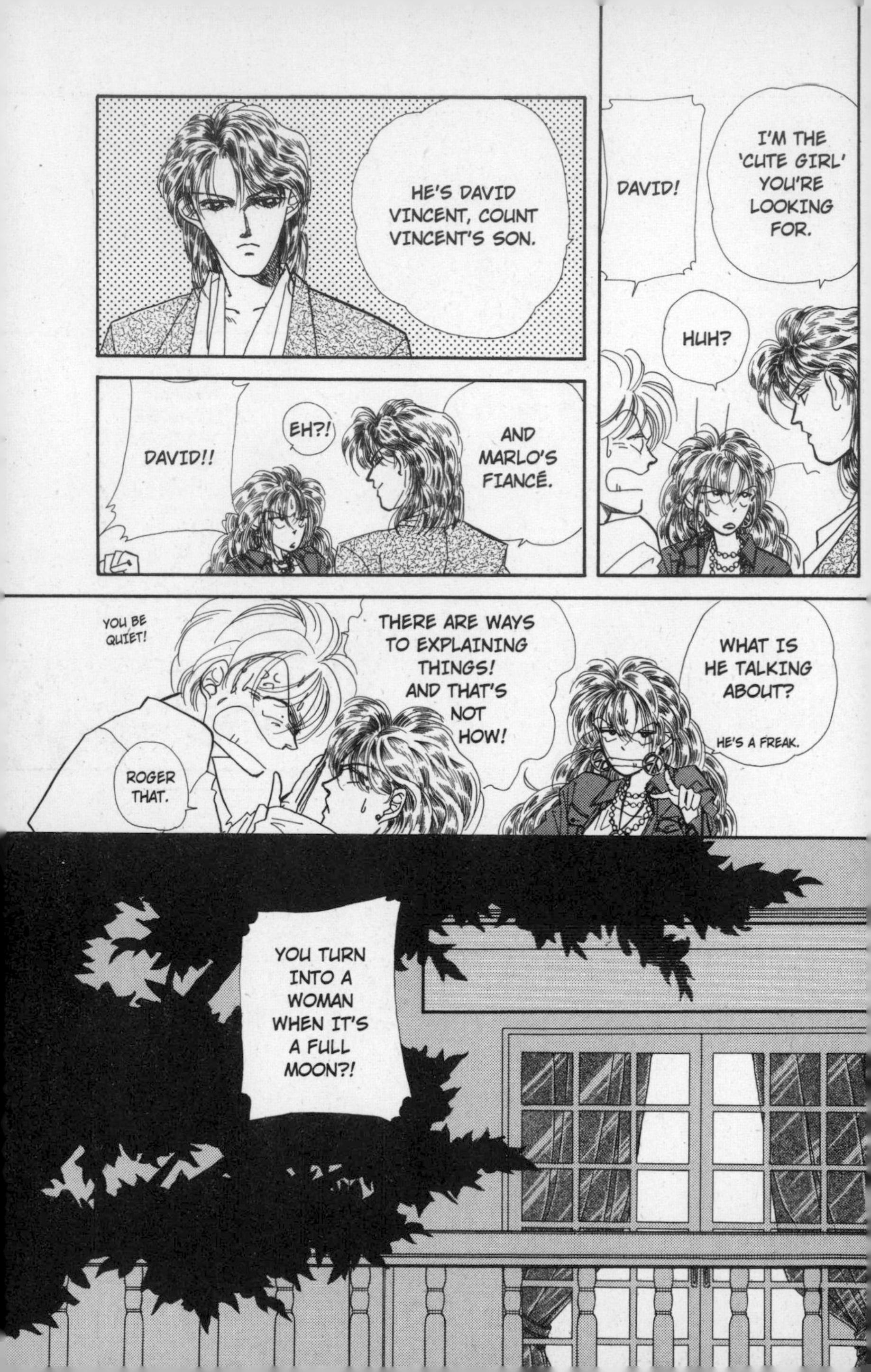
I'M THE 'CUTE GIRL' YOU'RE LOOKING FOR.
DAVID!
HUH?
HE'S DAVID VINCENT, COUNT VINCENT'S SON.
AND MARLO'S FIANCÉ.
EH?!
DAVID!!
WHAT IS HE TALKING ABOUT?
HE'S A FREAK.
THERE ARE WAYS TO EXPLAINING THINGS! AND THAT'S NOT HOW!
YOU BE QUIET!
ROGER THAT.
YOU TURN INTO A WOMAN WHEN IT'S A FULL MOON?!

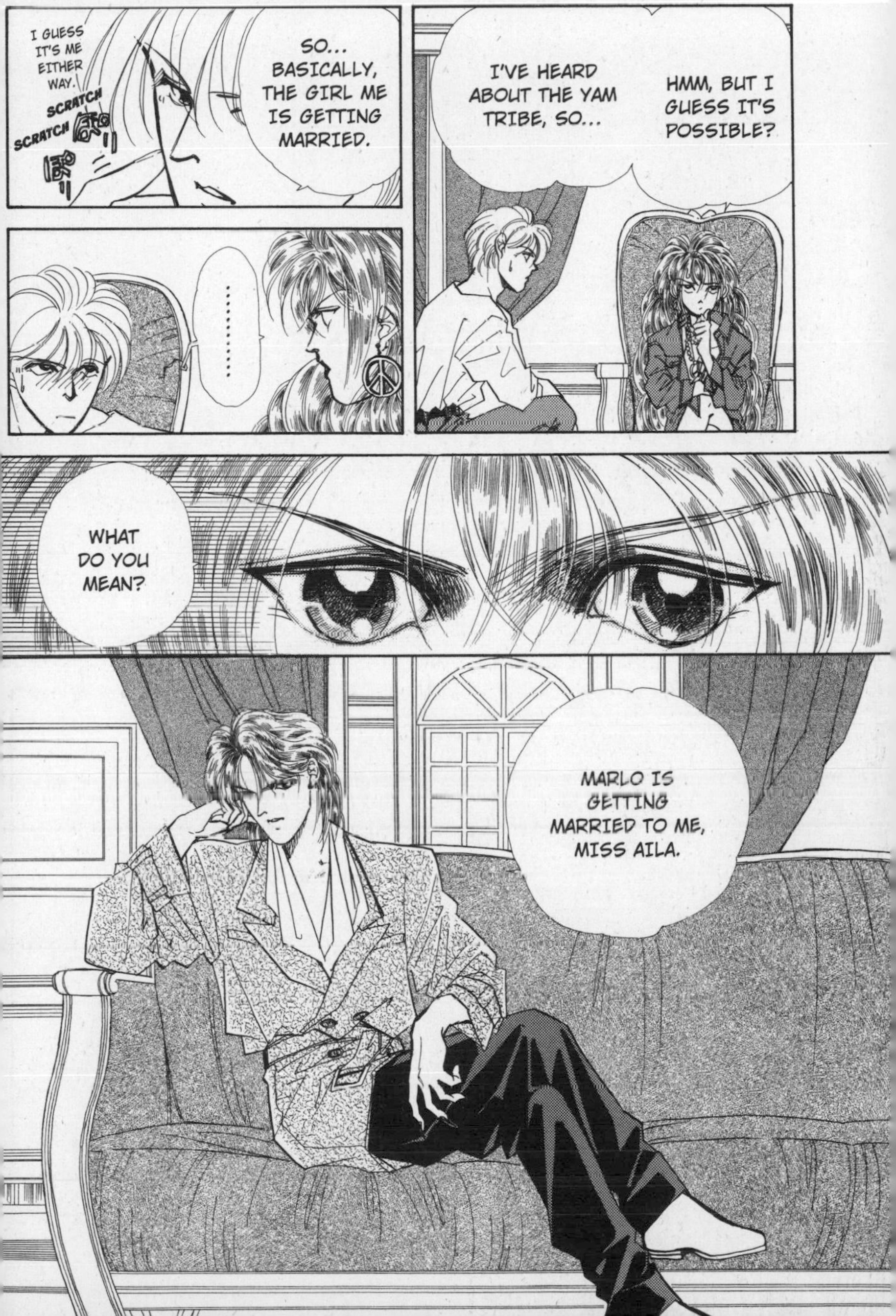
I'VE HEARD ABOUT THE YAM TRIBE, SO...
HMM, BUT I GUESS IT'S POSSIBLE?
SO... BASICALLY, THE GIRL ME IS GETTING MARRIED.
I GUESS IT'S ME EITHER WAY.
SCRATCH
SCRATCH
......
WHAT DO YOU MEAN?
MARLO IS GETTING MARRIED TO ME, MISS AILA.

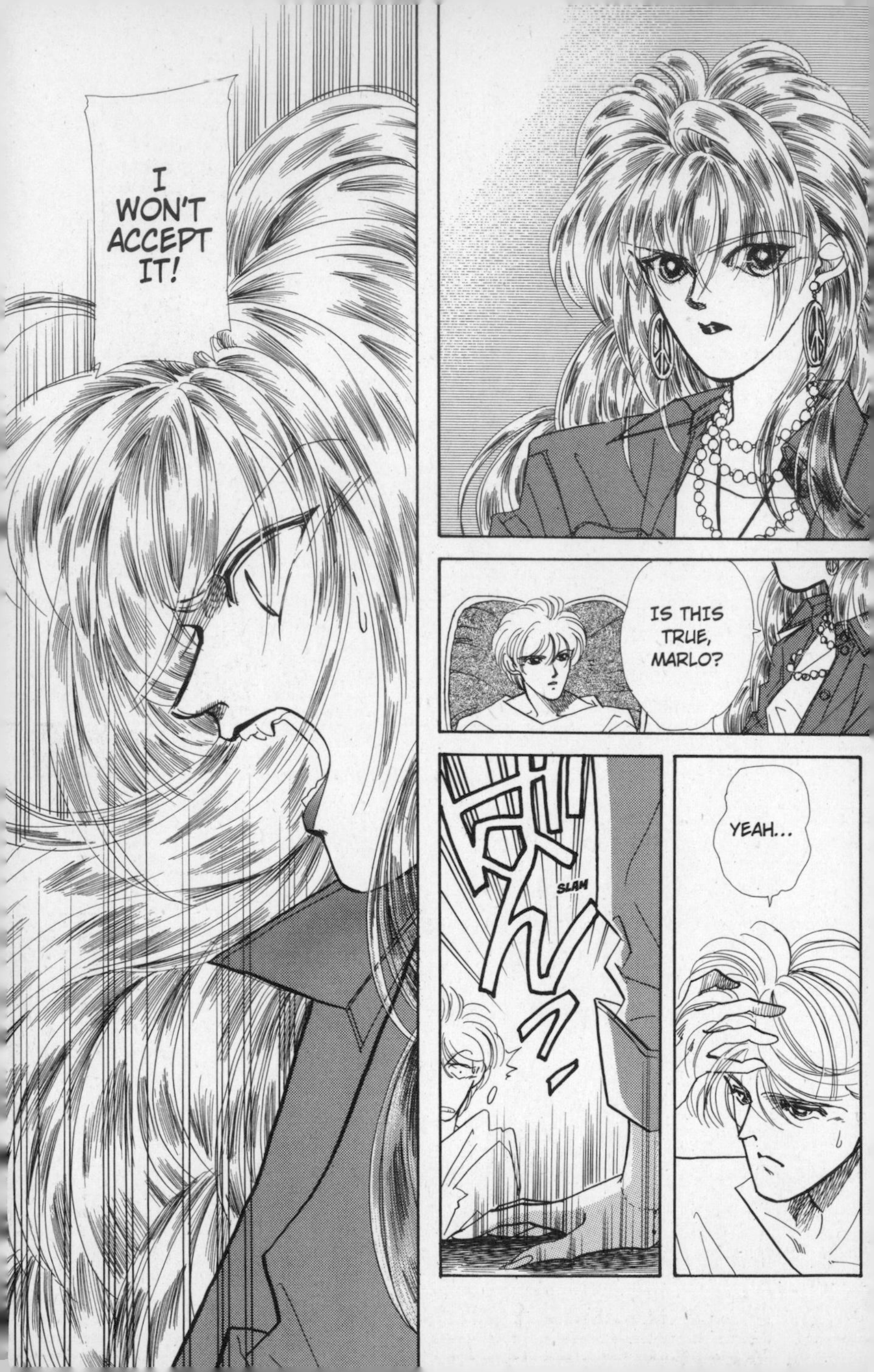
IS THIS TRUE, MARLO?
YEAH...
SLAM
I WON'T ACCEPT IT!

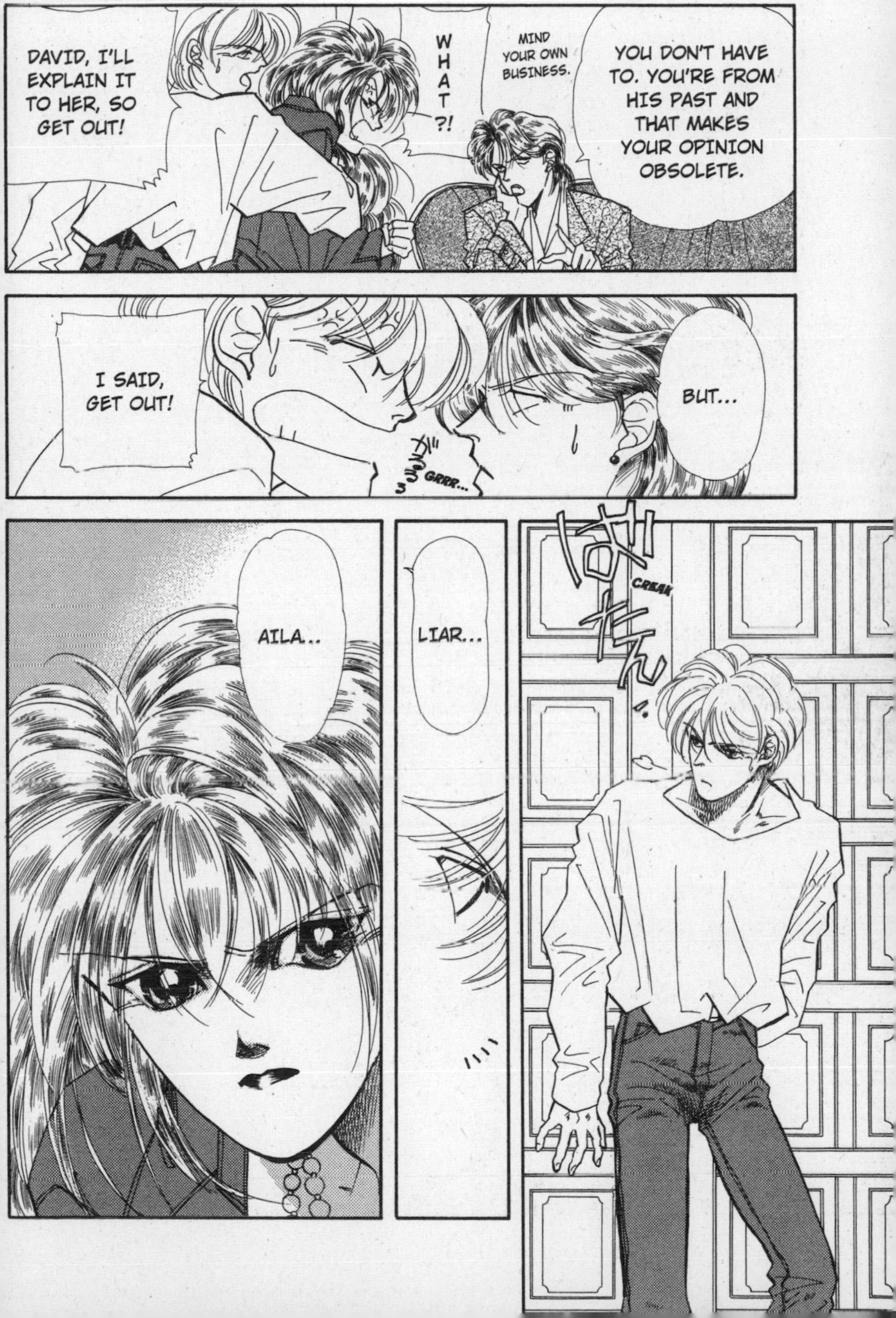

YOU DON'T HAVE TO. YOU'RE FROM HIS PAST AND THAT MAKES YOUR OPINION OBSOLETE.
MIND YOUR OWN BUSINESS.
WHAT?!
DAVID, I'LL EXPLAIN IT TO HER, SO GET OUT!
BUT...
I SAID, GET OUT!
GRRR...
ばたん
CREAK
LIAR...
AILA...

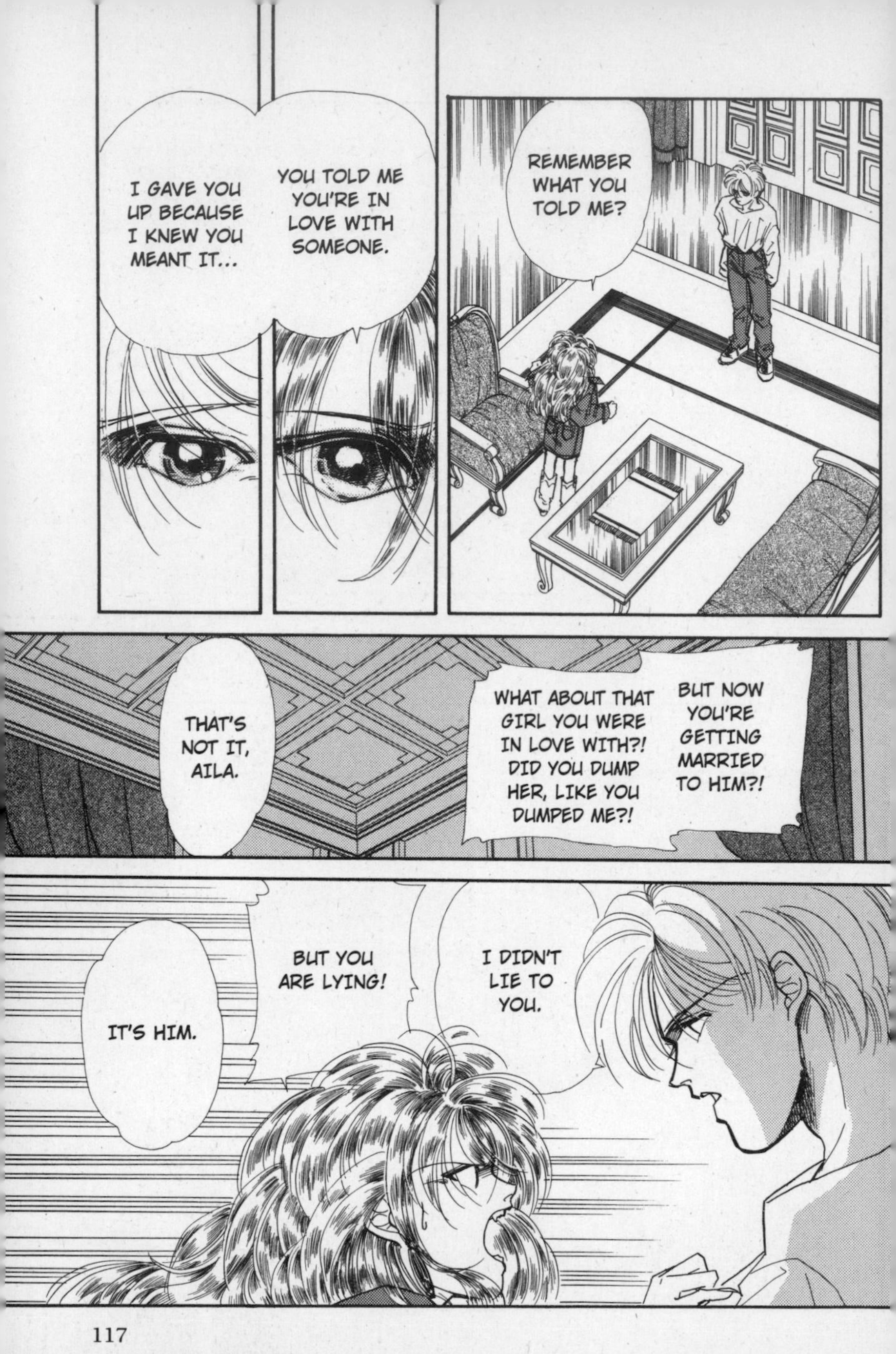
REMEMBER WHAT YOU TOLD ME?
YOU TOLD ME YOU'RE IN LOVE WITH SOMEONE.
I GAVE YOU UP BECAUSE I KNEW YOU MEANT IT...
BUT NOW YOU'RE GETTING MARRIED TO HIM?!
WHAT ABOUT THAT GIRL YOU WERE IN LOVE WITH?! DID YOU DUMP HER, LIKE YOU DUMPED ME?!
THAT'S NOT IT, AILA.
I DIDN'T LIE TO YOU.
BUT YOU ARE LYING!
IT'S HIM.

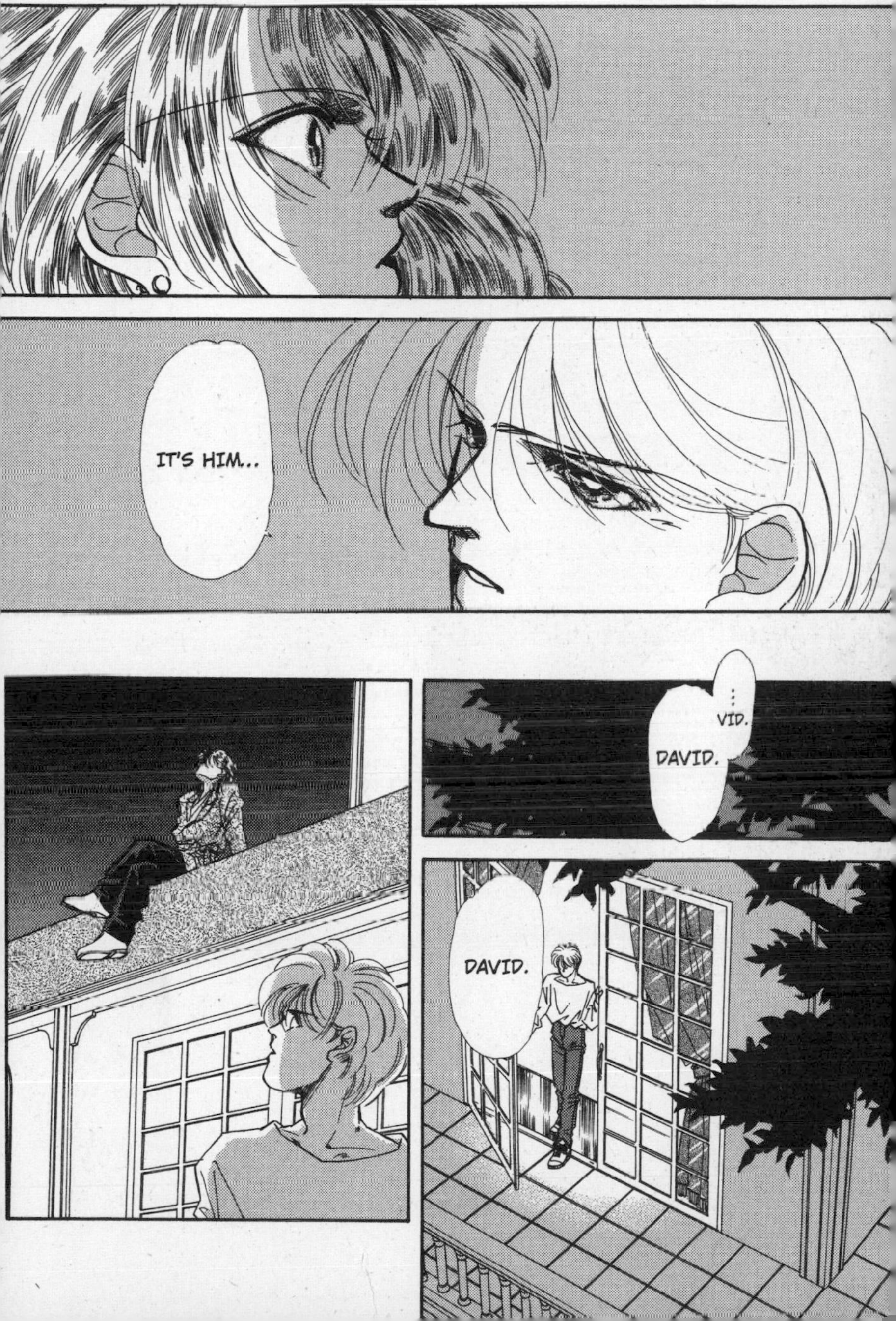
IT'S HIM...
...VID.
DAVID.
DAVID.

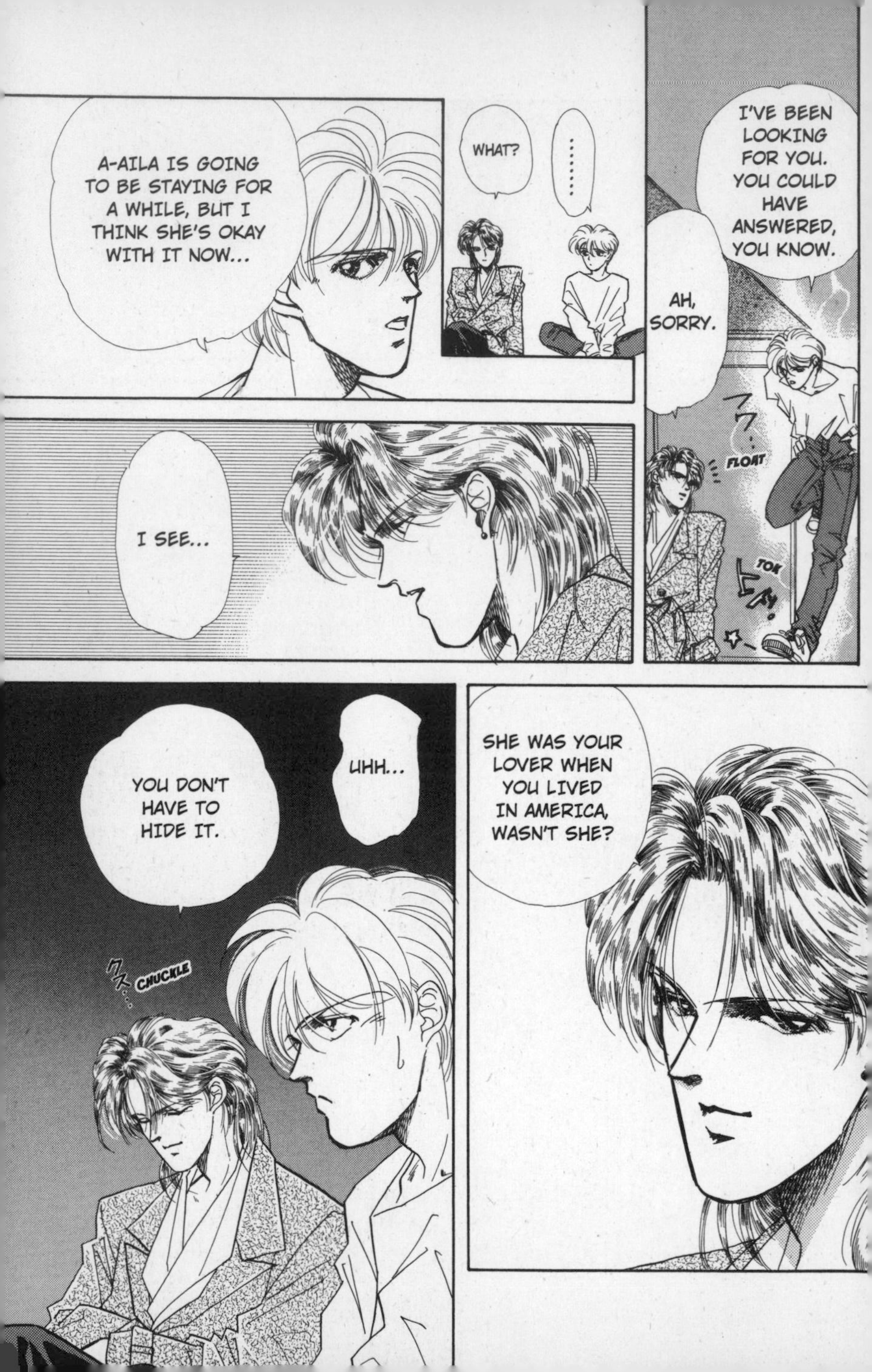
I'VE BEEN LOOKING FOR YOU. YOU COULD HAVE ANSWERED, YOU KNOW.
AH, SORRY.
フワ…
FLOAT
TOK
......
WHAT?
A-AILA IS GOING TO BE STAYING FOR A WHILE, BUT I THINK SHE'S OKAY WITH IT NOW...
I SEE...
SHE WAS YOUR LOVER WHEN YOU LIVED IN AMERICA, WASN'T SHE?
UHH...
YOU DON'T HAVE TO HIDE IT.
クス…
CHUCKLE

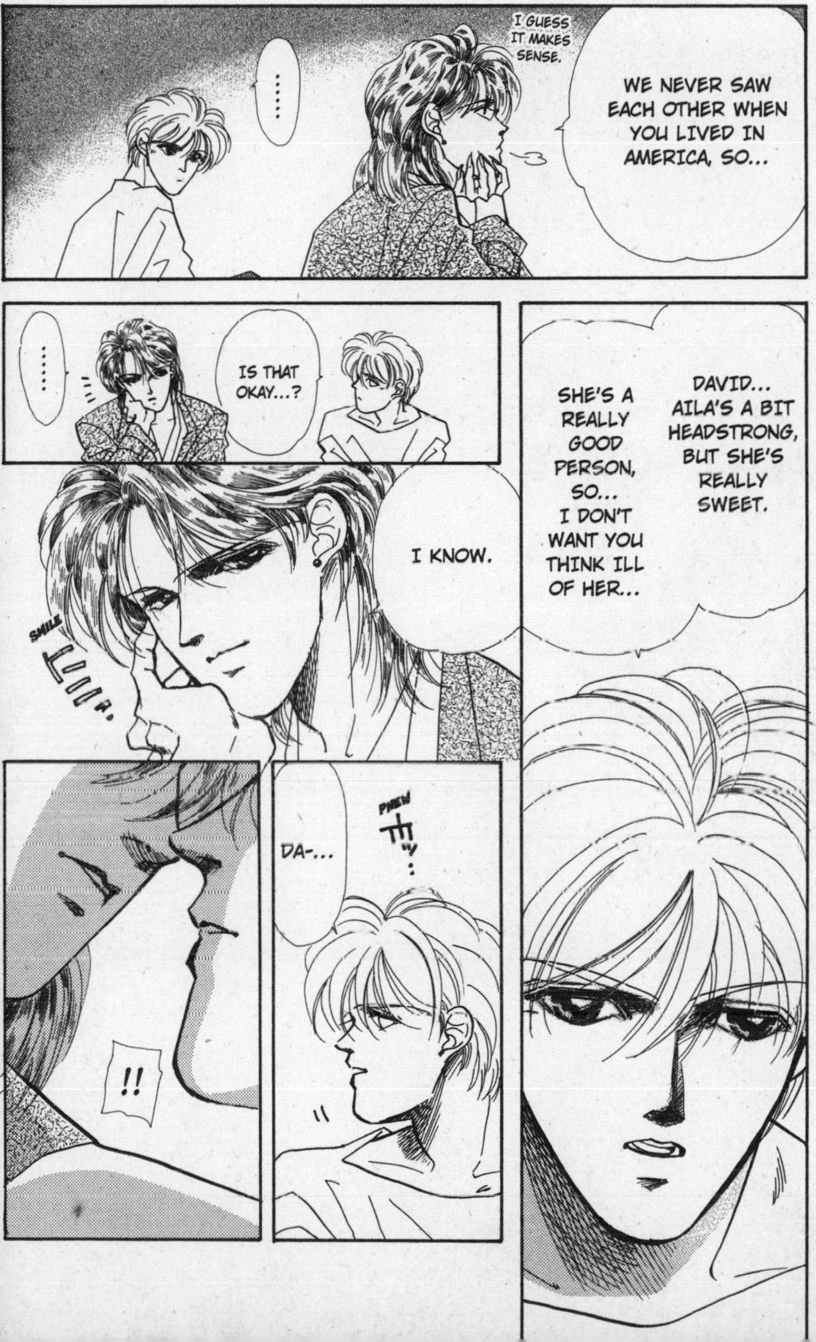
WE NEVER SAW EACH OTHER WHEN YOU LIVED IN AMERICA, SO...
I GUESS IT MAKES SENSE.
......
DAVID... AILA'S A BIT HEADSTRONG, BUT SHE'S REALLY SWEET.
SHE'S A REALLY GOOD PERSON, SO... I DON'T WANT YOU THINK ILL OF HER...
IS THAT OKAY...?
......
I KNOW.
SMILE
DA-...
PHEW
!!

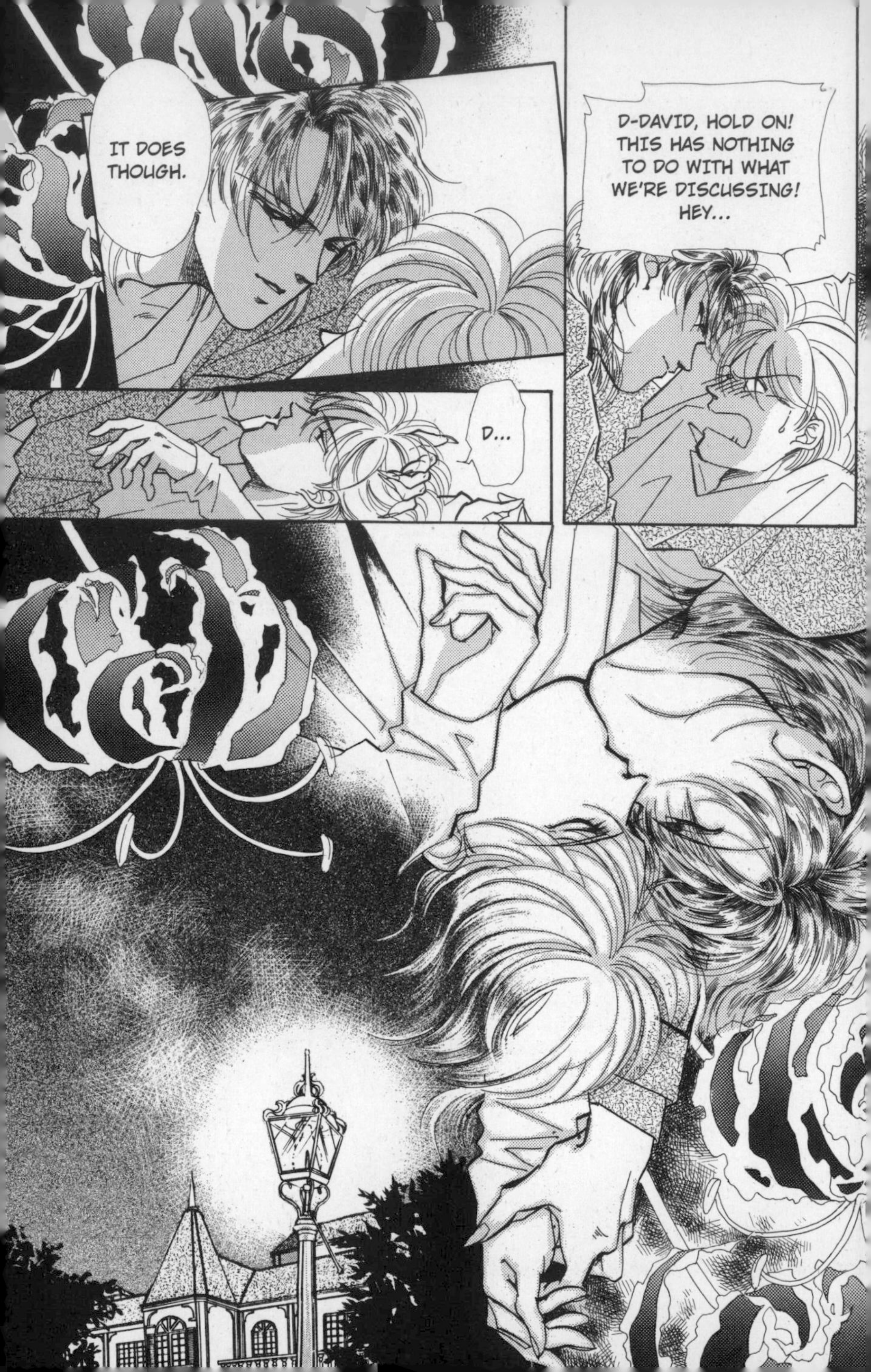
D-DAVID, HOLD ON! THIS HAS NOTHING TO DO WITH WHAT WE'RE DISCUSSING! HEY...
IT DOES THOUGH.
D...

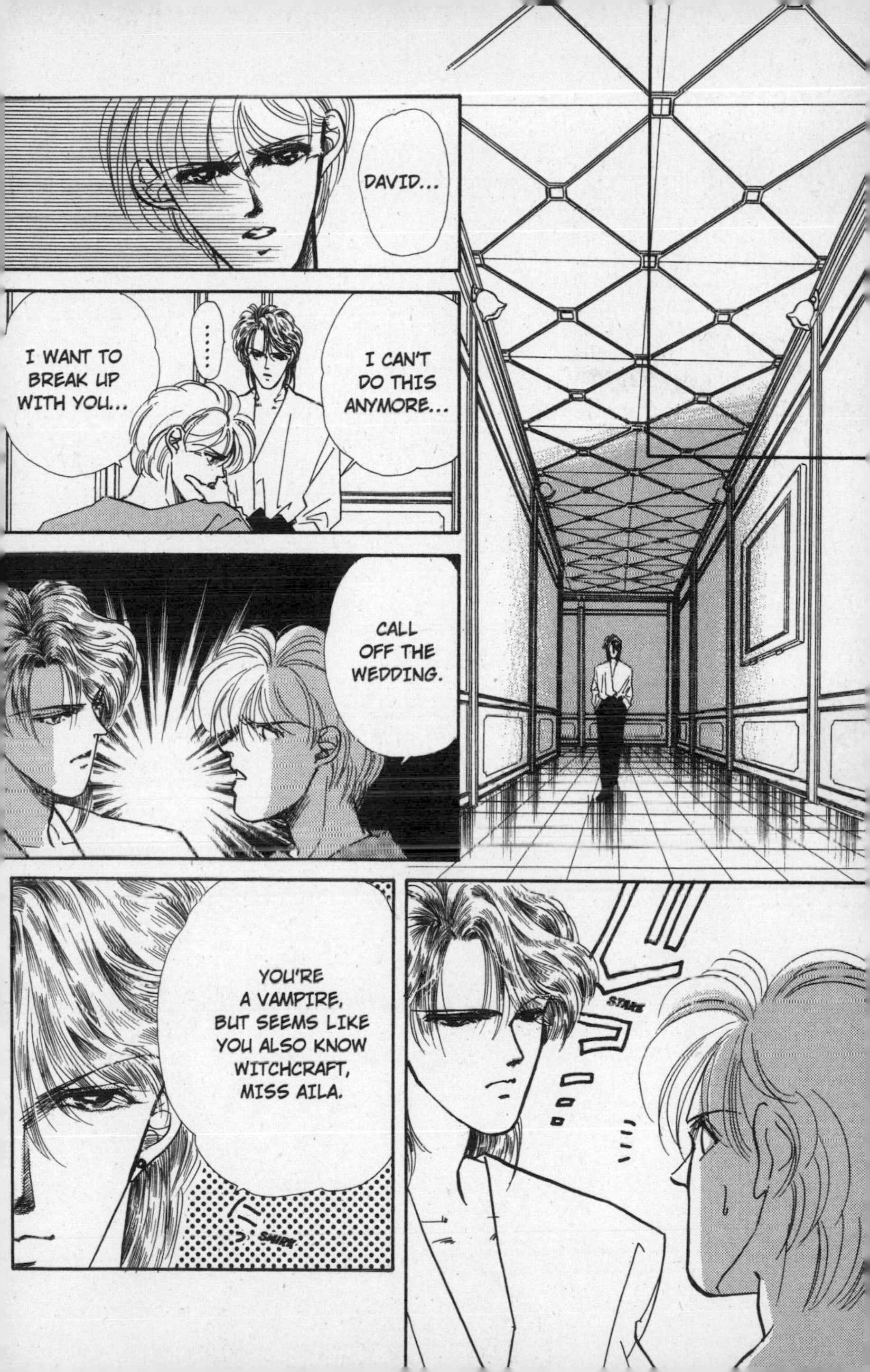
DAVID...
I CAN'T DO THIS ANYMORE...
......
I WANT TO BREAK UP WITH YOU...
CALL OFF THE WEDDING.
STARE
YOU'RE A VAMPIRE, BUT SEEMS LIKE YOU ALSO KNOW WITCHCRAFT, MISS AILA.
SHIRK

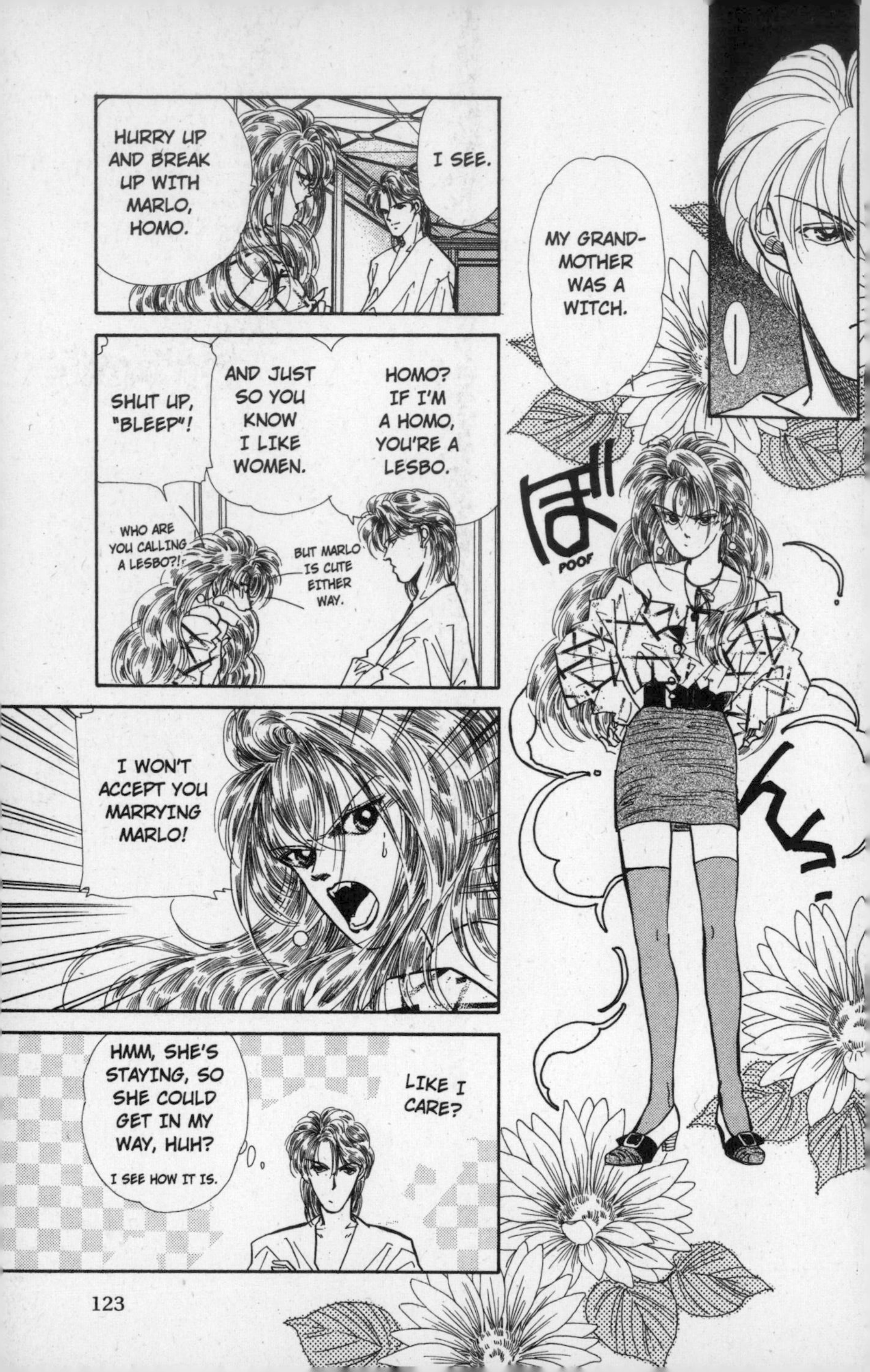
MY GRAND-MOTHER WAS A WITCH.
ぽ POOF
ん
I SEE.
HURRY UP AND BREAK UP WITH MARLO, HOMO.
HOMO? IF I'M A HOMO, YOU'RE A LESBO.
AND JUST SO YOU KNOW I LIKE WOMEN.
SHUT UP, "BLEEP"!
BUT MARLO IS CUTE EITHER WAY.
WHO ARE YOU CALLING A LESBO?!
I WON'T ACCEPT YOU MARRYING MARLO!
LIKE I CARE?
HMM, SHE'S STAYING, SO SHE COULD GET IN MY WAY, HUH?
I SEE HOW IT IS.

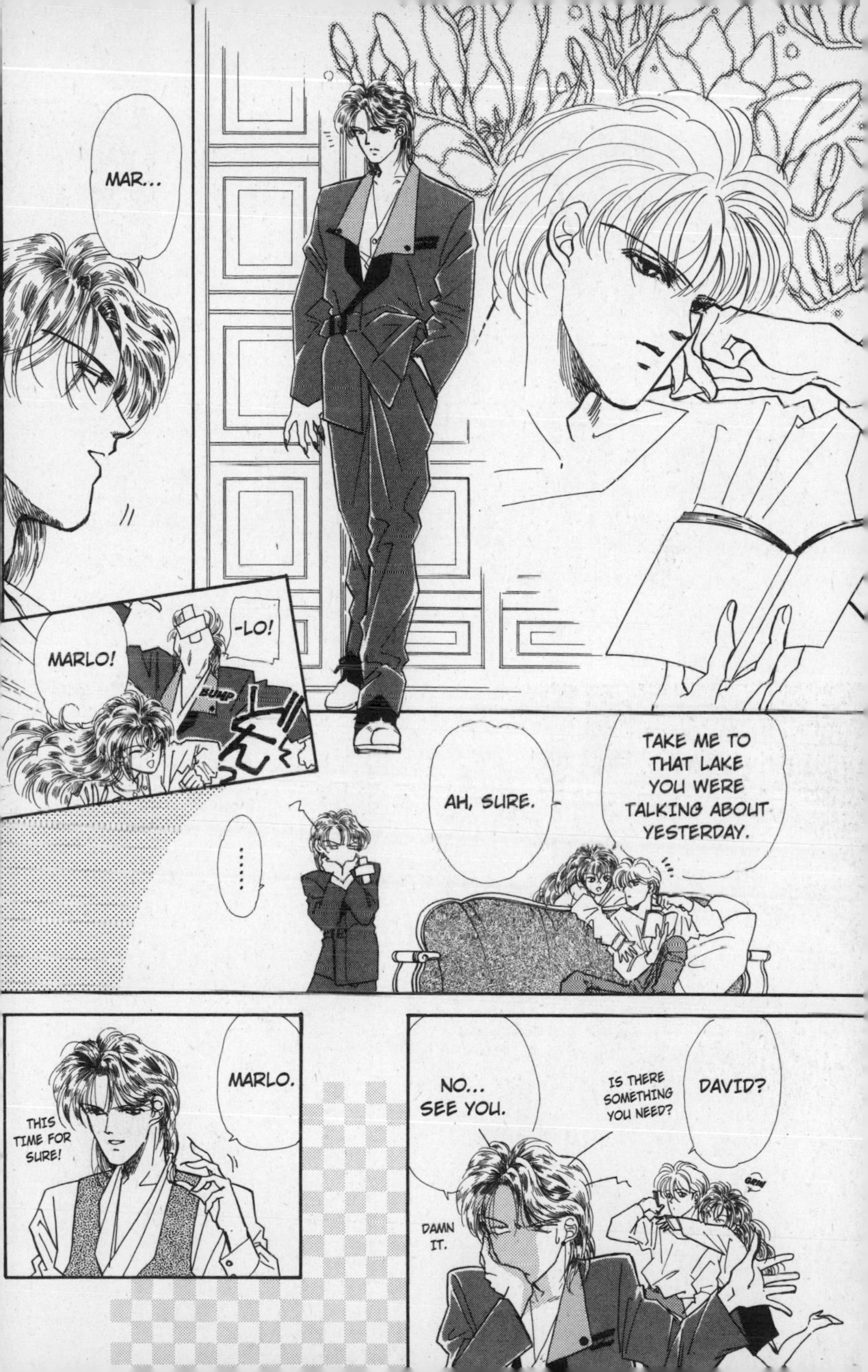
MAR...
-LO!
BUMP
MARLO!
TAKE ME TO THAT LAKE YOU WERE TALKING ABOUT YESTERDAY.
AH, SURE.
......
DAVID?
IS THERE SOMETHING YOU NEED?
NO... SEE YOU.
GRIN
DAMN IT.
MARLO.
THIS TIME FOR SURE!

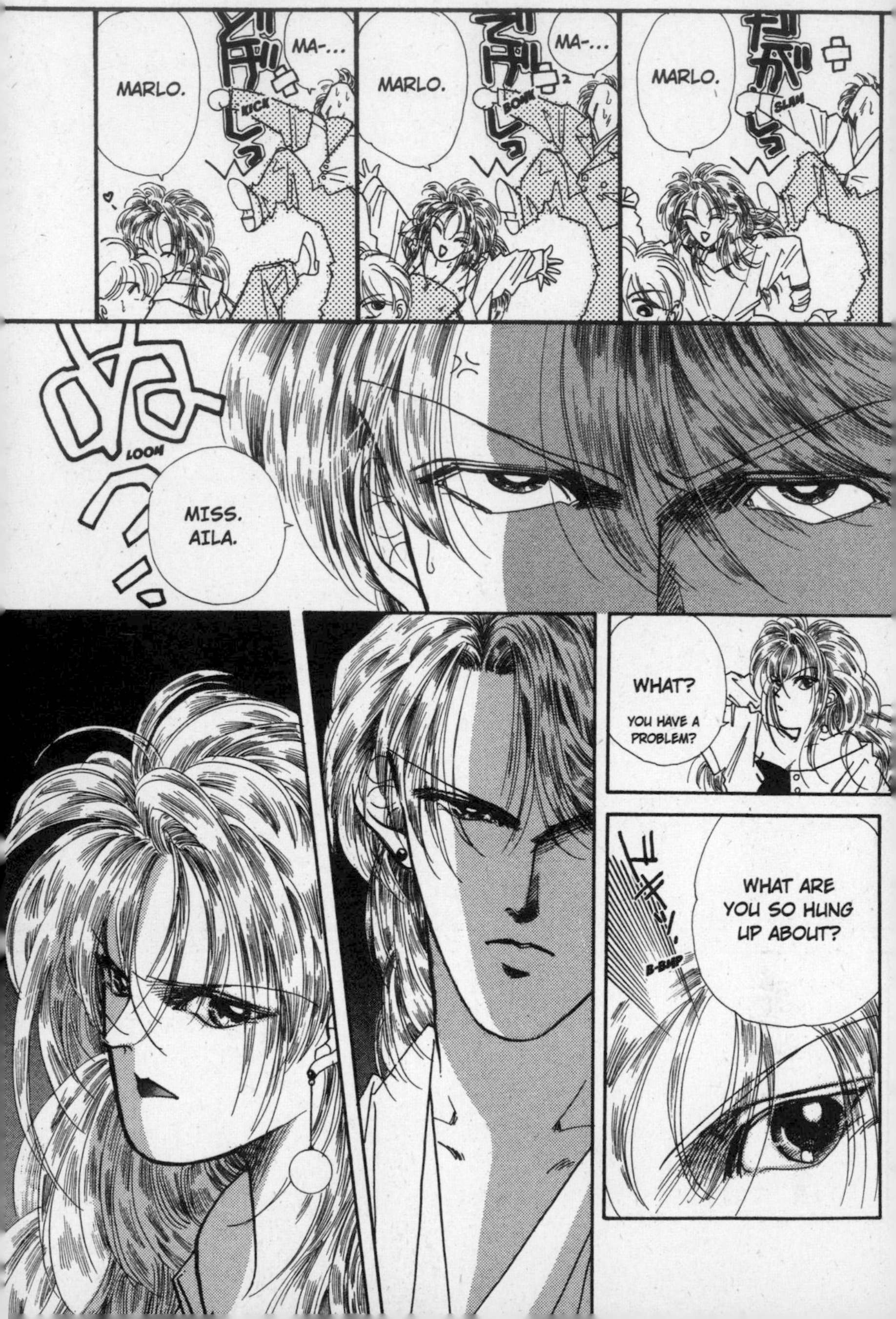
MARLO.
SLAM
MA-...
MARLO.
BONK
MA-...
MARLO.
KICK
MISS. AILA.
LOOM
WHAT?
YOU HAVE A PROBLEM?
WHAT ARE YOU SO HUNG UP ABOUT?
B-BMP

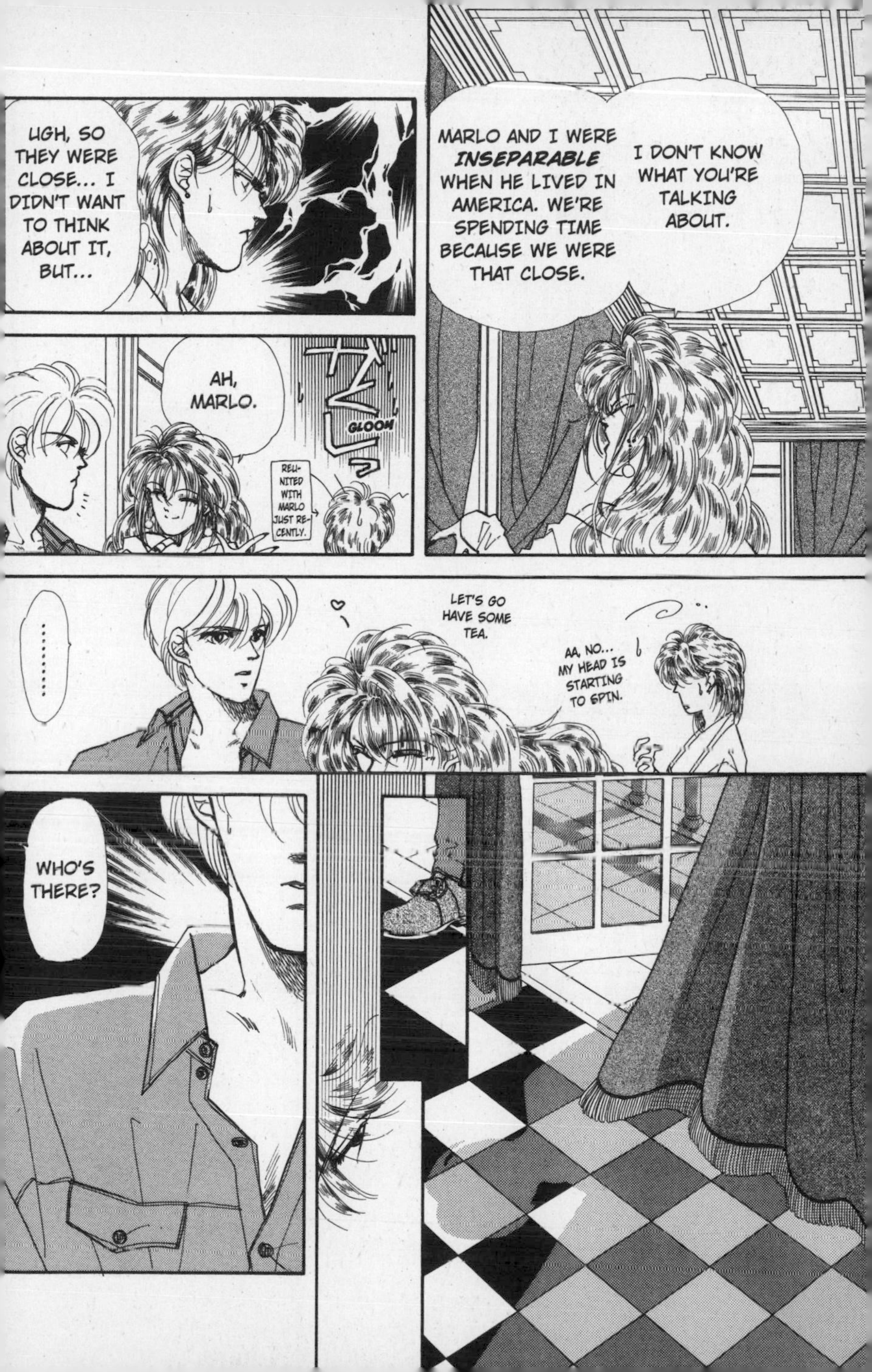
I DON'T KNOW WHAT YOU'RE TALKING ABOUT.
MARLO AND I WERE *INSEPARABLE* WHEN HE LIVED IN AMERICA. WE'RE SPENDING TIME BECAUSE WE WERE THAT CLOSE.
UGH, SO THEY WERE CLOSE... I DIDN'T WANT TO THINK ABOUT IT, BUT...
GLOOM
REU-NITED WITH MARLO JUST RE-CENTLY.
AH, MARLO.
AA, NO... MY HEAD IS STARTING TO SPIN.
LET'S GO HAVE SOME TEA.
......
WHO'S THERE?

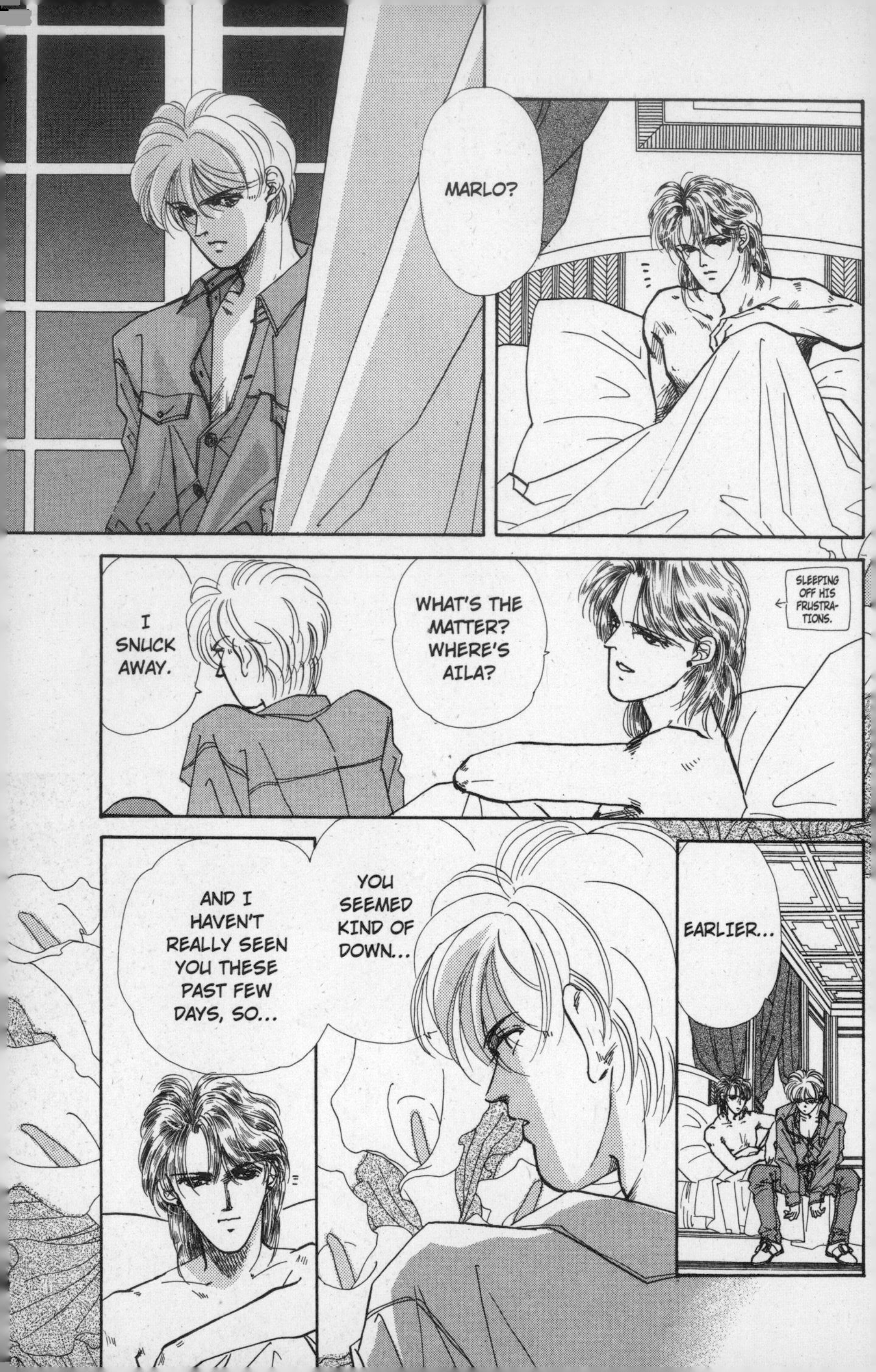
MARLO?
SLEEPING OFF HIS FRUSTRATIONS.
WHAT'S THE MATTER? WHERE'S AILA?
I SNUCK AWAY.
EARLIER...
YOU SEEMED KIND OF DOWN...
AND I HAVEN'T REALLY SEEN YOU THESE PAST FEW DAYS, SO...

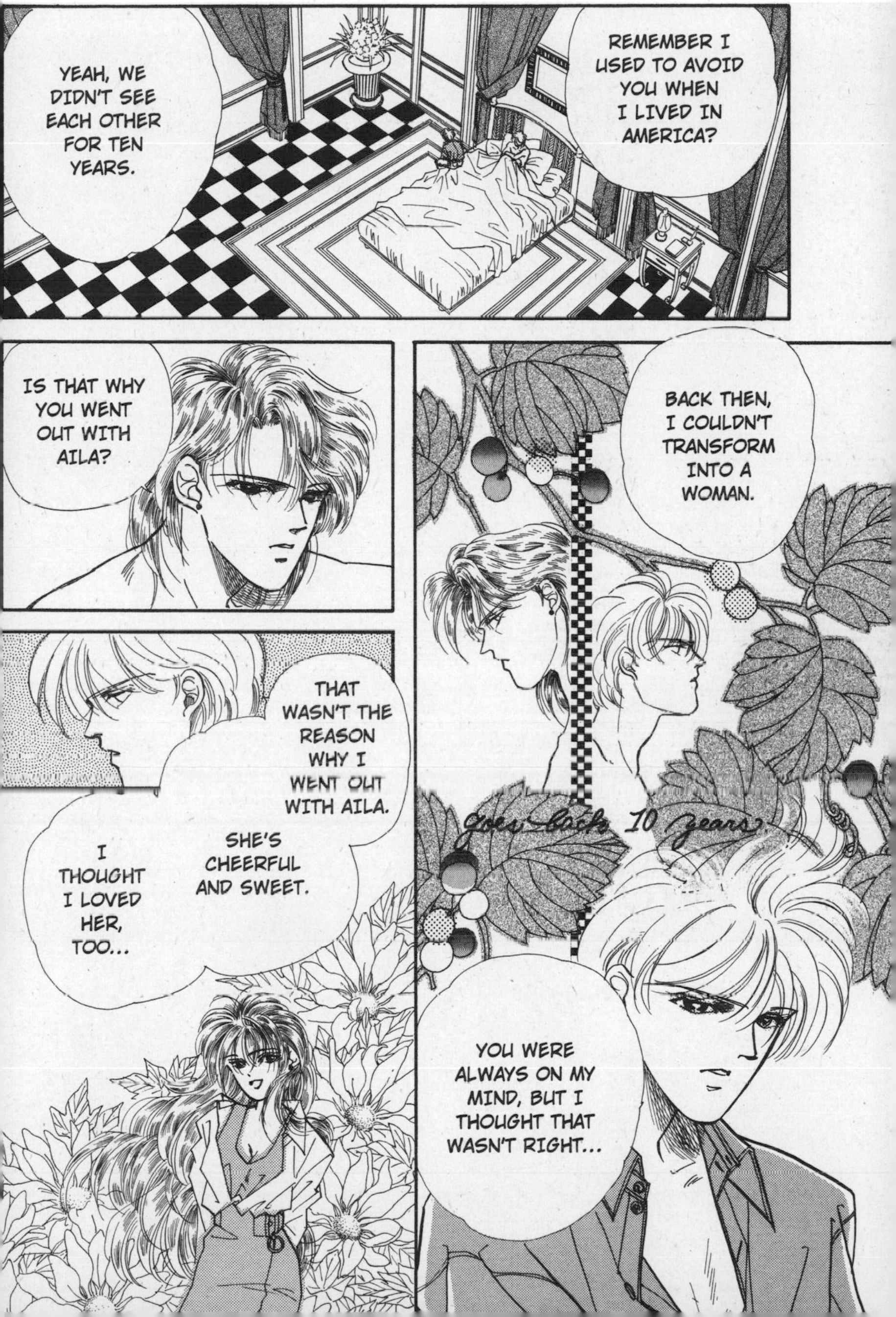
REMEMBER I USED TO AVOID YOU WHEN I LIVED IN AMERICA?
YEAH, WE DIDN'T SEE EACH OTHER FOR TEN YEARS.
BACK THEN, I COULDN'T TRANSFORM INTO A WOMAN.
goes back 10 years
YOU WERE ALWAYS ON MY MIND, BUT I THOUGHT THAT WASN'T RIGHT...
IS THAT WHY YOU WENT OUT WITH AILA?
THAT WASN'T THE REASON WHY I WENT OUT WITH AILA.
SHE'S CHEERFUL AND SWEET.
I THOUGHT I LOVED HER, TOO...

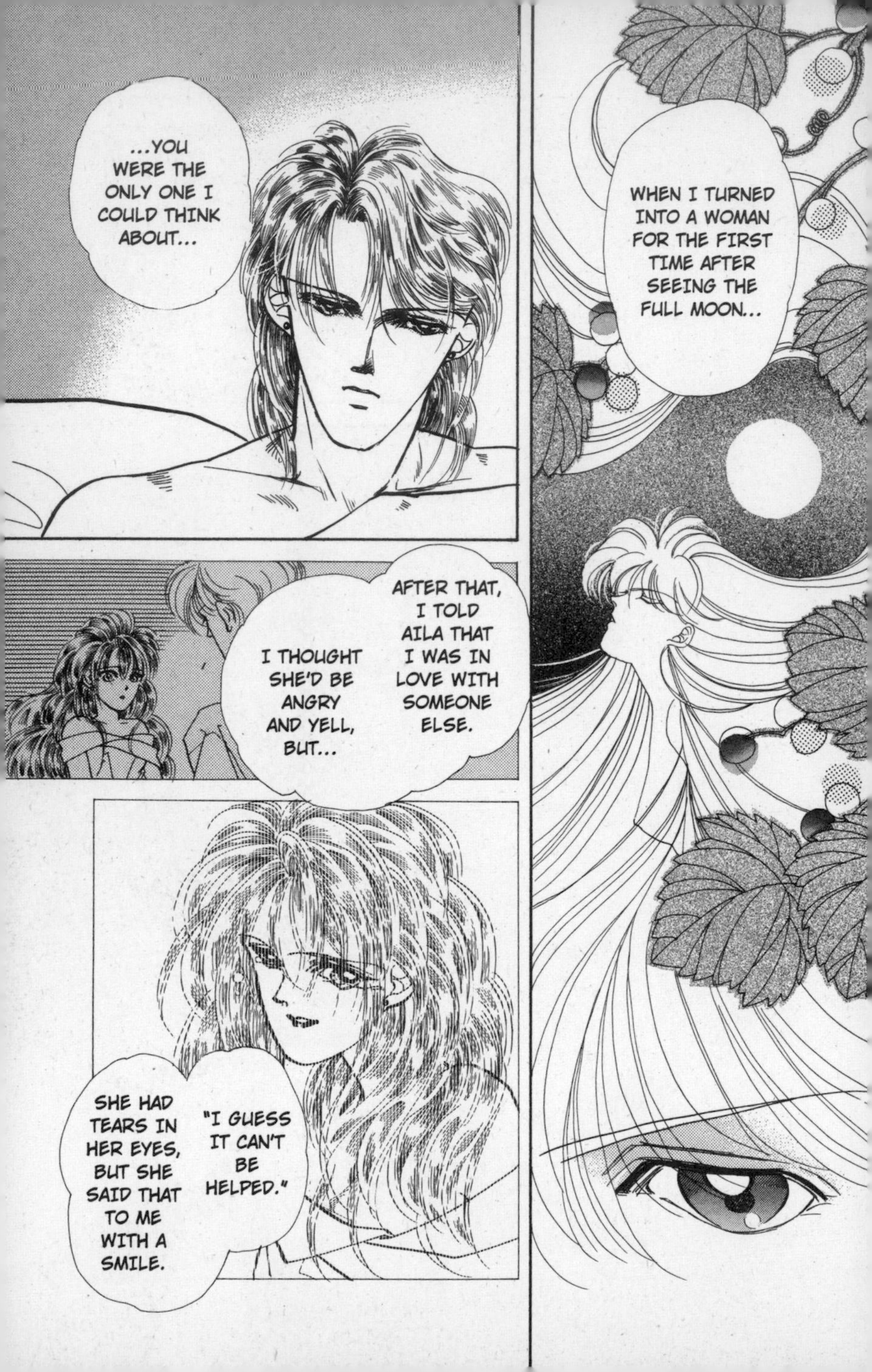
WHEN I TURNED INTO A WOMAN FOR THE FIRST TIME AFTER SEEING THE FULL MOON...
...YOU WERE THE ONLY ONE I COULD THINK ABOUT...
AFTER THAT, I TOLD AILA THAT I WAS IN LOVE WITH SOMEONE ELSE.
I THOUGHT SHE'D BE ANGRY AND YELL, BUT...
"I GUESS IT CAN'T BE HELPED."
SHE HAD TEARS IN HER EYES, BUT SHE SAID THAT TO ME WITH A SMILE.

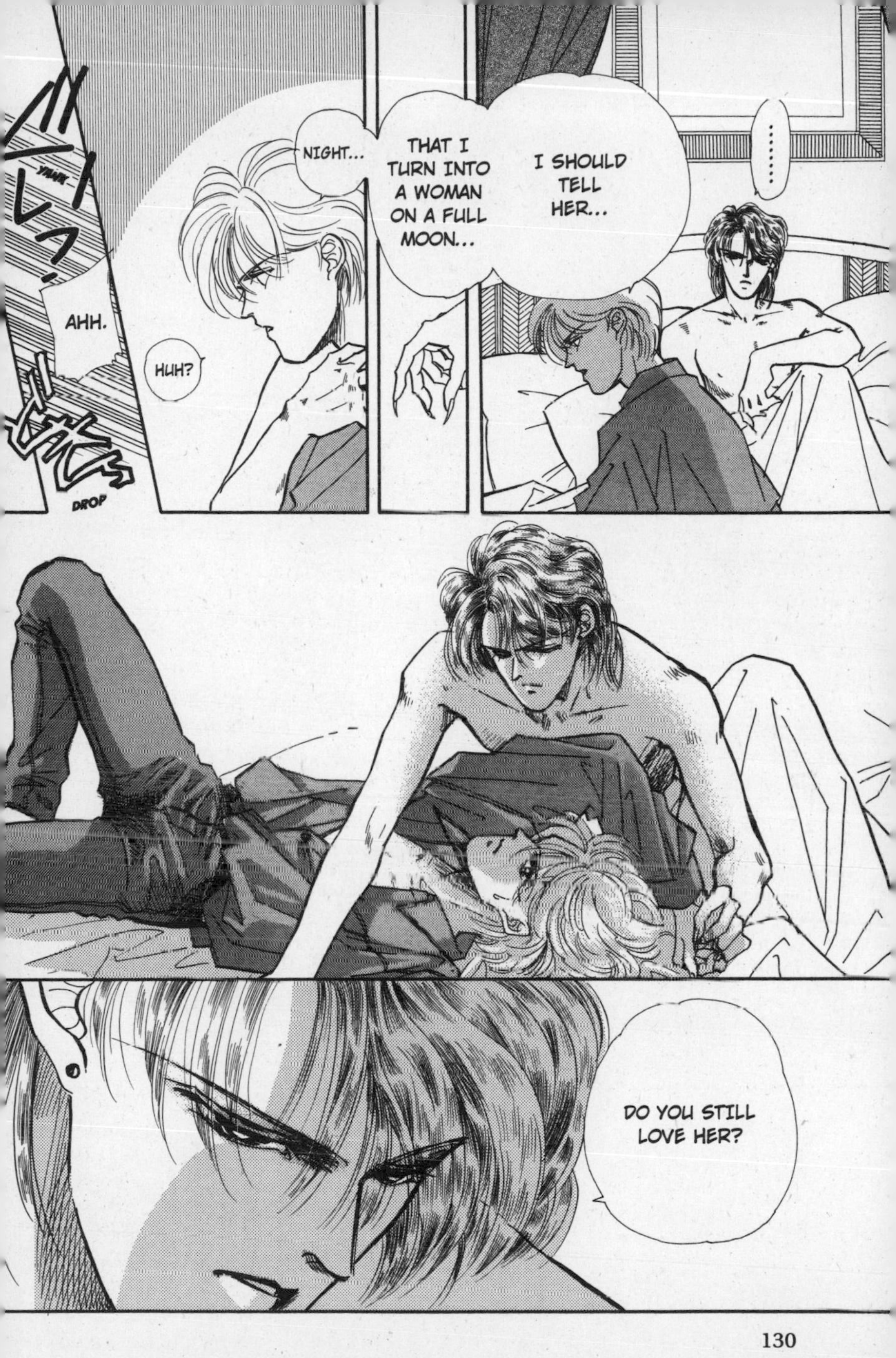
......
I SHOULD TELL HER...
THAT I TURN INTO A WOMAN ON A FULL MOON...
NIGHT...
YANK
AHH.
HUH?
DROP
DO YOU STILL LOVE HER?

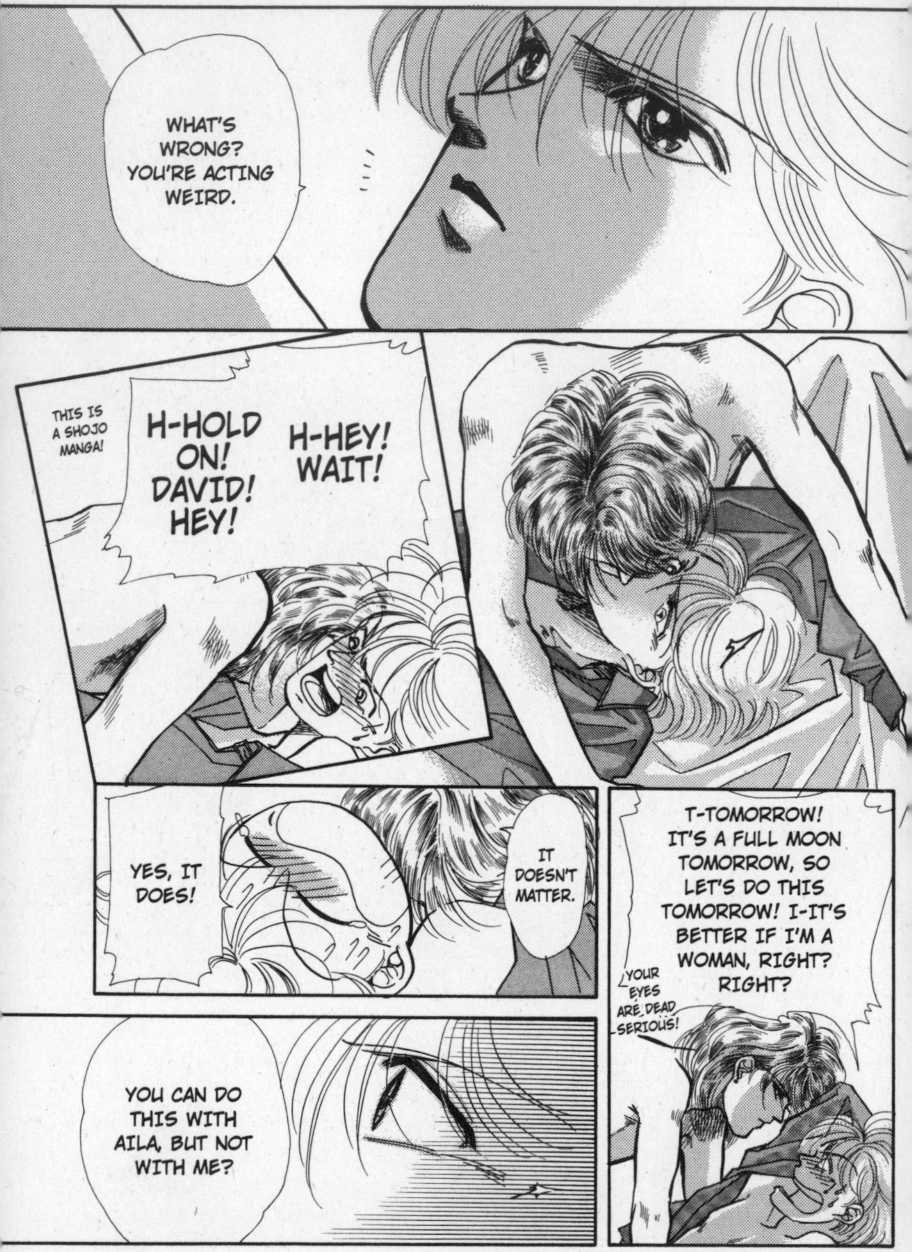

WHAT'S WRONG? YOU'RE ACTING WEIRD.
H-HEY! WAIT!
H-HOLD ON! DAVID! HEY!
THIS IS A SHOJO MANGA!
T-TOMORROW! IT'S A FULL MOON TOMORROW, SO LET'S DO THIS TOMORROW! I-IT'S BETTER IF I'M A WOMAN, RIGHT? RIGHT?
YOUR EYES ARE DEAD SERIOUS!
IT DOESN'T MATTER.
YES, IT DOES!
YOU CAN DO THIS WITH AILA, BUT NOT WITH ME?

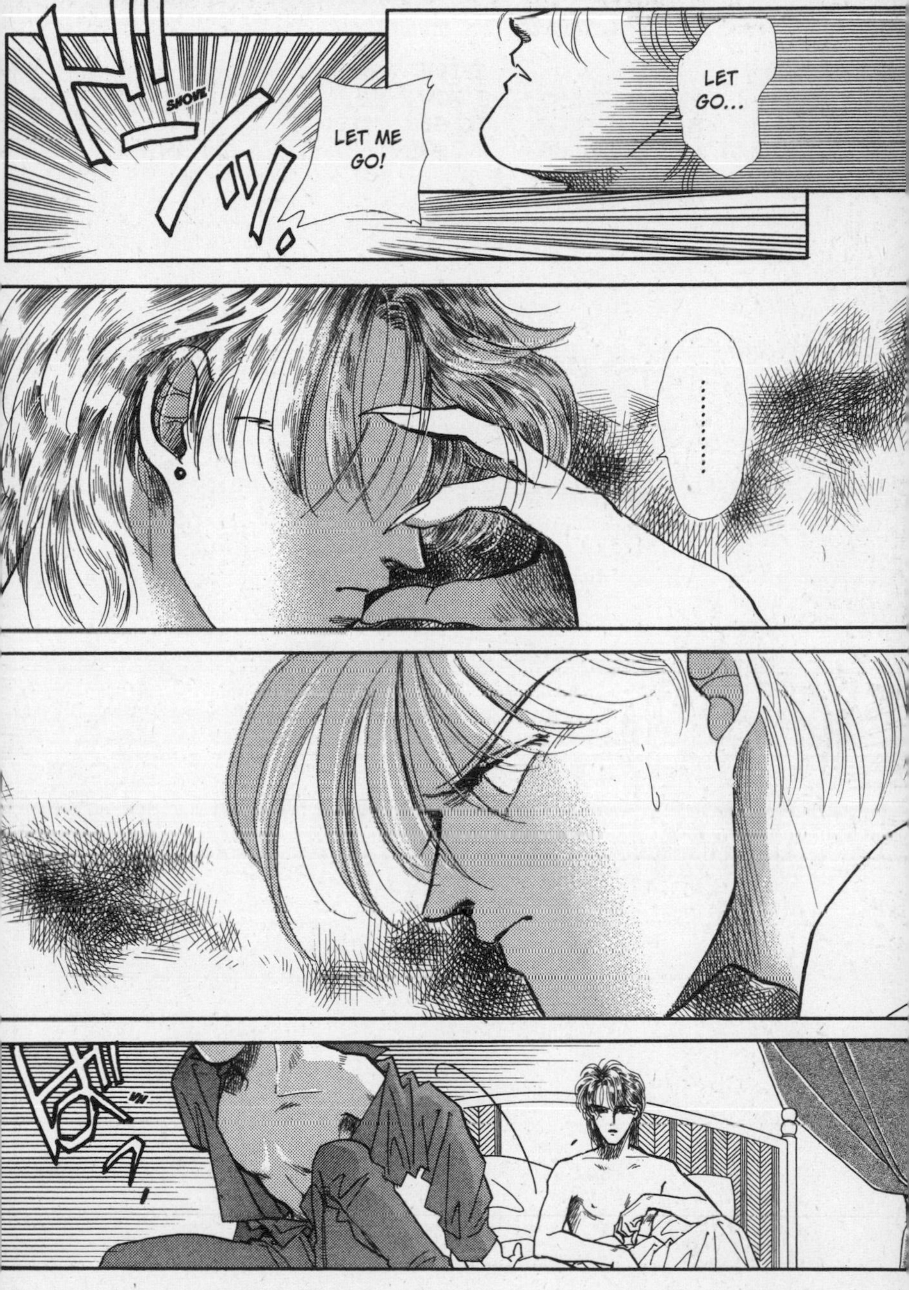
LET GO...
LET ME GO!
SHOVE
......
VH

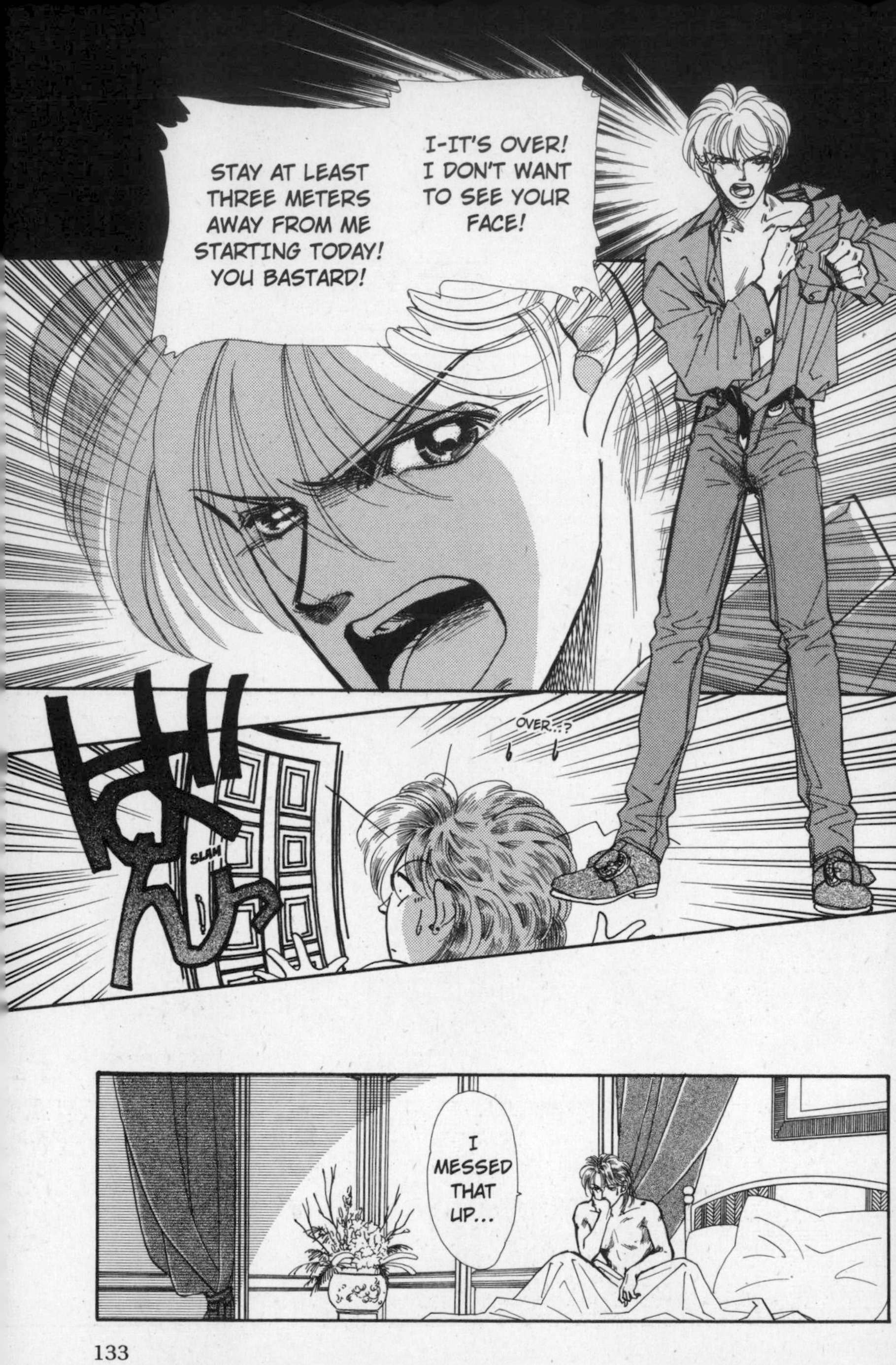
I-IT'S OVER! I DON'T WANT TO SEE YOUR FACE!
STAY AT LEAST THREE METERS AWAY FROM ME STARTING TODAY! YOU BASTARD!
OVER...?
SLAM
I MESSED THAT UP...

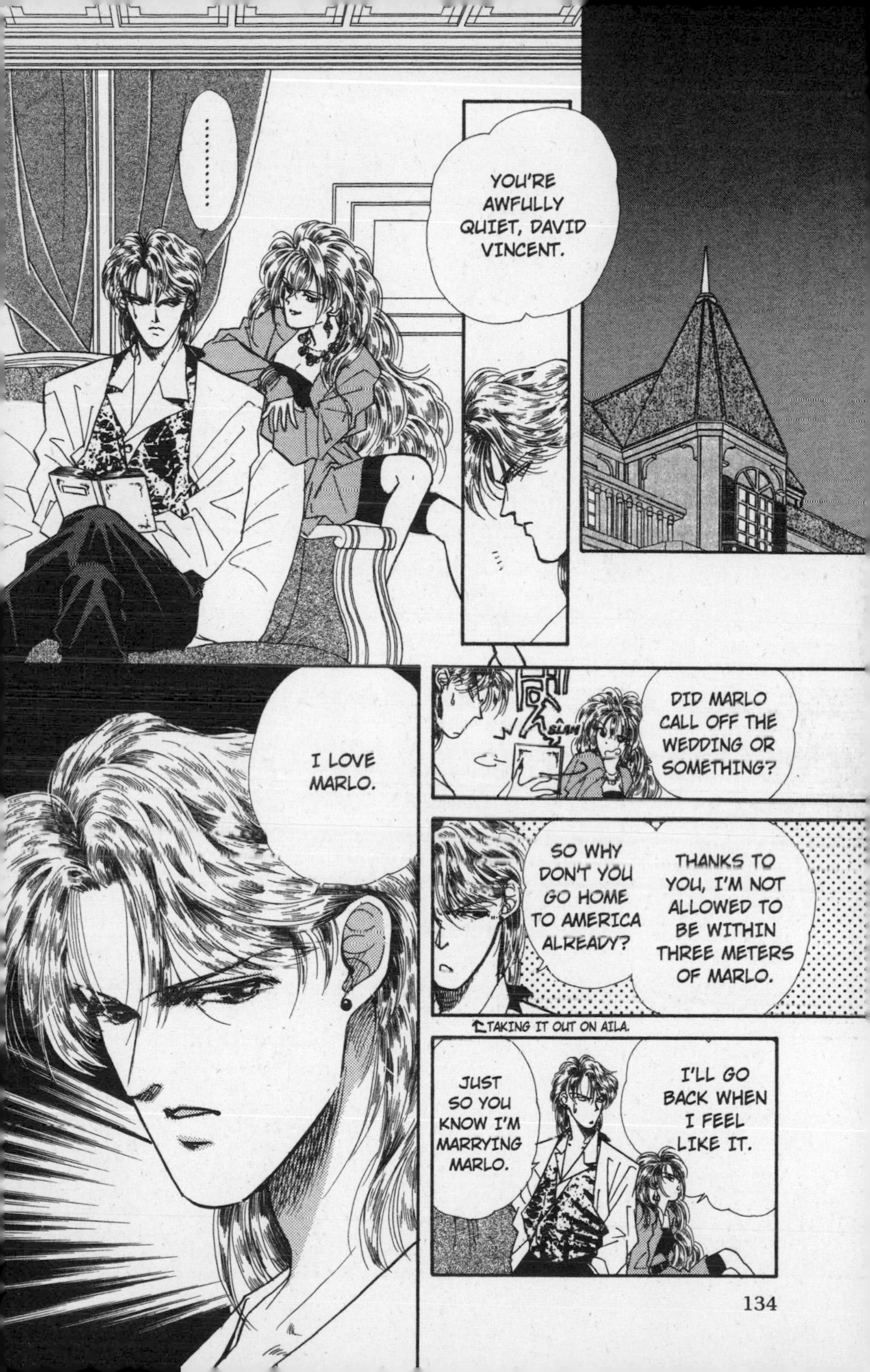
YOU'RE AWFULLY QUIET, DAVID VINCENT.
......
DID MARLO CALL OFF THE WEDDING OR SOMETHING?
BLAM
THANKS TO YOU, I'M NOT ALLOWED TO BE WITHIN THREE METERS OF MARLO.
SO WHY DON'T YOU GO HOME TO AMERICA ALREADY?
TAKING IT OUT ON AILA.
I'LL GO BACK WHEN I FEEL LIKE IT.
JUST SO YOU KNOW I'M MARRYING MARLO.
I LOVE MARLO.

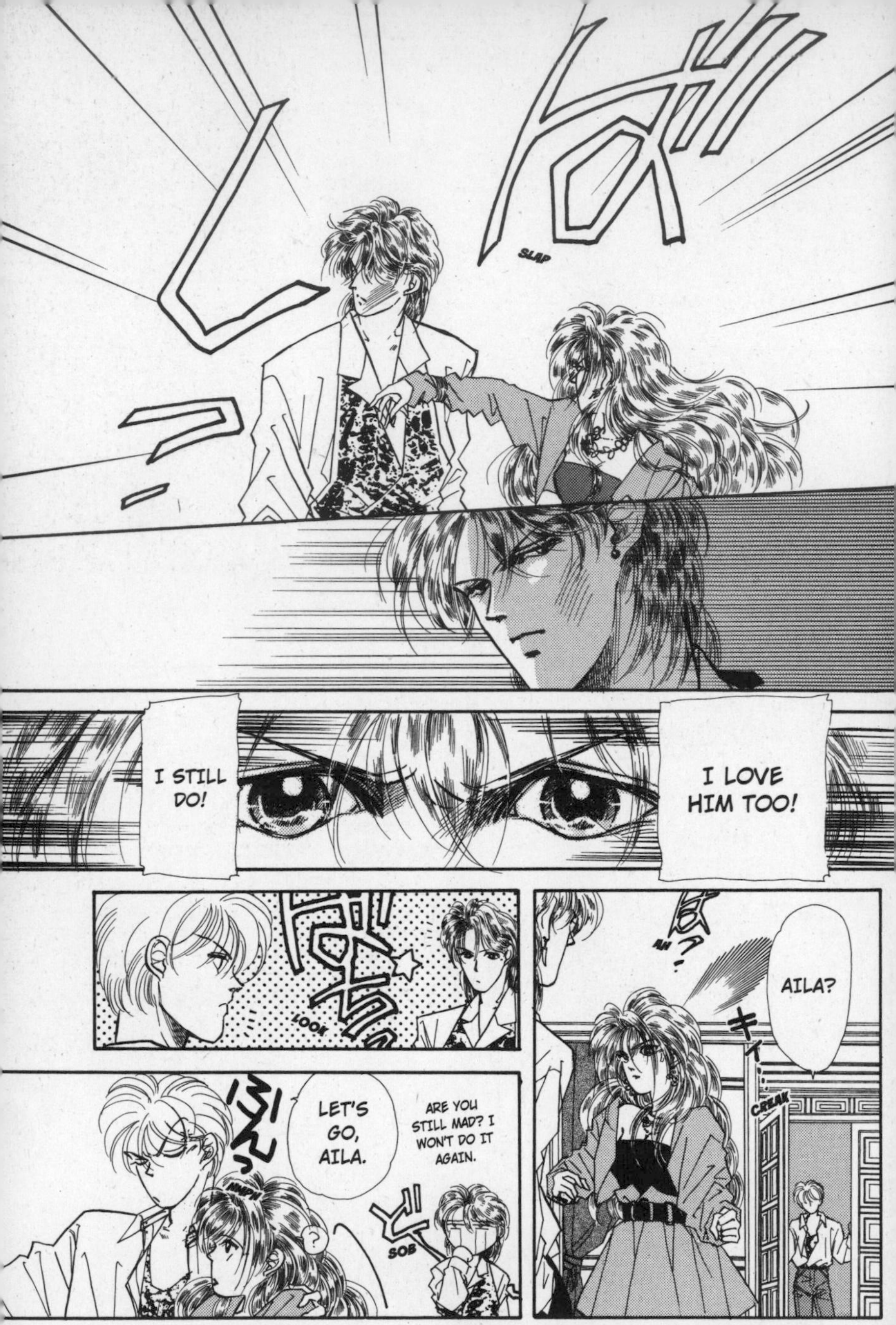
SLAP
I LOVE HIM TOO!
I STILL DO!
AH
AILA?
CREAK
LOOK
ARE YOU STILL MAD? I WON'T DO IT AGAIN.
SOB
LET'S GO, AILA.
HMPH

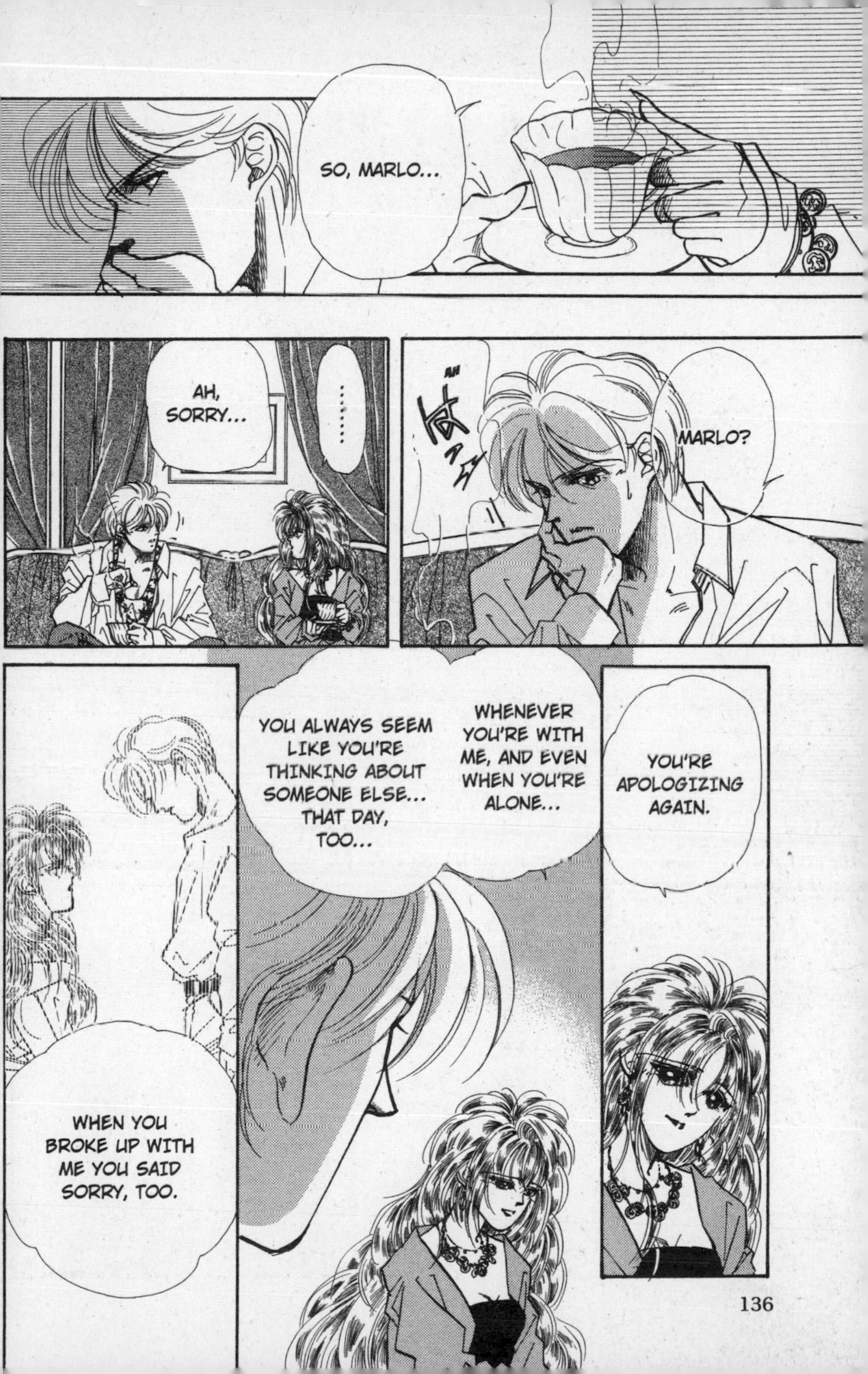
SO, MARLO...
MARLO?
......
AH, SORRY...
YOU'RE APOLOGIZING AGAIN.
WHENEVER YOU'RE WITH ME, AND EVEN WHEN YOU'RE ALONE...
YOU ALWAYS SEEM LIKE YOU'RE THINKING ABOUT SOMEONE ELSE... THAT DAY, TOO...
WHEN YOU BROKE UP WITH ME YOU SAID SORRY, TOO.

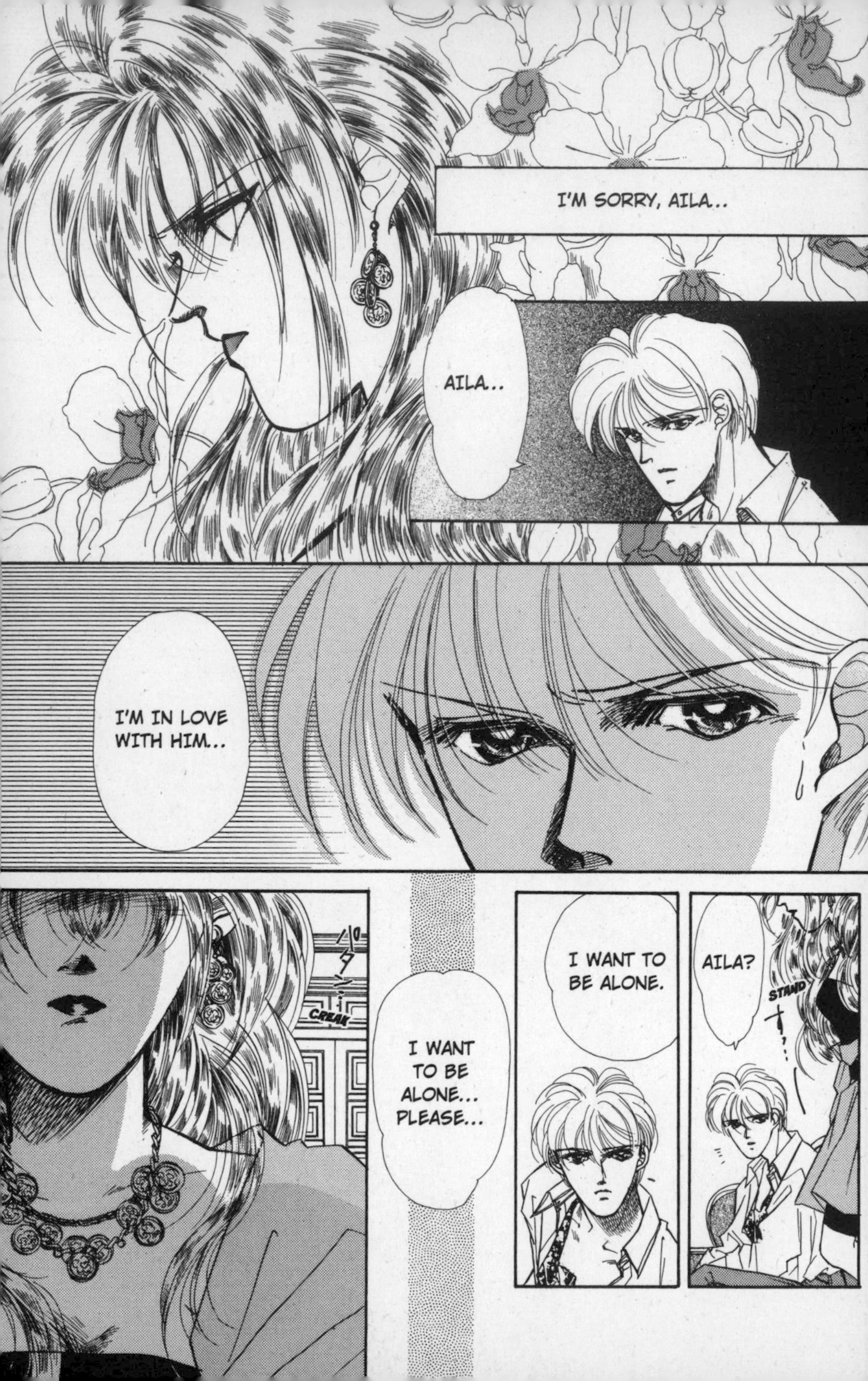
I'M SORRY, AILA...
AILA...
I'M IN LOVE WITH HIM...
AILA?
STAND
I WANT TO BE ALONE.
CREAK
I WANT TO BE ALONE... PLEASE...

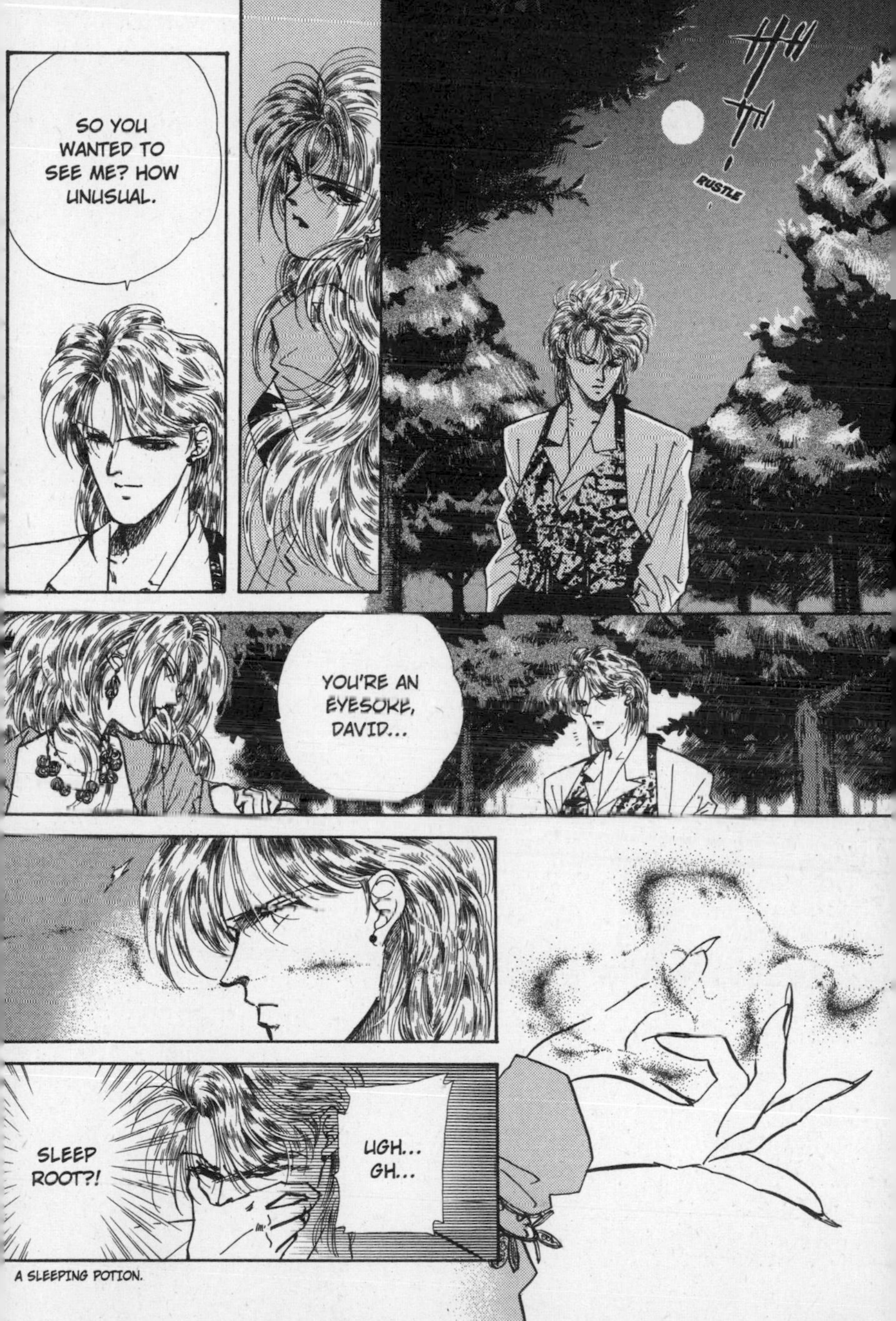
RUSTLE
SO YOU WANTED TO SEE ME? HOW UNUSUAL.
YOU'RE AN EYESORE, DAVID...
UGH... GH...
SLEEP ROOT?!

A SLEEPING POTION.

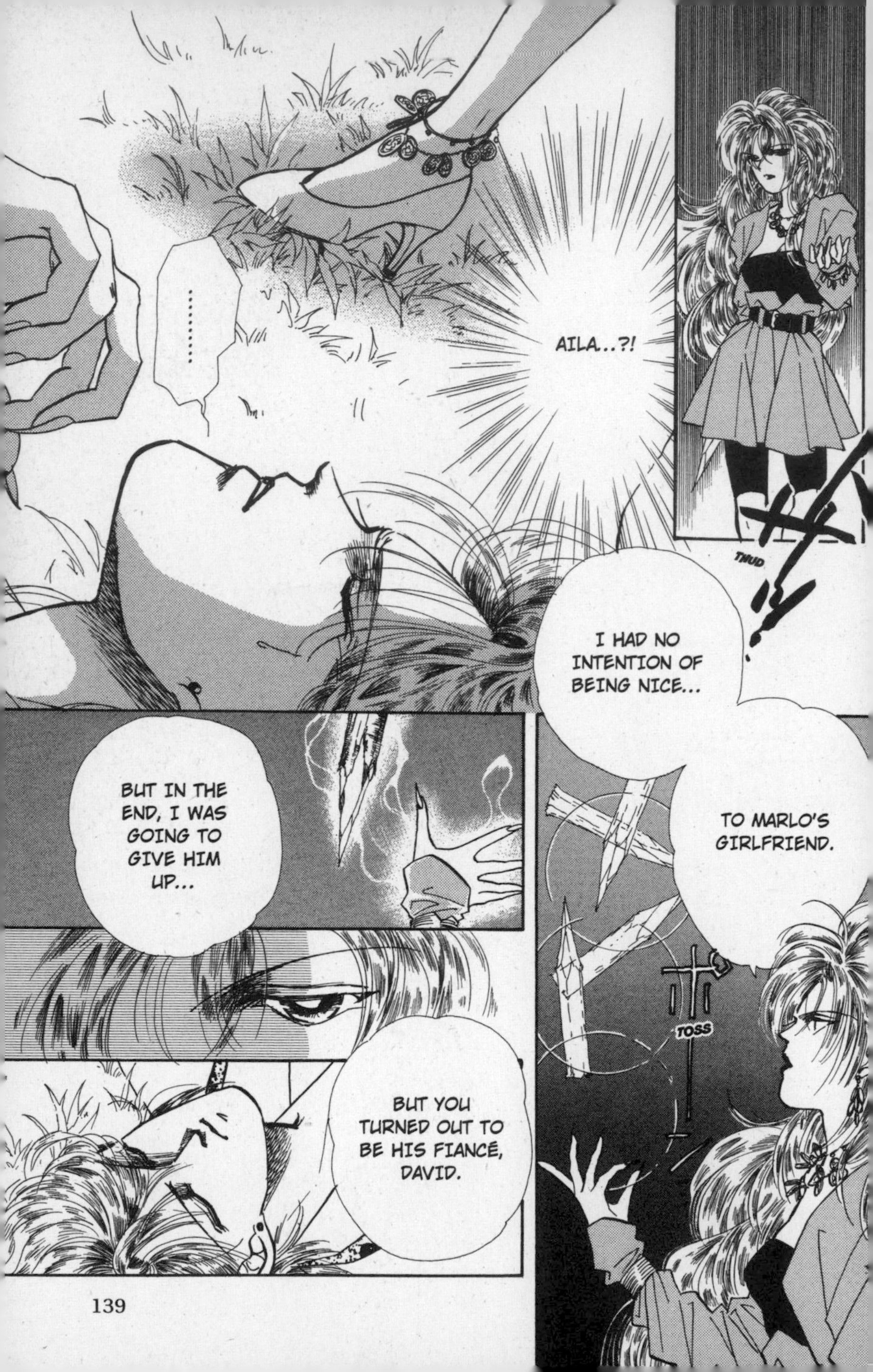
THUD
AILA..?!
......
I HAD NO INTENTION OF BEING NICE...
TO MARLO'S GIRLFRIEND.
TOSS
BUT IN THE END, I WAS GOING TO GIVE HIM UP...
BUT YOU TURNED OUT TO BE HIS FIANCÉ, DAVID.

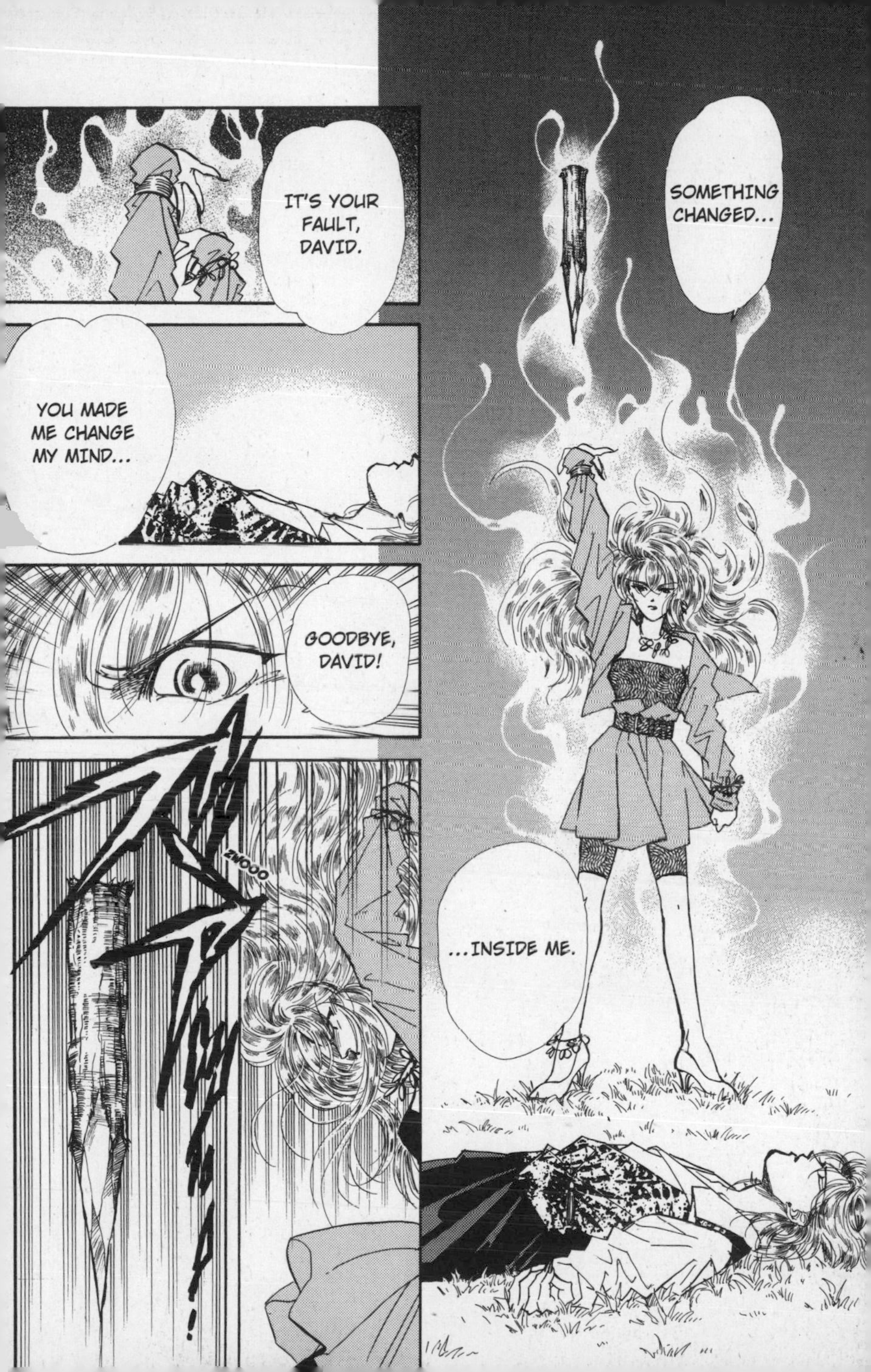
SOMETHING CHANGED...
...INSIDE ME.
IT'S YOUR FAULT, DAVID.
YOU MADE ME CHANGE MY MIND...
GOODBYE, DAVID!
ZWOOO

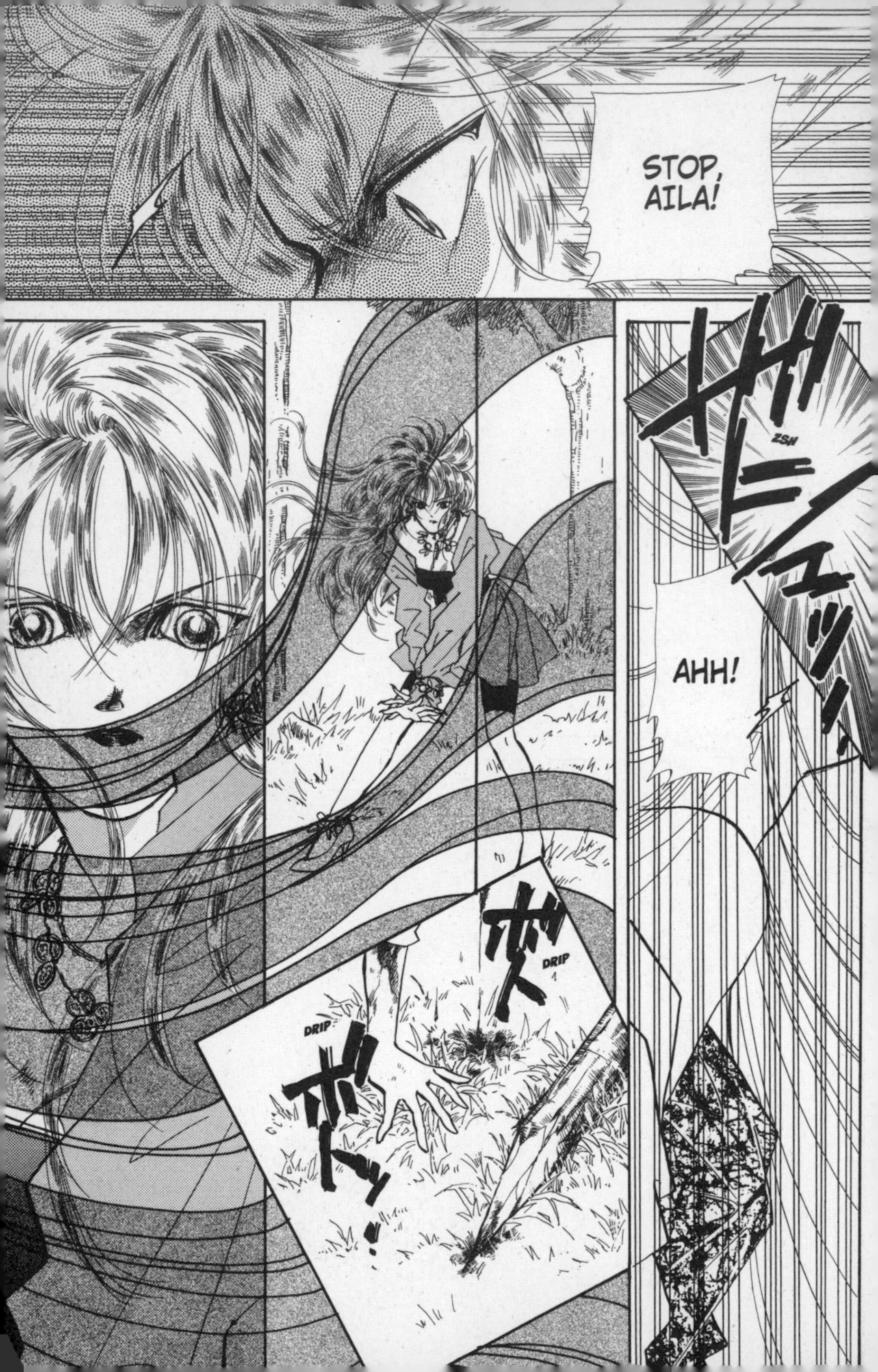
STOP, AILA!
ZSH
AHH!
DRIP
DRIP

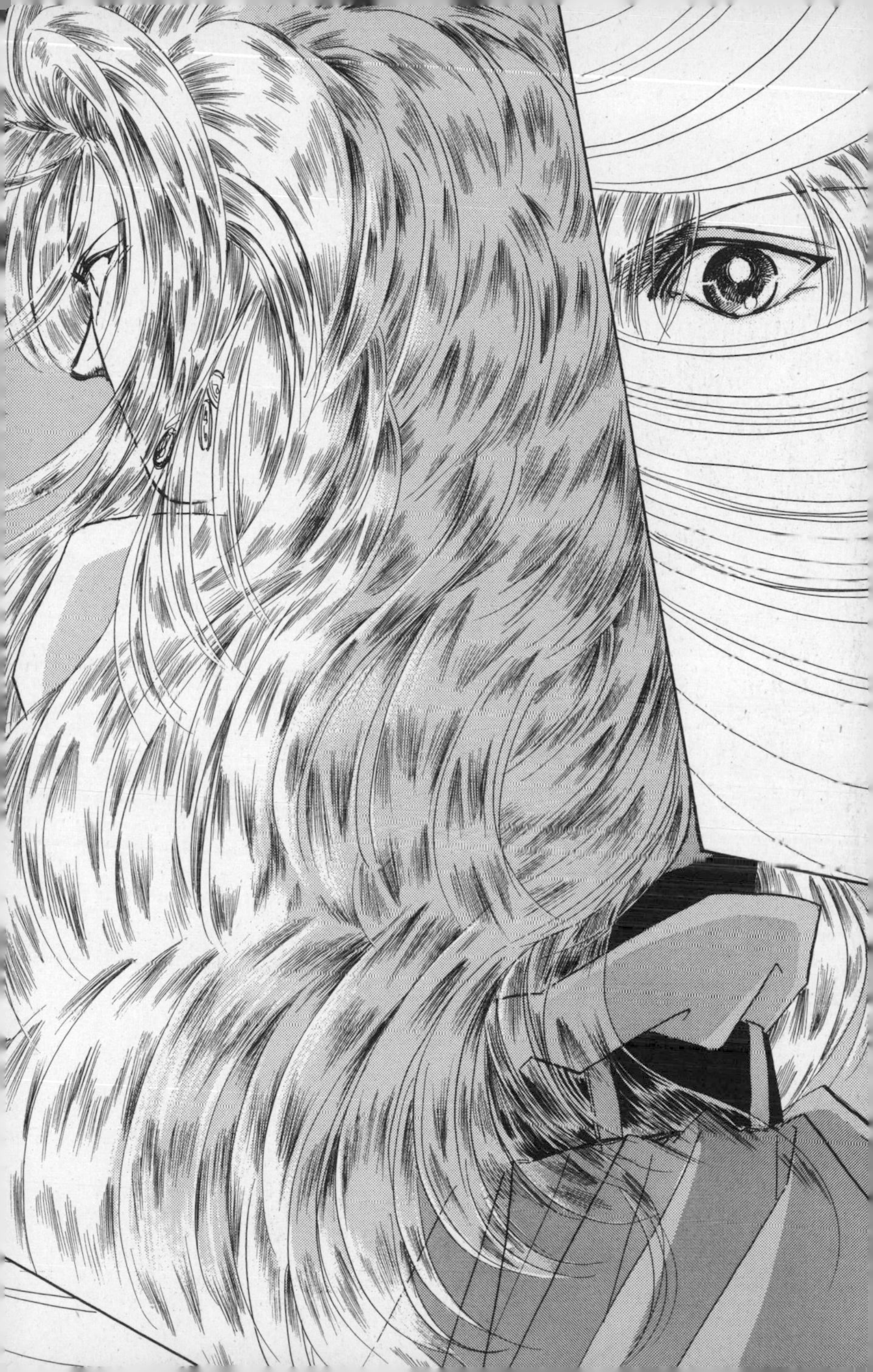

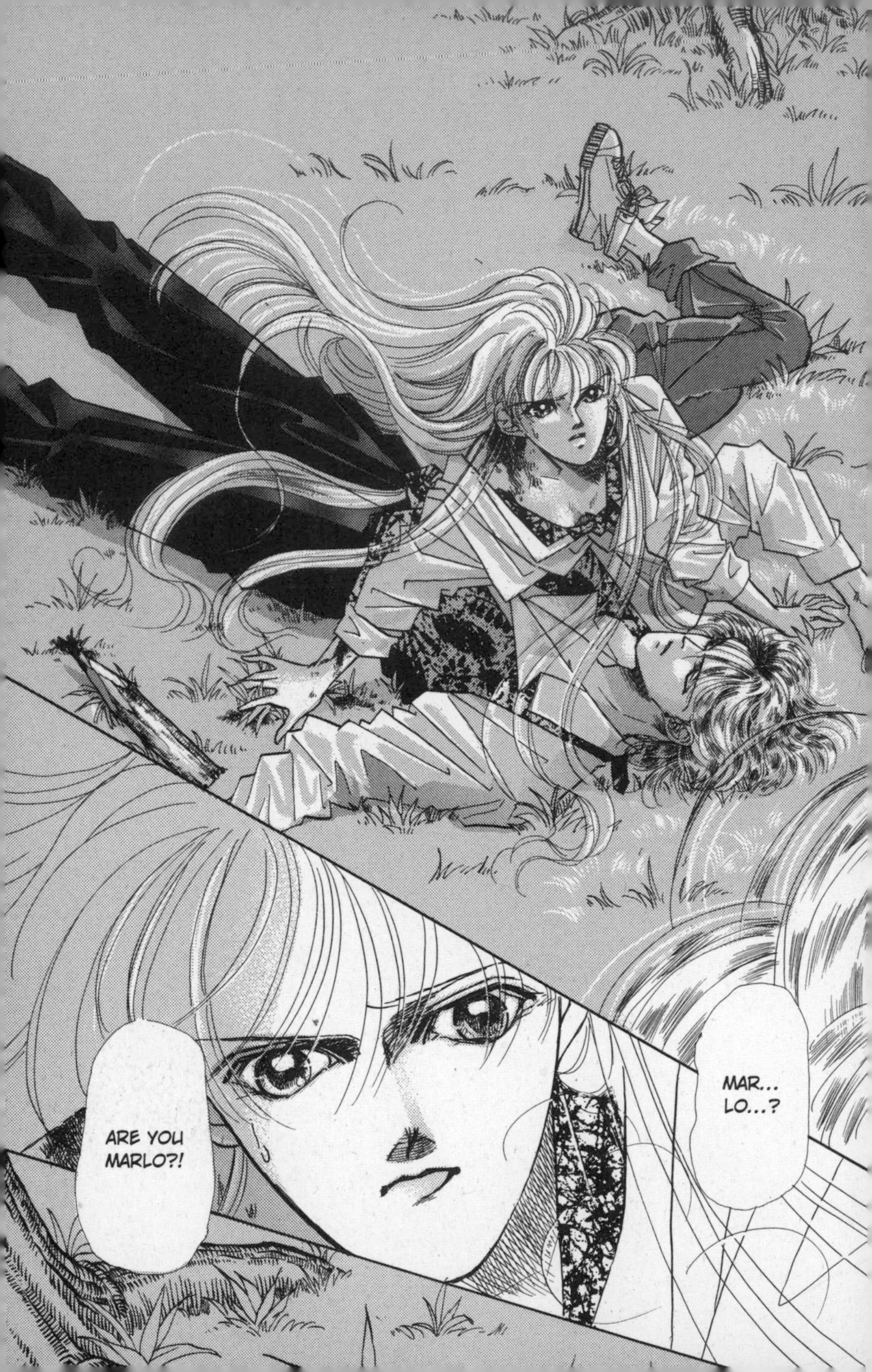
MAR... LO...?
ARE YOU MARLO?!

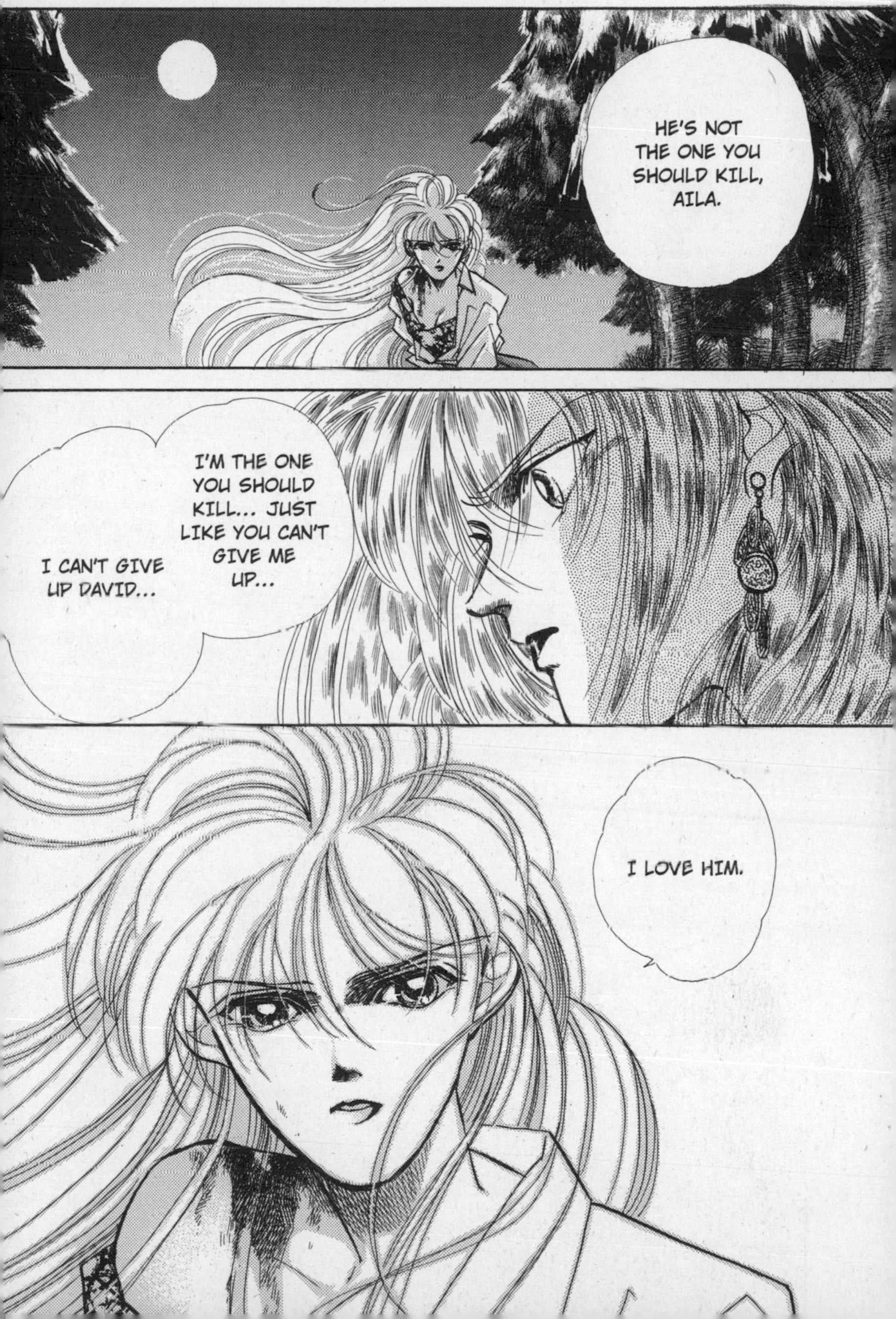
HE'S NOT THE ONE YOU SHOULD KILL, AILA.
I'M THE ONE YOU SHOULD KILL... JUST LIKE YOU CAN'T GIVE ME UP...
I CAN'T GIVE UP DAVID...
I LOVE HIM.

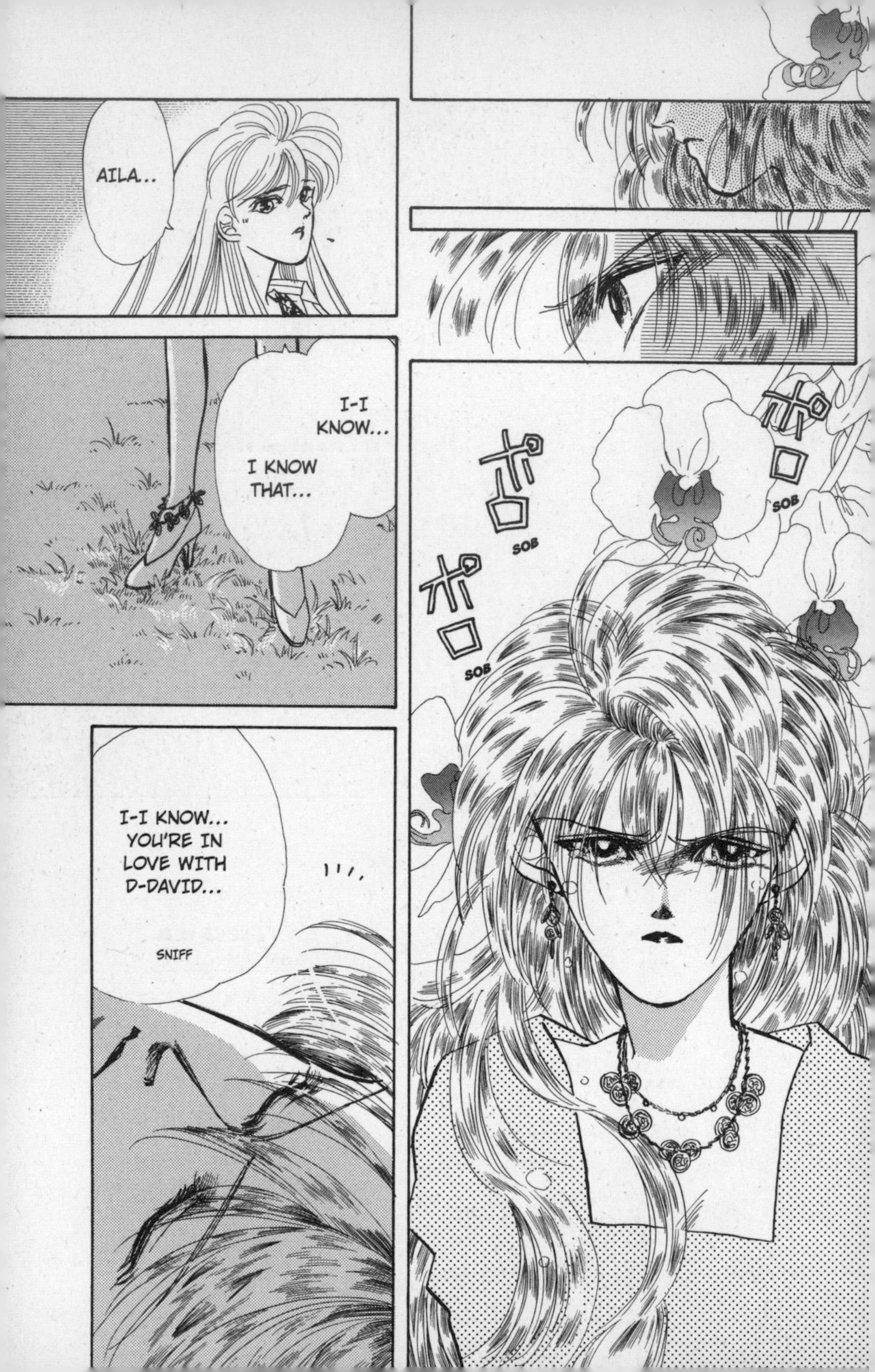
ポロ
SOB
ポロ
SOB
ポロ
SOB
AILA...
I-I KNOW...
I KNOW THAT...
I-I KNOW... YOU'RE IN LOVE WITH D-DAVID...
SNIFF

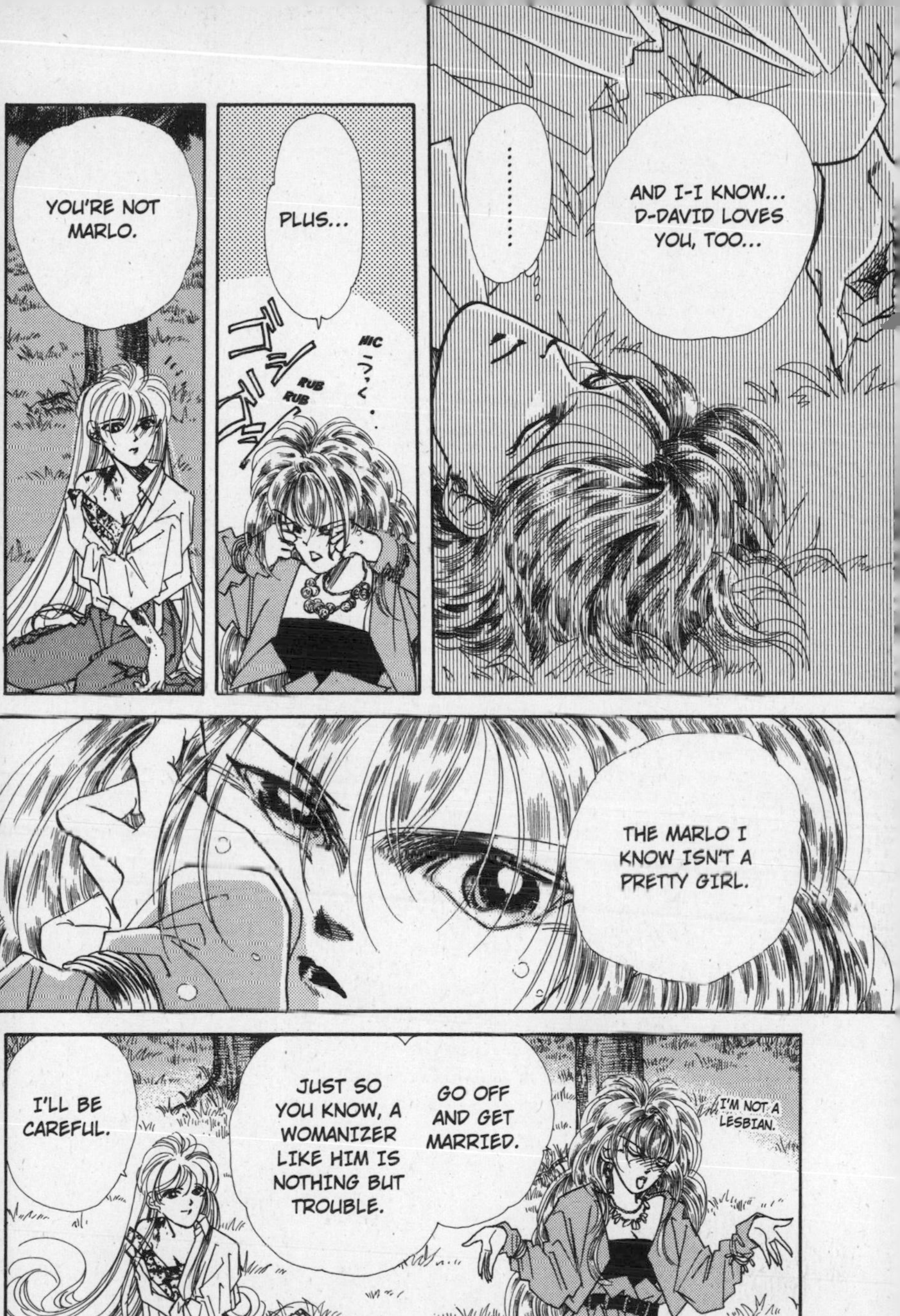
AND I-I KNOW... D-DAVID LOVES YOU, TOO...
......
PLUS...
HIC
RUB RUB
YOU'RE NOT MARLO.
THE MARLO I KNOW ISN'T A PRETTY GIRL.
I'M NOT A LESBIAN.
GO OFF AND GET MARRIED.
JUST SO YOU KNOW, A WOMANIZER LIKE HIM IS NOTHING BUT TROUBLE.
I'LL BE CAREFUL.

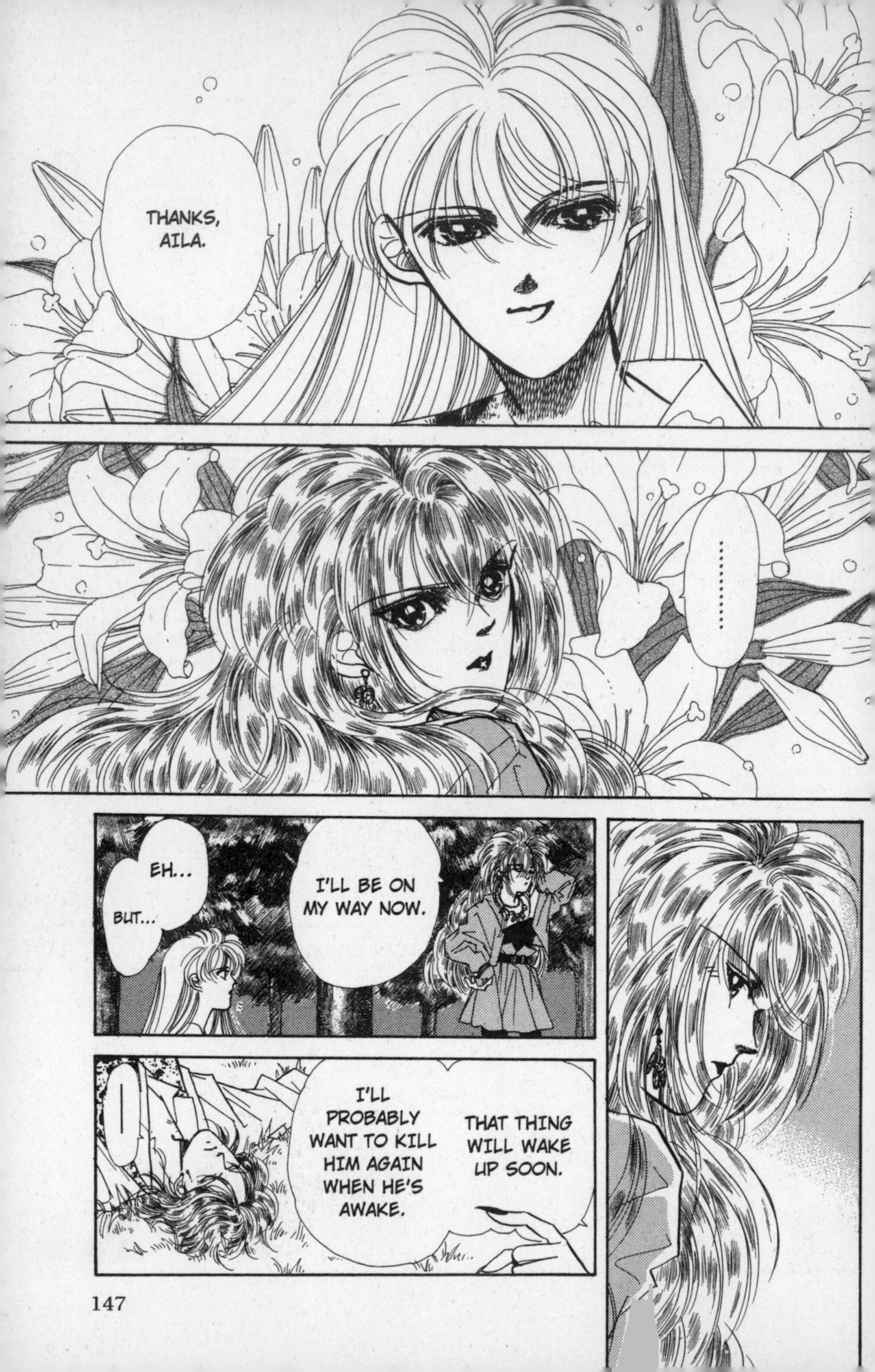
THANKS, AILA.
......
I'LL BE ON MY WAY NOW.
EH... BUT...
THAT THING WILL WAKE UP SOON.
I'LL PROBABLY WANT TO KILL HIM AGAIN WHEN HE'S AWAKE.

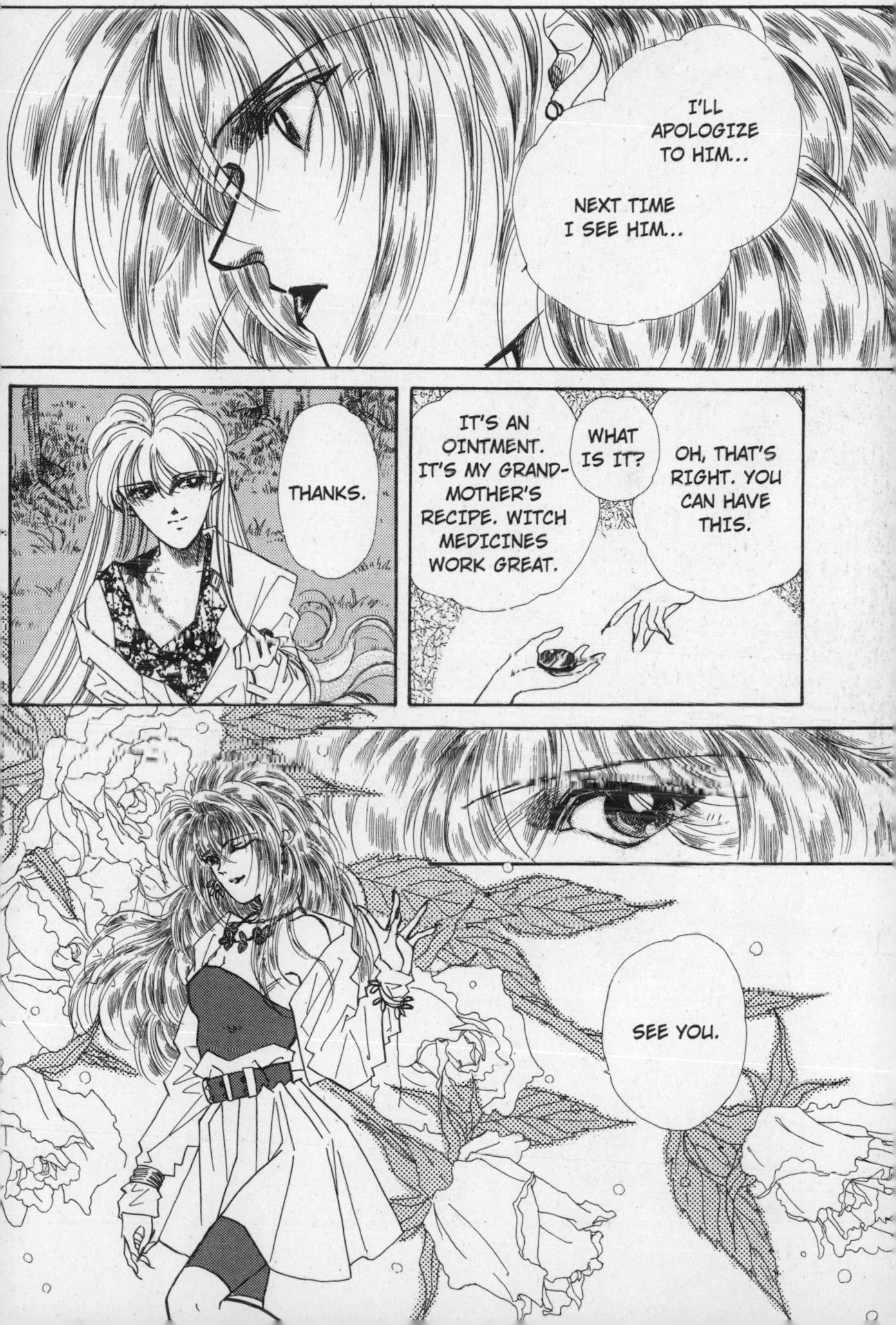
I'LL APOLOGIZE TO HIM...
NEXT TIME I SEE HIM...
OH, THAT'S RIGHT. YOU CAN HAVE THIS.
WHAT IS IT?
IT'S AN OINTMENT. IT'S MY GRAND-MOTHER'S RECIPE. WITCH MEDICINES WORK GREAT.
THANKS.
SEE YOU.

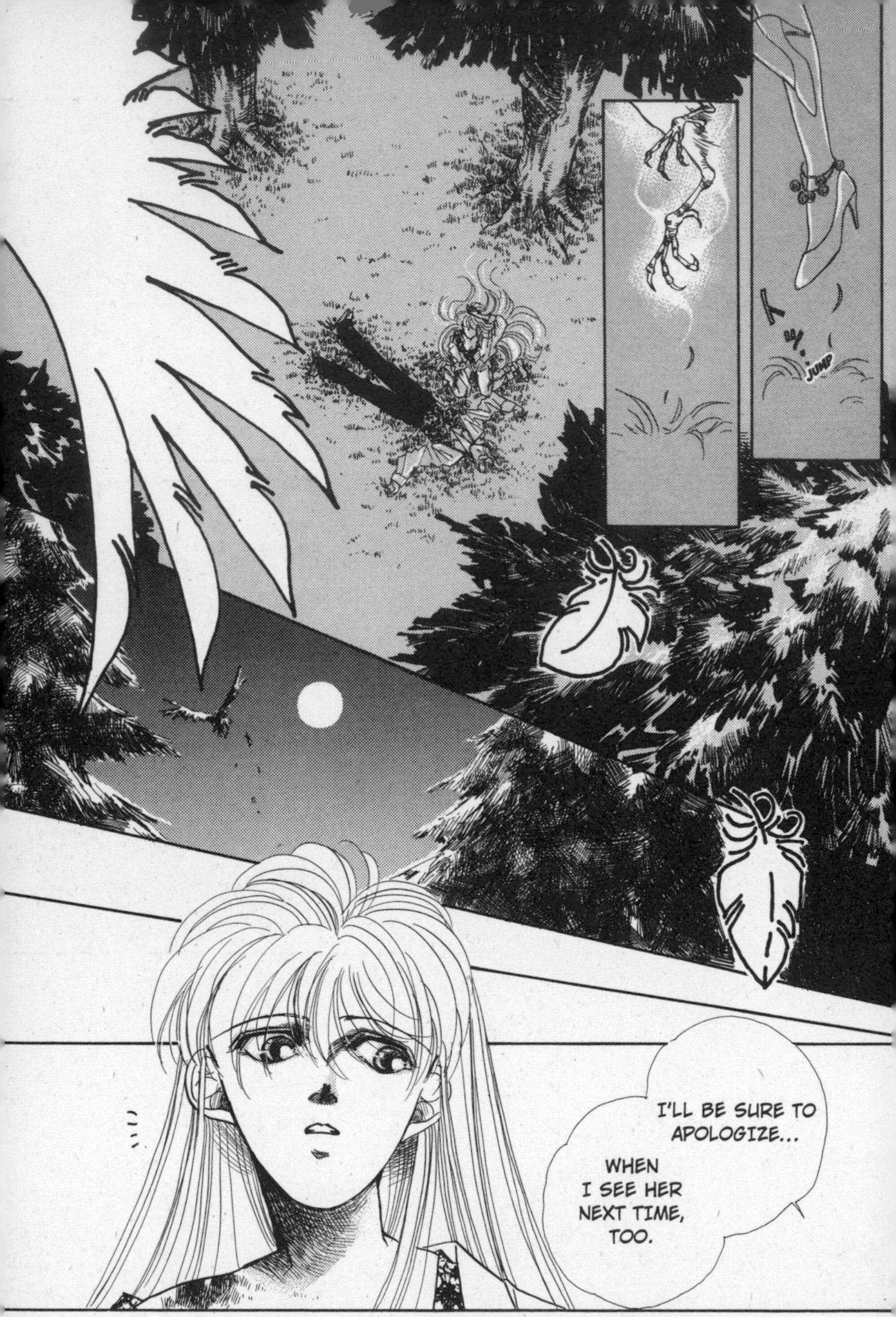
JUMP
I'LL BE SURE TO APOLOGIZE...
WHEN I SEE HER NEXT TIME, TOO.

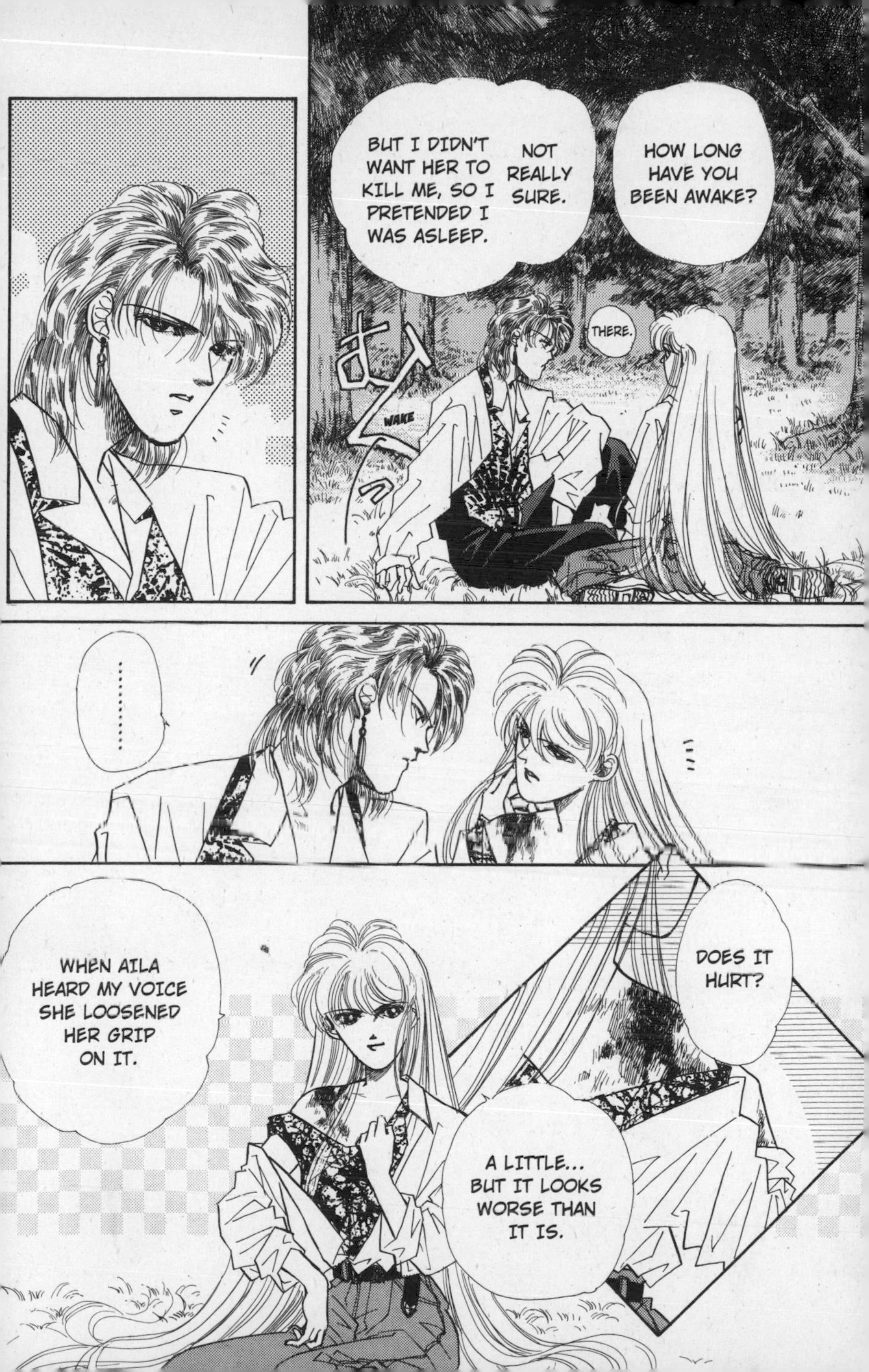
HOW LONG HAVE YOU BEEN AWAKE?
NOT REALLY SURE.
BUT I DIDN'T WANT HER TO KILL ME, SO I PRETENDED I WAS ASLEEP.
THERE.
WAKE
......
DOES IT HURT?
A LITTLE... BUT IT LOOKS WORSE THAN IT IS.
WHEN AILA HEARD MY VOICE SHE LOOSENED HER GRIP ON IT.

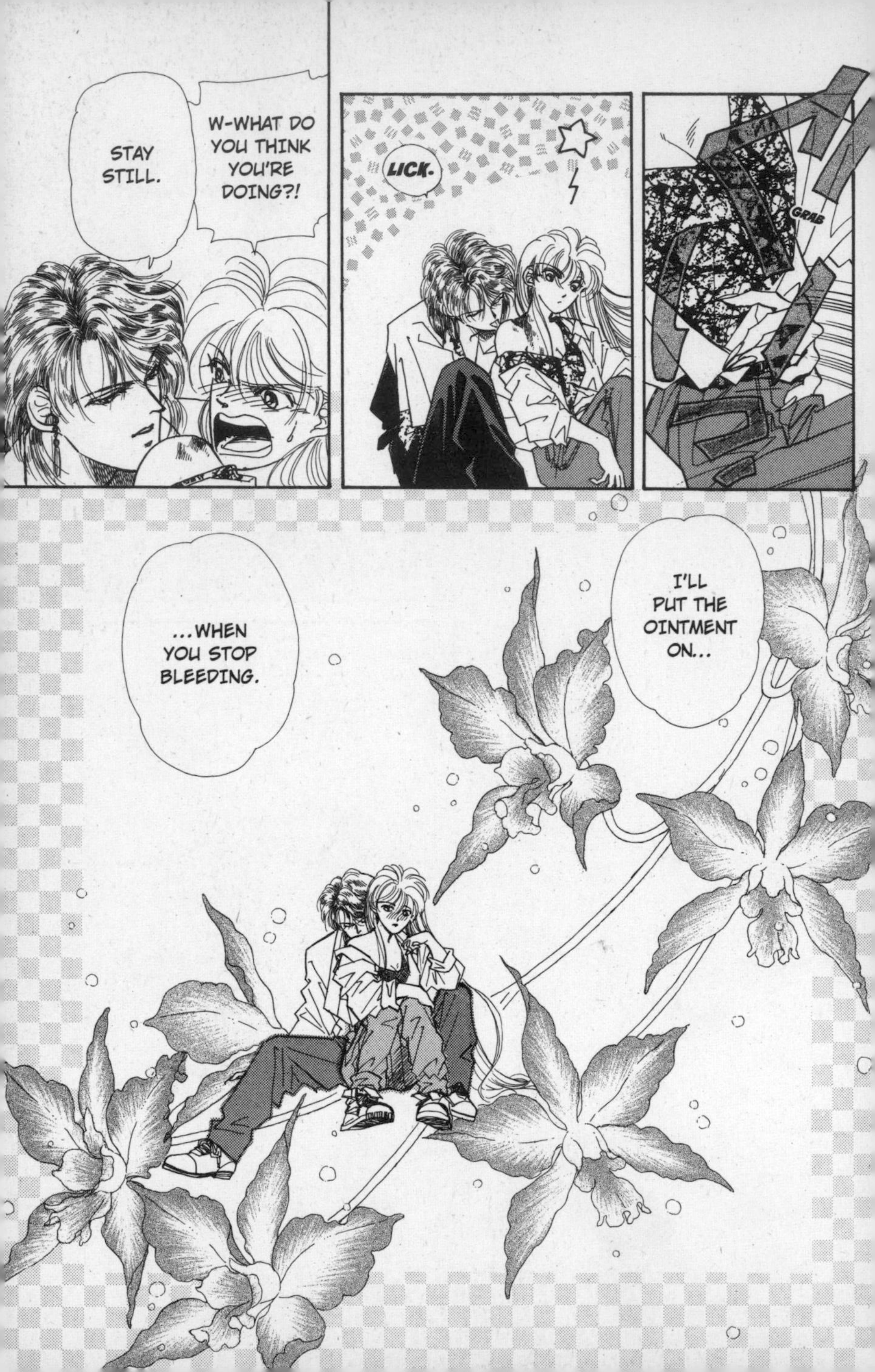
GRAB
LICK.
W-WHAT DO YOU THINK YOU'RE DOING?!
STAY STILL.
I'LL PUT THE OINTMENT ON...
...WHEN YOU STOP BLEEDING.

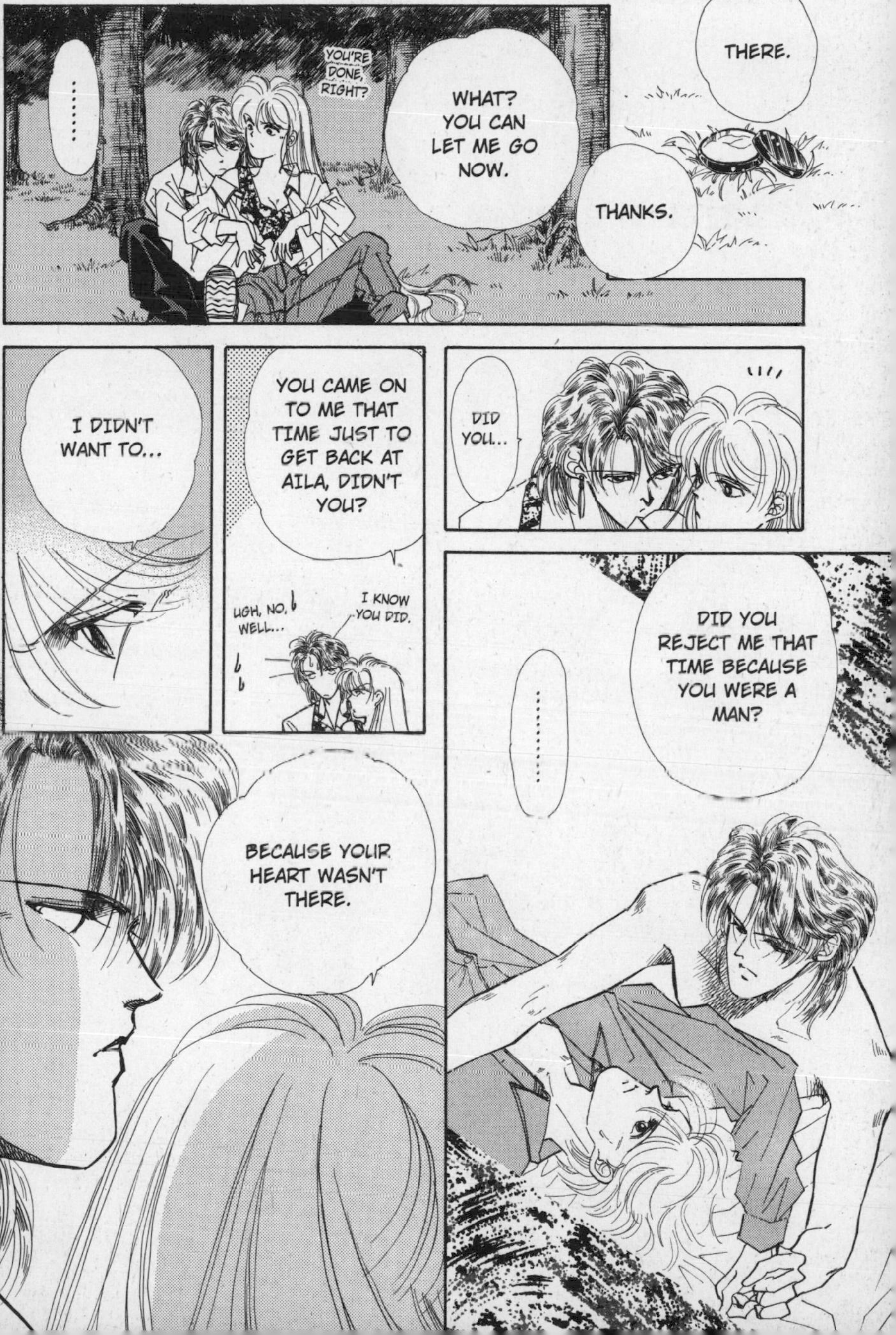
THERE.
THANKS.
WHAT? YOU CAN LET ME GO NOW.
YOU'RE DONE, RIGHT?
......
!
DID YOU...
YOU CAME ON TO ME THAT TIME JUST TO GET BACK AT AILA, DIDN'T YOU?
I KNOW YOU DID.
UGH, NO, WELL...
I DIDN'T WANT TO...
BECAUSE YOUR HEART WASN'T THERE.
DID YOU REJECT ME THAT TIME BECAUSE YOU WERE A MAN?
......

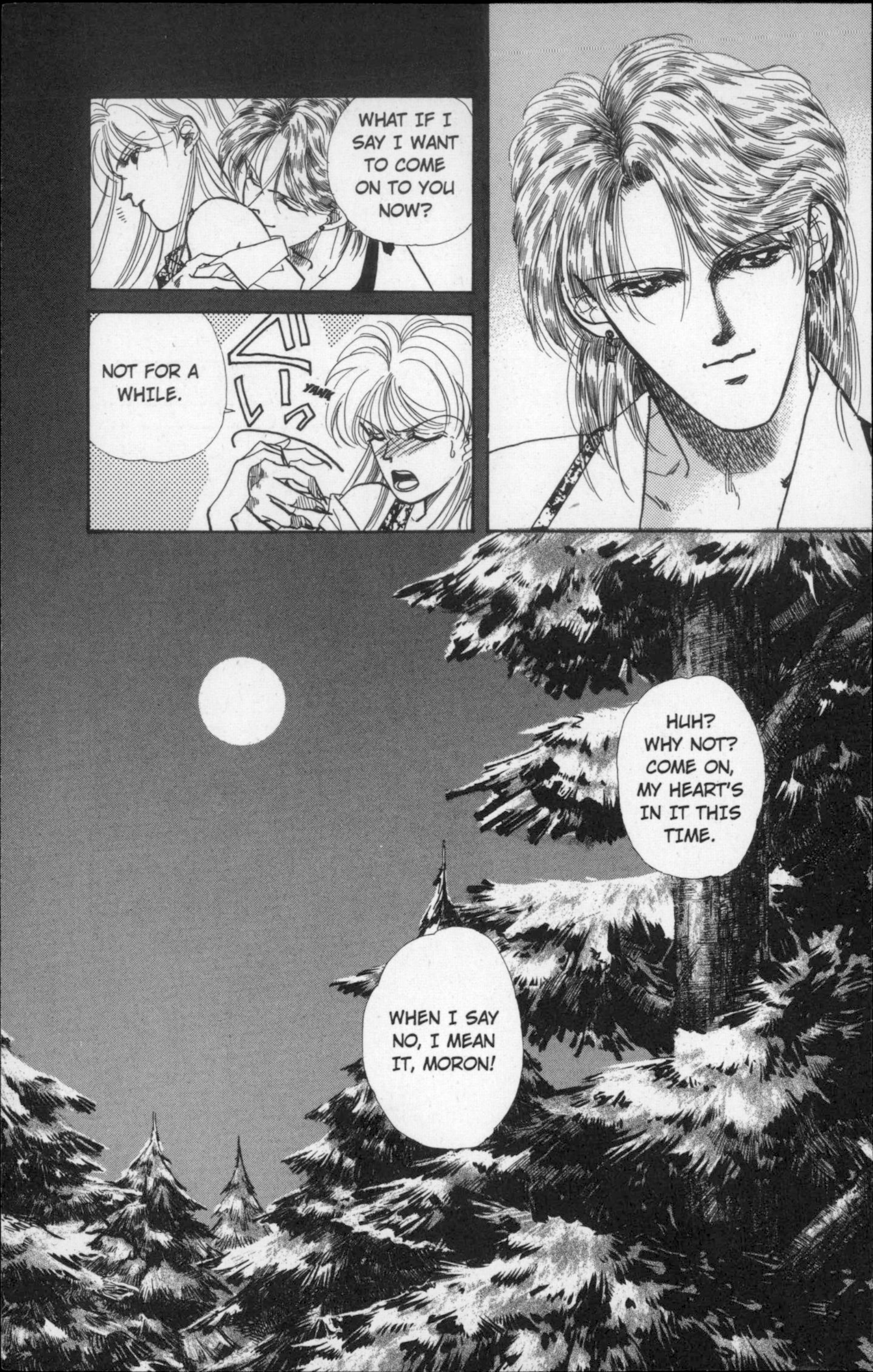
WHAT IF I SAY I WANT TO COME ON TO YOU NOW?
NOT FOR A WHILE.
YANK
HUH? WHY NOT? COME ON, MY HEART'S IN IT THIS TIME.
WHEN I SAY NO, I MEAN IT, MORON!

Whisper to Me
at
Full Moon Night

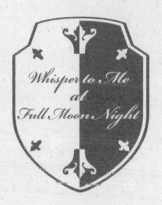

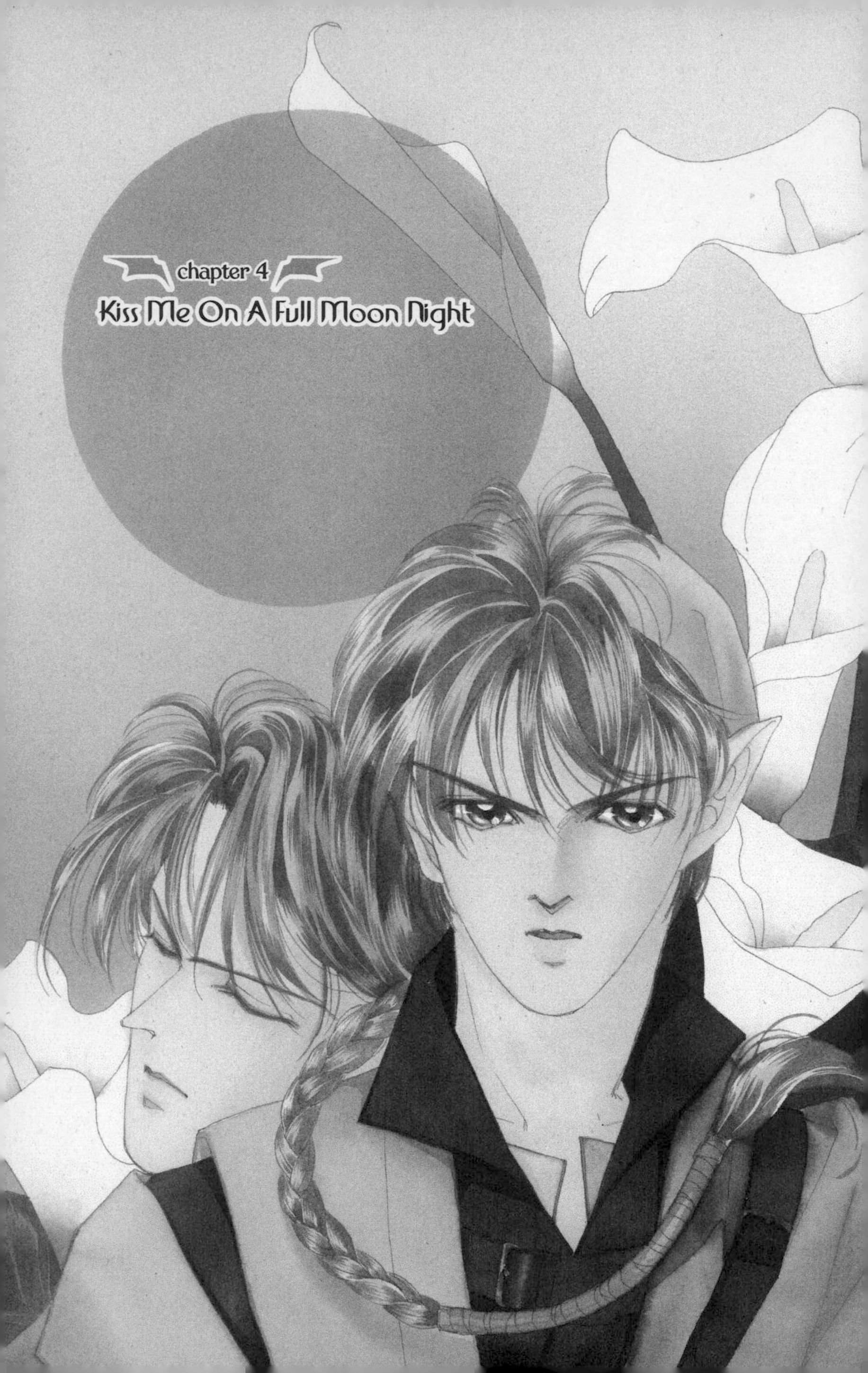
chapter 4
Kiss Me On A Full Moon Night

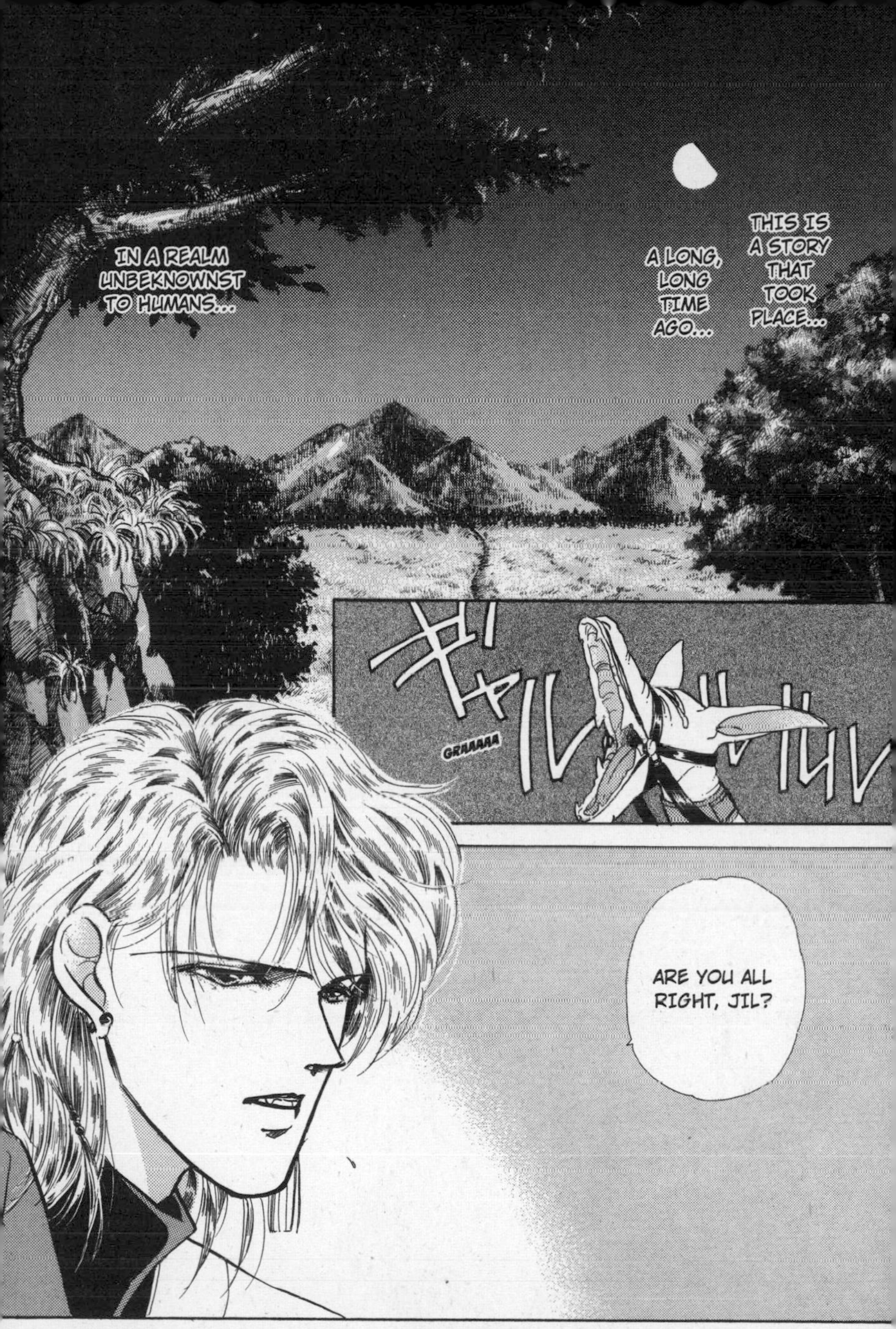
THIS IS A STORY THAT TOOK PLACE...
A LONG, LONG TIME AGO...
IN A REALM UNBEKNOWNST TO HUMANS...
GRAAAAAA
ARE YOU ALL RIGHT, JIL?

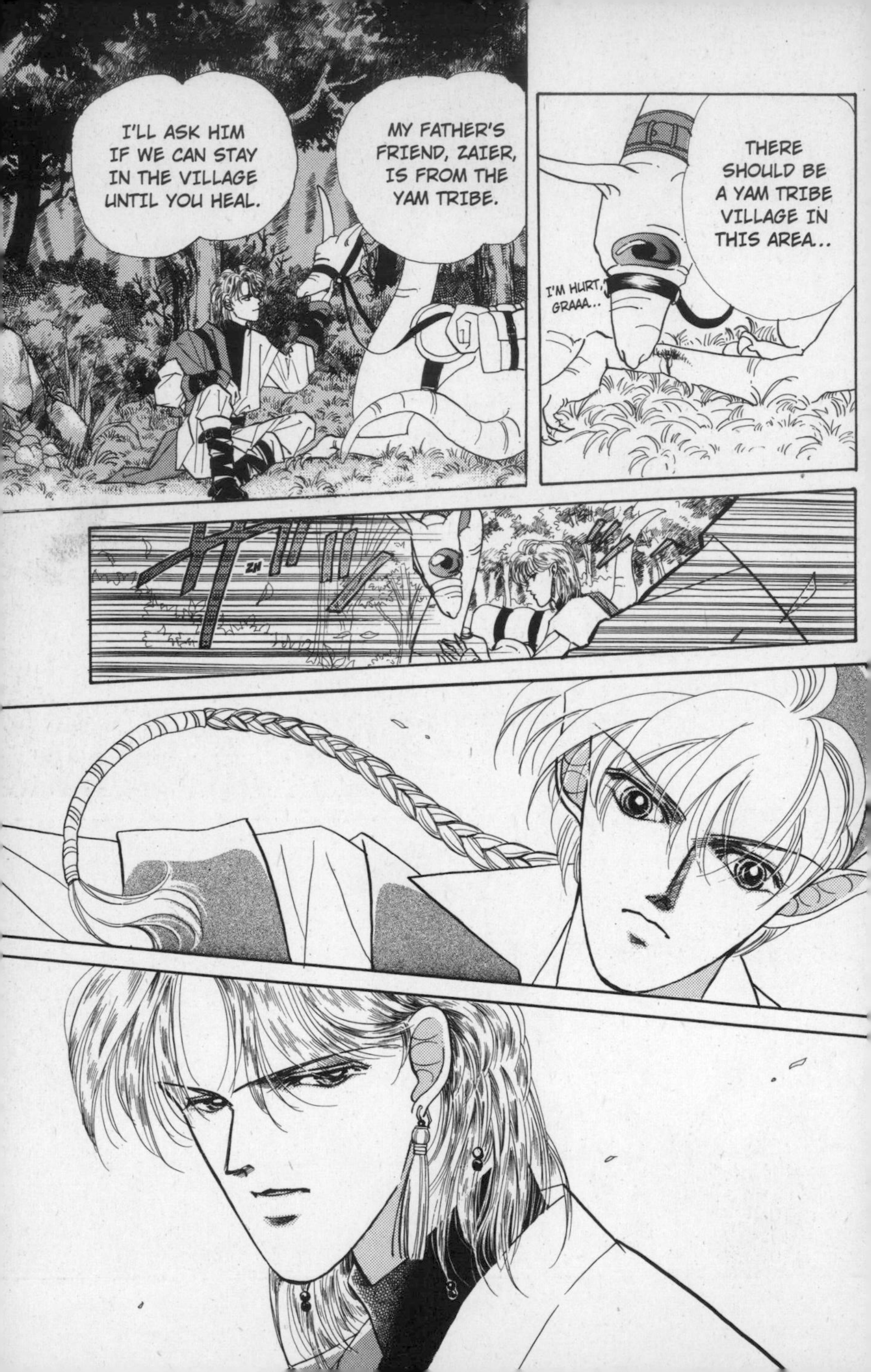
THERE SHOULD BE A YAM TRIBE VILLAGE IN THIS AREA...
I'M HURT, GRAAA...
MY FATHER'S FRIEND, ZAIER, IS FROM THE YAM TRIBE.
I'LL ASK HIM IF WE CAN STAY IN THE VILLAGE UNTIL YOU HEAL.
ZH

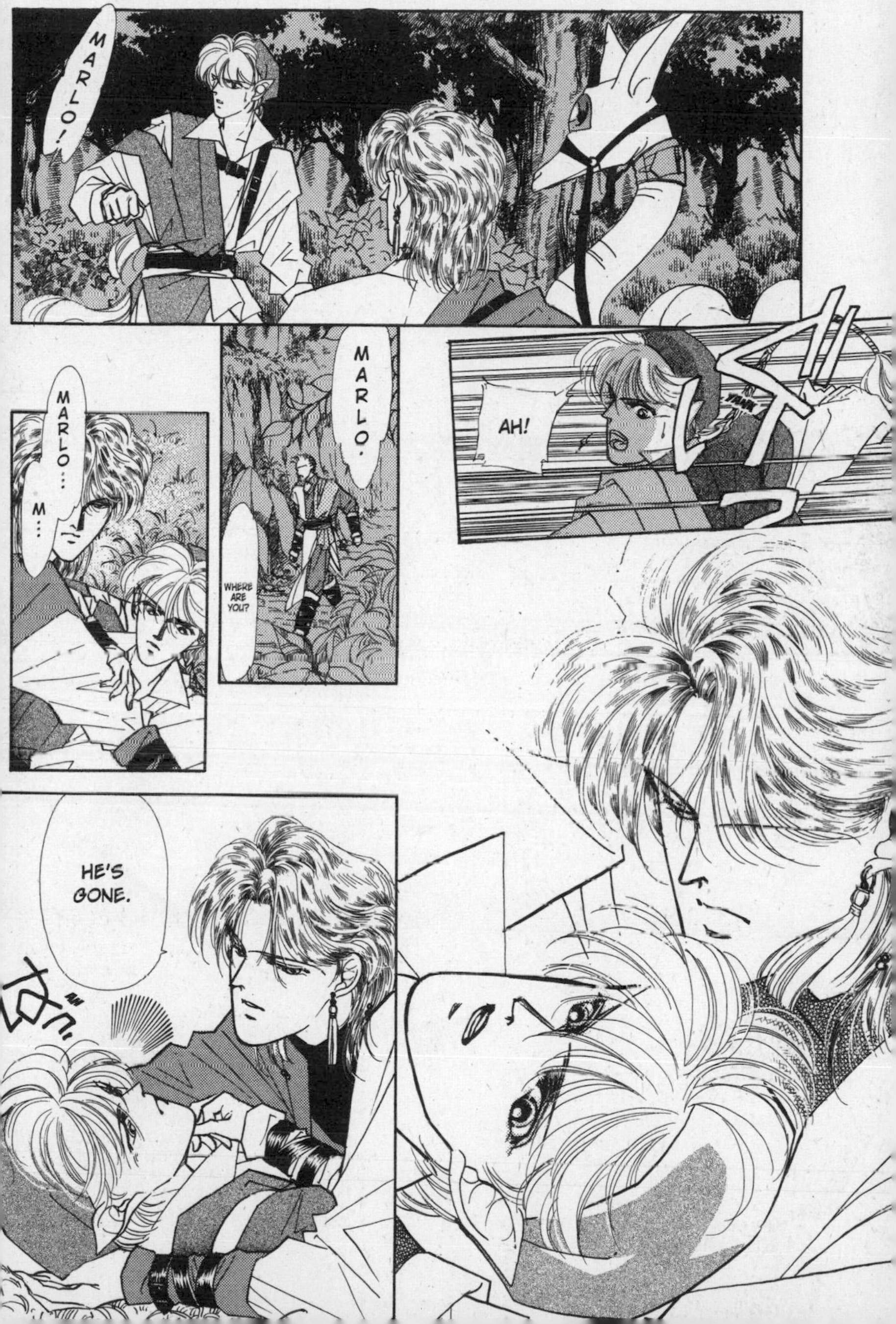
MARLO!
AH!
MARLO.
WHERE ARE YOU?
MARLO... M...
HE'S GONE.

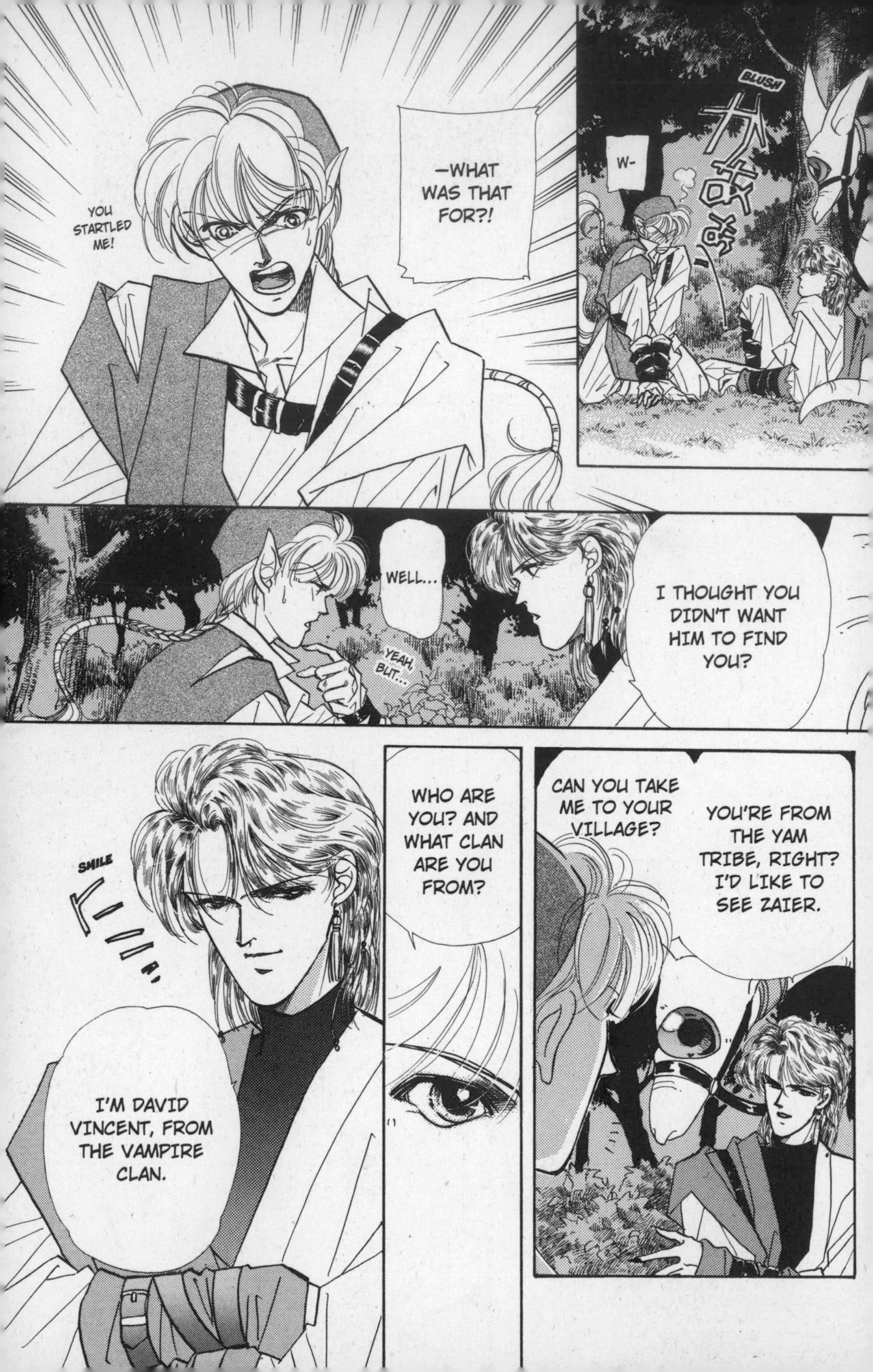
BLUSH
W-
—WHAT WAS THAT FOR?!
YOU STARTLED ME!
I THOUGHT YOU DIDN'T WANT HIM TO FIND YOU?
WELL...
YEAH, BUT...
YOU'RE FROM THE YAM TRIBE, RIGHT? I'D LIKE TO SEE ZAIER.
CAN YOU TAKE ME TO YOUR VILLAGE?
WHO ARE YOU? AND WHAT CLAN ARE YOU FROM?
SMILE
I'M DAVID VINCENT, FROM THE VAMPIRE CLAN.

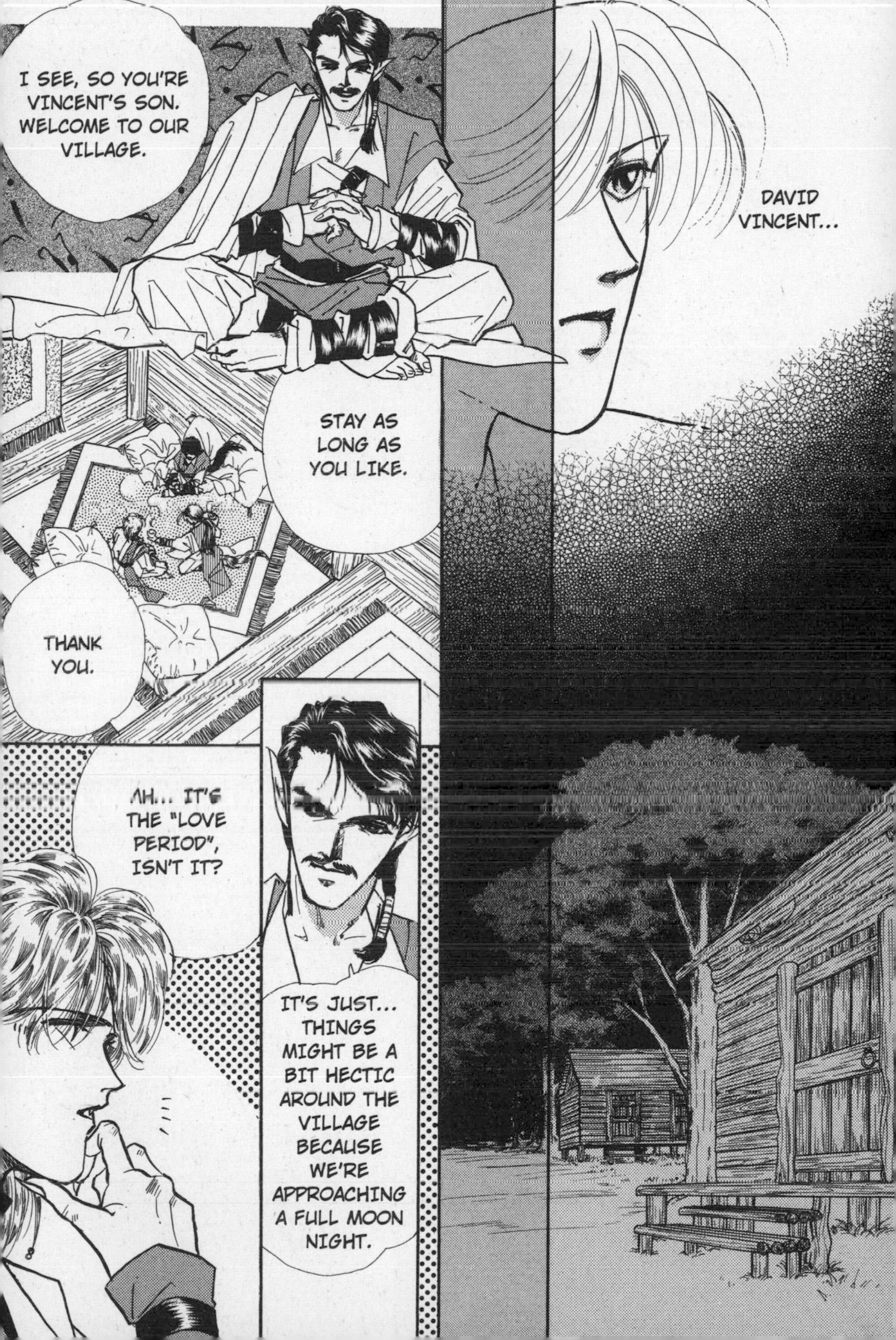
DAVID VINCENT...
I SEE, SO YOU'RE VINCENT'S SON. WELCOME TO OUR VILLAGE.
STAY AS LONG AS YOU LIKE.
THANK YOU.
AH... IT'S THE "LOVE PERIOD", ISN'T IT?
IT'S JUST... THINGS MIGHT BE A BIT HECTIC AROUND THE VILLAGE BECAUSE WE'RE APPROACHING A FULL MOON NIGHT.

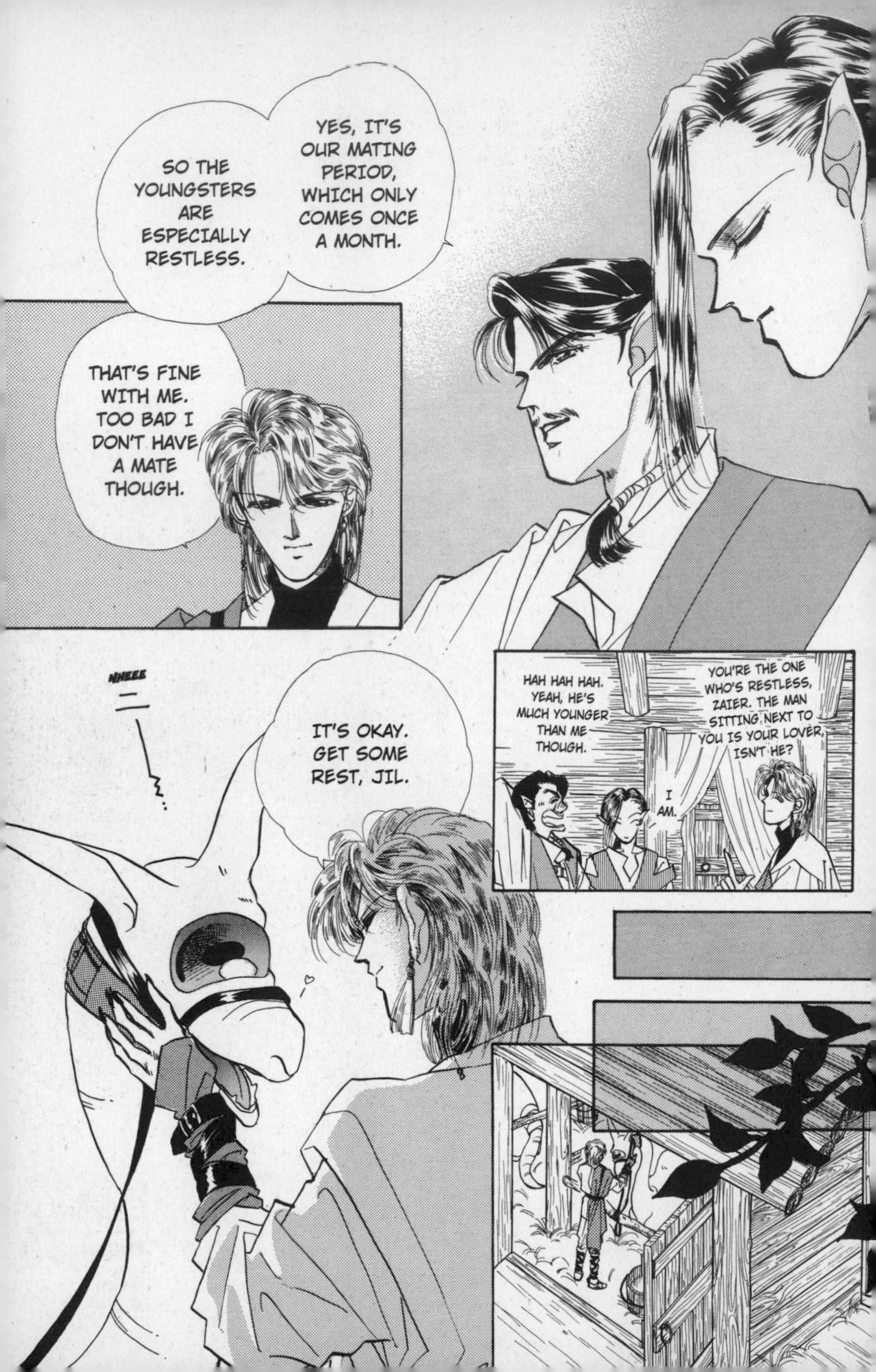
YES, IT'S OUR MATING PERIOD, WHICH ONLY COMES ONCE A MONTH.
SO THE YOUNGSTERS ARE ESPECIALLY RESTLESS.
THAT'S FINE WITH ME. TOO BAD I DON'T HAVE A MATE THOUGH.
YOU'RE THE ONE WHO'S RESTLESS, ZAIER. THE MAN SITTING NEXT TO YOU IS YOUR LOVER, ISN'T HE?
HAH HAH HAH. YEAH, HE'S MUCH YOUNGER THAN ME THOUGH.
I AM.
IT'S OKAY. GET SOME REST, JIL.
NHEEE

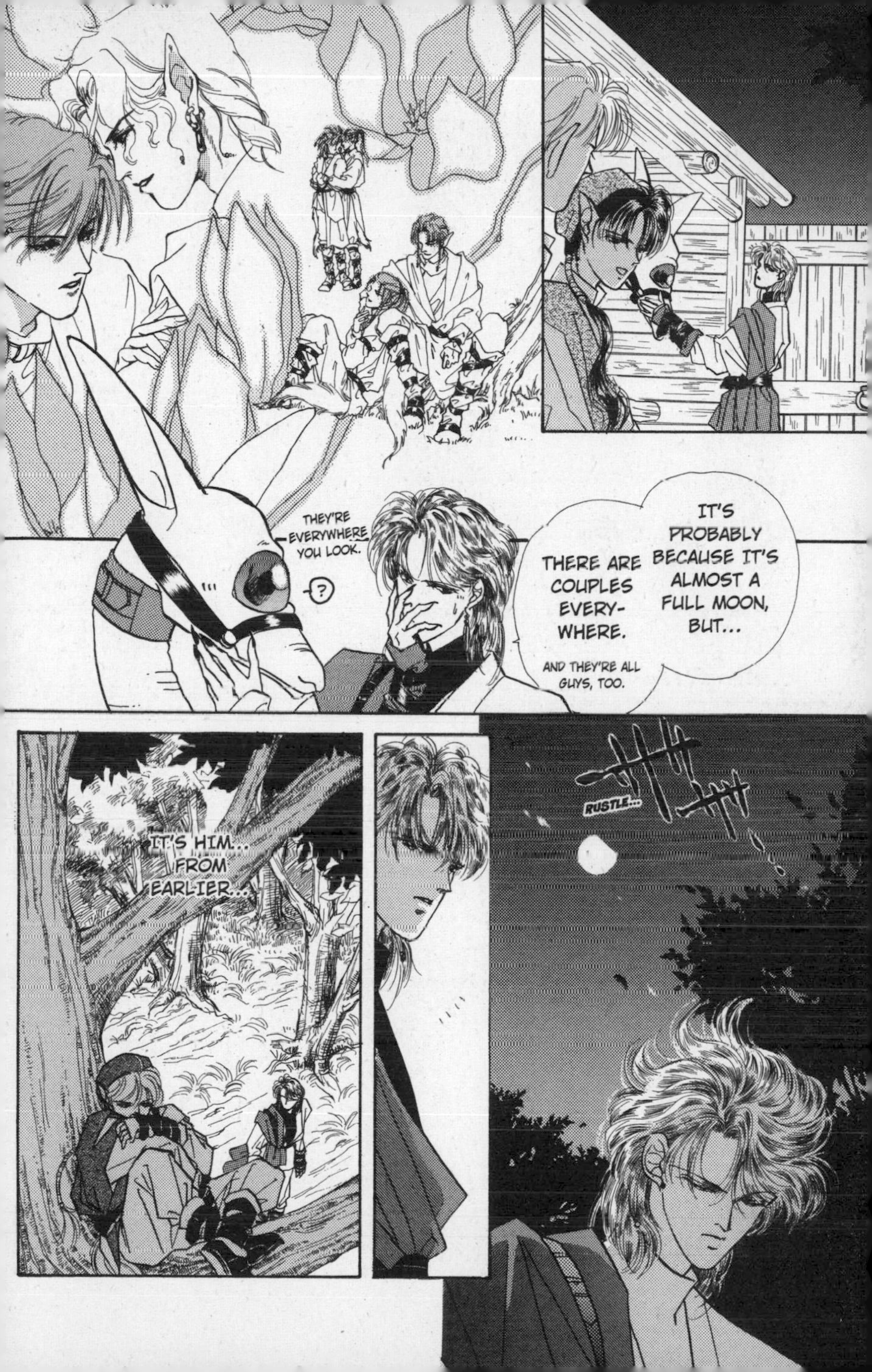
IT'S PROBABLY BECAUSE IT'S ALMOST A FULL MOON, BUT...
THERE ARE COUPLES EVERY-WHERE.
AND THEY'RE ALL GUYS, TOO.
THEY'RE EVERYWHERE YOU LOOK.
?
RUSTLE...
IT'S HIM... FROM EARLIER...

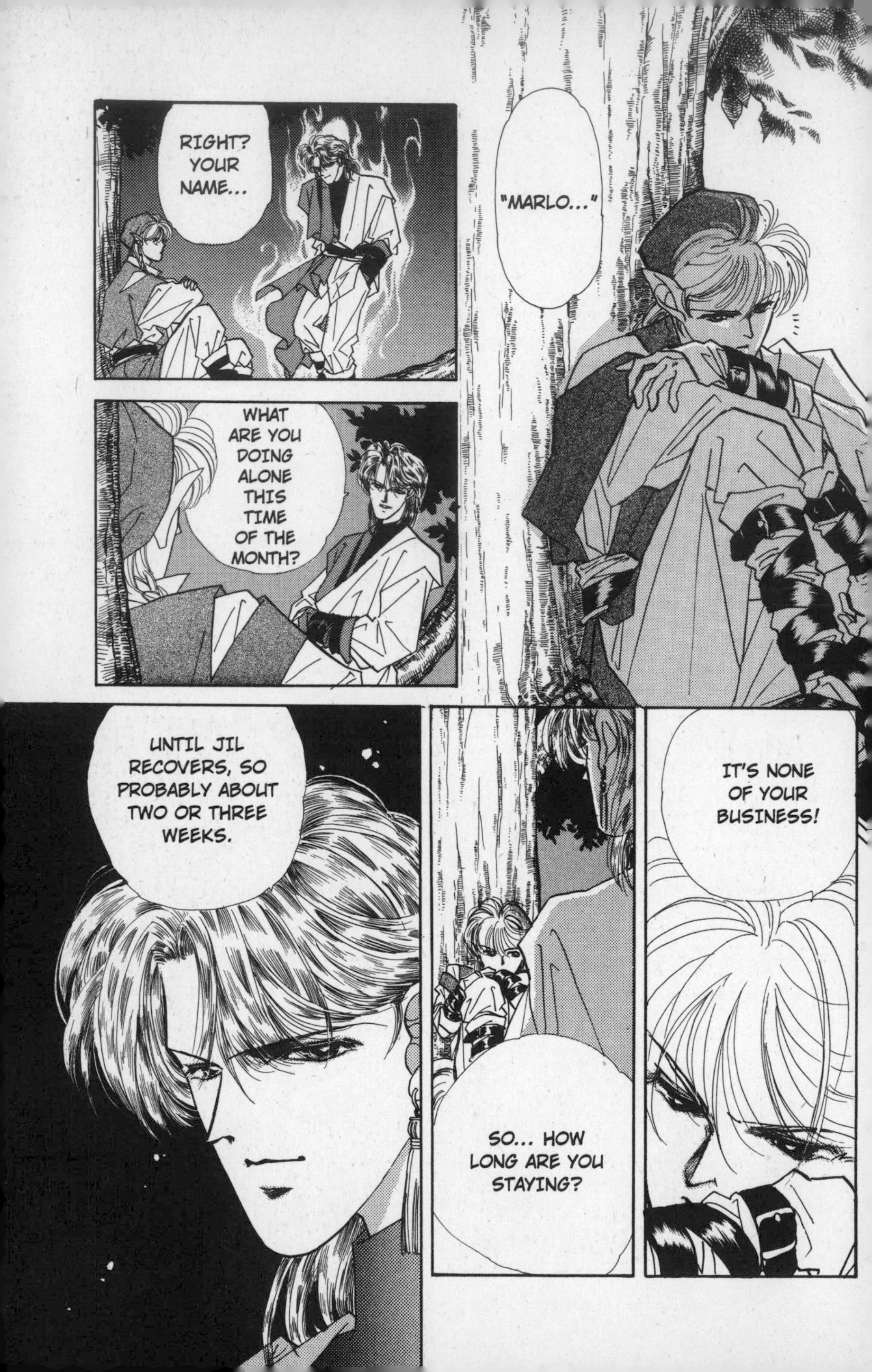
"MARLO..."
RIGHT? YOUR NAME...
WHAT ARE YOU DOING ALONE THIS TIME OF THE MONTH?
IT'S NONE OF YOUR BUSINESS!
SO... HOW LONG ARE YOU STAYING?
UNTIL JIL RECOVERS, SO PROBABLY ABOUT TWO OR THREE WEEKS.

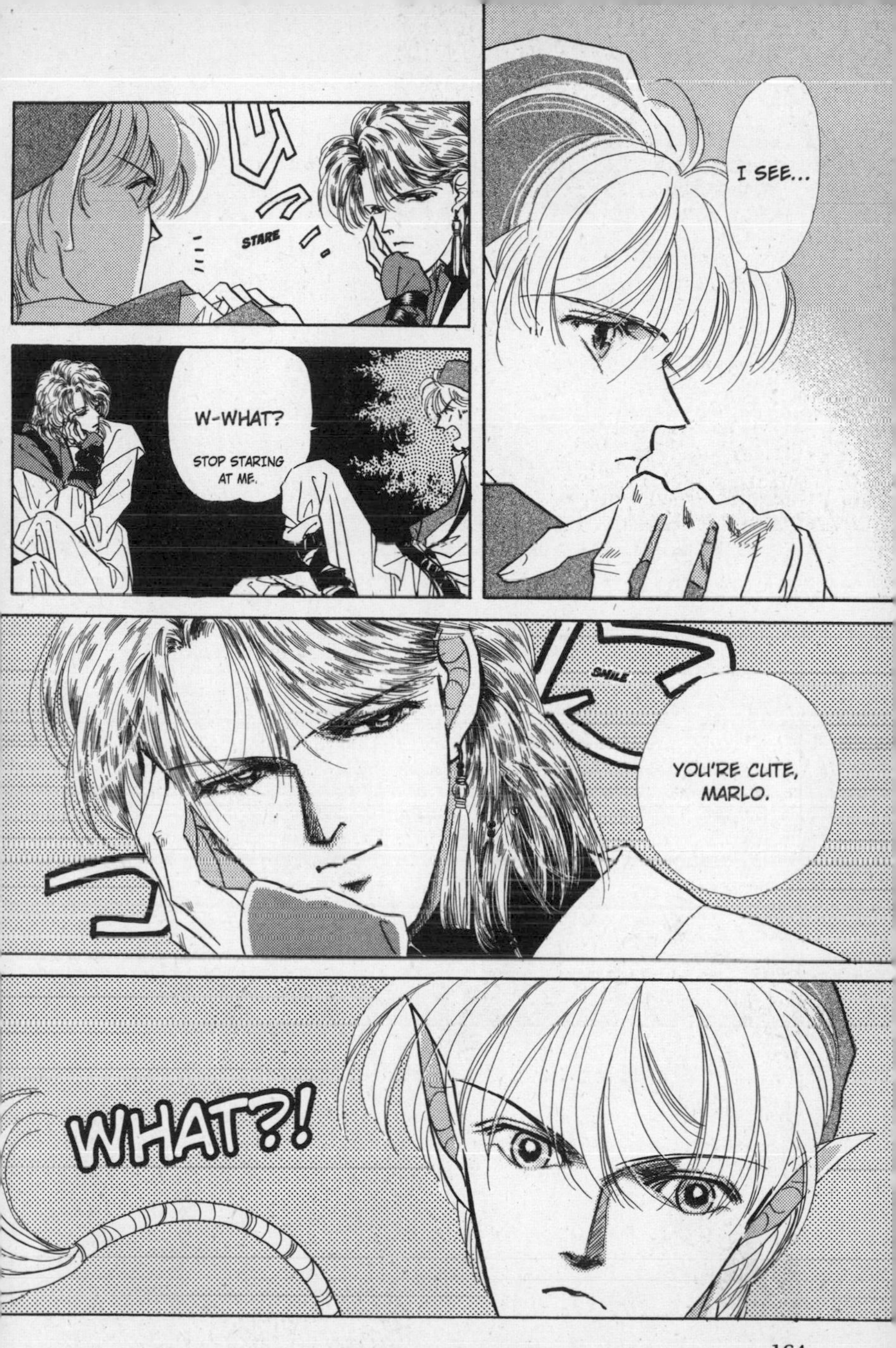
I SEE...
STARE
W-WHAT?
STOP STARING AT ME.
SMILE
YOU'RE CUTE, MARLO.
WHAT?!

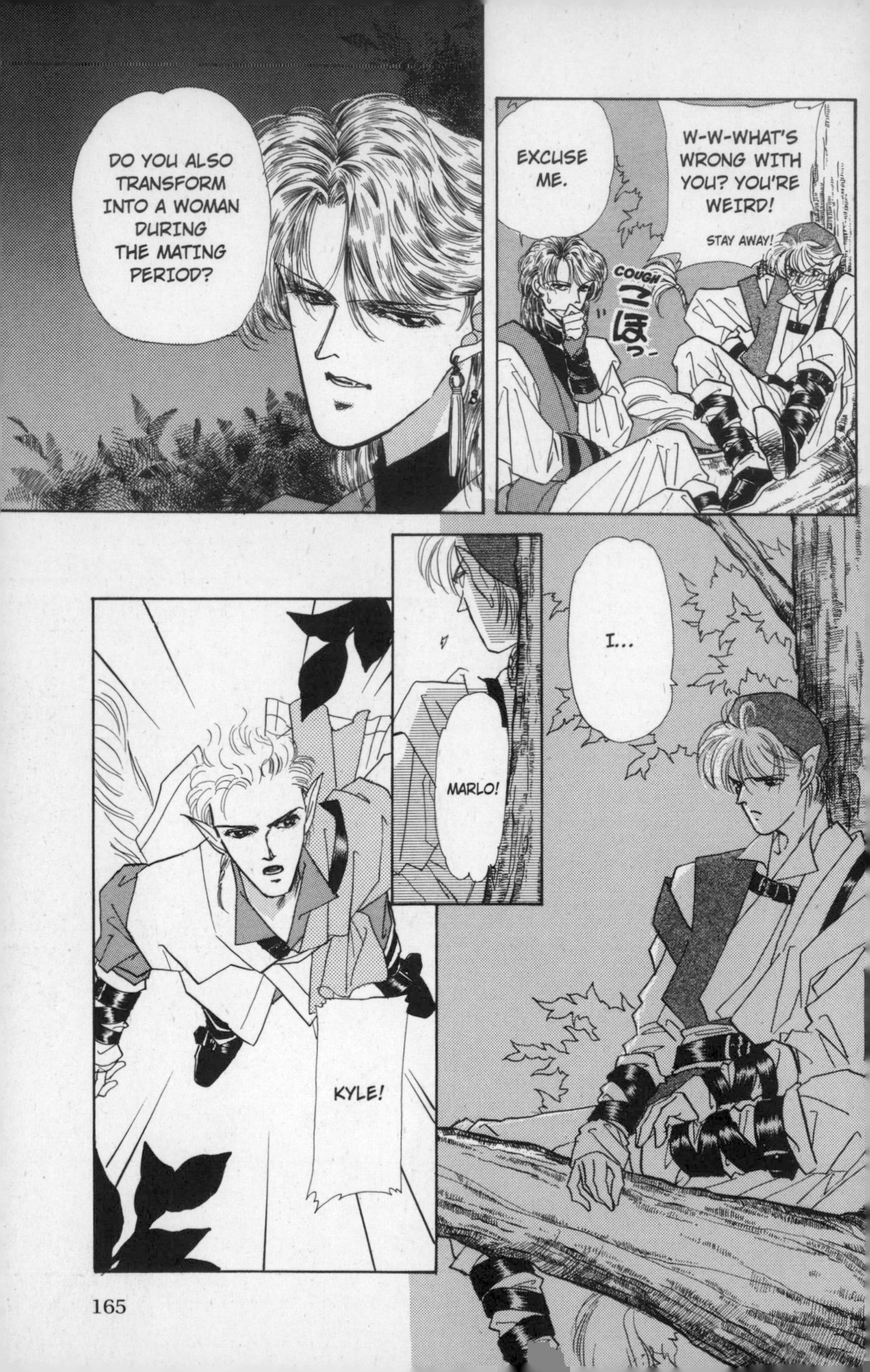
W-W-WHAT'S WRONG WITH YOU? YOU'RE WEIRD!
STAY AWAY!
EXCUSE ME.
COUGH
こほっ
DO YOU ALSO TRANSFORM INTO A WOMAN DURING THE MATING PERIOD?
I...
MARLO!
KYLE!

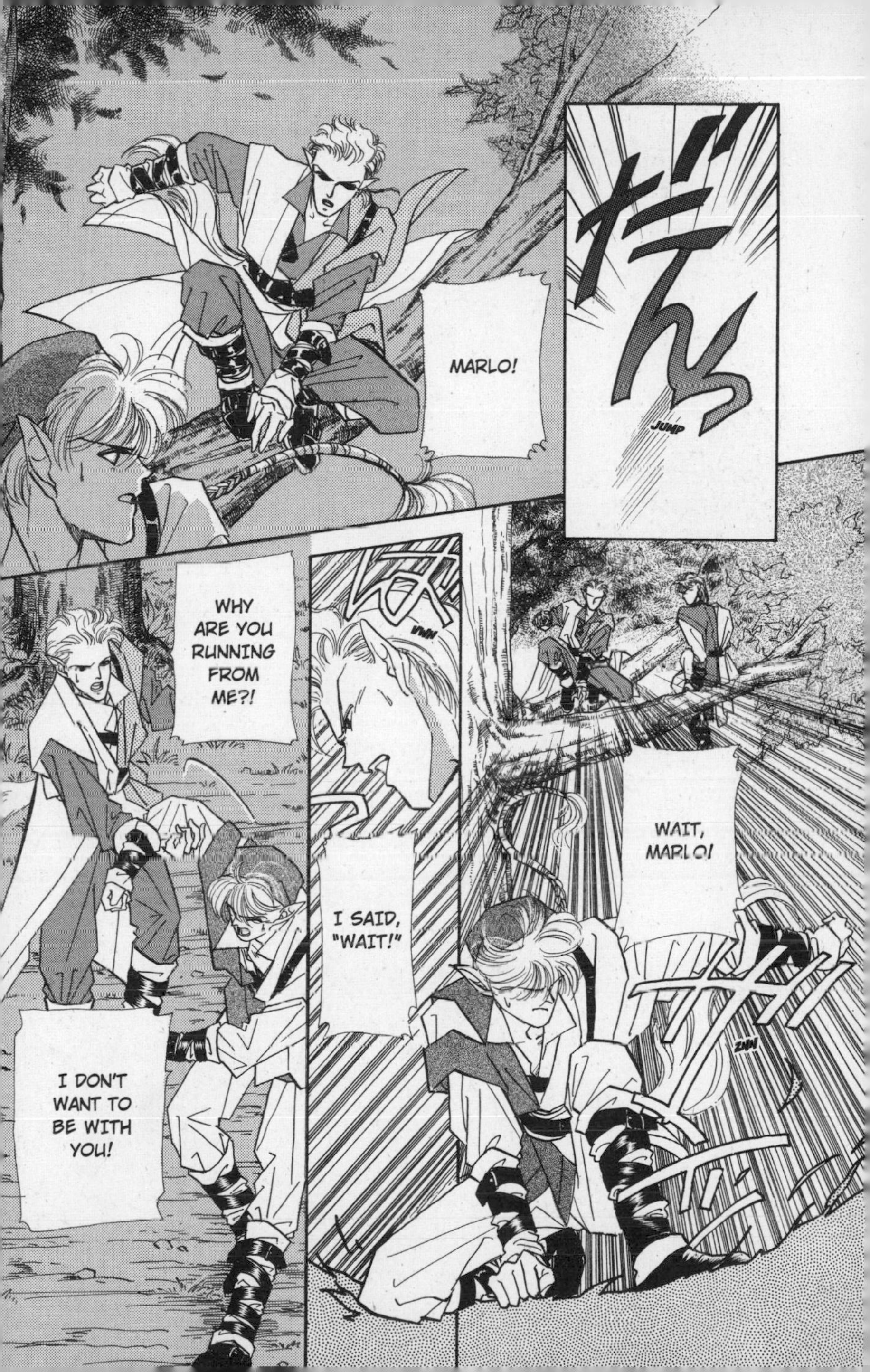
JUMP
MARLO!
WAIT, MARLO!
ZINN
VNN
I SAID, "WAIT!"
WHY ARE YOU RUNNING FROM ME?!
I DON'T WANT TO BE WITH YOU!

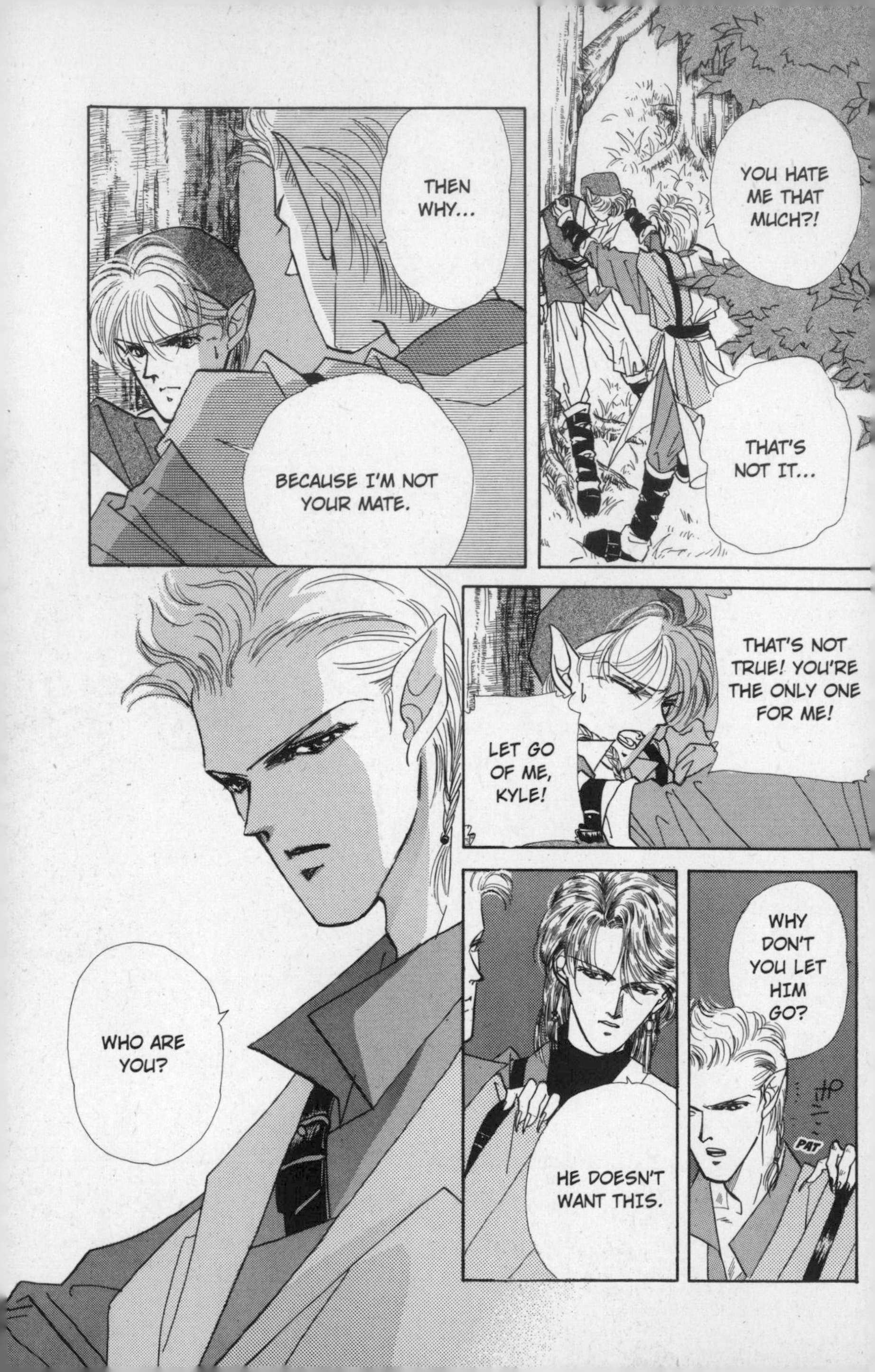
YOU HATE ME THAT MUCH?!
THAT'S NOT IT...
THEN WHY...
BECAUSE I'M NOT YOUR MATE.
THAT'S NOT TRUE! YOU'RE THE ONLY ONE FOR ME!
LET GO OF ME, KYLE!
WHY DON'T YOU LET HIM GO?
PAT
HE DOESN'T WANT THIS.
WHO ARE YOU?

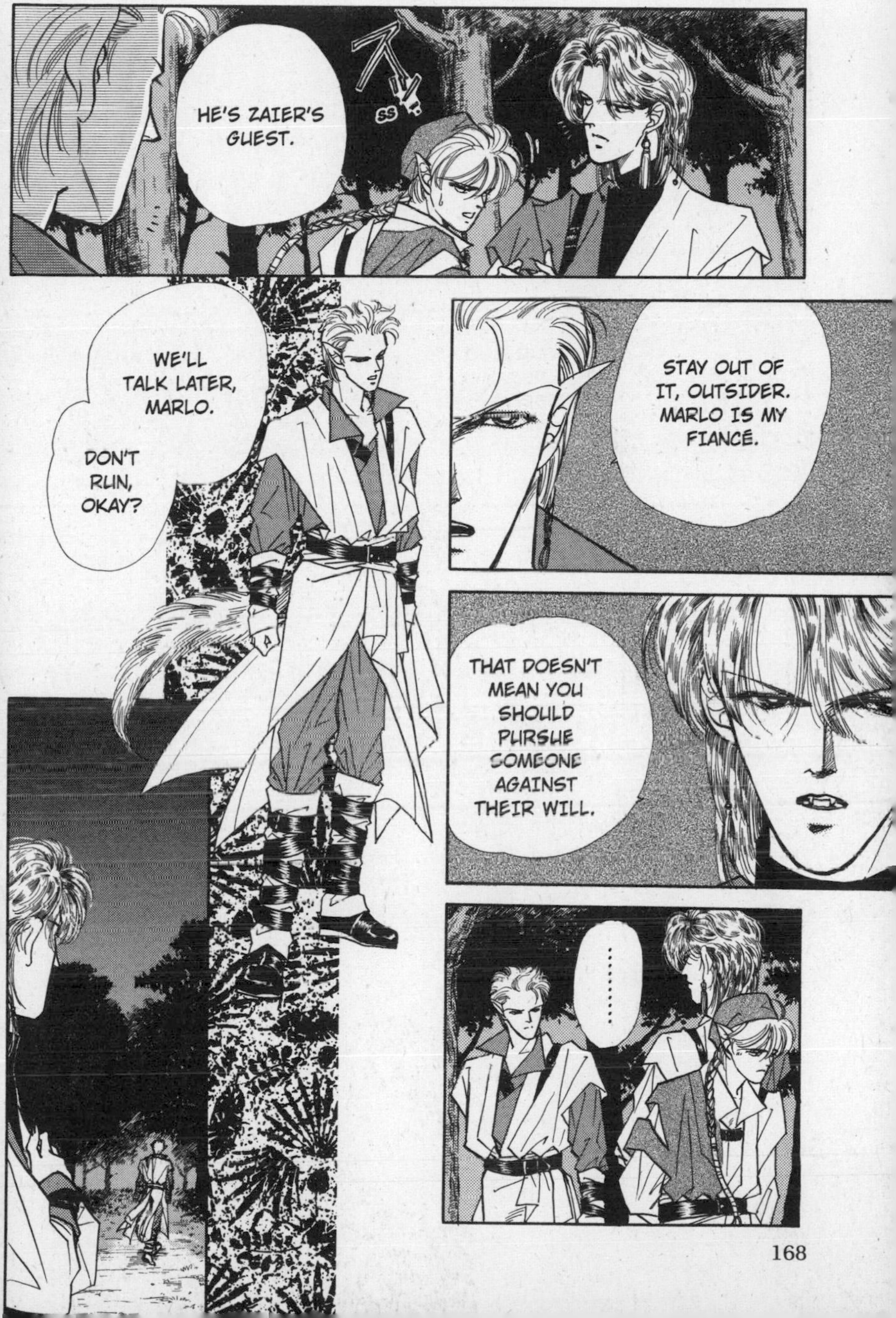
HE'S ZAIER'S GUEST.
SS
STAY OUT OF IT, OUTSIDER. MARLO IS MY FIANCÉ.
THAT DOESN'T MEAN YOU SHOULD PURSUE SOMEONE AGAINST THEIR WILL.
......
WE'LL TALK LATER, MARLO.
DON'T RUN, OKAY?

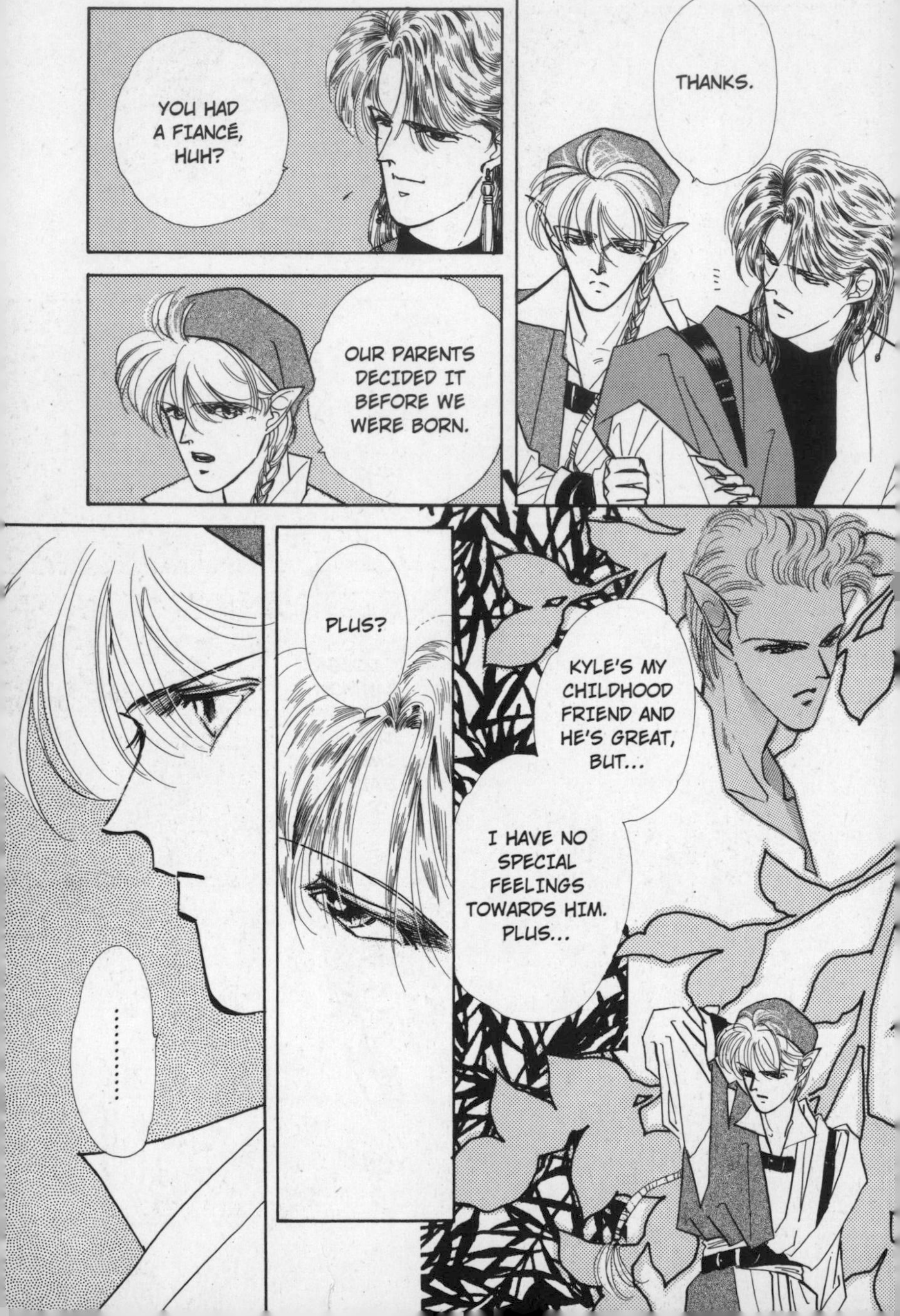
THANKS.
YOU HAD A FIANCÉ, HUH?
OUR PARENTS DECIDED IT BEFORE WE WERE BORN.
KYLE'S MY CHILDHOOD FRIEND AND HE'S GREAT, BUT...
I HAVE NO SPECIAL FEELINGS TOWARDS HIM. PLUS...
PLUS?
......

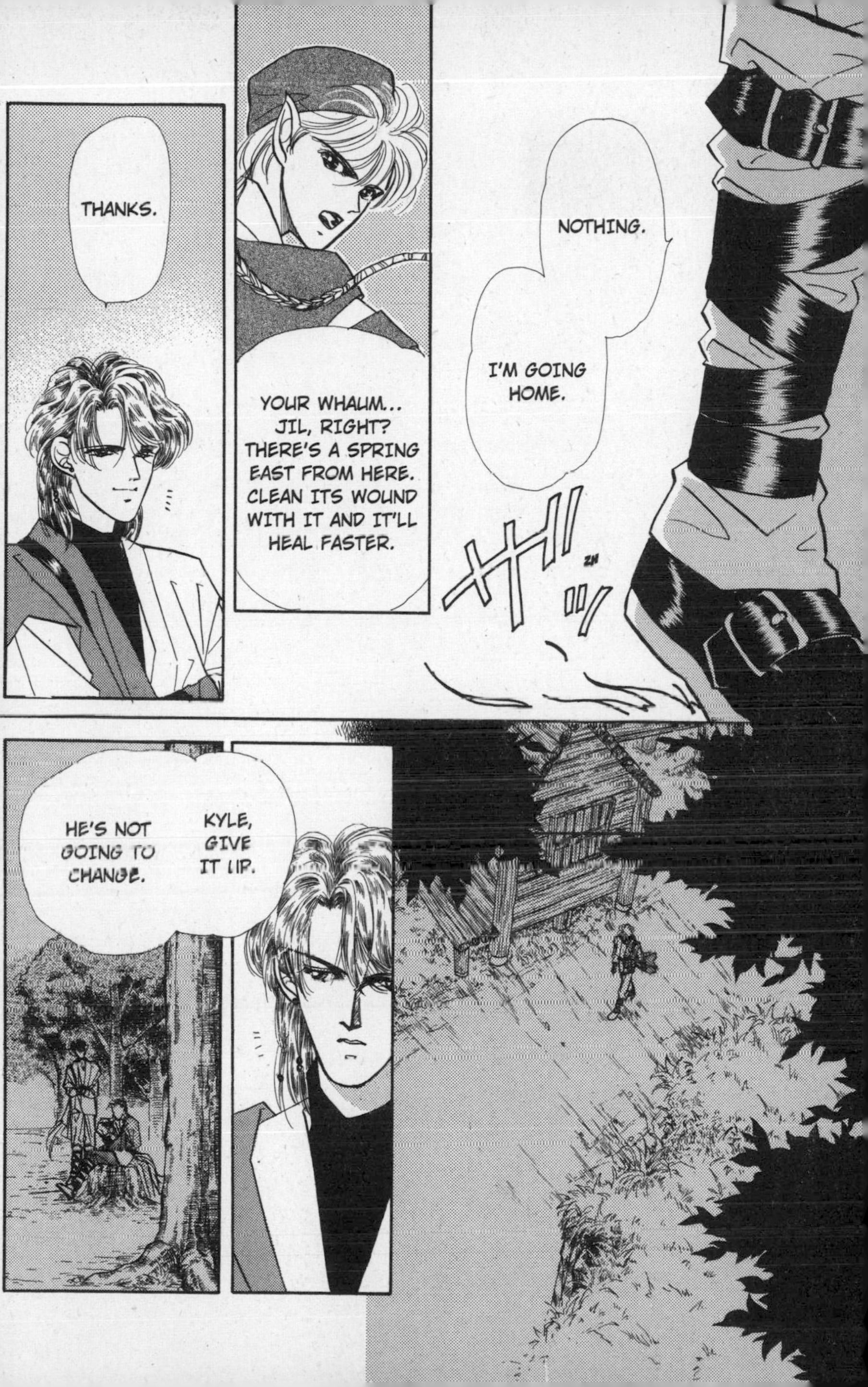
NOTHING.
I'M GOING HOME.
YOUR WHAUM... JIL, RIGHT? THERE'S A SPRING EAST FROM HERE. CLEAN ITS WOUND WITH IT AND IT'LL HEAL FASTER.
THANKS.
KYLE, GIVE IT UP.
HE'S NOT GOING TO CHANGE.

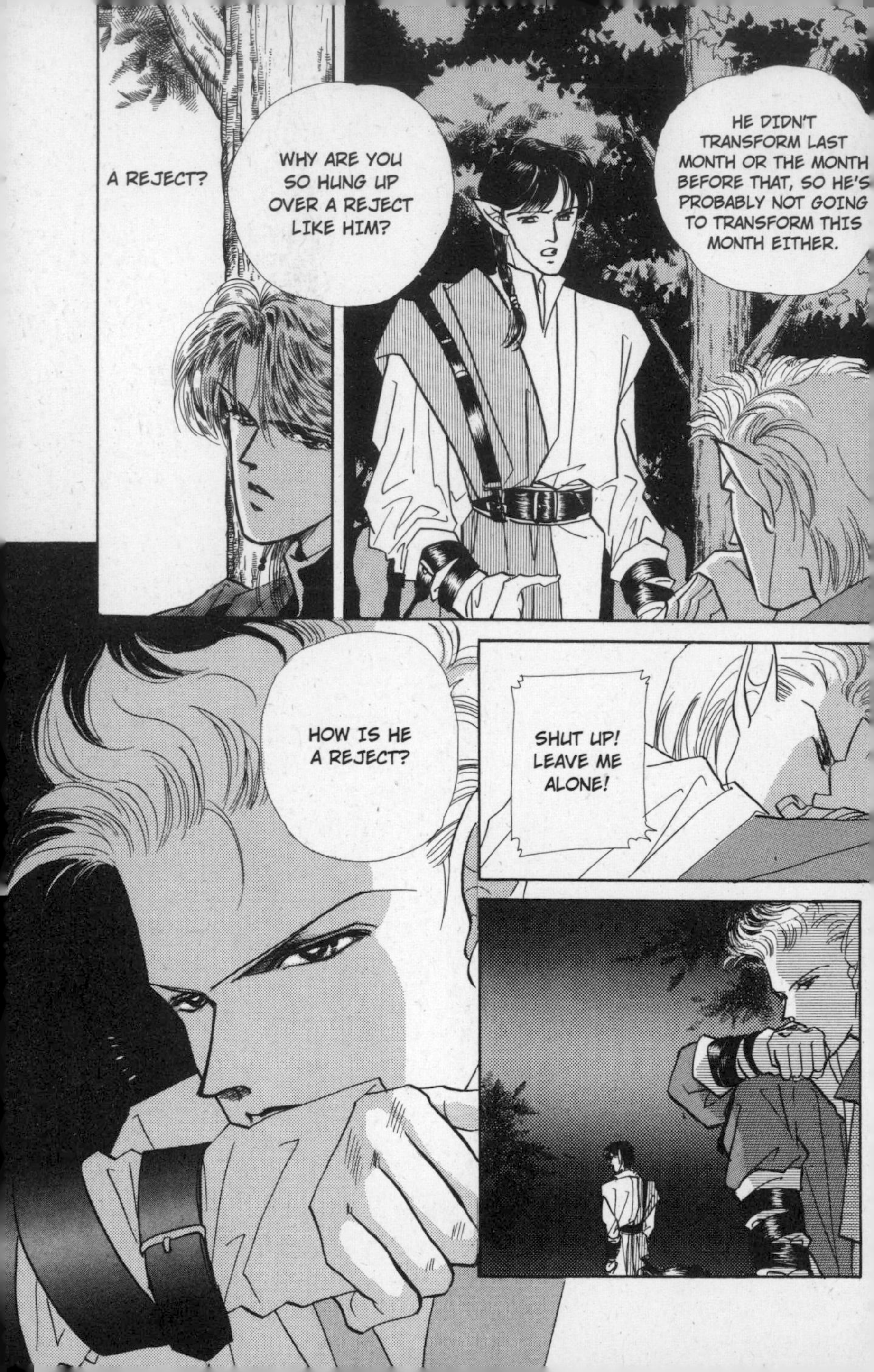
HE DIDN'T TRANSFORM LAST MONTH OR THE MONTH BEFORE THAT, SO HE'S PROBABLY NOT GOING TO TRANSFORM THIS MONTH EITHER.
WHY ARE YOU SO HUNG UP OVER A REJECT LIKE HIM?
A REJECT?
SHUT UP! LEAVE ME ALONE!
HOW IS HE A REJECT?

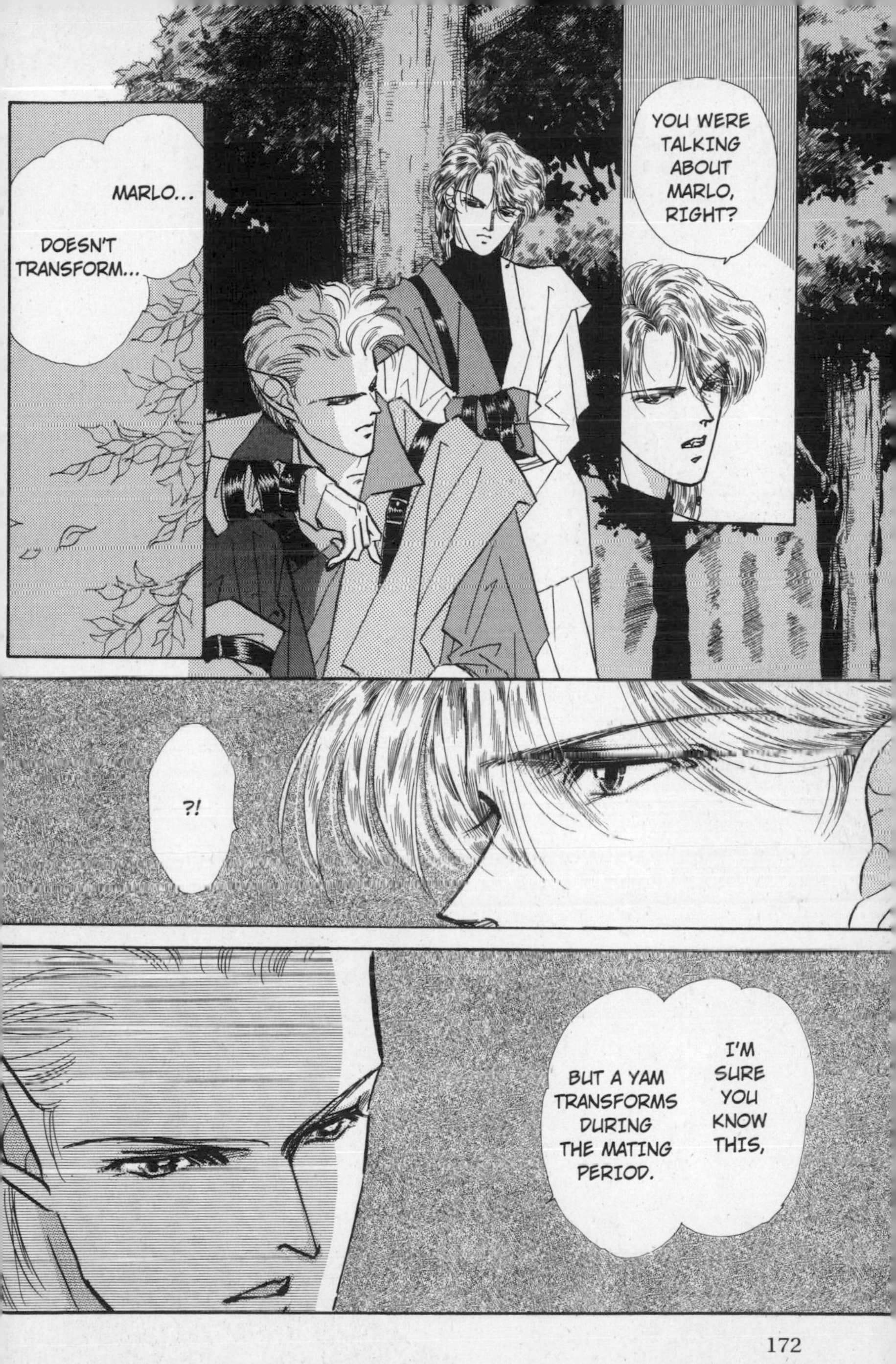
YOU WERE TALKING ABOUT MARLO, RIGHT?
MARLO...
DOESN'T TRANSFORM...
?!
I'M SURE YOU KNOW THIS,
BUT A YAM TRANSFORMS DURING THE MATING PERIOD.

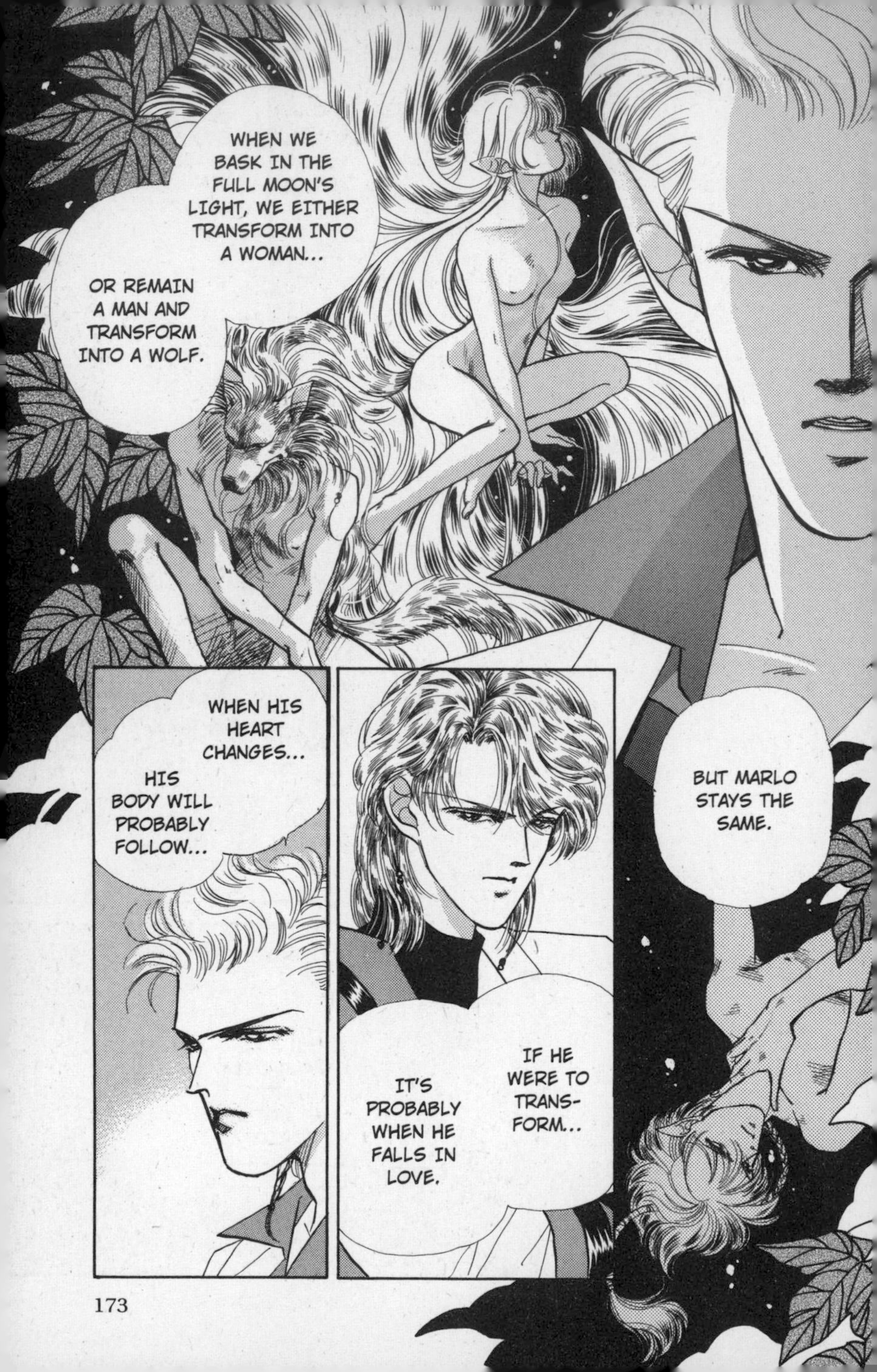
WHEN WE BASK IN THE FULL MOON'S LIGHT, WE EITHER TRANSFORM INTO A WOMAN...
OR REMAIN A MAN AND TRANSFORM INTO A WOLF.
BUT MARLO STAYS THE SAME.
IF HE WERE TO TRANS-FORM...
IT'S PROBABLY WHEN HE FALLS IN LOVE.
WHEN HIS HEART CHANGES...
HIS BODY WILL PROBABLY FOLLOW...

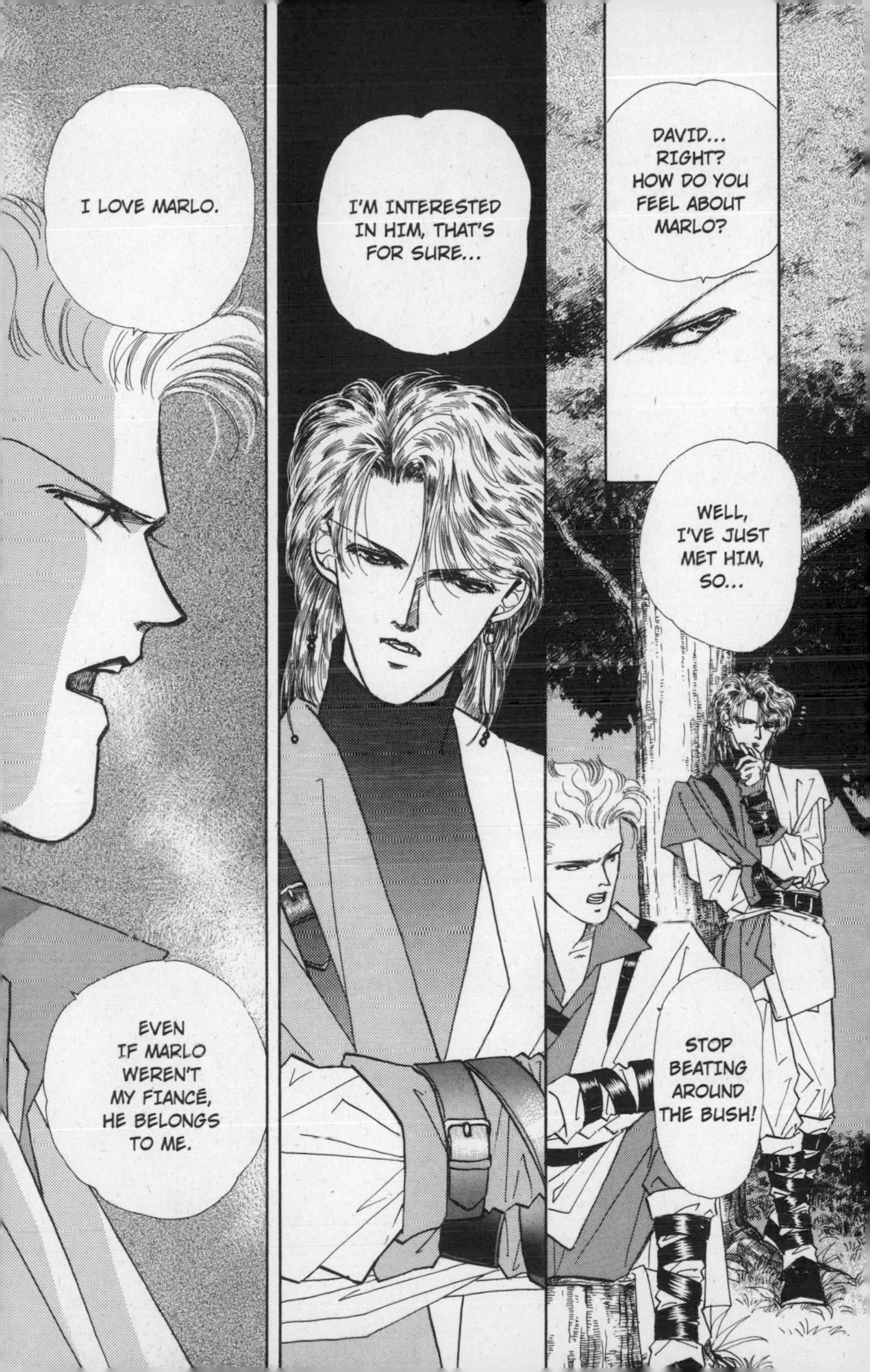
DAVID... RIGHT? HOW DO YOU FEEL ABOUT MARLO?
WELL, I'VE JUST MET HIM, SO...
STOP BEATING AROUND THE BUSH!
I'M INTERESTED IN HIM, THAT'S FOR SURE...
I LOVE MARLO.
EVEN IF MARLO WEREN'T MY FIANCÉ, HE BELONGS TO ME.

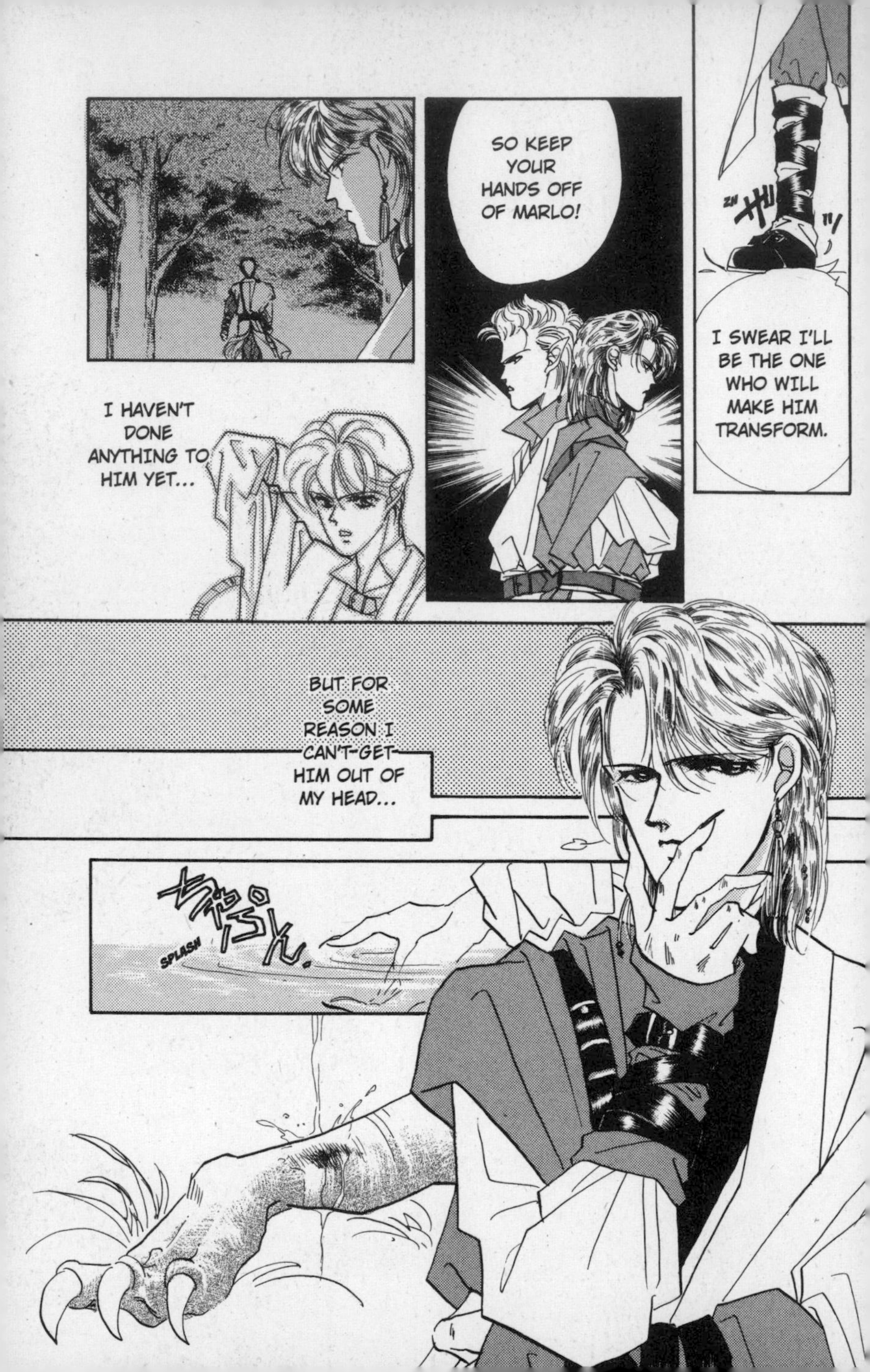
I SWEAR I'LL BE THE ONE WHO WILL MAKE HIM TRANSFORM.
SO KEEP YOUR HANDS OFF OF MARLO!
I HAVEN'T DONE ANYTHING TO HIM YET...
BUT FOR SOME REASON I CAN'T GET HIM OUT OF MY HEAD...
SPLASH

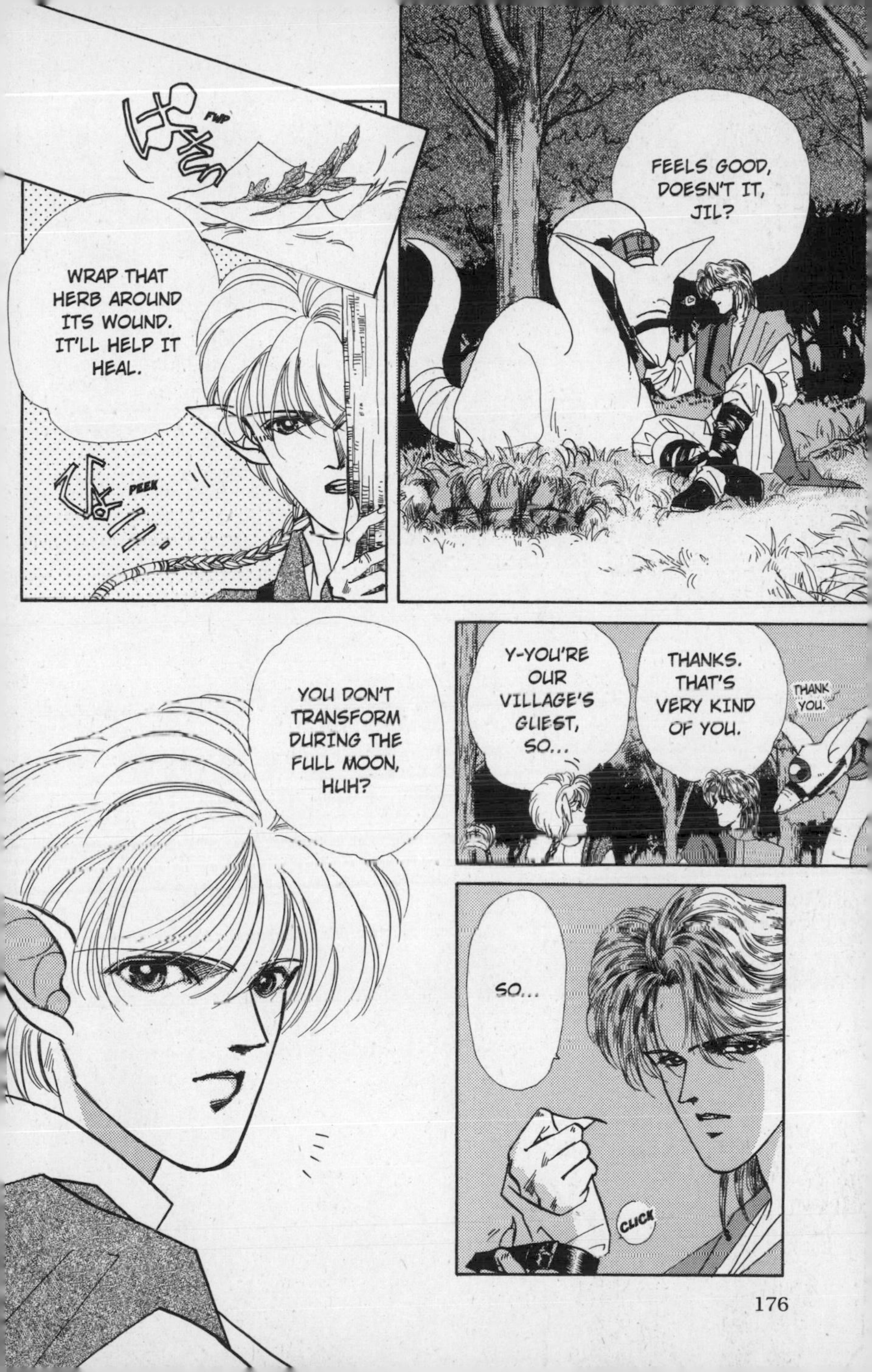
FEELS GOOD, DOESN'T IT, JIL?
FWP
WRAP THAT HERB AROUND ITS WOUND. IT'LL HELP IT HEAL.
PEEK
THANK YOU.
THANKS. THAT'S VERY KIND OF YOU.
Y-YOU'RE OUR VILLAGE'S GUEST, SO...
SO...
CLICK
YOU DON'T TRANSFORM DURING THE FULL MOON, HUH?

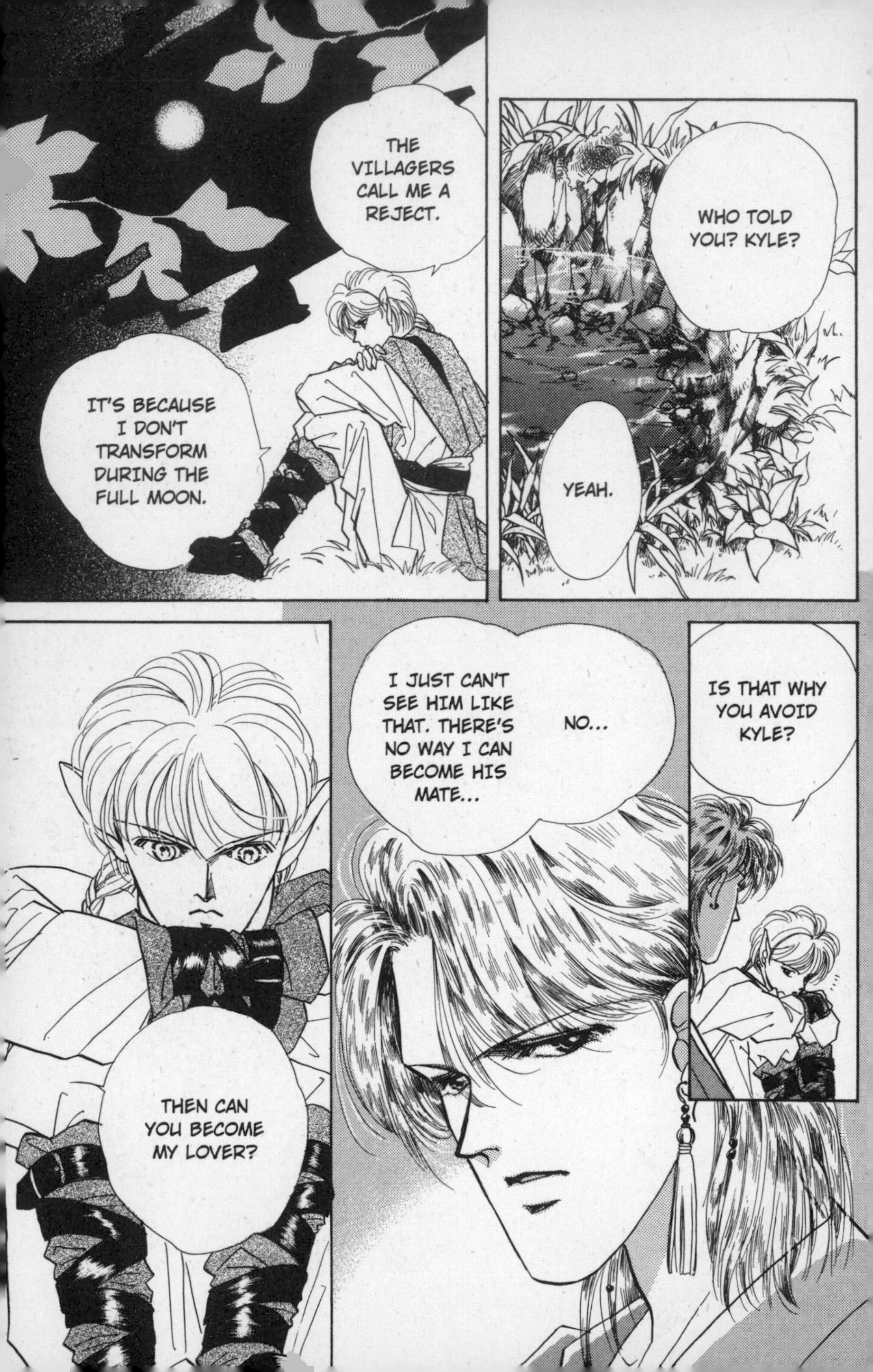
WHO TOLD YOU? KYLE?
YEAH.
THE VILLAGERS CALL ME A REJECT.
IT'S BECAUSE I DON'T TRANSFORM DURING THE FULL MOON.
IS THAT WHY YOU AVOID KYLE?
NO...
I JUST CAN'T SEE HIM LIKE THAT. THERE'S NO WAY I CAN BECOME HIS MATE...
THEN CAN YOU BECOME MY LOVER?

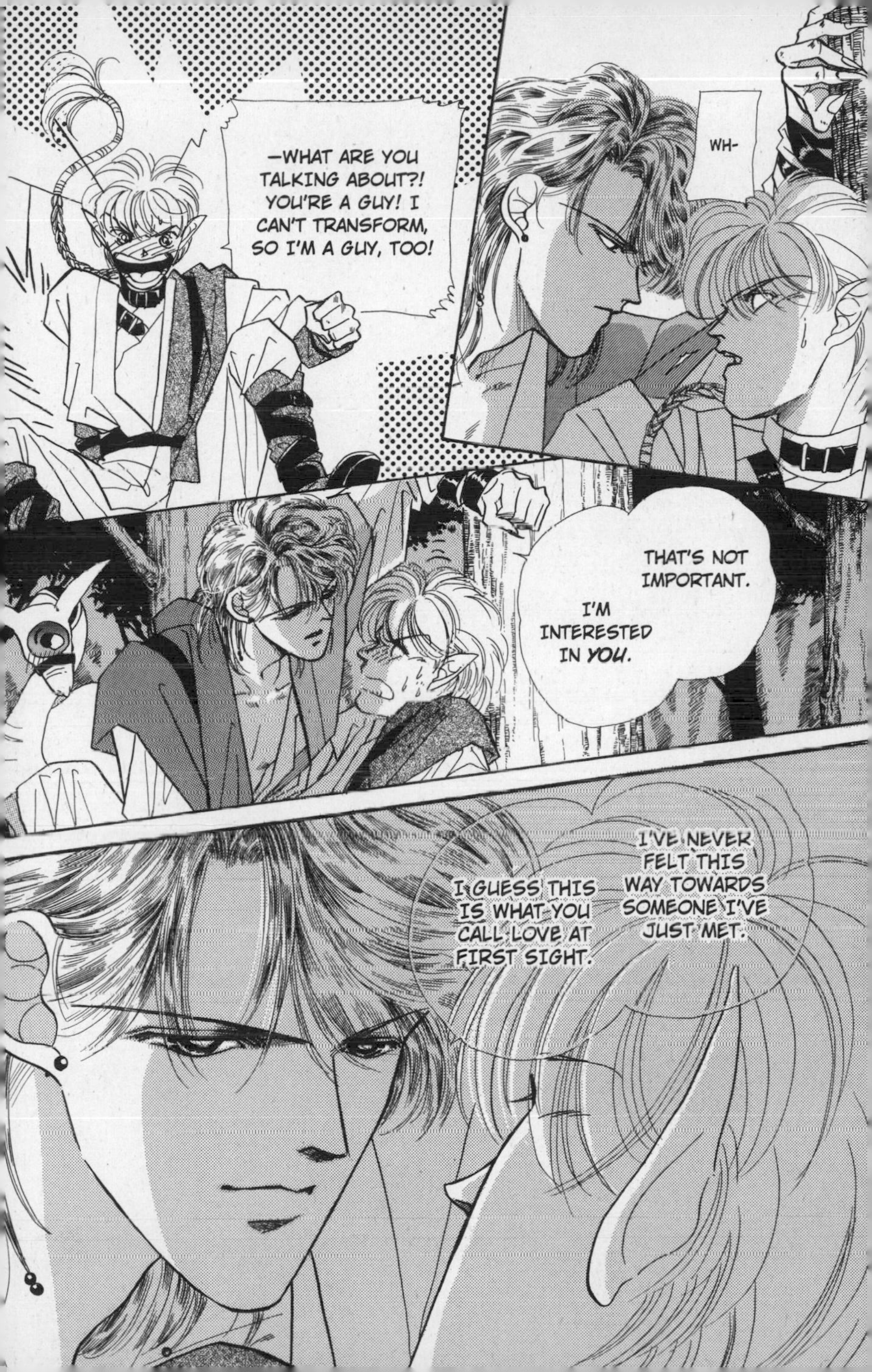

WH-
—WHAT ARE YOU TALKING ABOUT?! YOU'RE A GUY! I CAN'T TRANSFORM, SO I'M A GUY, TOO!
THAT'S NOT IMPORTANT.
I'M INTERESTED IN *YOU*.
I'VE NEVER FELT THIS WAY TOWARDS SOMEONE I'VE JUST MET.
I GUESS THIS IS WHAT YOU CALL LOVE AT FIRST SIGHT.

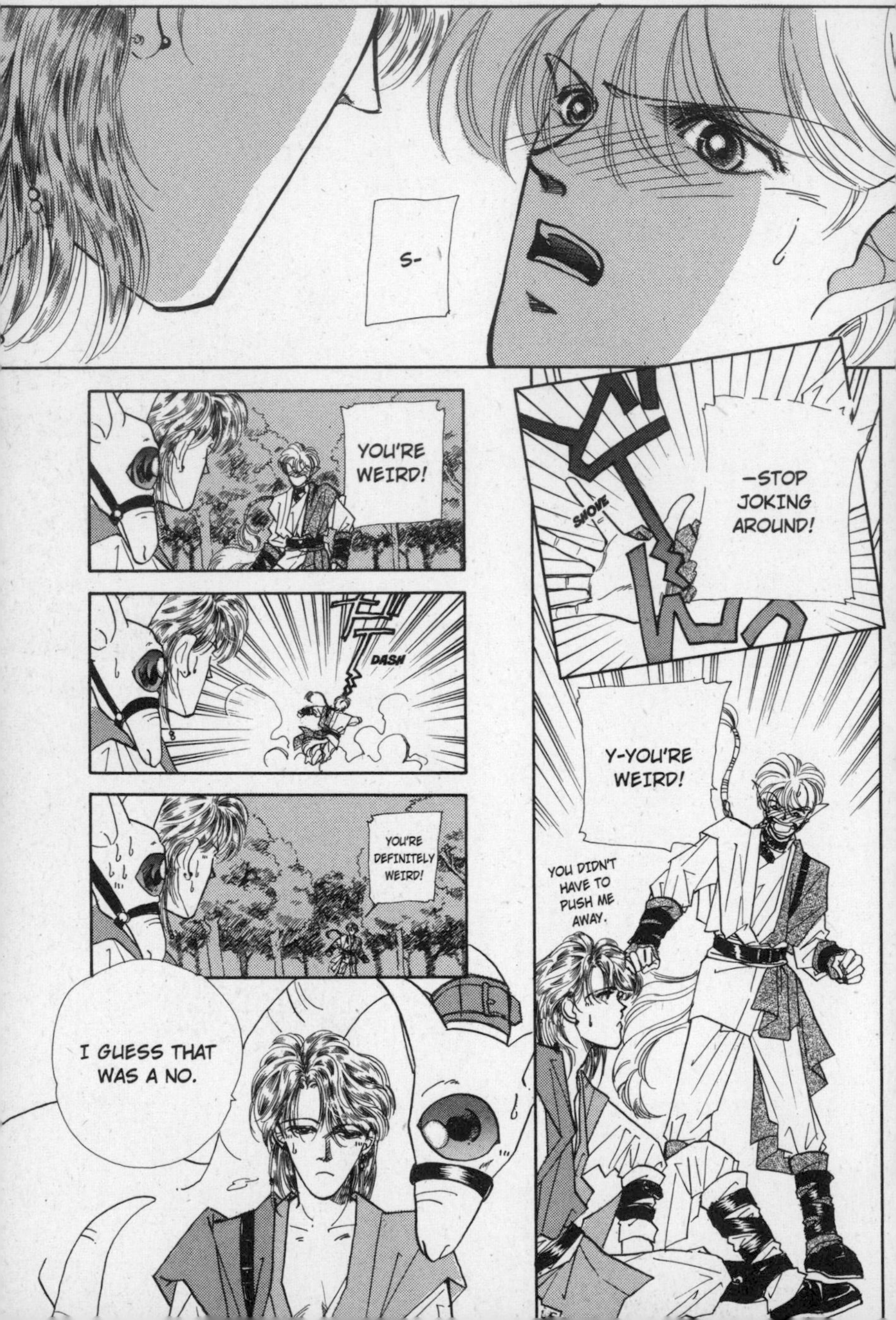
S-
SHOVE
—STOP JOKING AROUND!
Y-YOU'RE WEIRD!
YOU DIDN'T HAVE TO PUSH ME AWAY.
YOU'RE WEIRD!
DASH
YOU'RE DEFINITELY WEIRD!
I GUESS THAT WAS A NO.

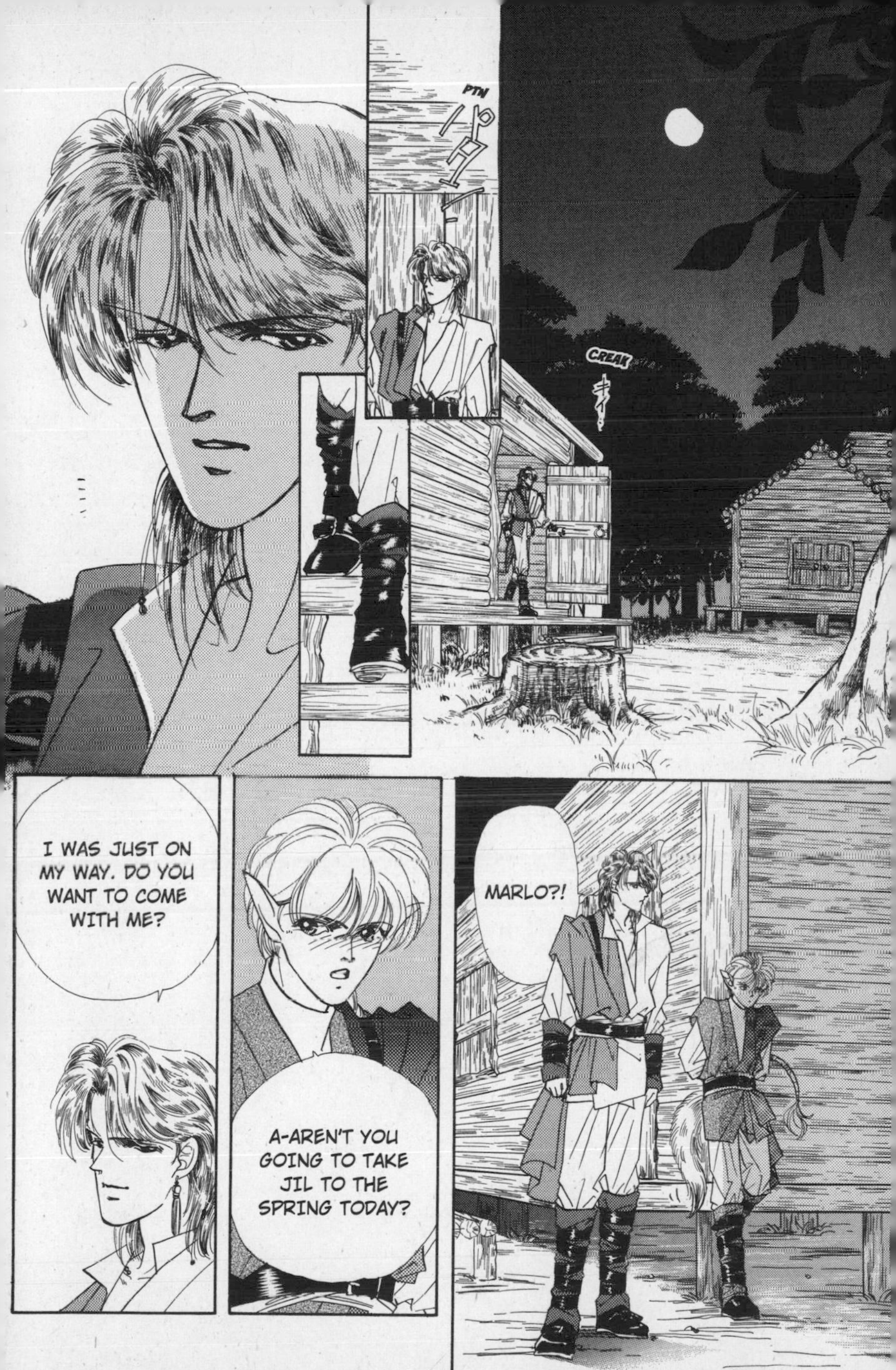
CREAK
PTN
MARLO?!
A-AREN'T YOU GOING TO TAKE JIL TO THE SPRING TODAY?
I WAS JUST ON MY WAY. DO YOU WANT TO COME WITH ME?

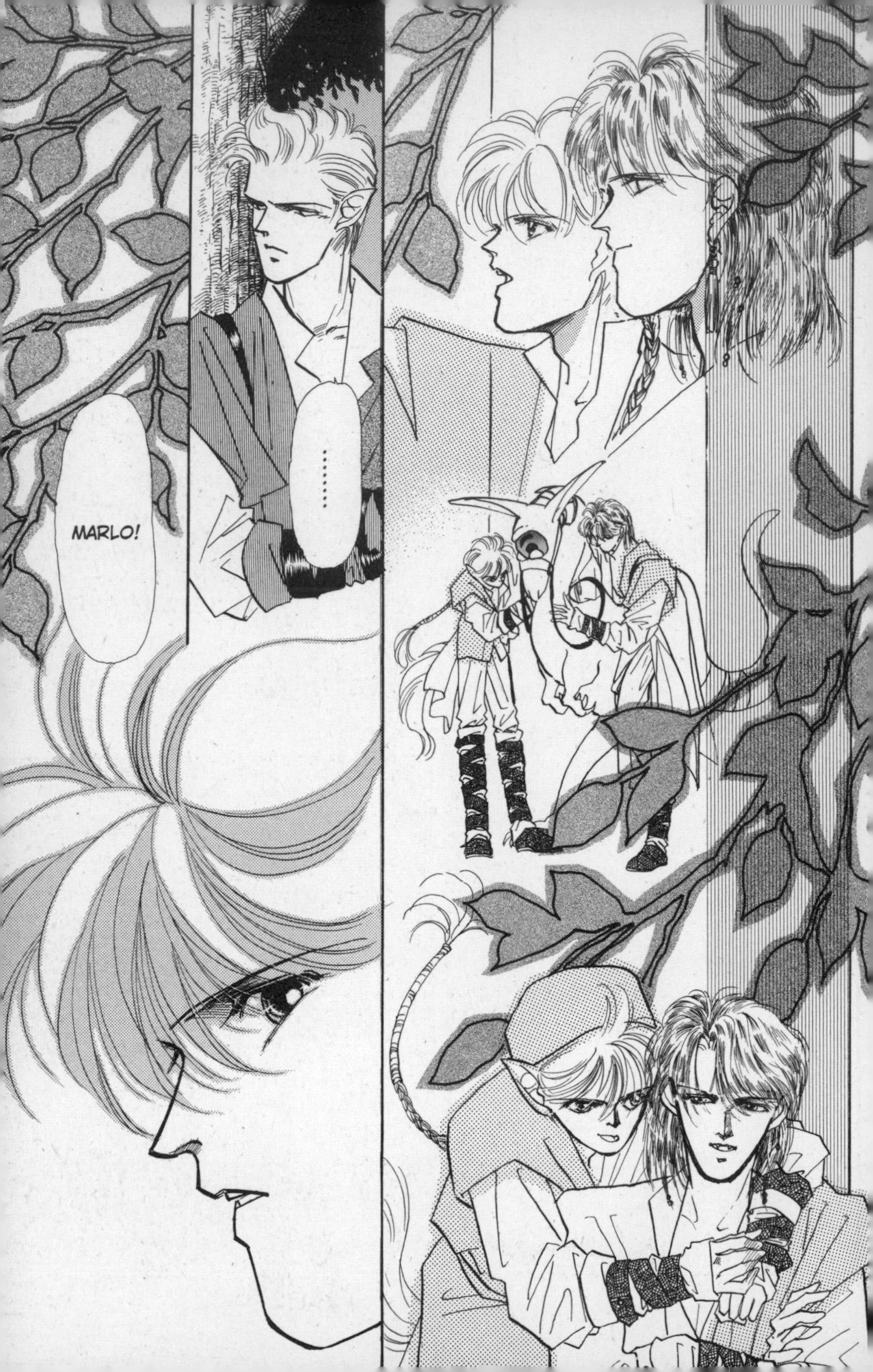
......
MARLO!

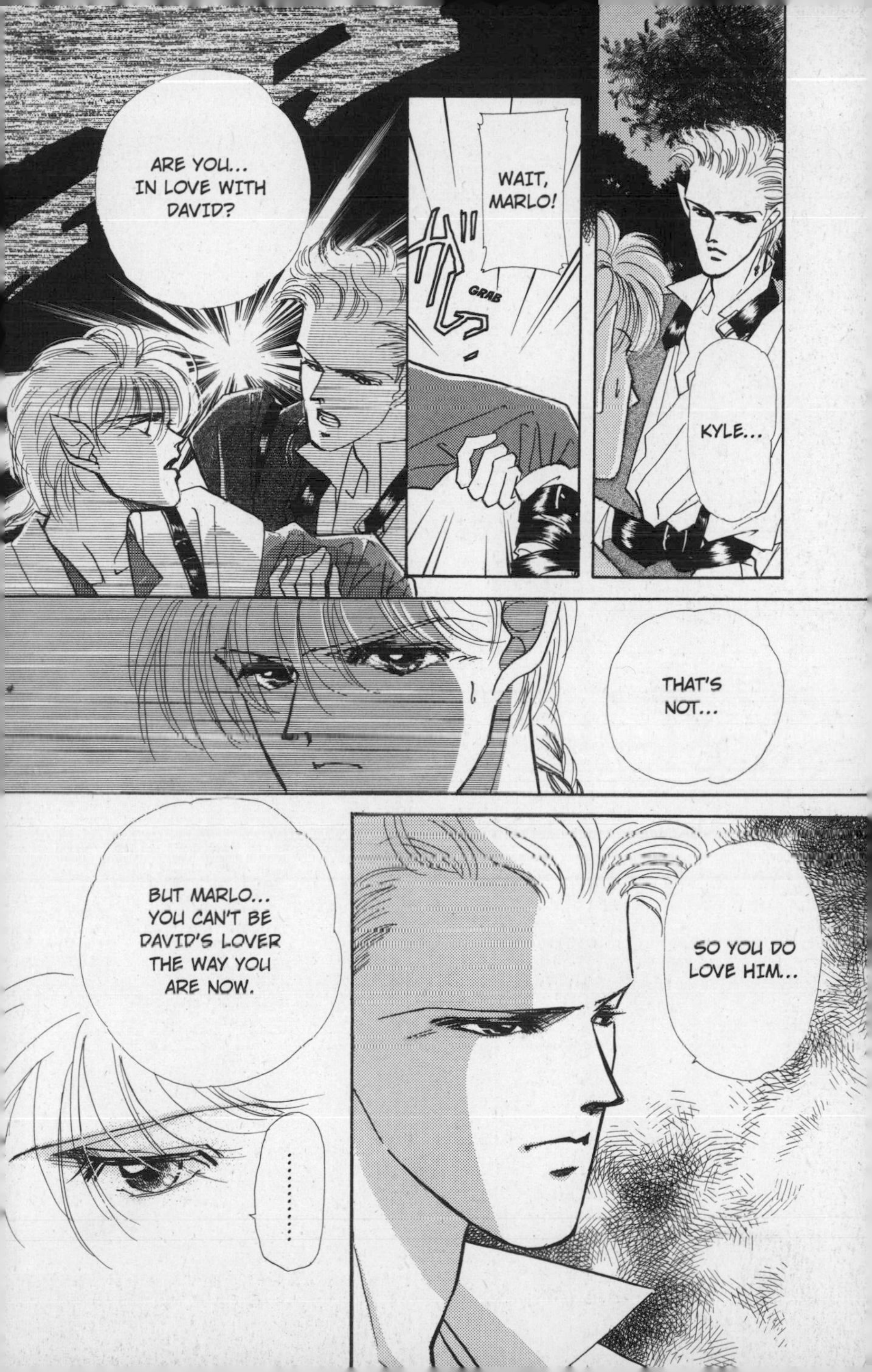
KYLE...
WAIT, MARLO!
GRAB
ARE YOU... IN LOVE WITH DAVID?
THAT'S NOT...
SO YOU DO LOVE HIM...
BUT MARLO... YOU CAN'T BE DAVID'S LOVER THE WAY YOU ARE NOW.
......

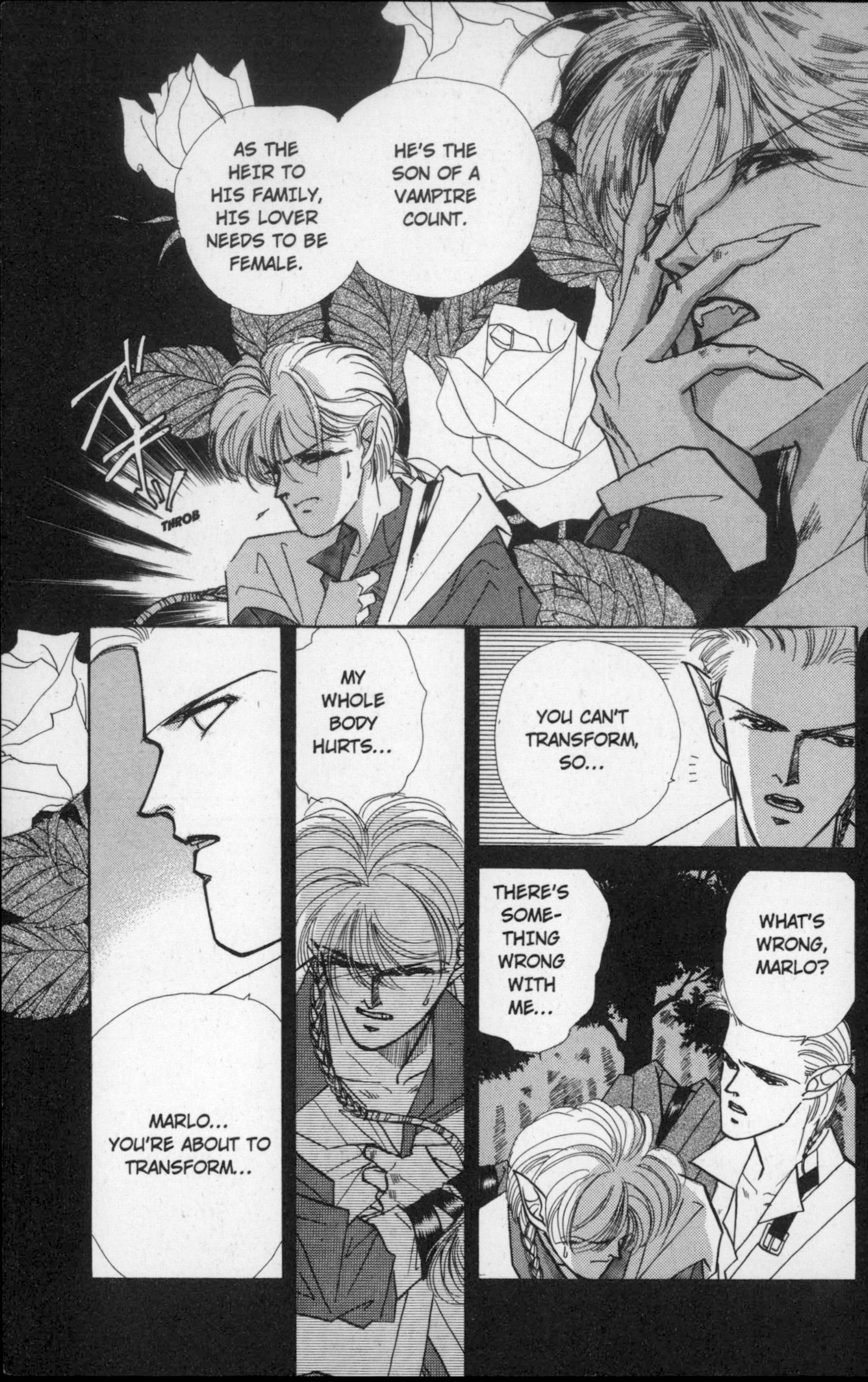
HE'S THE SON OF A VAMPIRE COUNT.
AS THE HEIR TO HIS FAMILY, HIS LOVER NEEDS TO BE FEMALE.
THROB
YOU CAN'T TRANSFORM, SO...
WHAT'S WRONG, MARLO?
THERE'S SOME-THING WRONG WITH ME...
MY WHOLE BODY HURTS...
MARLO... YOU'RE ABOUT TO TRANSFORM...

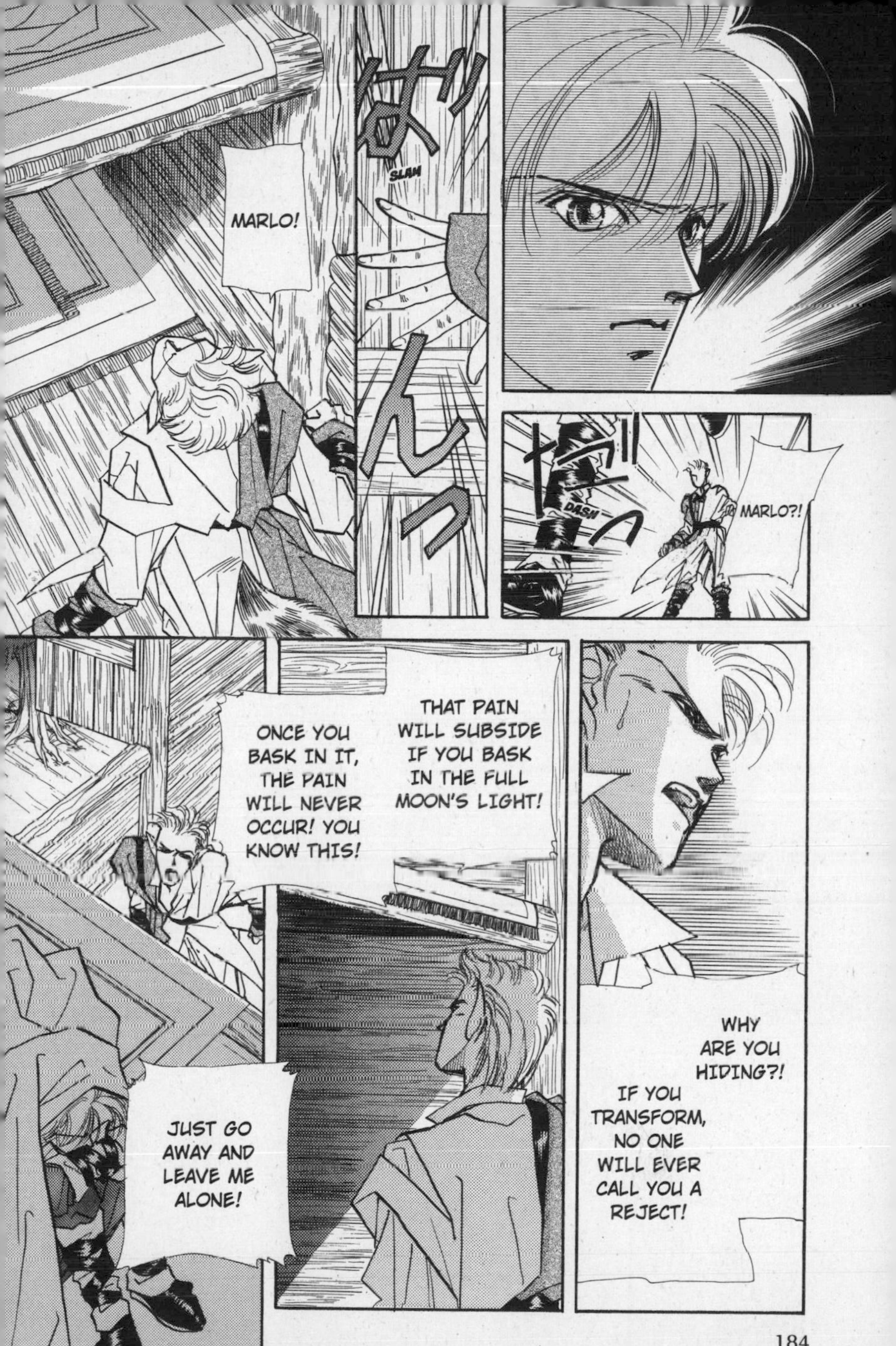
DASH
MARLO?!
SLAM
MARLO!
WHY ARE YOU HIDING?!
IF YOU TRANSFORM, NO ONE WILL EVER CALL YOU A REJECT!
THAT PAIN WILL SUBSIDE IF YOU BASK IN THE FULL MOON'S LIGHT!
ONCE YOU BASK IN IT, THE PAIN WILL NEVER OCCUR! YOU KNOW THIS!
JUST GO AWAY AND LEAVE ME ALONE!

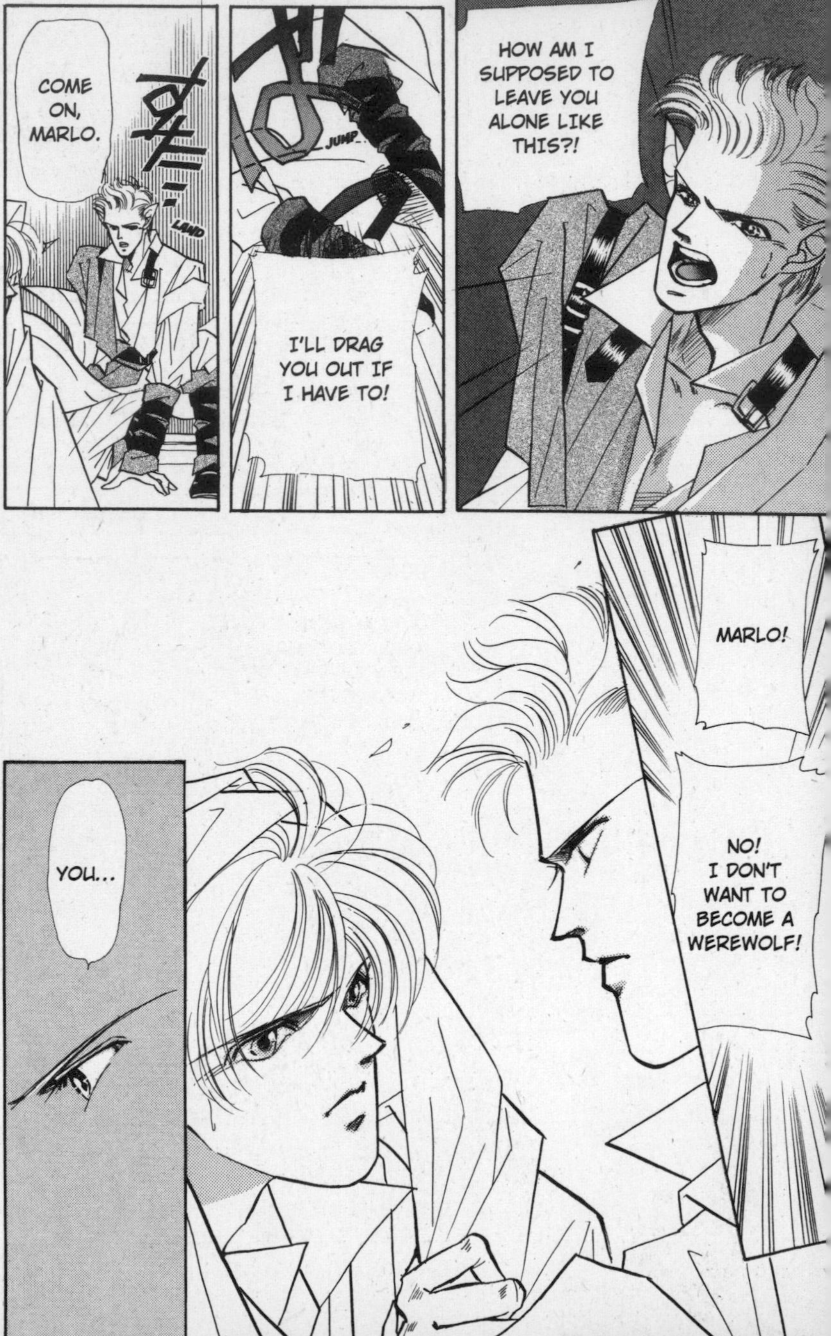
HOW AM I SUPPOSED TO LEAVE YOU ALONE LIKE THIS?!
JUMP
I'LL DRAG YOU OUT IF I HAVE TO!
COME ON, MARLO.
LAND
MARLO!
NO! I DON'T WANT TO BECOME A WEREWOLF!
YOU...

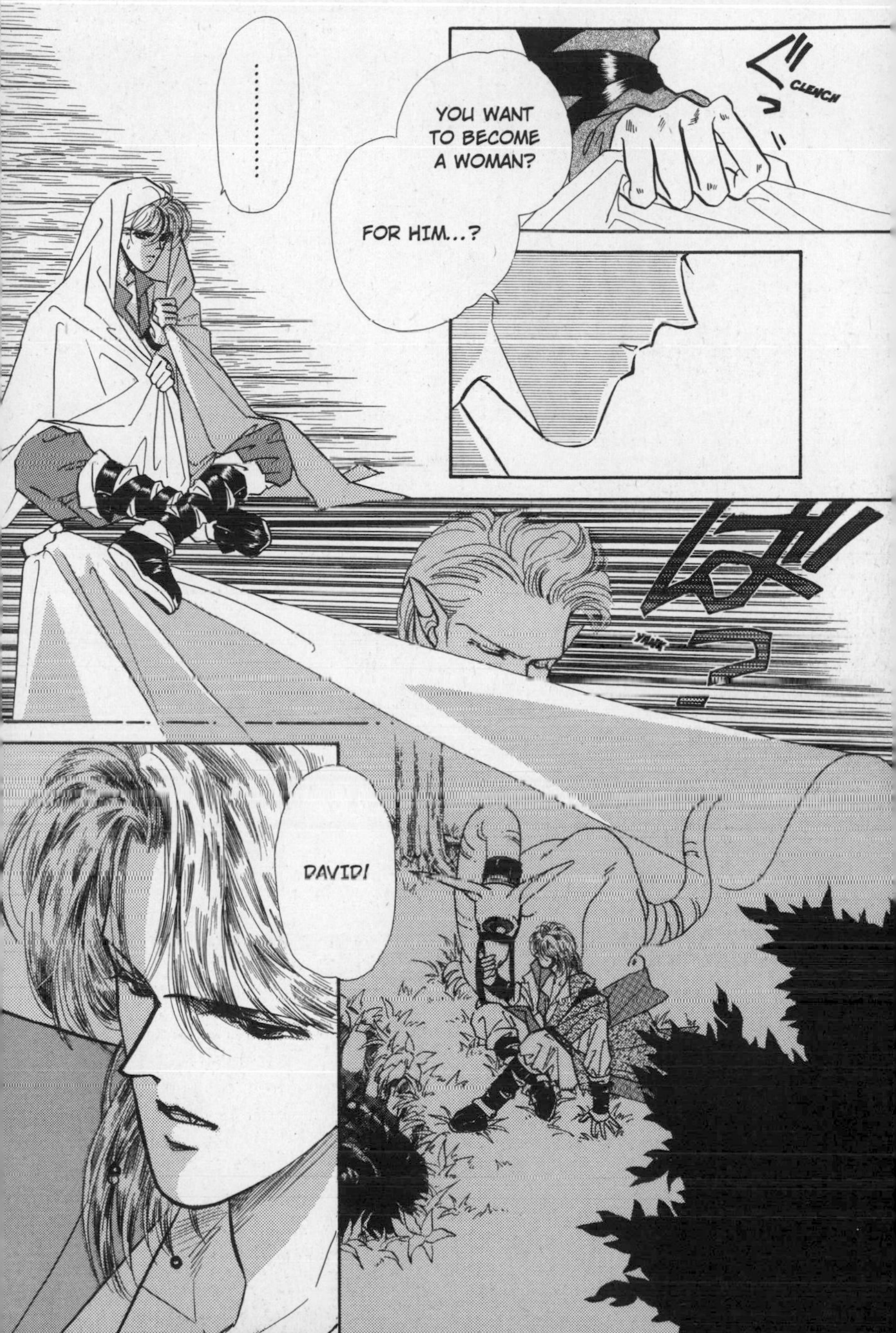
CLENCH
YOU WANT TO BECOME A WOMAN?
FOR HIM...?
......
YANK
DAVID!

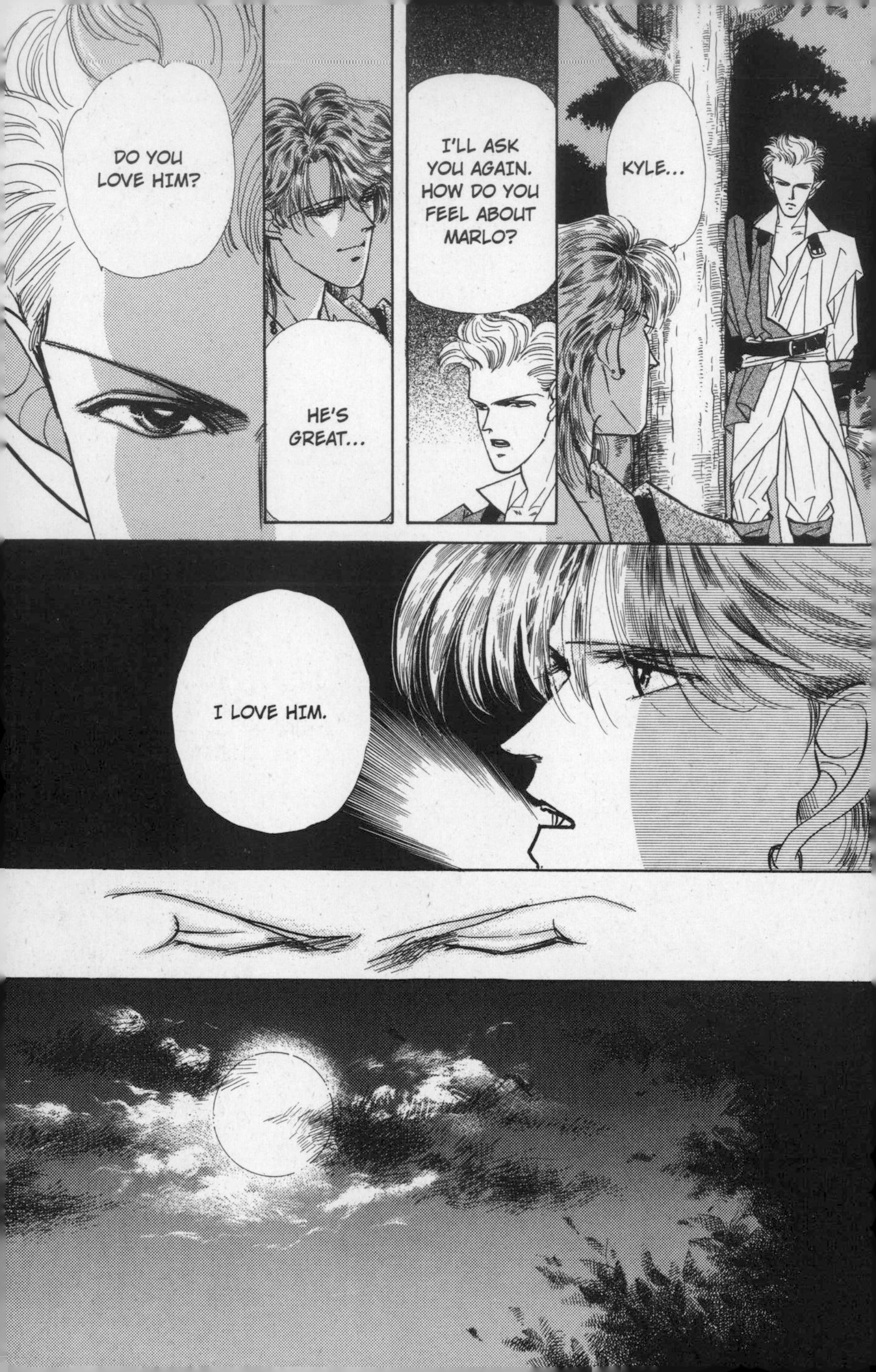
KYLE...
I'LL ASK YOU AGAIN. HOW DO YOU FEEL ABOUT MARLO?
HE'S GREAT...
DO YOU LOVE HIM?
I LOVE HIM.

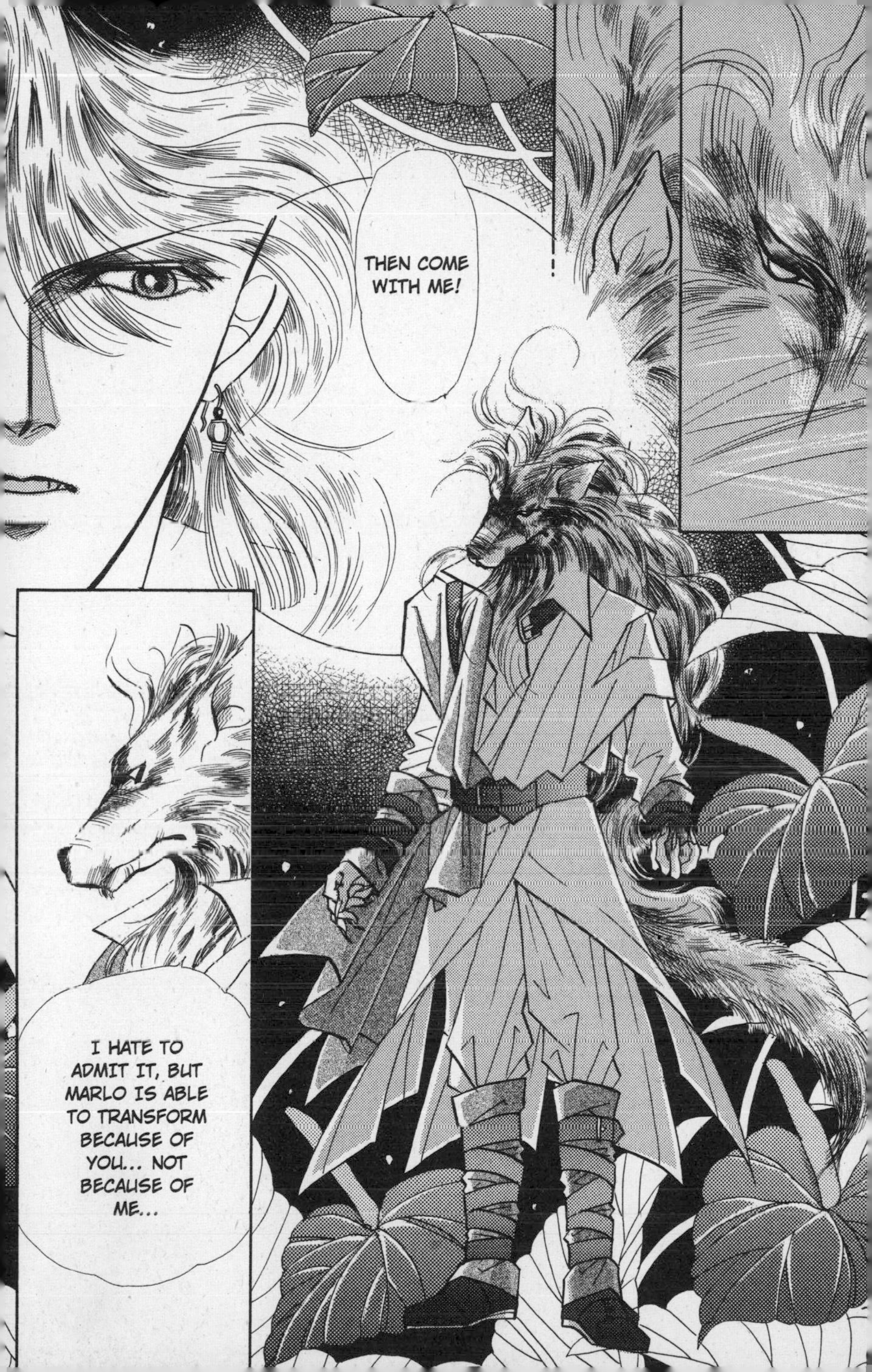
THEN COME WITH ME!
I HATE TO ADMIT IT, BUT MARLO IS ABLE TO TRANSFORM BECAUSE OF YOU... NOT BECAUSE OF ME...

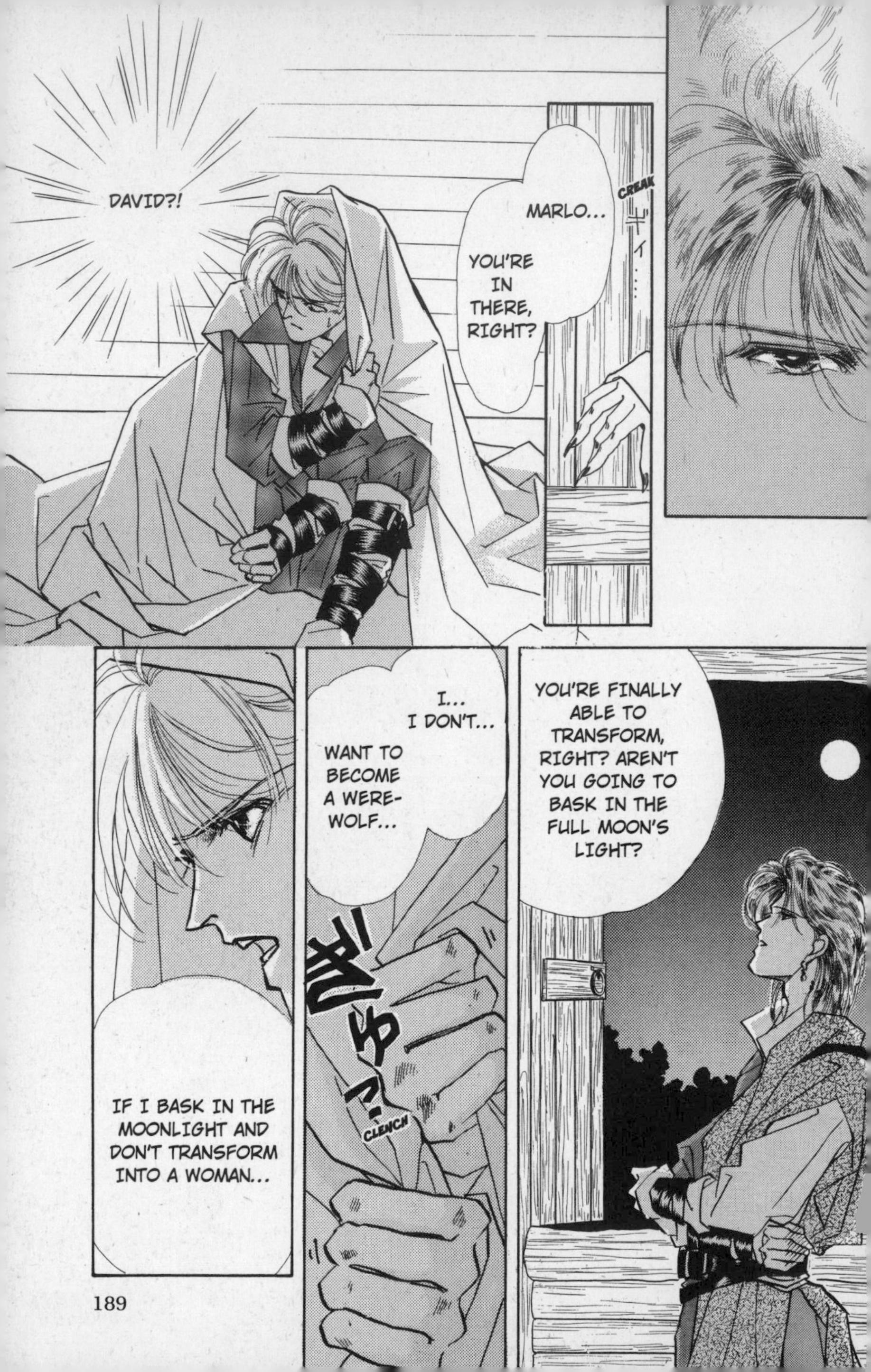
CREAK
ギイ…
MARLO…
YOU'RE IN THERE, RIGHT?
DAVID?!
YOU'RE FINALLY ABLE TO TRANSFORM, RIGHT? AREN'T YOU GOING TO BASK IN THE FULL MOON'S LIGHT?
I… I DON'T…
WANT TO BECOME A WERE-WOLF…
ぎゅっ
CLENCH
IF I BASK IN THE MOONLIGHT AND DON'T TRANSFORM INTO A WOMAN…

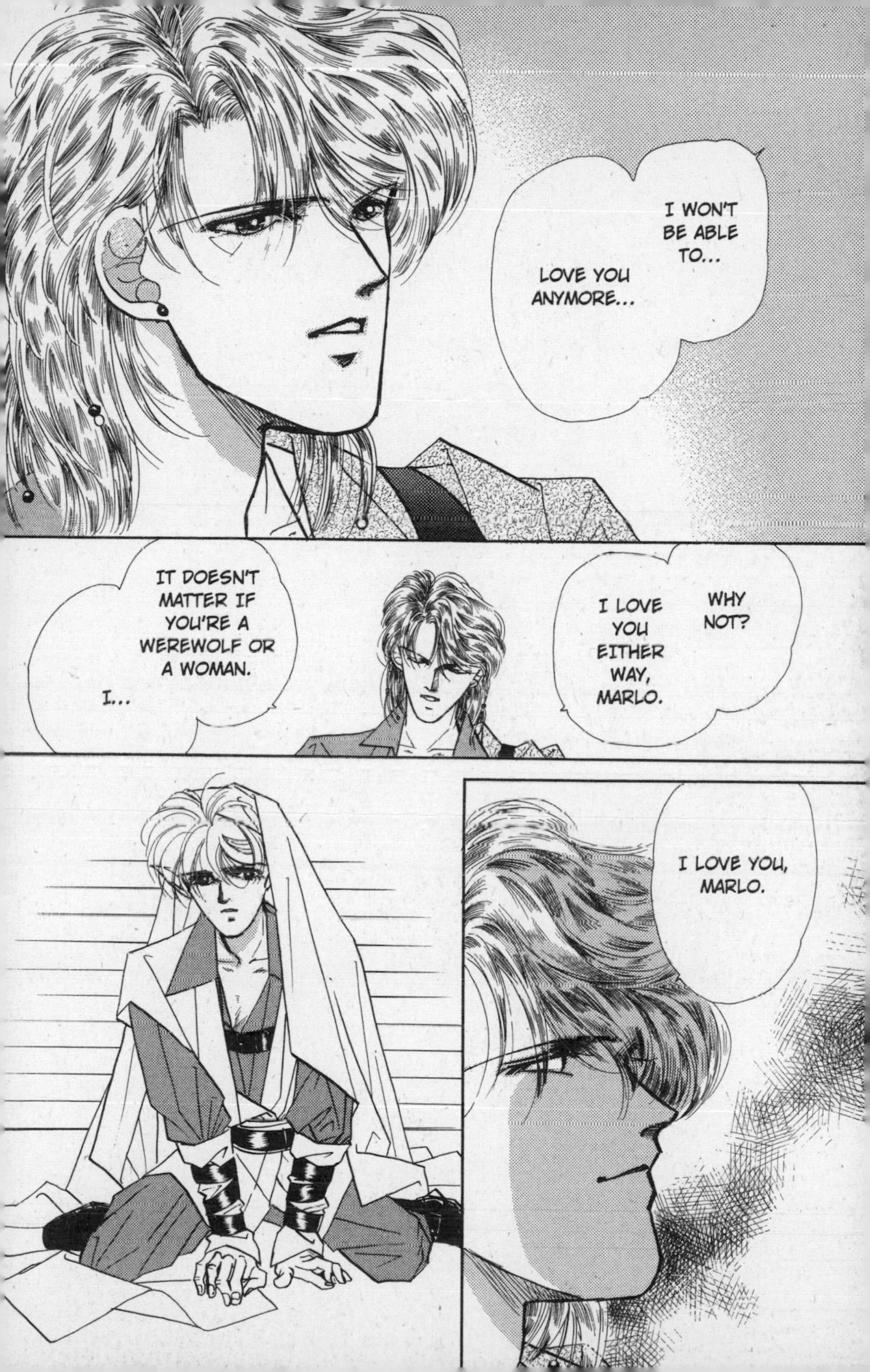
I WON'T BE ABLE TO...
LOVE YOU ANYMORE...
WHY NOT?
I LOVE YOU EITHER WAY, MARLO.
IT DOESN'T MATTER IF YOU'RE A WEREWOLF OR A WOMAN.
I...
I LOVE YOU, MARLO.

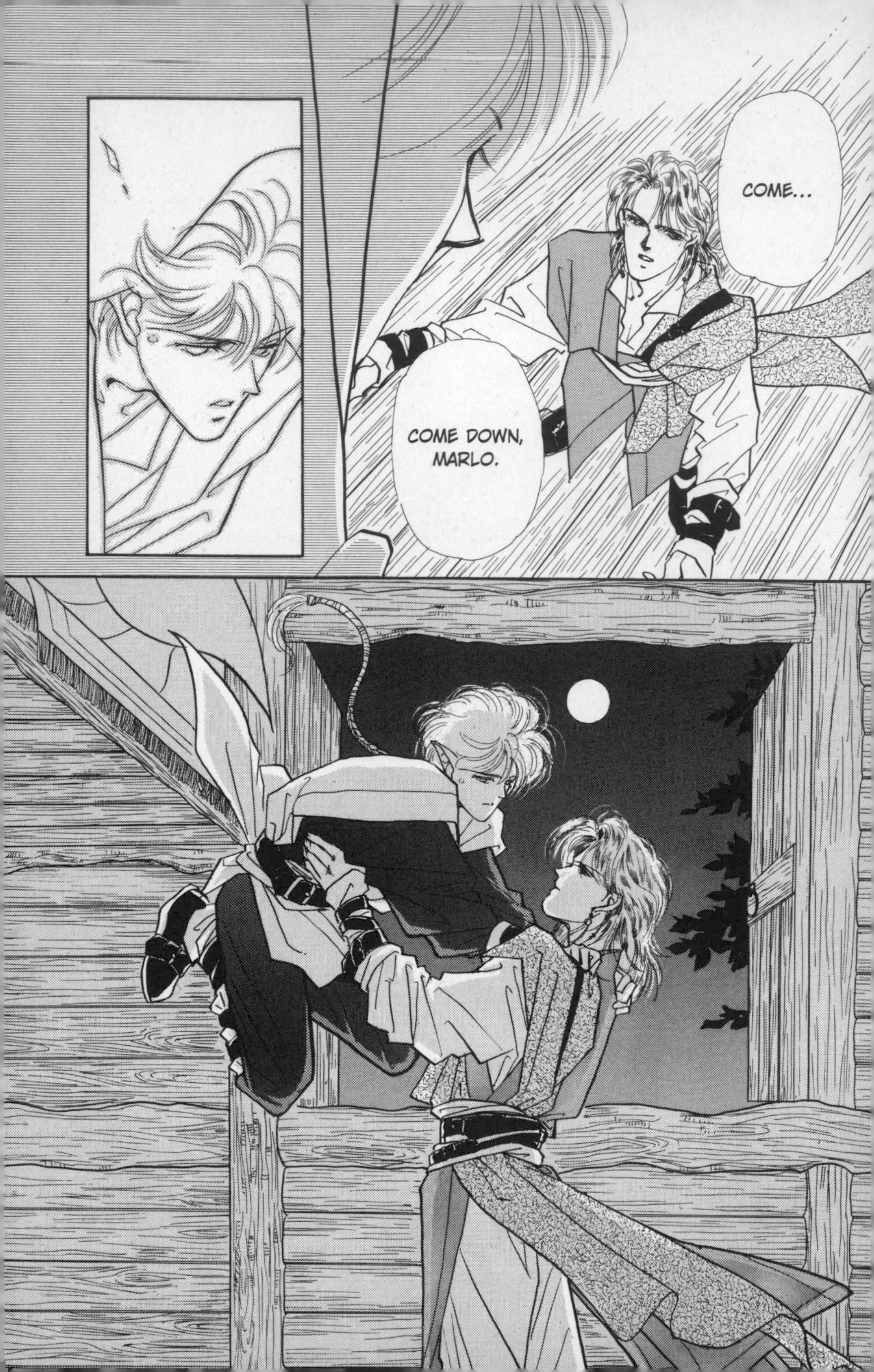
COME...
COME DOWN, MARLO.

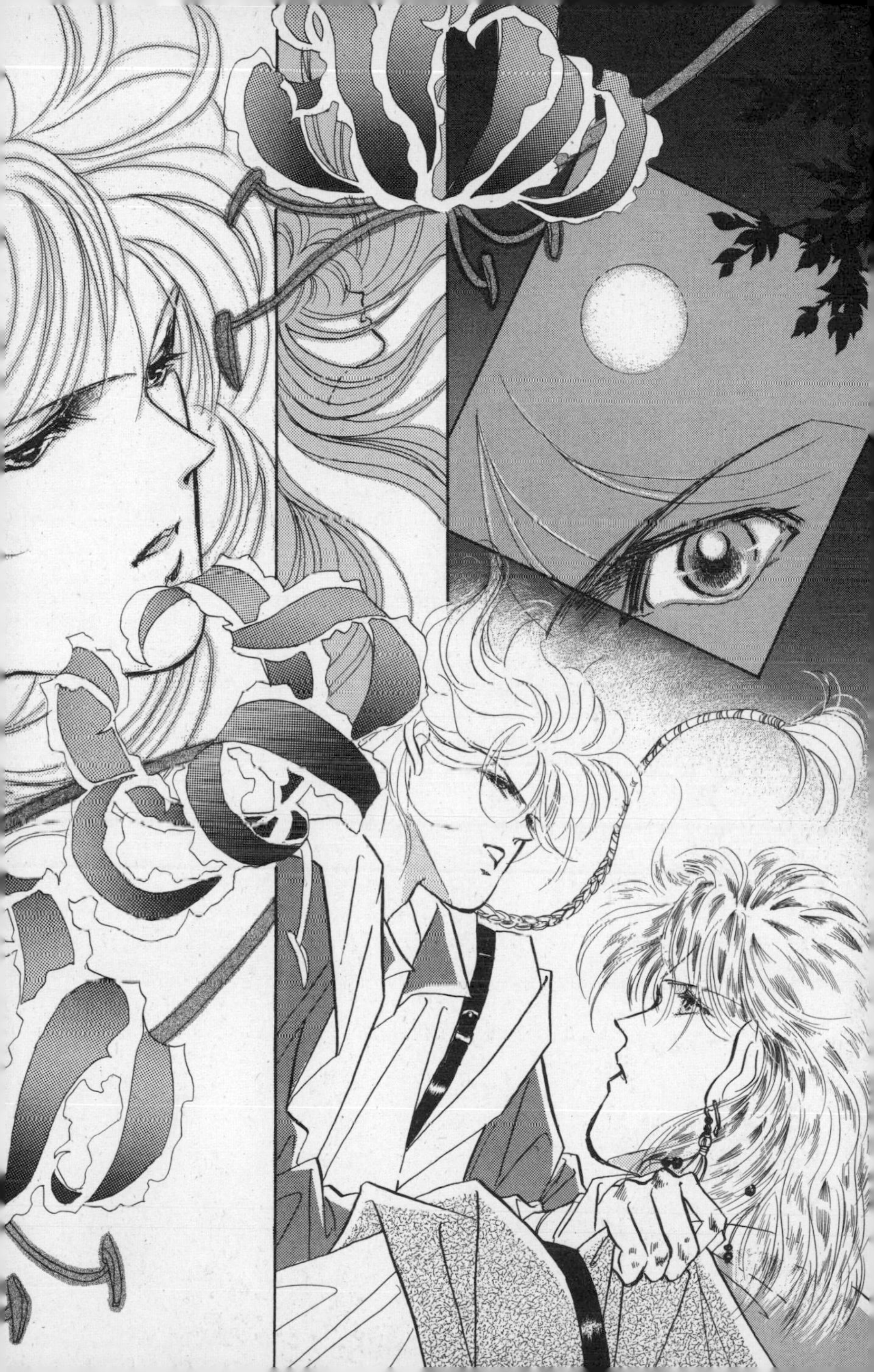

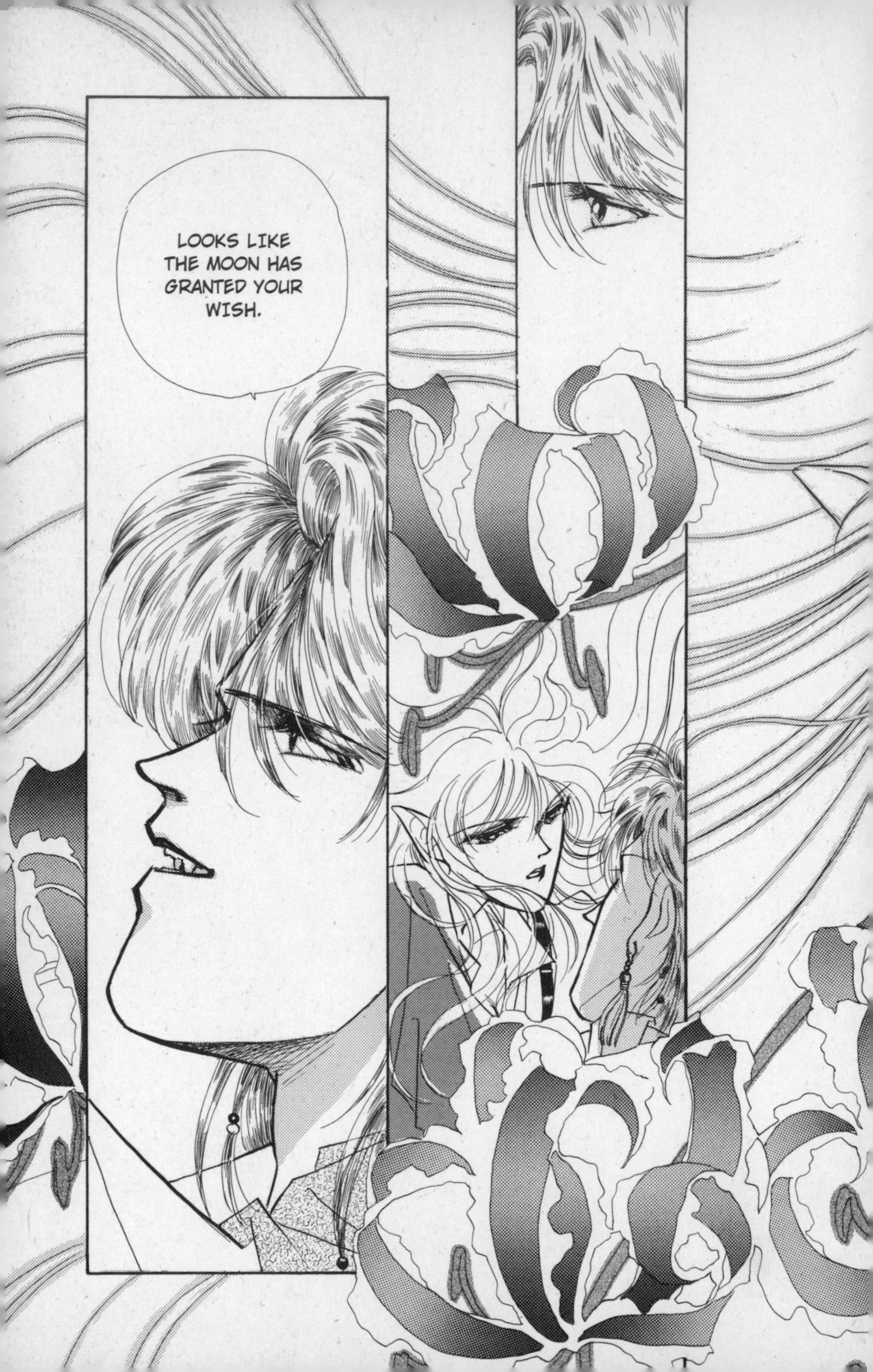
LOOKS LIKE
THE MOON HAS
GRANTED YOUR
WISH.

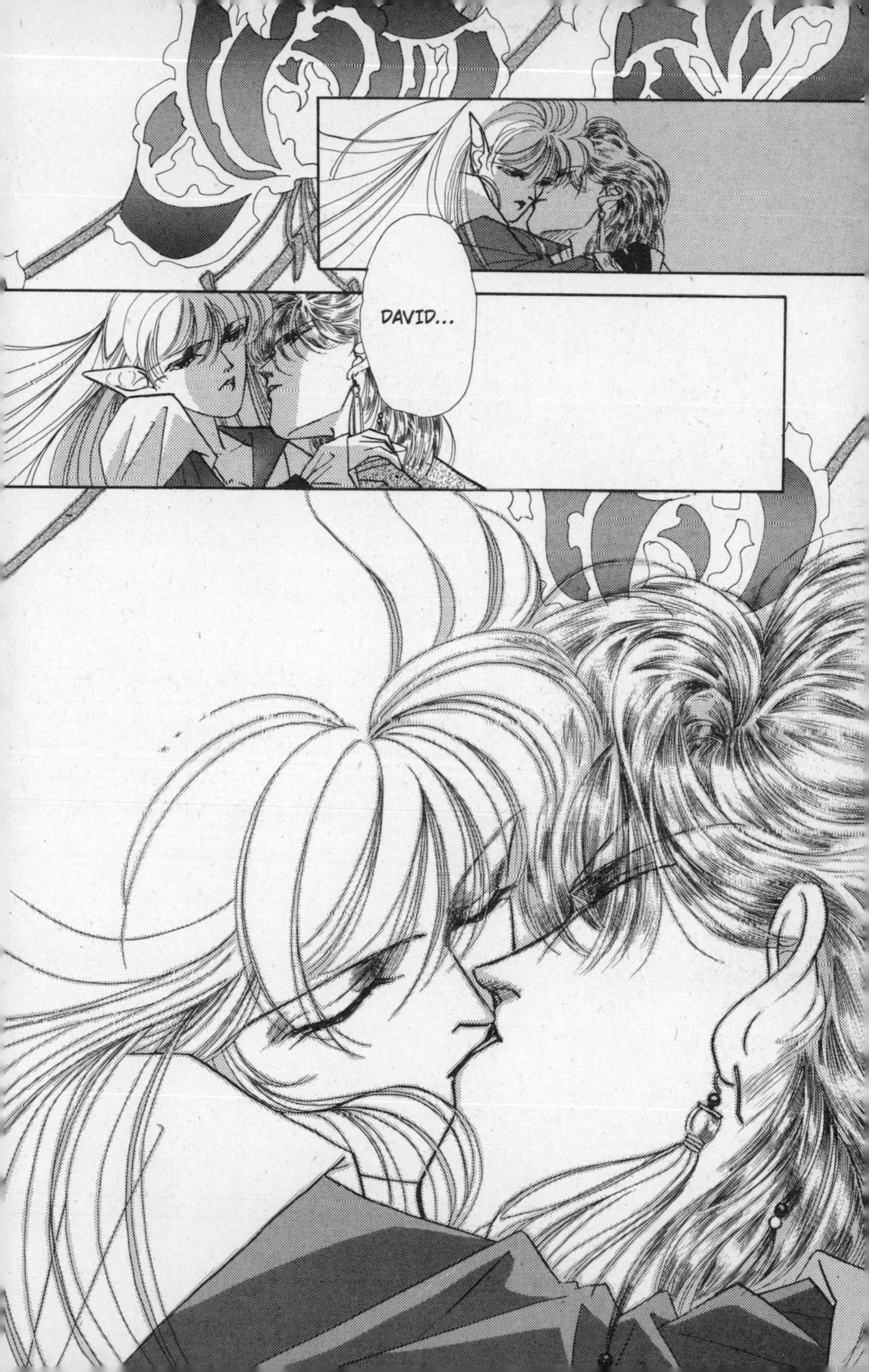
DAVID...

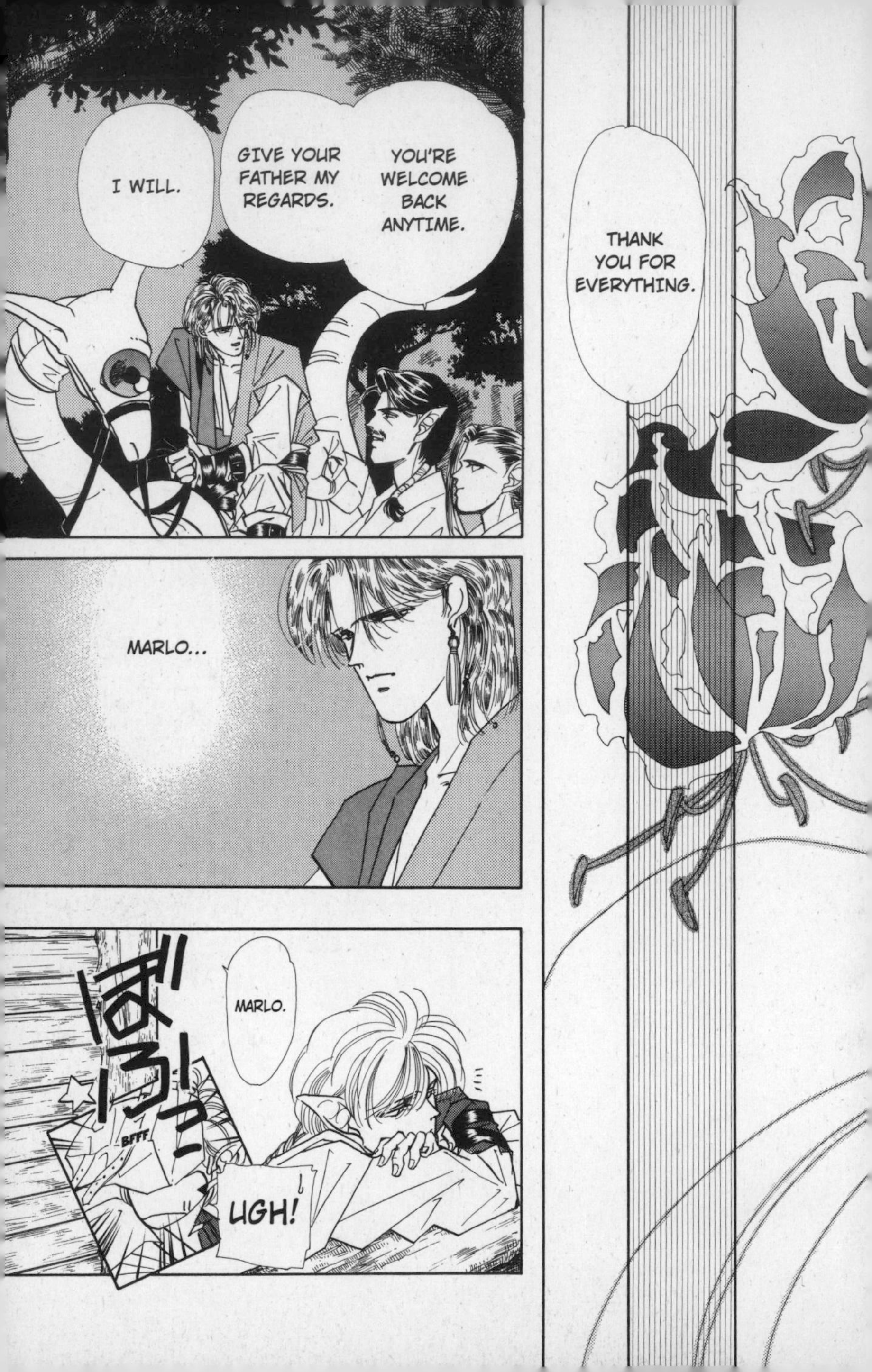
THANK YOU FOR EVERYTHING.
YOU'RE WELCOME BACK ANYTIME.
GIVE YOUR FATHER MY REGARDS.
I WILL.
MARLO...
MARLO.
BFFF
UGH!

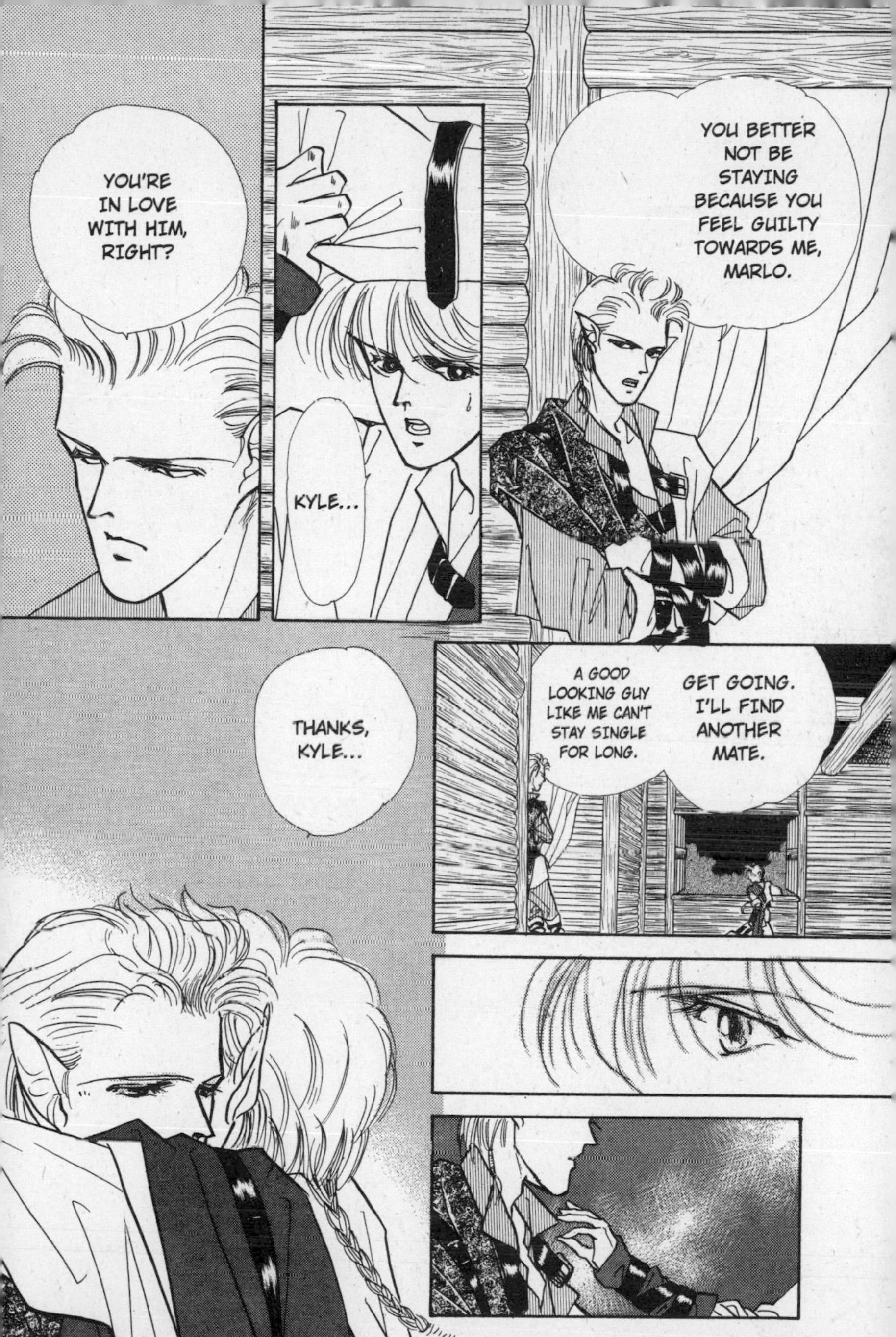
YOU BETTER NOT BE STAYING BECAUSE YOU FEEL GUILTY TOWARDS ME, MARLO.
KYLE...
YOU'RE IN LOVE WITH HIM, RIGHT?
GET GOING. I'LL FIND ANOTHER MATE.
A GOOD LOOKING GUY LIKE ME CAN'T STAY SINGLE FOR LONG.
THANKS, KYLE...

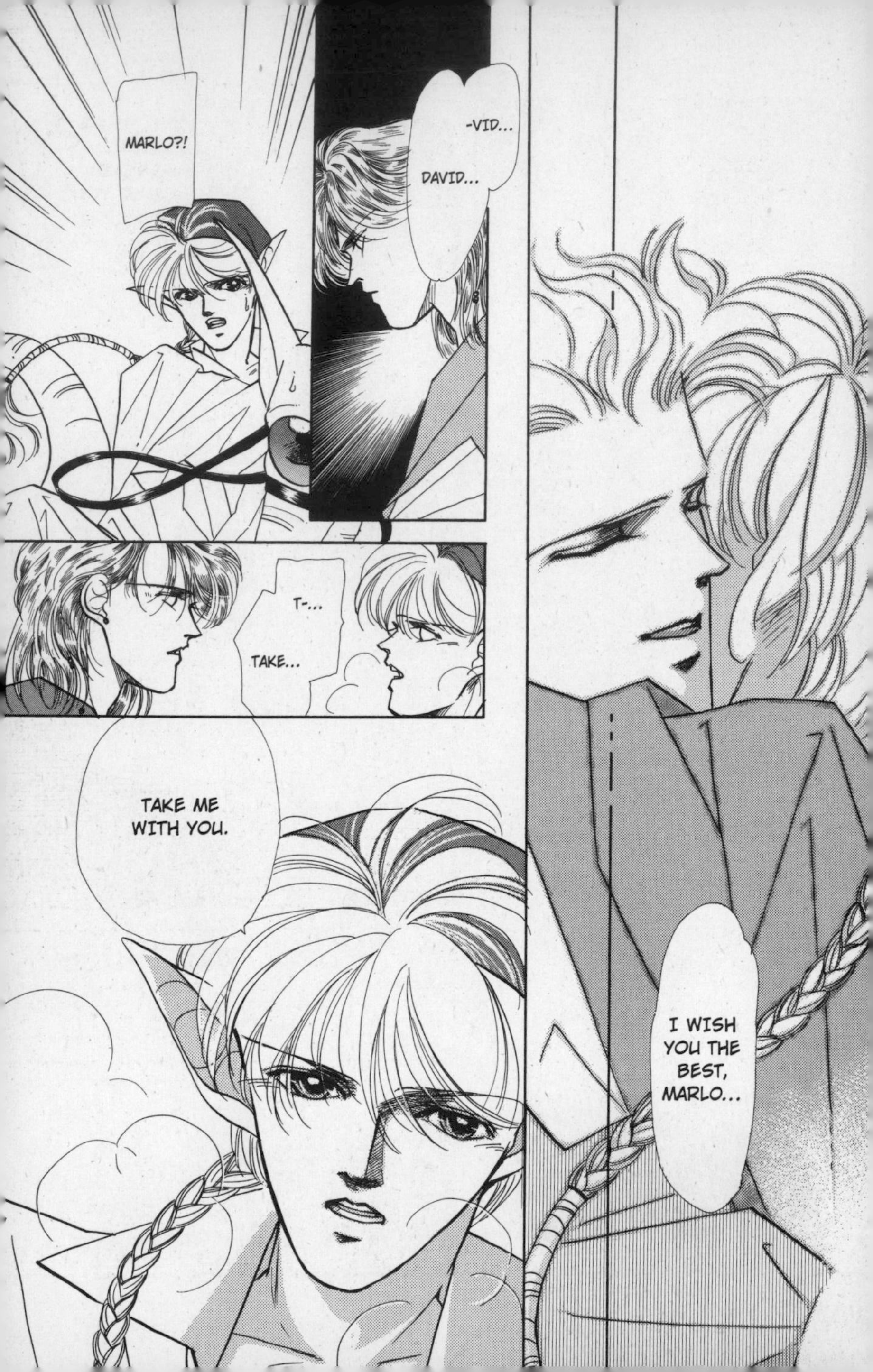
I WISH YOU THE BEST, MARLO...
-VID...
DAVID...
MARLO?!
T-...
TAKE...
TAKE ME WITH YOU.

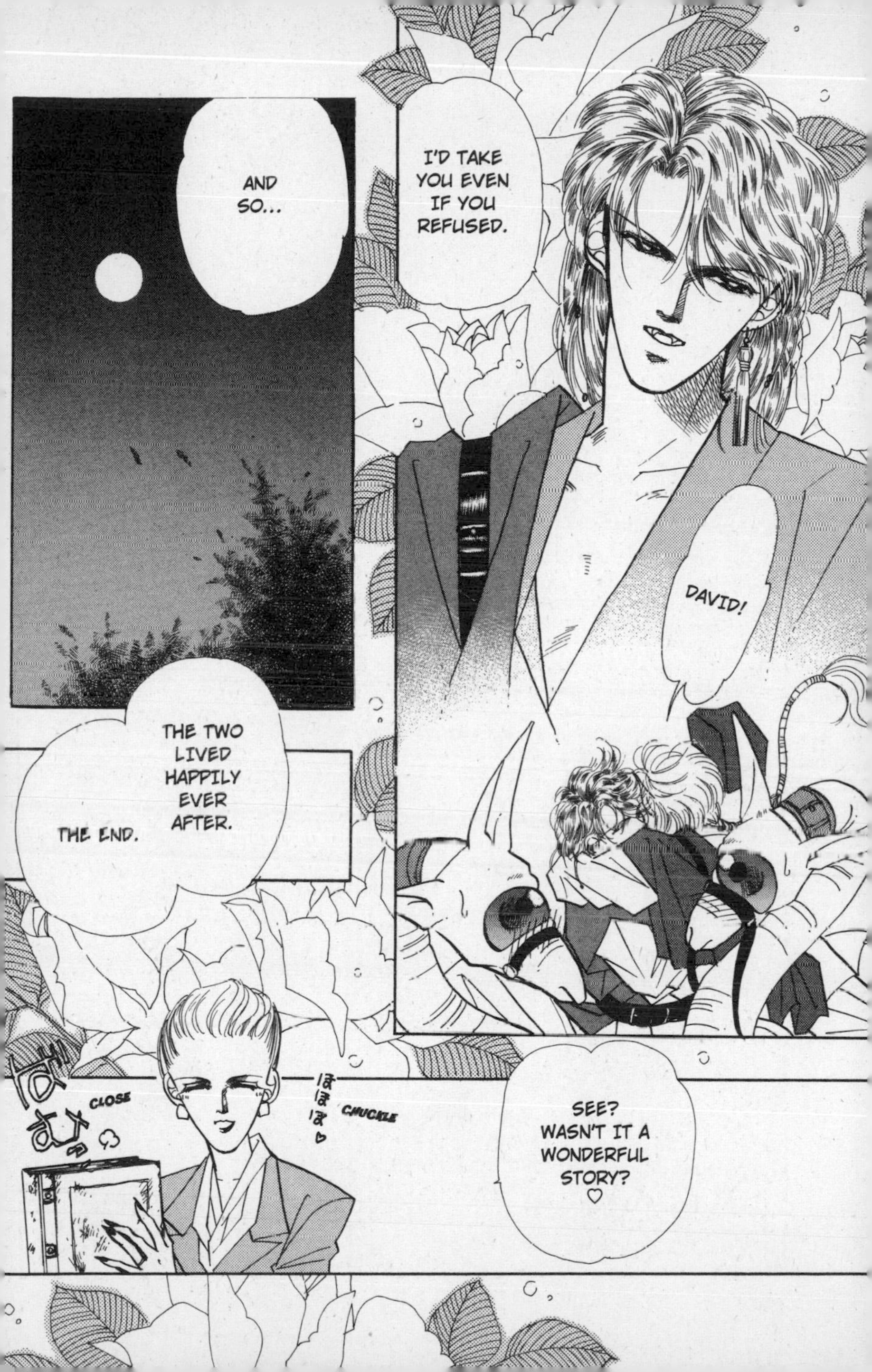
I'D TAKE YOU EVEN IF YOU REFUSED.
DAVID!
AND SO...
THE TWO LIVED HAPPILY EVER AFTER.
THE END.
SEE? WASN'T IT A WONDERFUL STORY? ♡
ほほほ♡
CHUCKLE
CLOSE

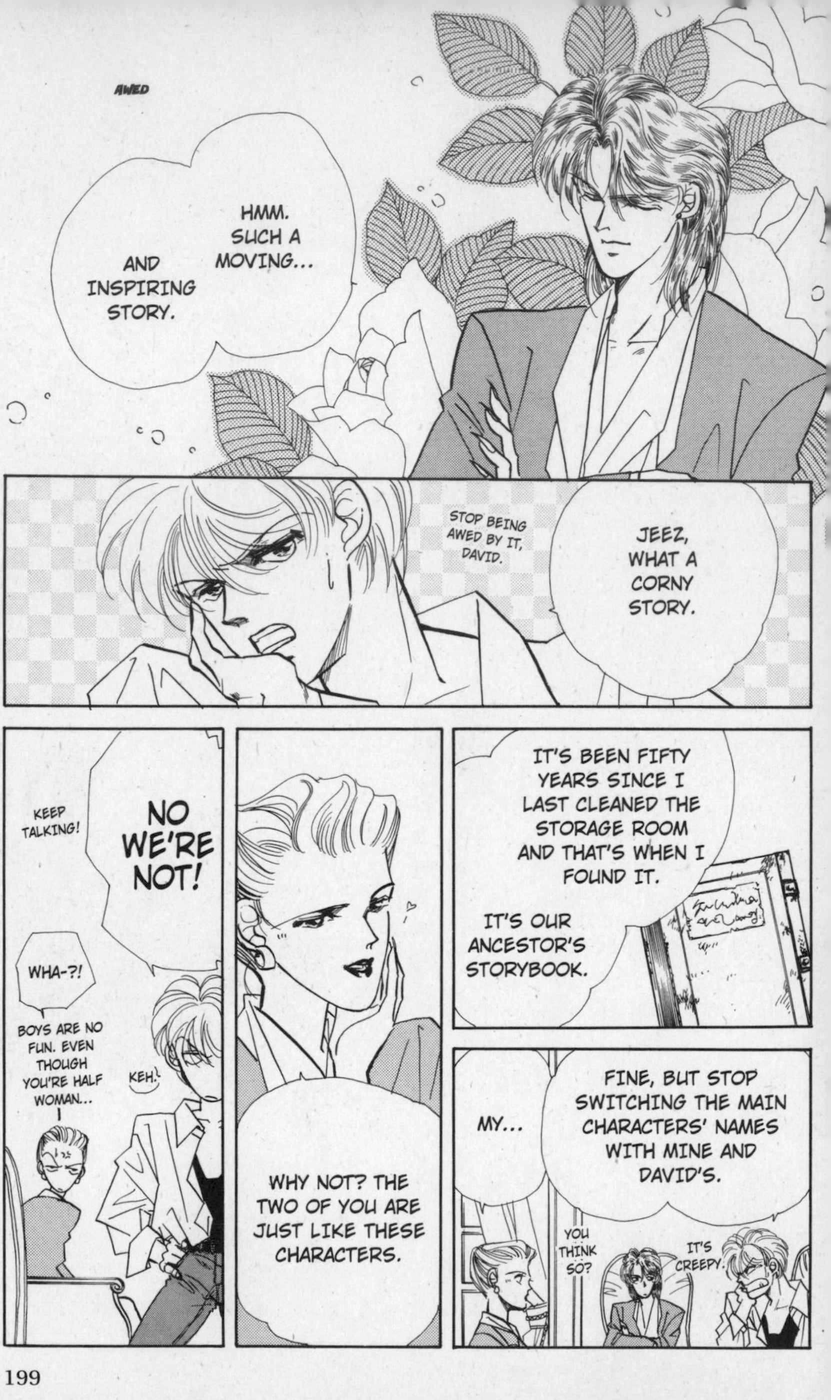
AWED
HMM. SUCH A MOVING... AND INSPIRING STORY.
JEEZ, WHAT A CORNY STORY.
STOP BEING AWED BY IT, DAVID.
IT'S BEEN FIFTY YEARS SINCE I LAST CLEANED THE STORAGE ROOM AND THAT'S WHEN I FOUND IT.
IT'S OUR ANCESTOR'S STORYBOOK.
FINE, BUT STOP SWITCHING THE MAIN CHARACTERS' NAMES WITH MINE AND DAVID'S.
MY...
IT'S CREEPY.
YOU THINK SO?
WHY NOT? THE TWO OF YOU ARE JUST LIKE THESE CHARACTERS.
NO WE'RE NOT!
KEEP TALKING!
WHA-?!
KEH.
BOYS ARE NO FUN. EVEN THOUGH YOU'RE HALF WOMAN...

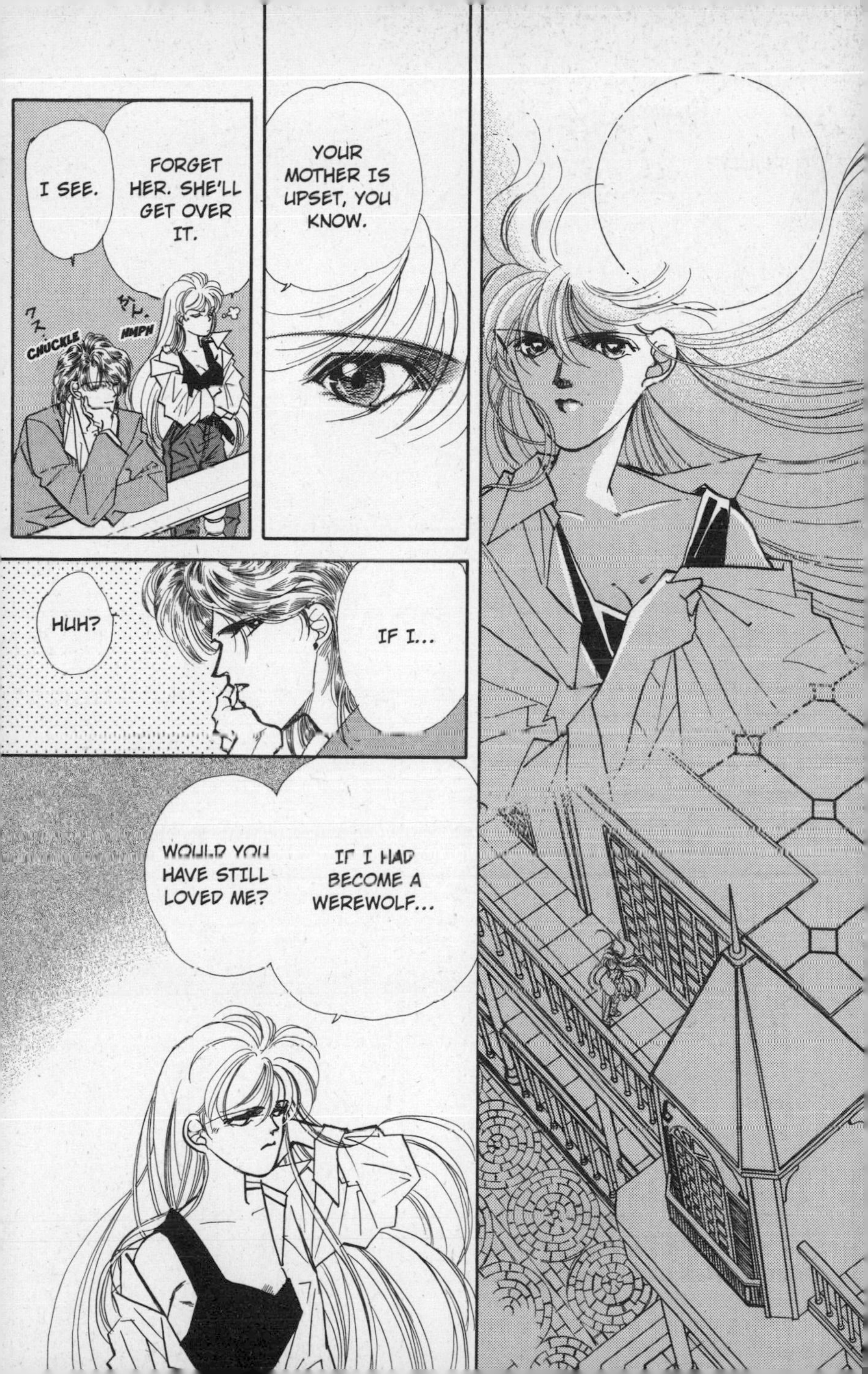
YOUR MOTHER IS UPSET, YOU KNOW.
FORGET HER. SHE'LL GET OVER IT.
I SEE.
HMPH
CHUCKLE
IF I...
HUH?
IF I HAD BECOME A WEREWOLF...
WOULD YOU HAVE STILL LOVED ME?

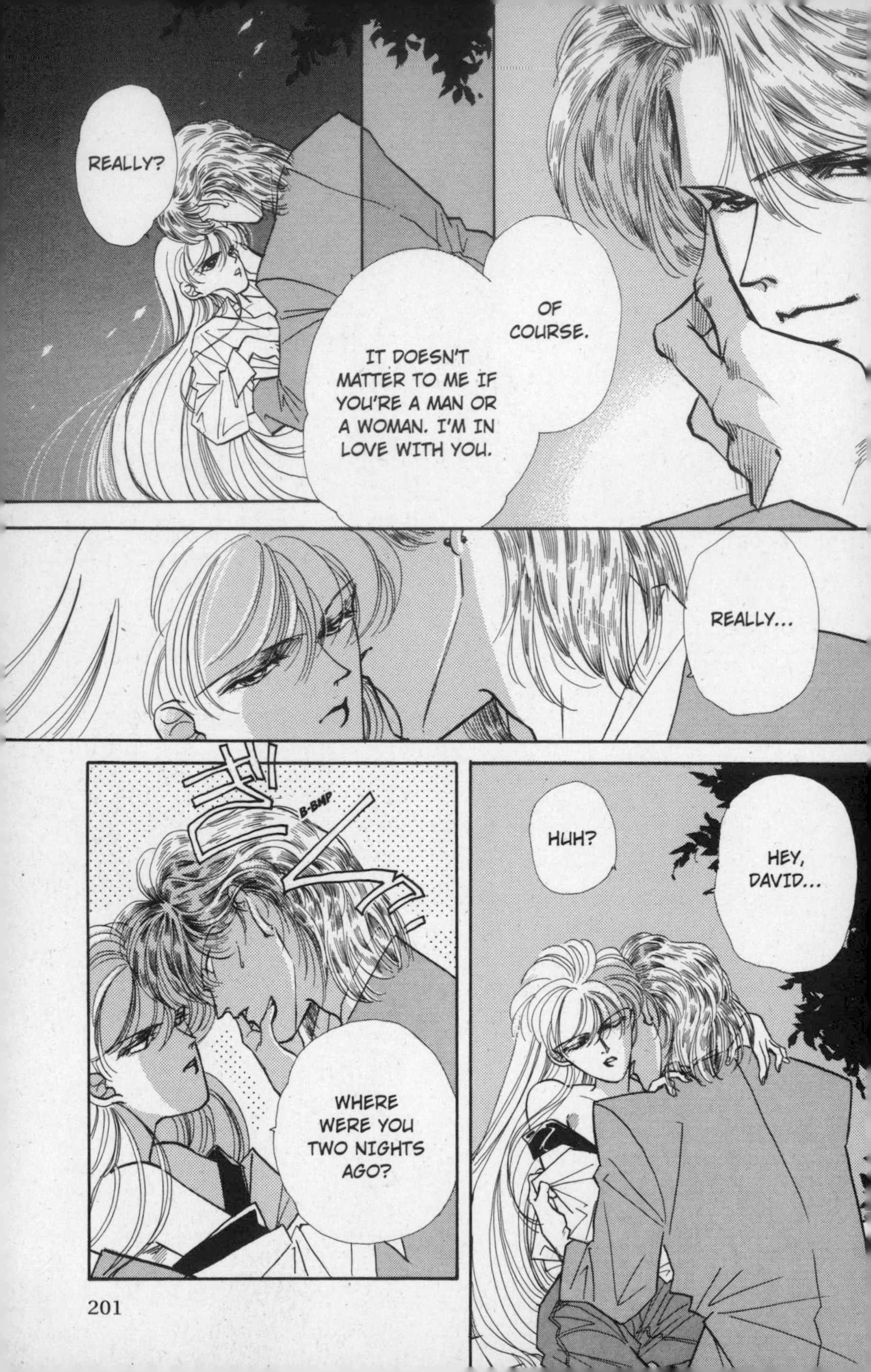
REALLY?
OF COURSE.
IT DOESN'T MATTER TO ME IF YOU'RE A MAN OR A WOMAN. I'M IN LOVE WITH YOU.
REALLY...
HEY, DAVID...
HUH?
B-BMP
WHERE WERE YOU TWO NIGHTS AGO?

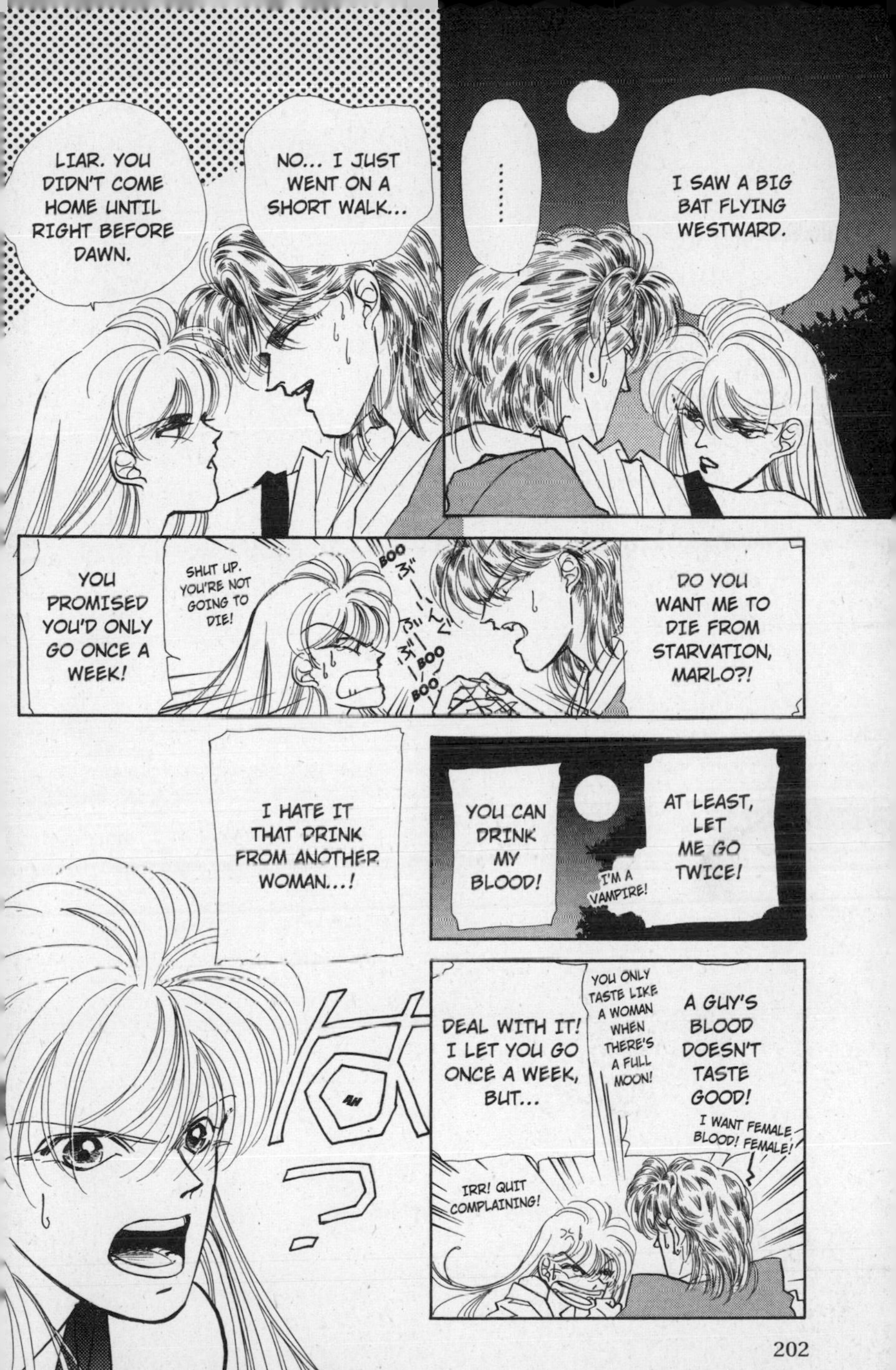
I SAW A BIG BAT FLYING WESTWARD.
......
NO... I JUST WENT ON A SHORT WALK...
LIAR. YOU DIDN'T COME HOME UNTIL RIGHT BEFORE DAWN.
DO YOU WANT ME TO DIE FROM STARVATION, MARLO?!
BOO BOO BOO
SHUT UP. YOU'RE NOT GOING TO DIE!
YOU PROMISED YOU'D ONLY GO ONCE A WEEK!
AT LEAST, LET ME GO TWICE!
I'M A VAMPIRE!
YOU CAN DRINK MY BLOOD!
A GUY'S BLOOD DOESN'T TASTE GOOD!
I WANT FEMALE BLOOD! FEMALE!
YOU ONLY TASTE LIKE A WOMAN WHEN THERE'S A FULL MOON!
DEAL WITH IT! I LET YOU GO ONCE A WEEK, BUT...
IRR! QUIT COMPLAINING!
I HATE IT THAT DRINK FROM ANOTHER WOMAN...!
AH

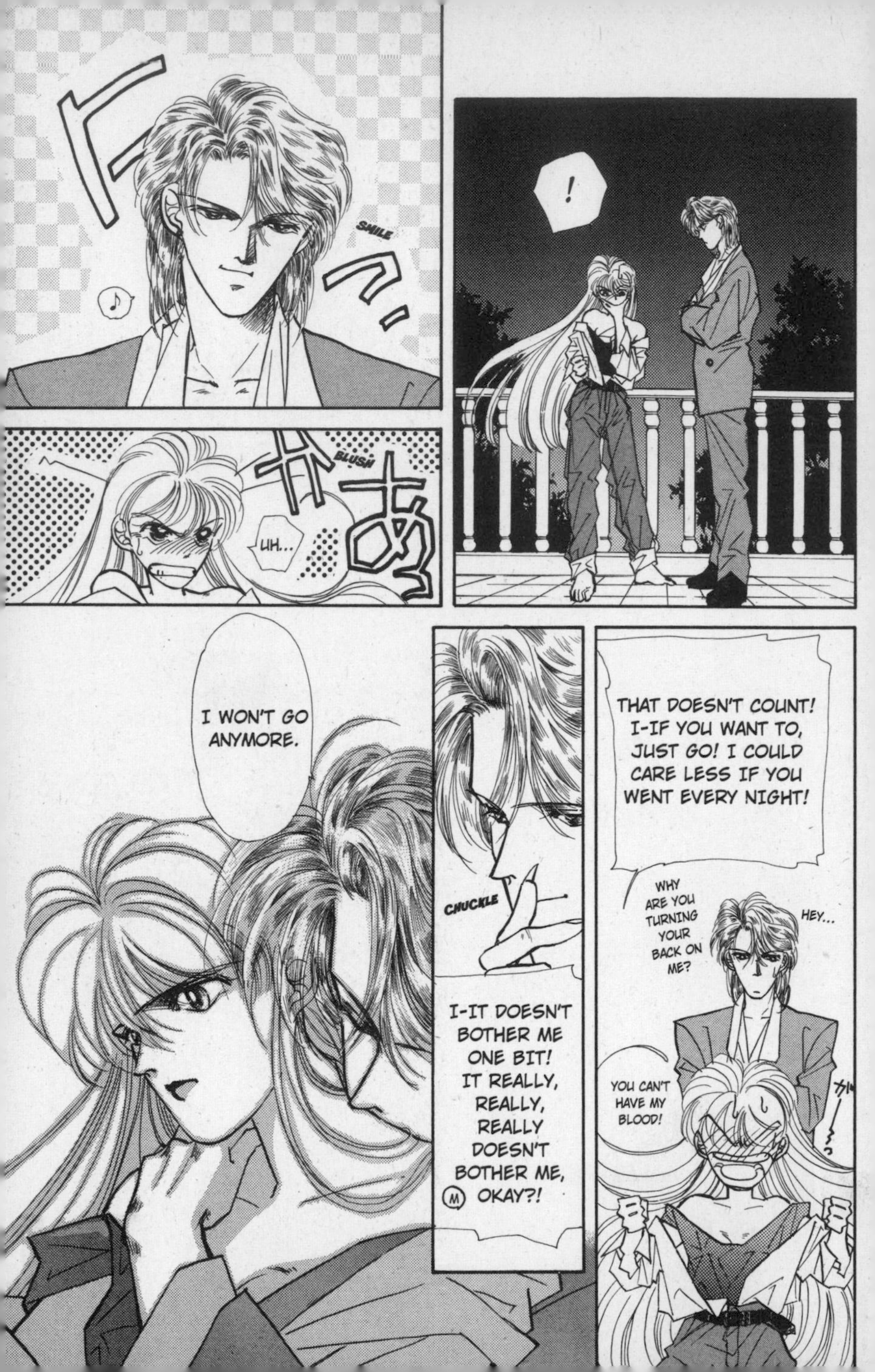
!
SMILE
♪
BLUSH
UH...
THAT DOESN'T COUNT! I-IF YOU WANT TO, JUST GO! I COULD CARE LESS IF YOU WENT EVERY NIGHT!
HEY...
WHY ARE YOU TURNING YOUR BACK ON ME?
YOU CAN'T HAVE MY BLOOD!
CHUCKLE
I-IT DOESN'T BOTHER ME ONE BIT! IT REALLY, REALLY, REALLY DOESN'T BOTHER ME, OKAY?!
I WON'T GO ANYMORE.

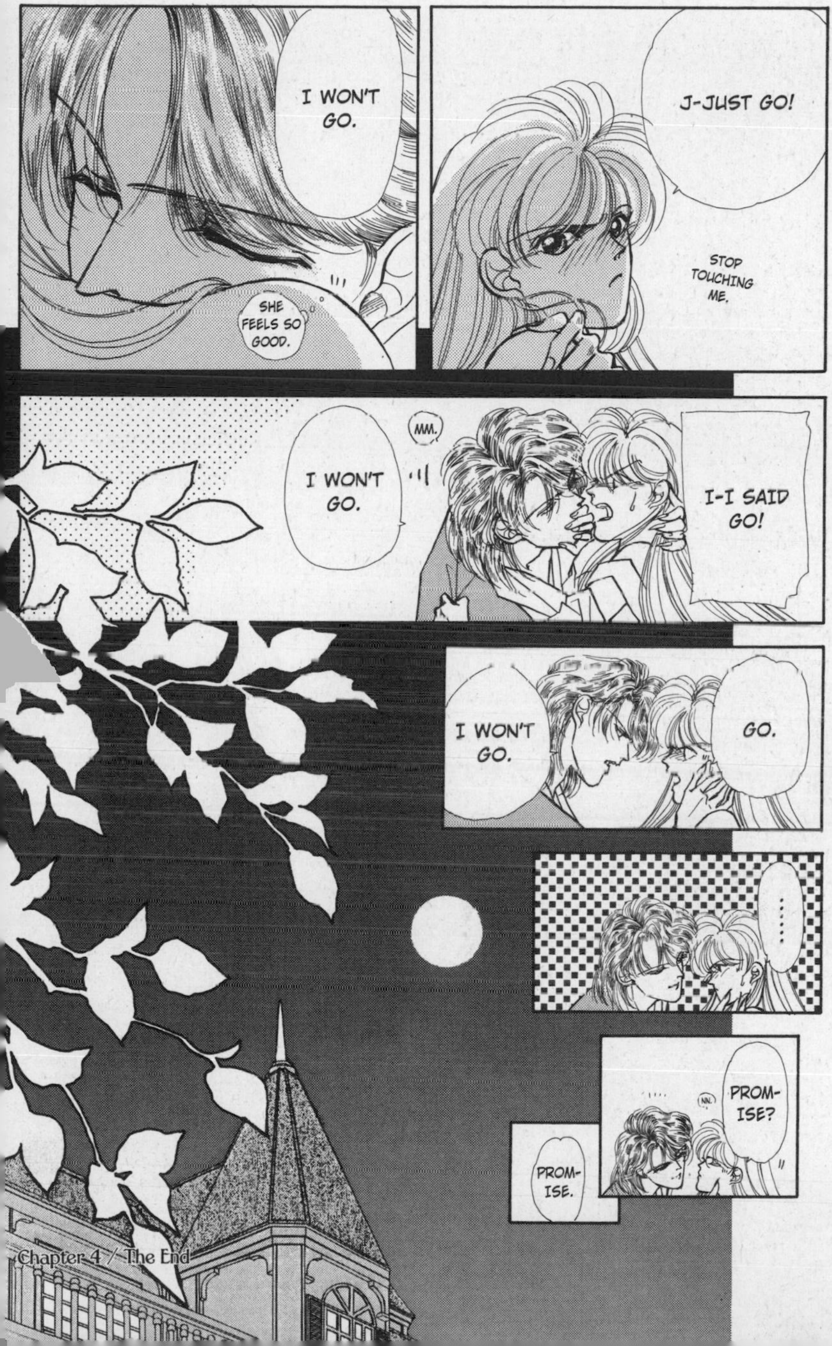
J-JUST GO!
STOP TOUCHING ME.
I WON'T GO.
SHE FEELS SO GOOD.
I-I SAID GO!
MM.
I WON'T GO.
GO.
I WON'T GO.
......
PROMISE?
NN.
PROMISE.
Chapter 4 / The End

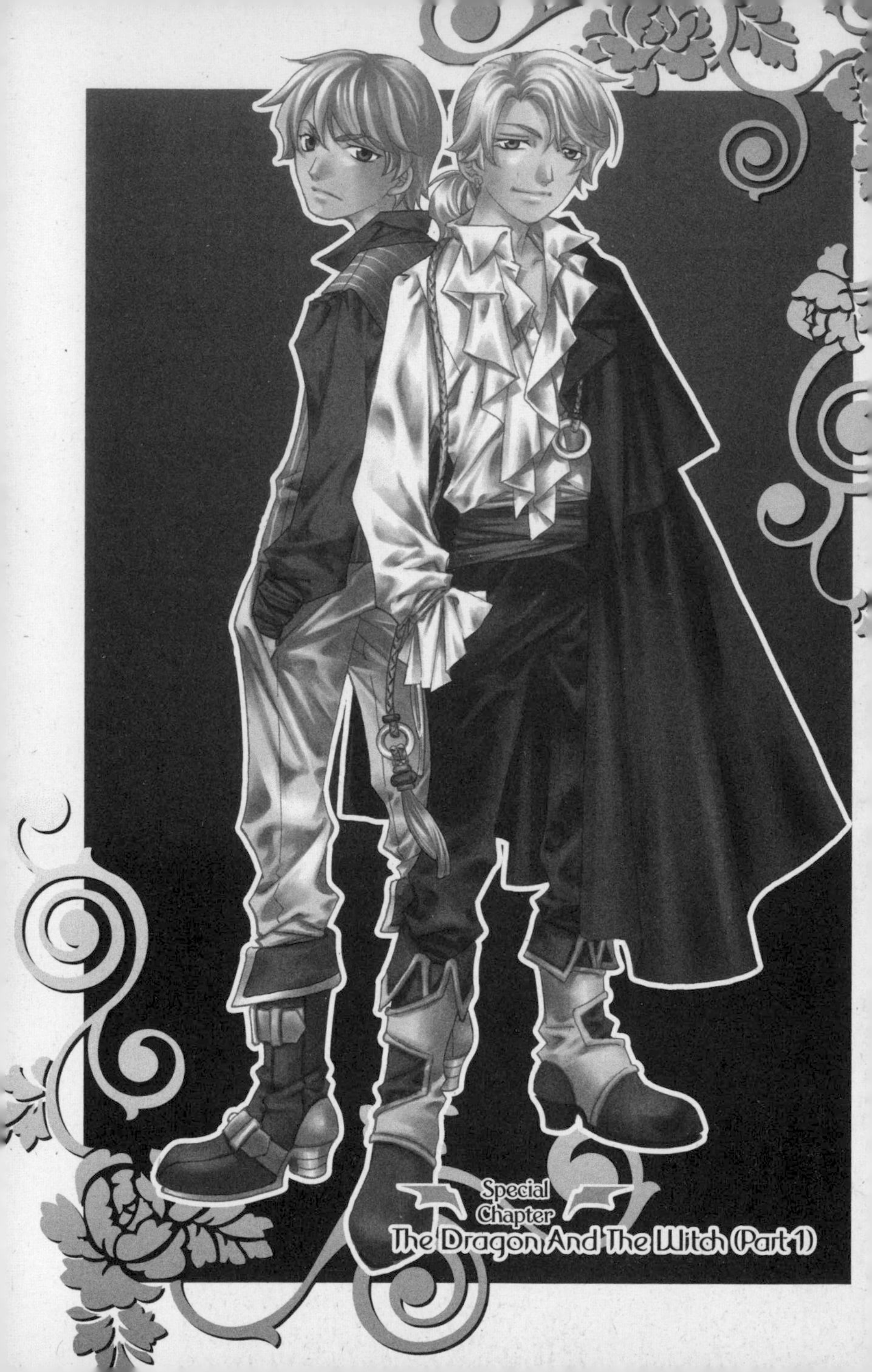
Special Chapter
The Dragon And The Witch (Part 1)

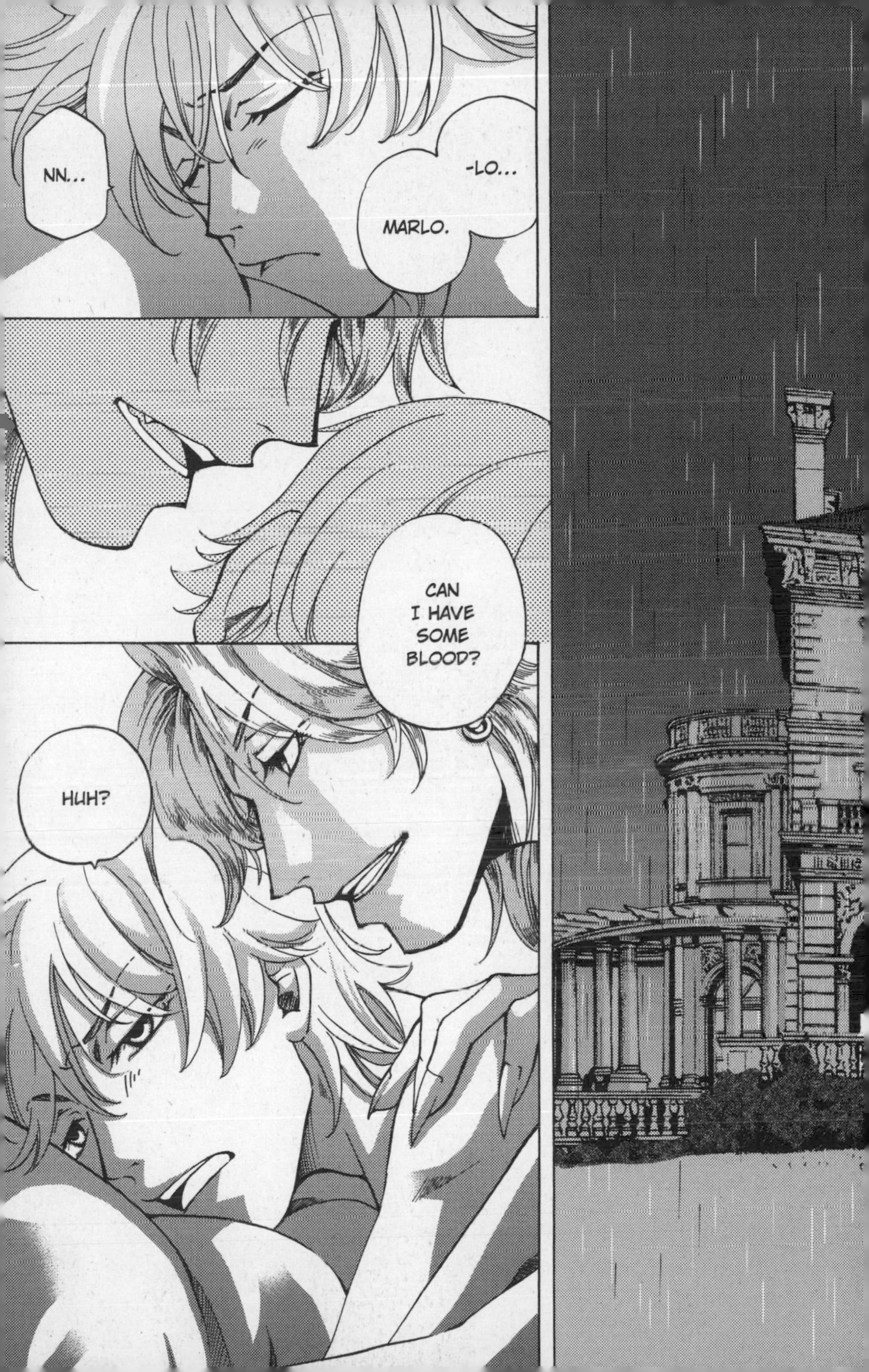
-LO...
MARLO.
NN...
CAN I HAVE SOME BLOOD?
HUH?

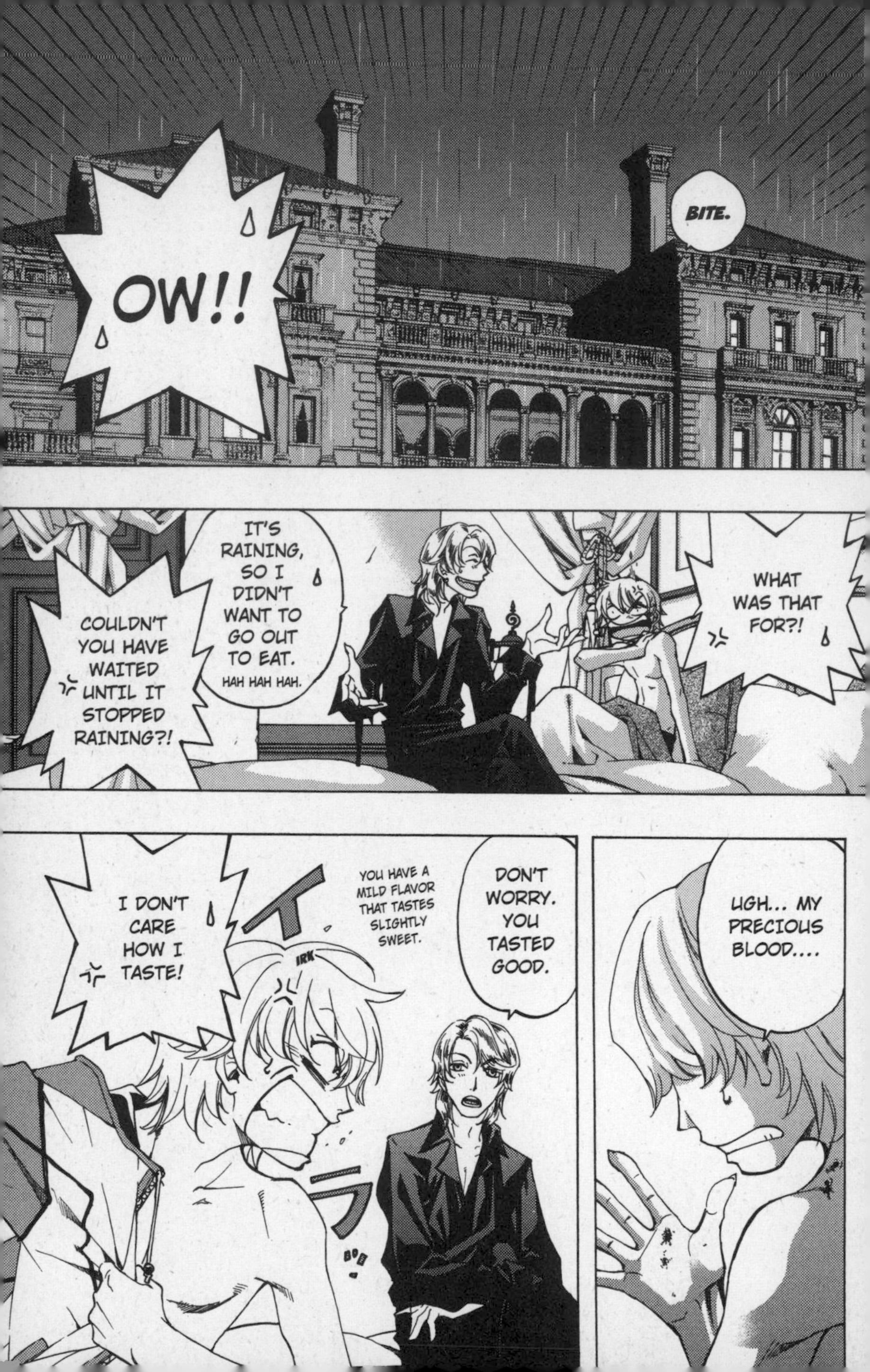
BITE.
OW!!
WHAT WAS THAT FOR?!
IT'S RAINING, SO I DIDN'T WANT TO GO OUT TO EAT. HAH HAH HAH.
COULDN'T YOU HAVE WAITED UNTIL IT STOPPED RAINING?!
UGH... MY PRECIOUS BLOOD....
DON'T WORRY. YOU TASTED GOOD.
YOU HAVE A MILD FLAVOR THAT TASTES SLIGHTLY SWEET.
IRK
I DON'T CARE HOW I TASTE!

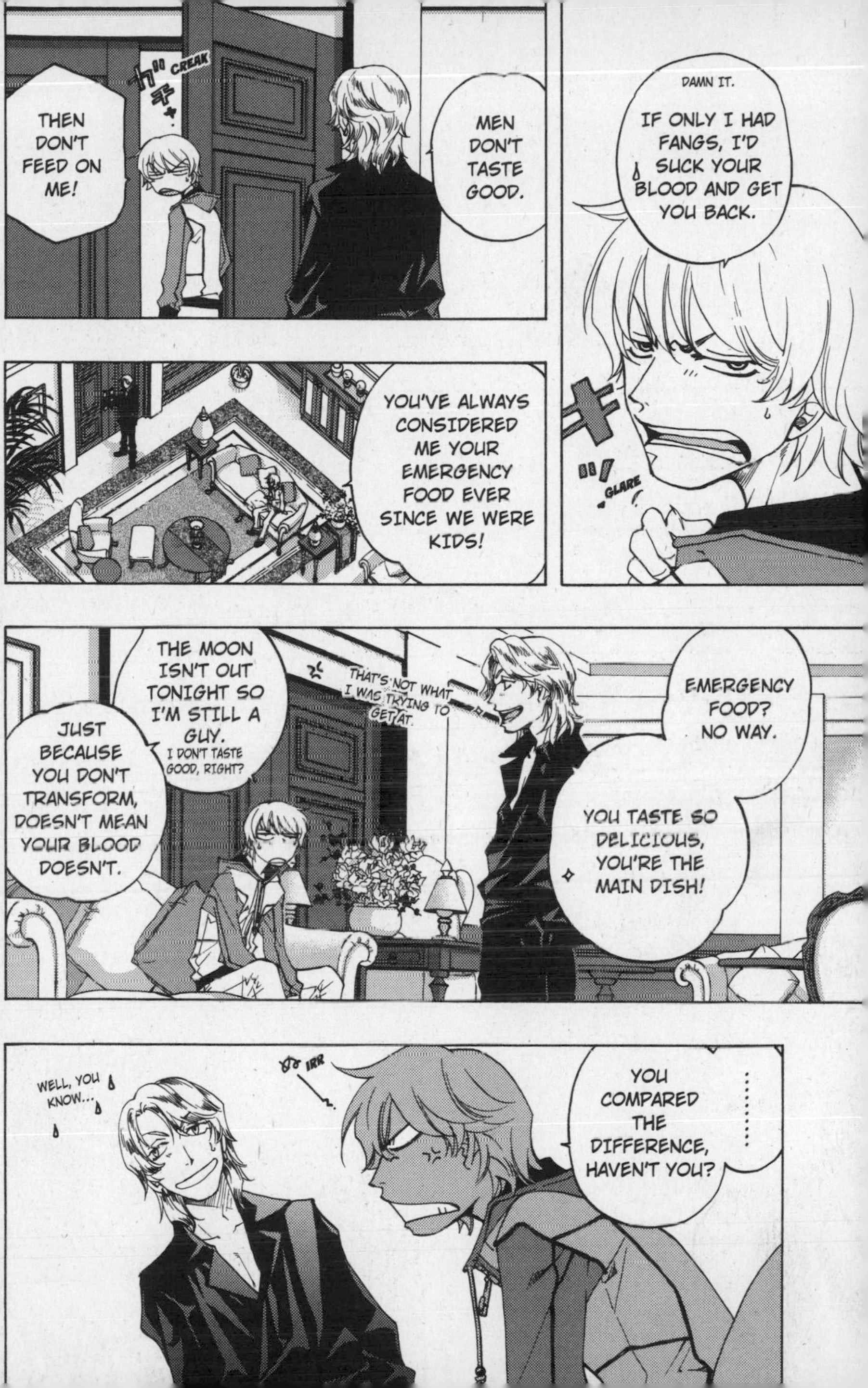
DAMN IT.
IF ONLY I HAD FANGS, I'D SUCK YOUR BLOOD AND GET YOU BACK.
GLARE
MEN DON'T TASTE GOOD.
CREAK
THEN DON'T FEED ON ME!
YOU'VE ALWAYS CONSIDERED ME YOUR EMERGENCY FOOD EVER SINCE WE WERE KIDS!
EMERGENCY FOOD? NO WAY.
YOU TASTE SO DELICIOUS, YOU'RE THE MAIN DISH!
THAT'S NOT WHAT I WAS TRYING TO GET AT.
THE MOON ISN'T OUT TONIGHT SO I'M STILL A GUY.
I DON'T TASTE GOOD, RIGHT?
JUST BECAUSE YOU DON'T TRANSFORM, DOESN'T MEAN YOUR BLOOD DOESN'T.
......
YOU COMPARED THE DIFFERENCE, HAVEN'T YOU?
IRR
WELL, YOU KNOW...

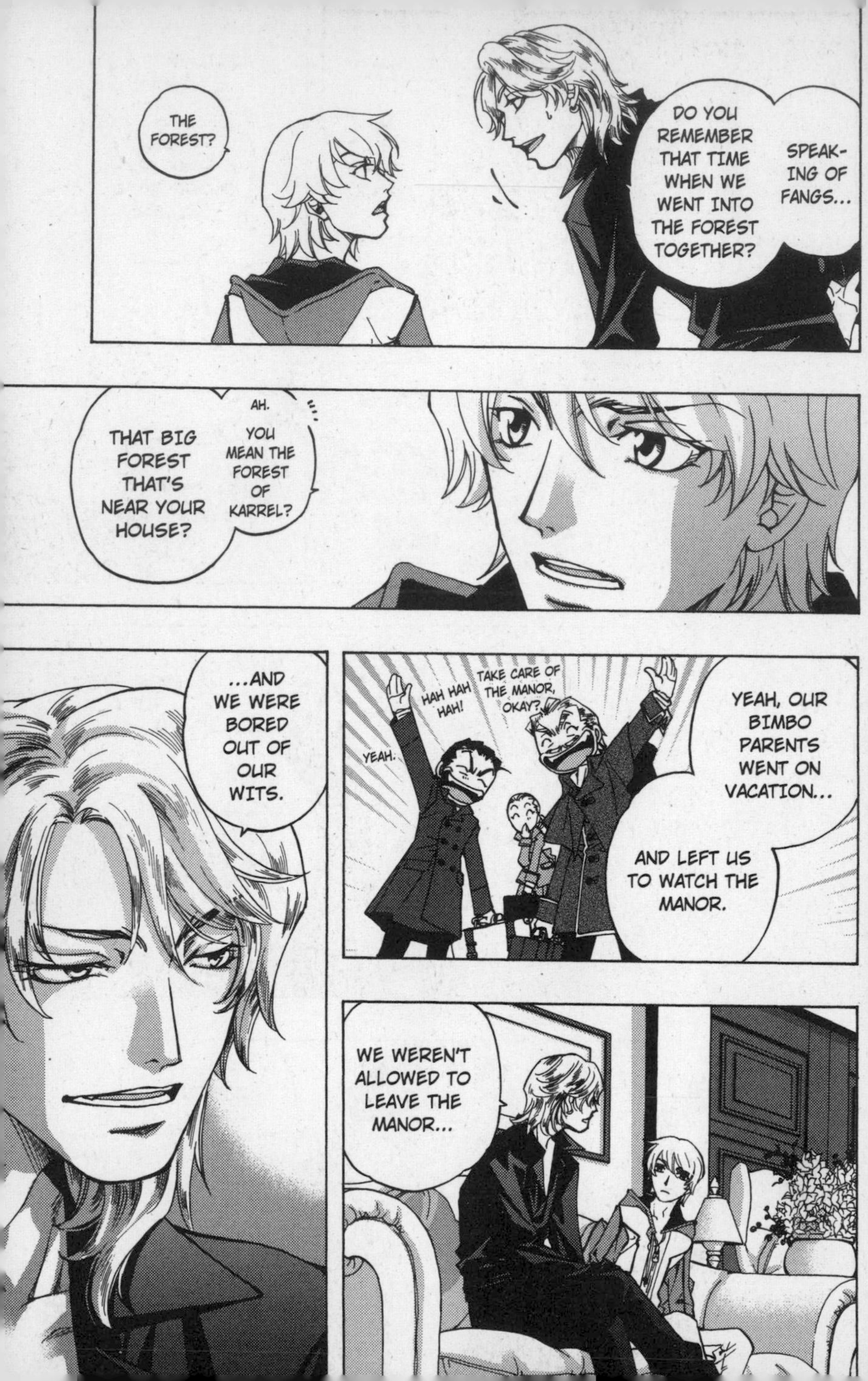
SPEAK-ING OF FANGS...
DO YOU REMEMBER THAT TIME WHEN WE WENT INTO THE FOREST TOGETHER?
THE FOREST?
AH.
YOU MEAN THE FOREST OF KARREL?
THAT BIG FOREST THAT'S NEAR YOUR HOUSE?
YEAH, OUR BIMBO PARENTS WENT ON VACATION...
AND LEFT US TO WATCH THE MANOR.
TAKE CARE OF THE MANOR, OKAY?
HAH HAH HAH!
YEAH.
WE WEREN'T ALLOWED TO LEAVE THE MANOR...
...AND WE WERE BORED OUT OF OUR WITS.

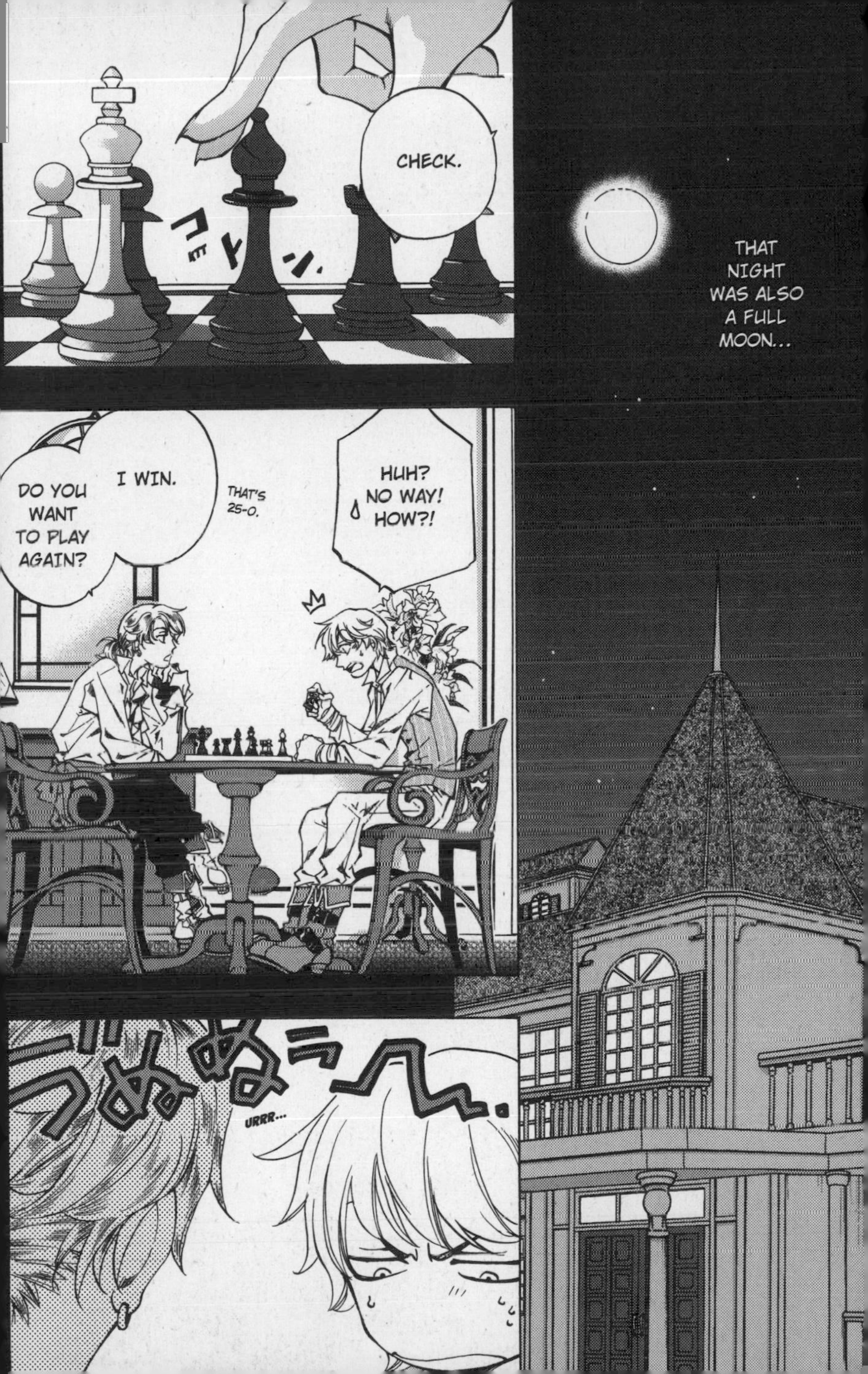
THAT NIGHT WAS ALSO A FULL MOON...
CHECK.
コトッ
KTT
HUH? NO WAY! HOW?!
THAT'S 25-0.
I WIN.
DO YOU WANT TO PLAY AGAIN?
URRR...

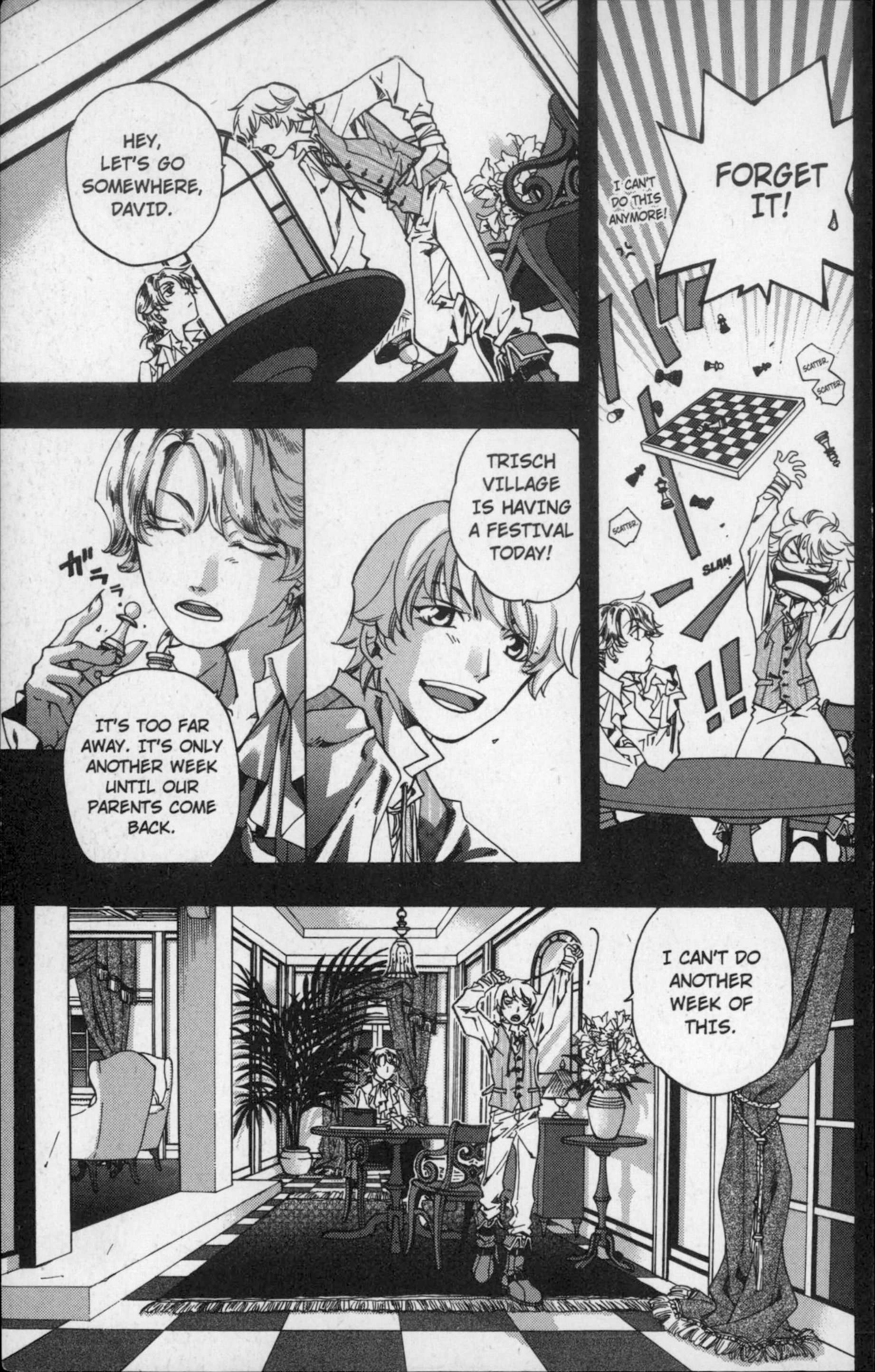
FORGET IT!
I CAN'T DO THIS ANYMORE!
SCATTER, SCATTER
SCATTER
SLAM
!!
HEY, LET'S GO SOMEWHERE, DAVID.
TRISCH VILLAGE IS HAVING A FESTIVAL TODAY!
ガララ
IT'S TOO FAR AWAY. IT'S ONLY ANOTHER WEEK UNTIL OUR PARENTS COME BACK.
I CAN'T DO ANOTHER WEEK OF THIS.

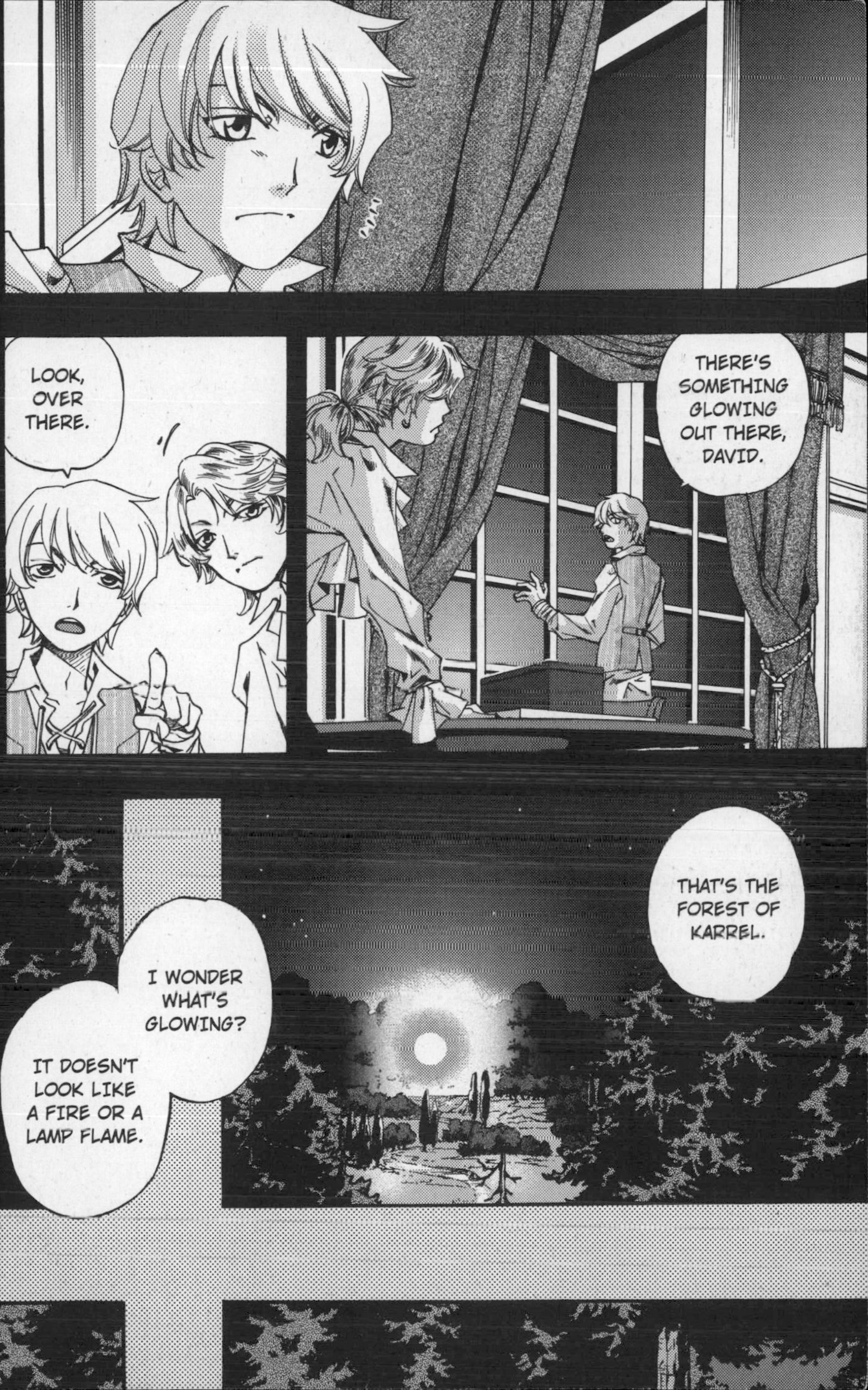
THERE'S SOMETHING GLOWING OUT THERE, DAVID.
LOOK, OVER THERE.
THAT'S THE FOREST OF KARREL.
I WONDER WHAT'S GLOWING?
IT DOESN'T LOOK LIKE A FIRE OR A LAMP FLAME.

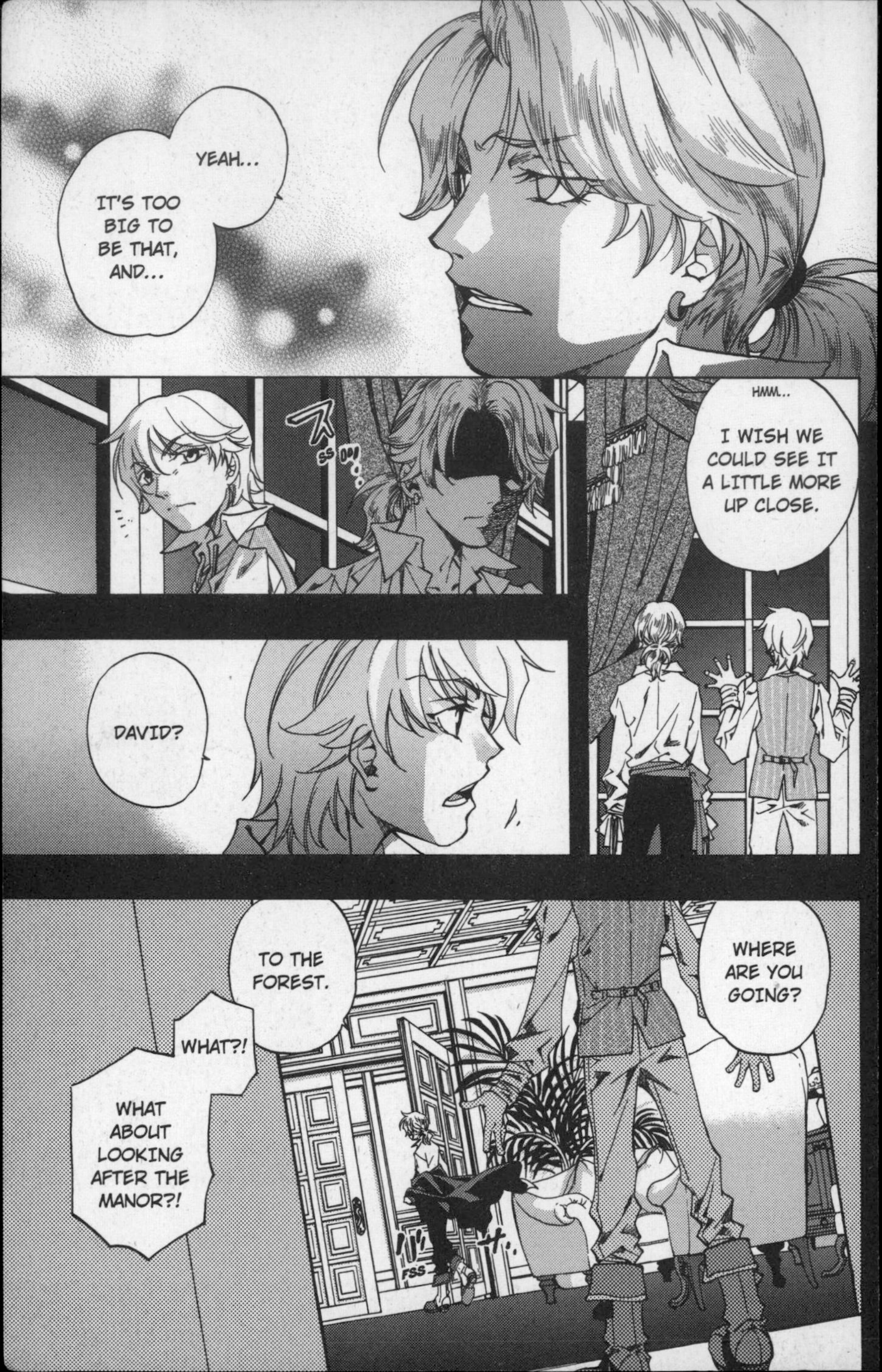
YEAH...
IT'S TOO BIG TO BE THAT, AND...
HMM..
I WISH WE COULD SEE IT A LITTLE MORE UP CLOSE.
DAVID?
WHERE ARE YOU GOING?
TO THE FOREST.
WHAT?!
WHAT ABOUT LOOKING AFTER THE MANOR?!
FSS

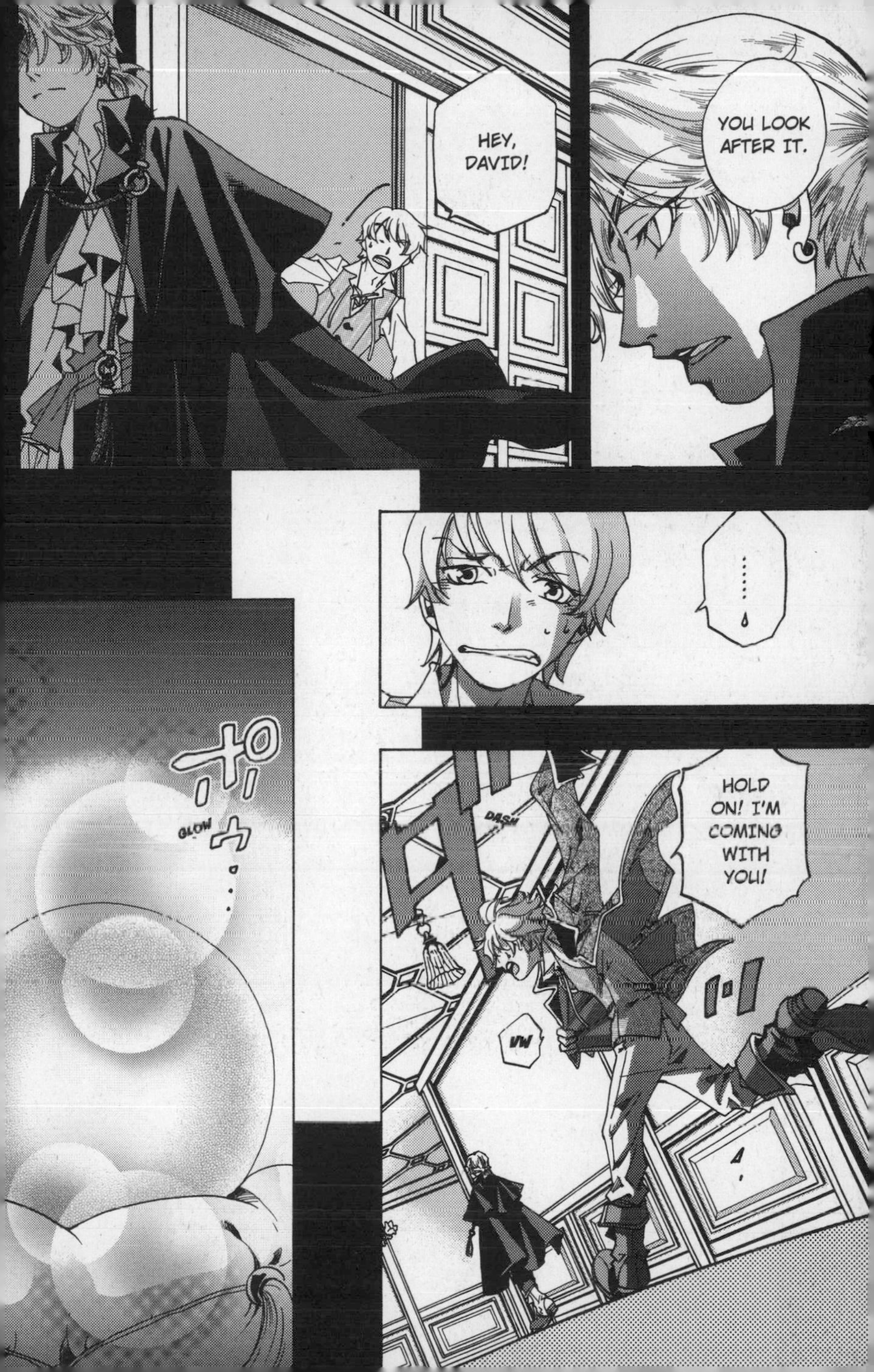
YOU LOOK AFTER IT.
HEY, DAVID!
......
HOLD ON! I'M COMING WITH YOU!
DASH
VW
GLOW

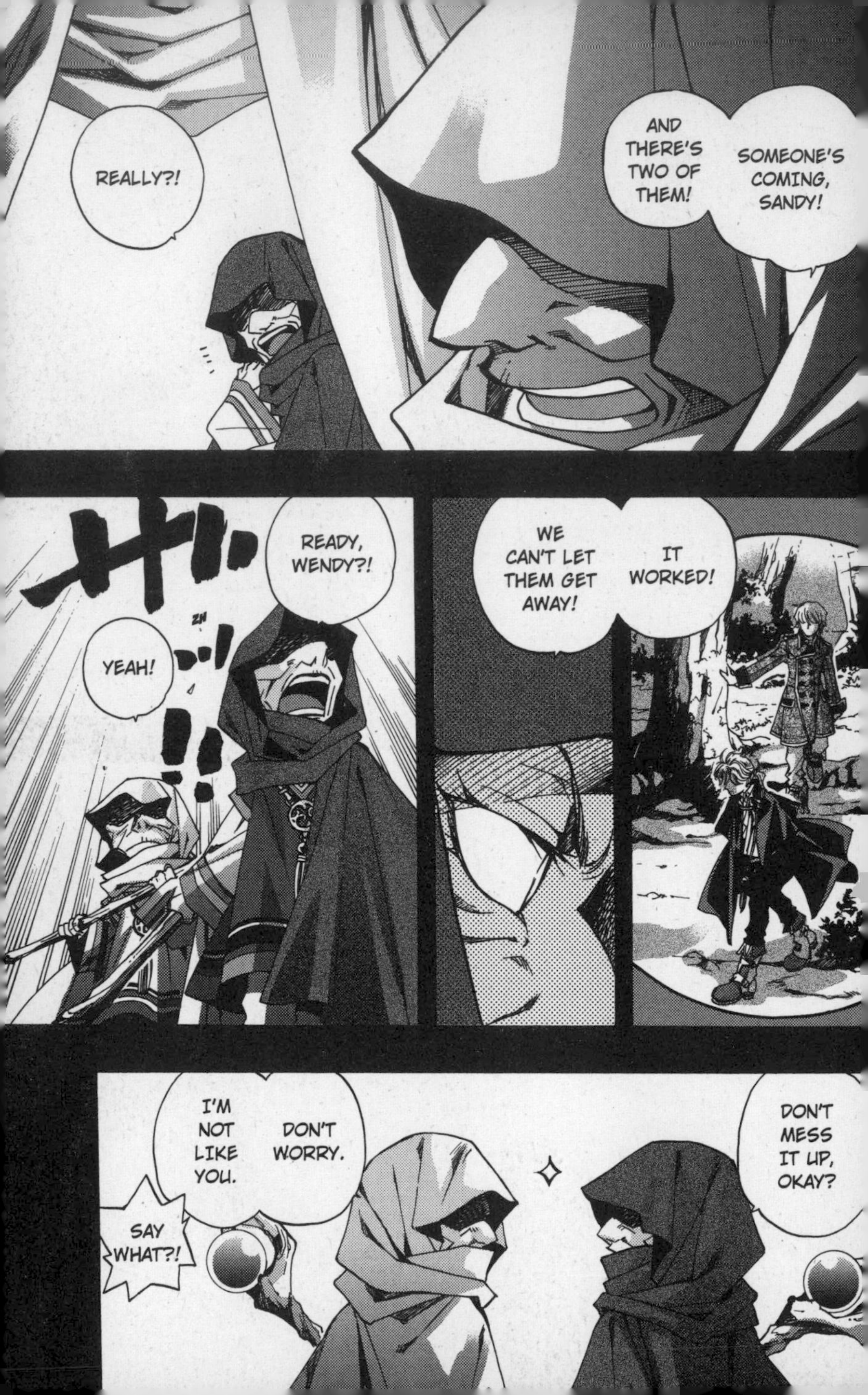
SOMEONE'S COMING, SANDY!
AND THERE'S TWO OF THEM!
REALLY?!
IT WORKED!
WE CAN'T LET THEM GET AWAY!
READY, WENDY?!
YEAH!
DON'T MESS IT UP, OKAY?
DON'T WORRY.
I'M NOT LIKE YOU.
SAY WHAT?!

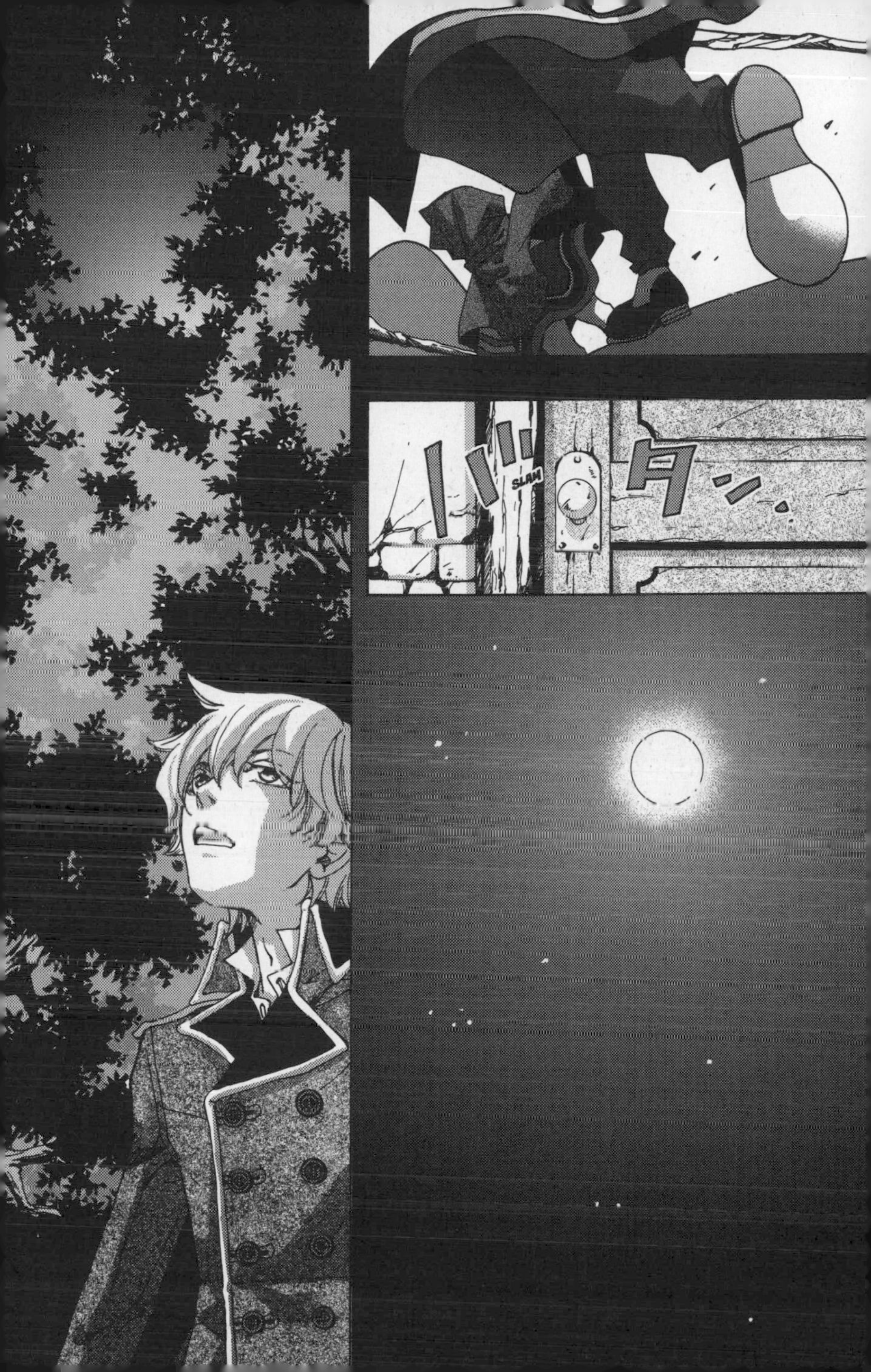
SLAM

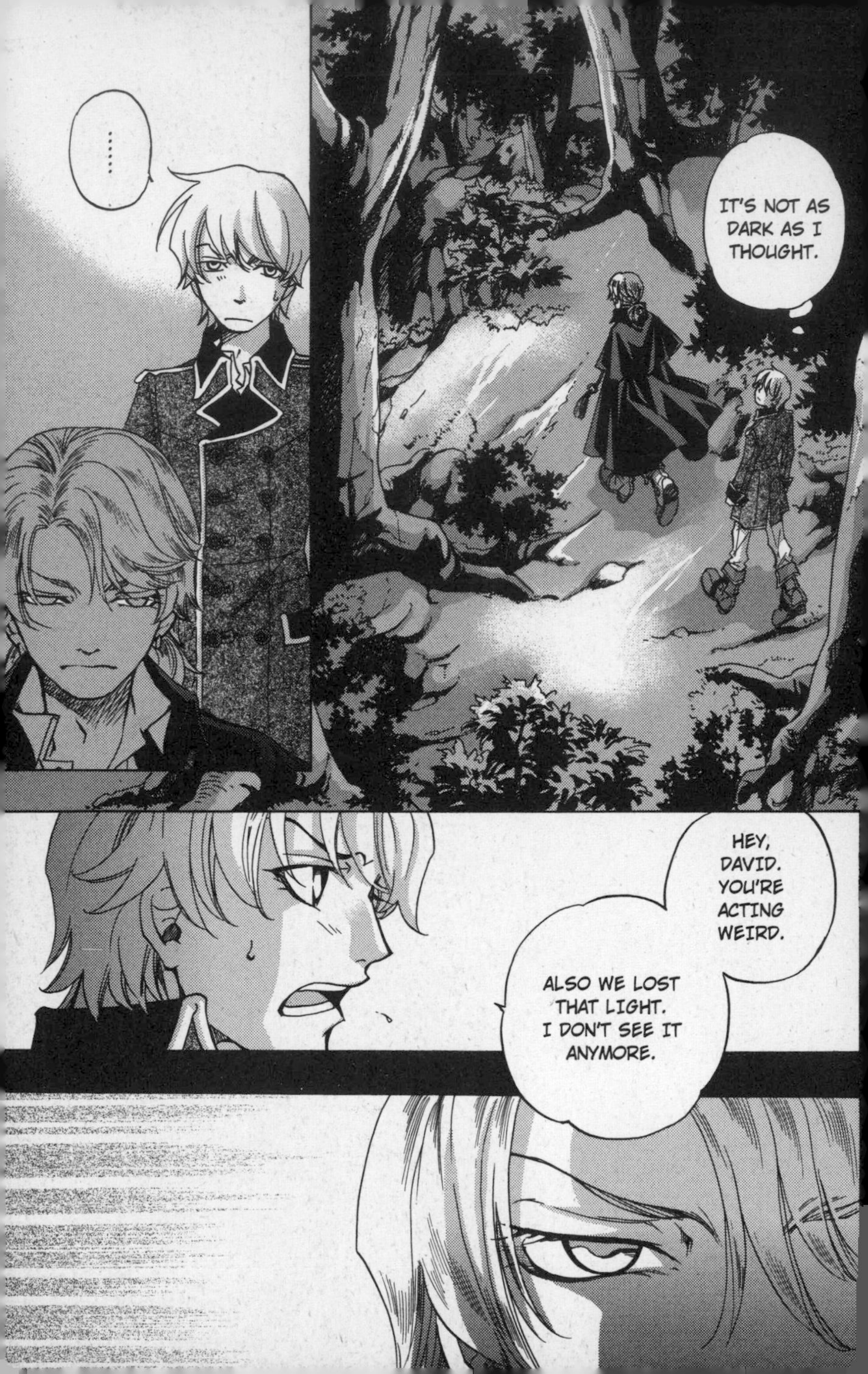
IT'S NOT AS DARK AS I THOUGHT.
......
HEY, DAVID. YOU'RE ACTING WEIRD.
ALSO WE LOST THAT LIGHT. I DON'T SEE IT ANYMORE.

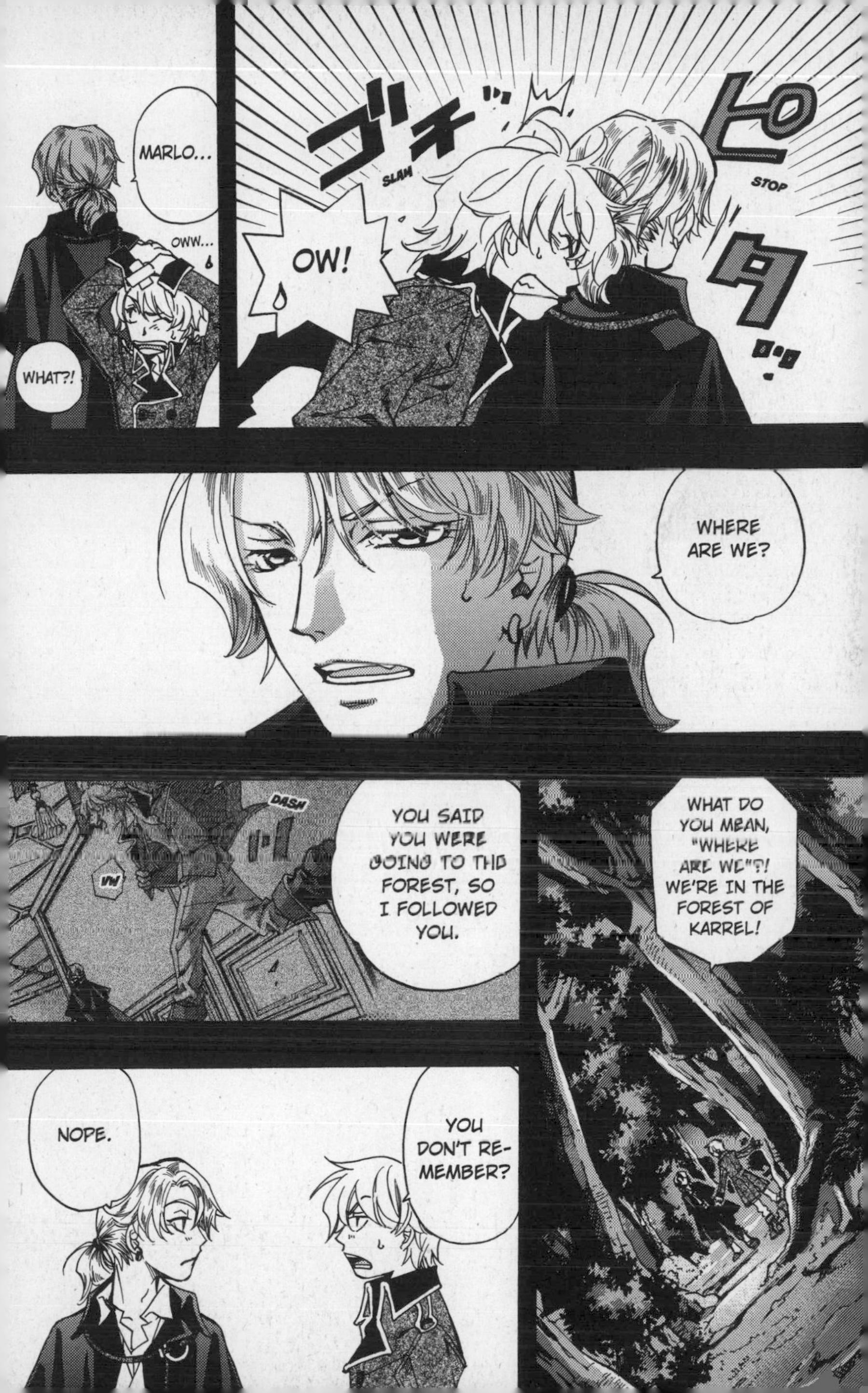
STOP
SLAM
OW!
MARLO...
OWW...
WHAT?!
WHERE ARE WE?
WHAT DO YOU MEAN, "WHERE ARE WE"?! WE'RE IN THE FOREST OF KARREL!
DASH
YOU SAID YOU WERE GOING TO THE FOREST, SO I FOLLOWED YOU.
VW
YOU DON'T RE-MEMBER?
NOPE.

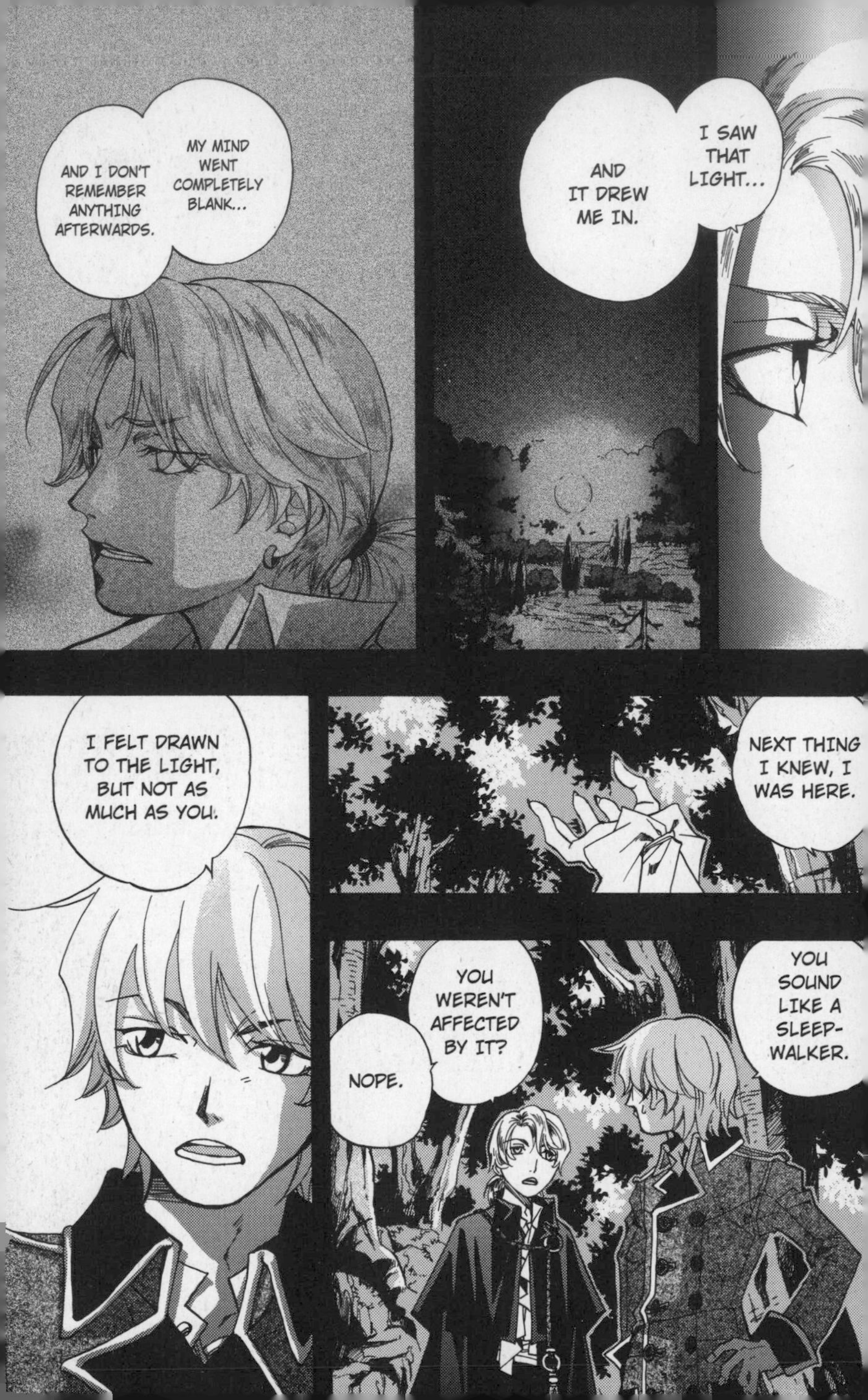
I SAW THAT LIGHT...
AND IT DREW ME IN.
MY MIND WENT COMPLETELY BLANK...
AND I DON'T REMEMBER ANYTHING AFTERWARDS.
NEXT THING I KNEW, I WAS HERE.
YOU SOUND LIKE A SLEEP-WALKER.
YOU WEREN'T AFFECTED BY IT?
NOPE.
I FELT DRAWN TO THE LIGHT, BUT NOT AS MUCH AS YOU.

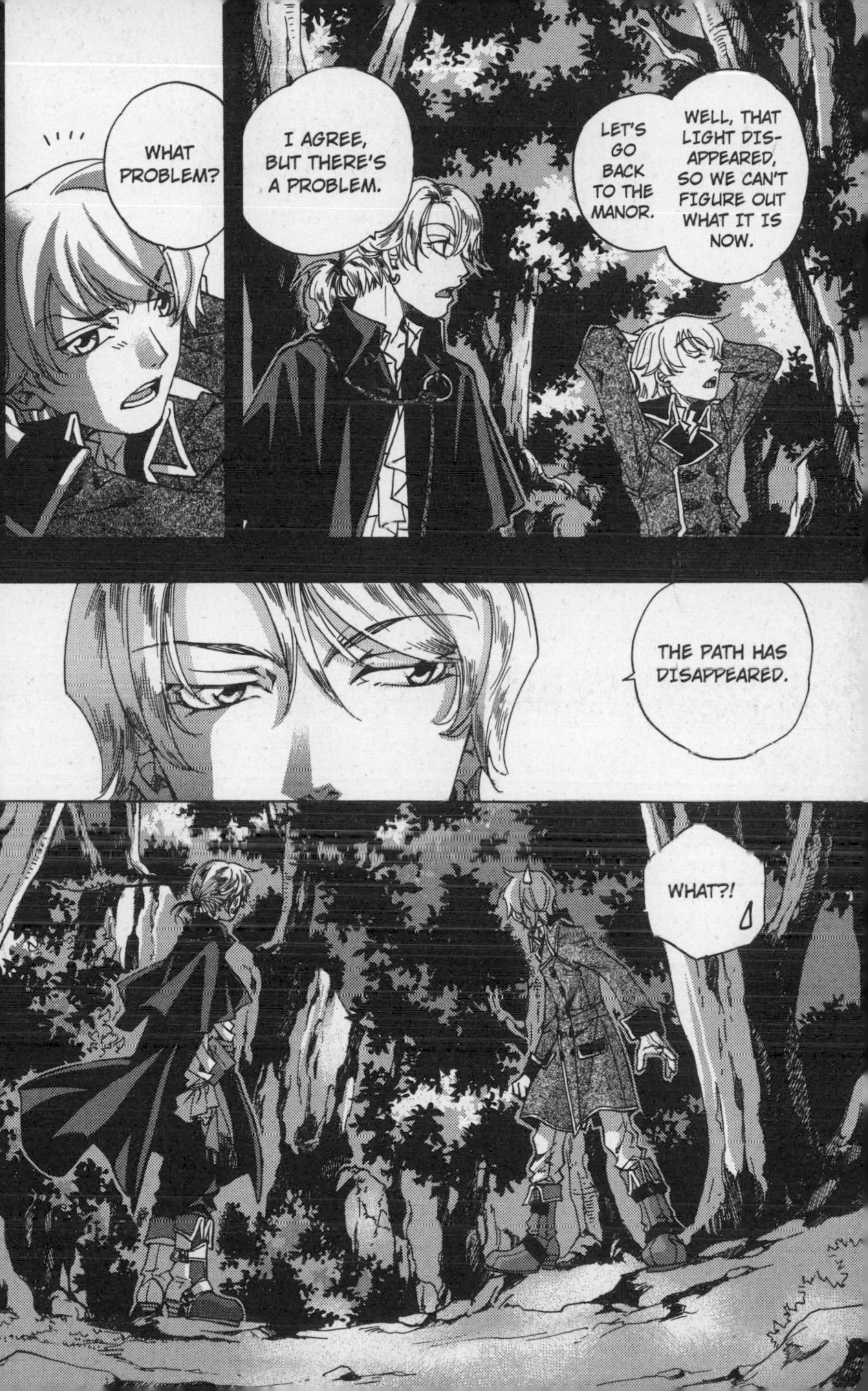
WELL, THAT LIGHT DIS-APPEARED, SO WE CAN'T FIGURE OUT WHAT IT IS NOW.
LET'S GO BACK TO THE MANOR.
I AGREE, BUT THERE'S A PROBLEM.
WHAT PROBLEM?
THE PATH HAS DISAPPEARED.
WHAT?!

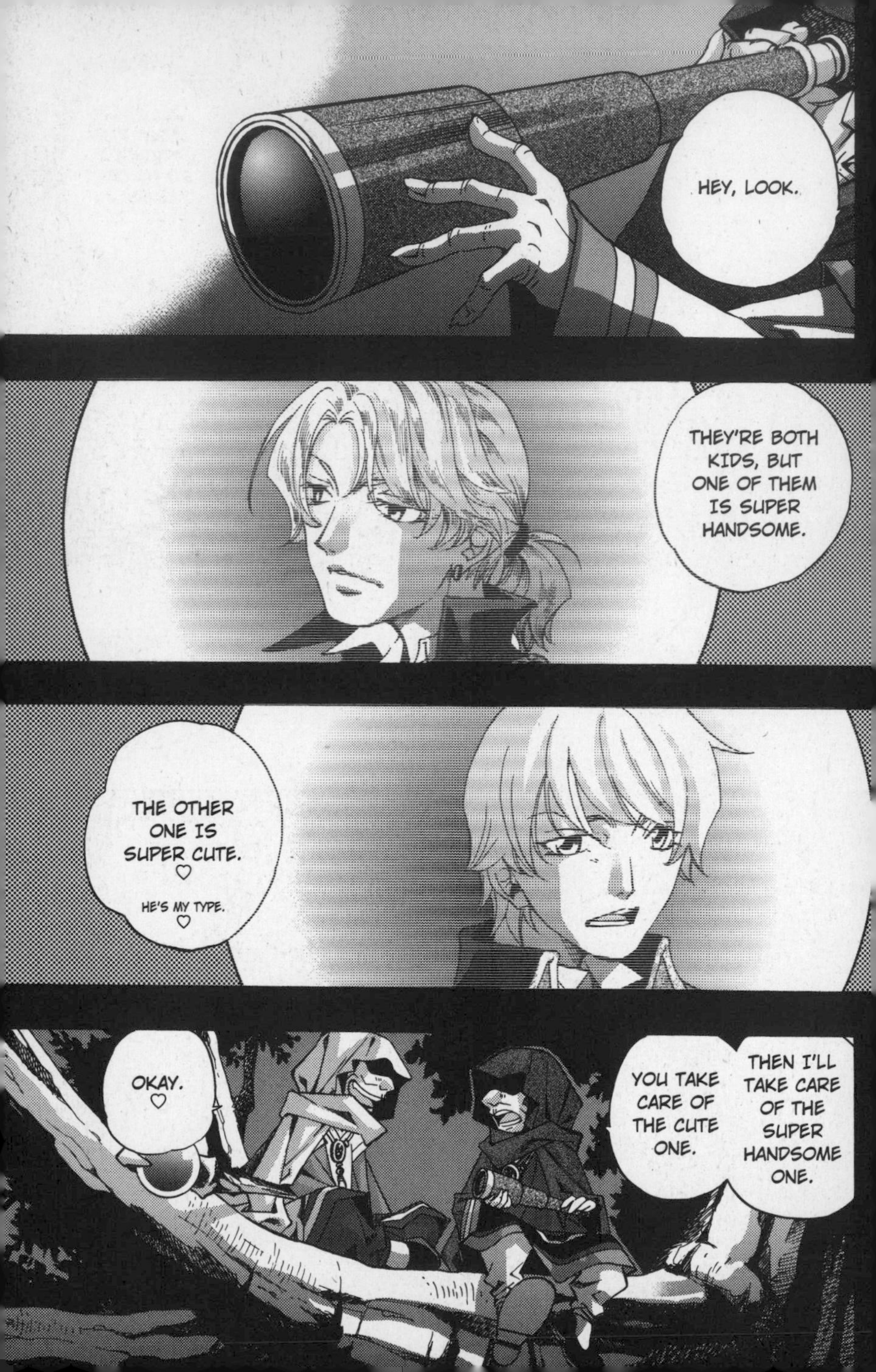
HEY, LOOK.
THEY'RE BOTH KIDS, BUT ONE OF THEM IS SUPER HANDSOME.
THE OTHER ONE IS SUPER CUTE. ♡
HE'S MY TYPE. ♡
THEN I'LL TAKE CARE OF THE SUPER HANDSOME ONE.
YOU TAKE CARE OF THE CUTE ONE.
OKAY. ♡

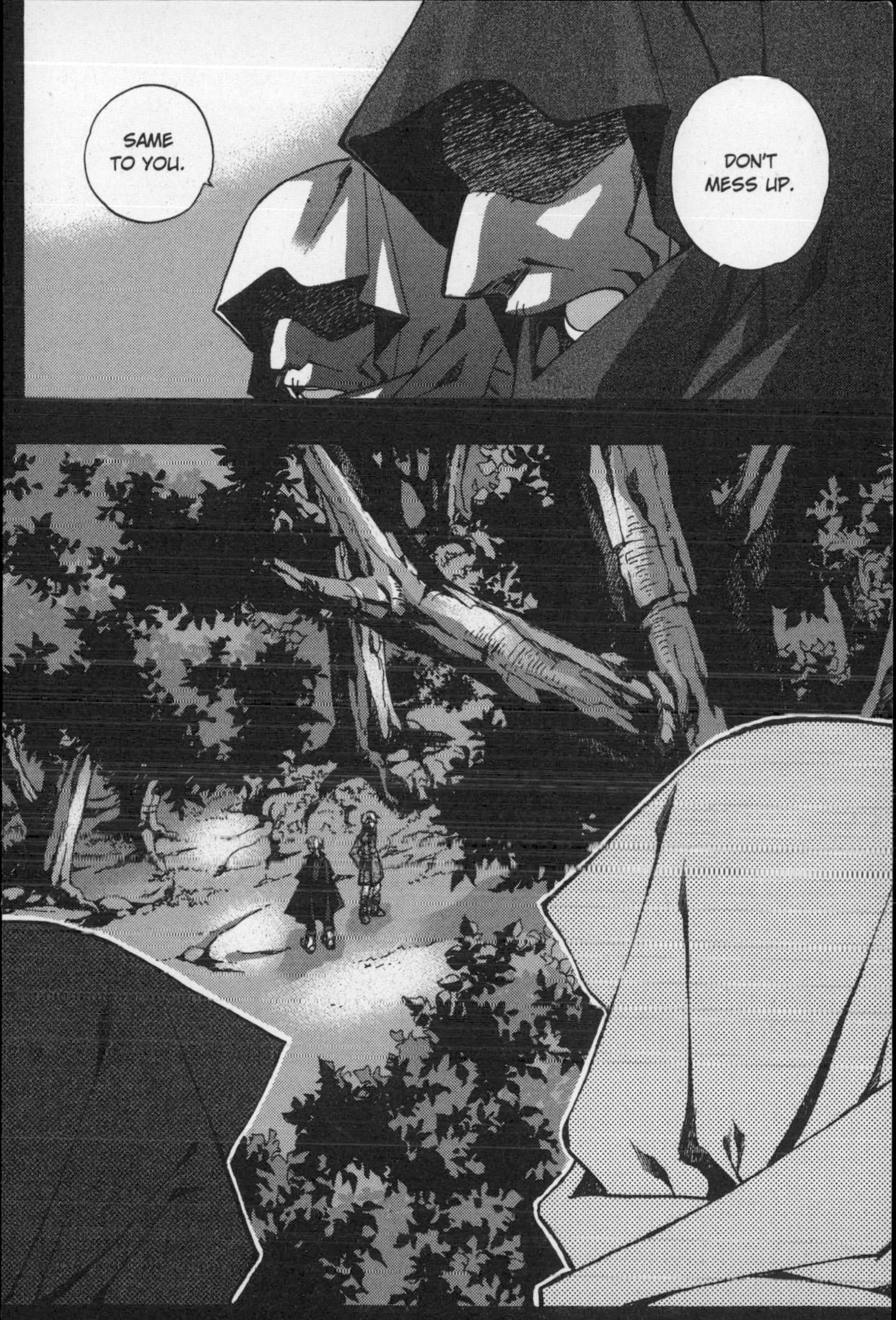
DON'T MESS UP.
SAME TO YOU.

Continued in Volume 2

Whisper to Me
at
Full Moon Night

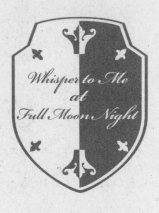

SANAMI MATOH

From Oita Prefecture, now residing in
Saitama Prefecture.

Her debut manga is *Tenshi no Soba*
(Akita Publishing Co.), published in the
September 1990 issue of Bonita. Her works
are both shojo and BL manga, and her best
known works include *Pengin no Ousama,
Tenryuu, FAKE, @Full Moon,* etc.

Preview of
UNTIL THE FULL MOON
volume 2

We're pleased to present you a preview from volume 2.
Please check our website, www.kodanshacomics.com,
to see when this volume will be available in English.
For now you'll have to make do with Japanese!

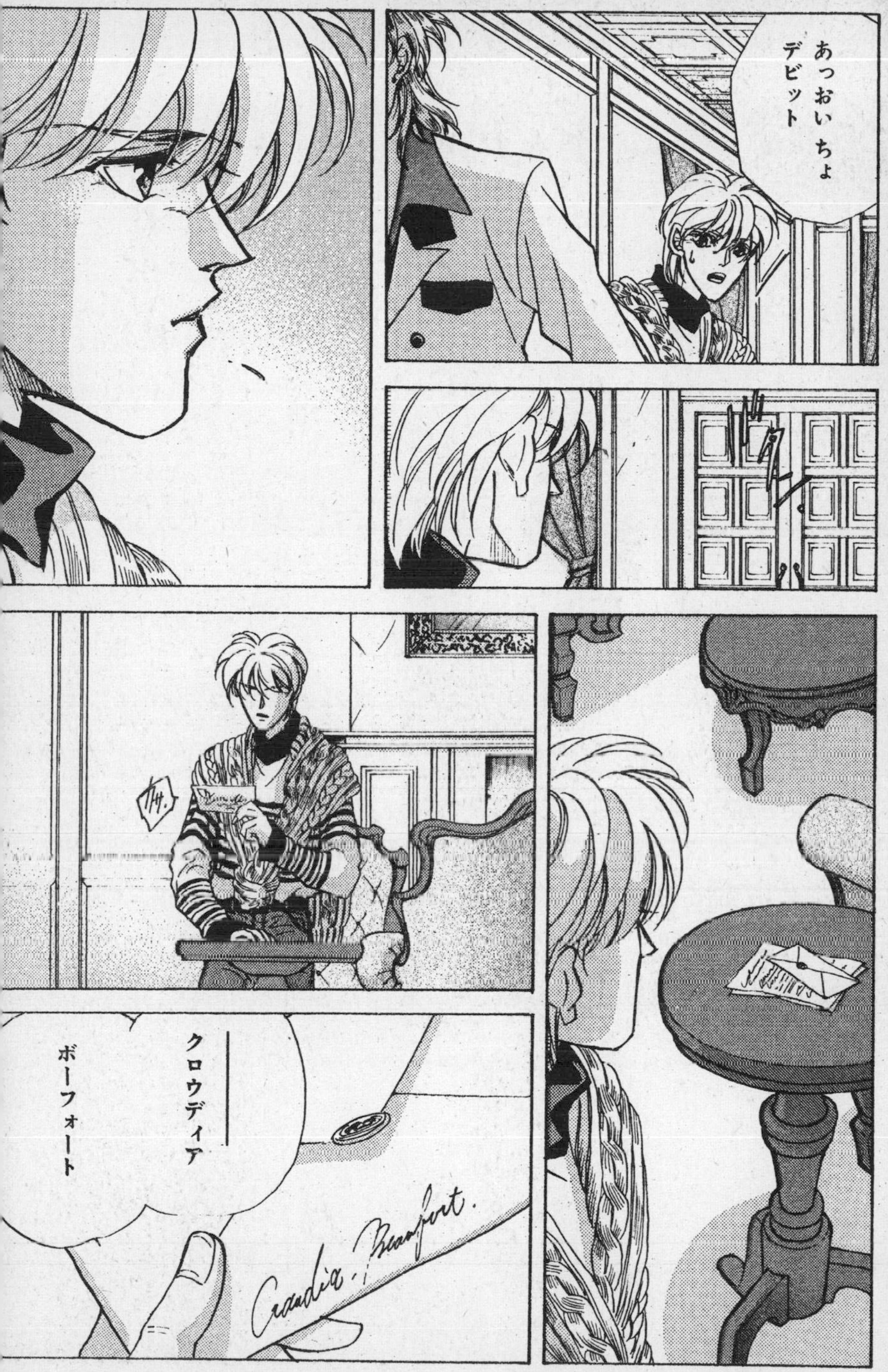
あっおい ちょ
デビット
クロウディア
ボーフォート
Claudia. Beaufort.

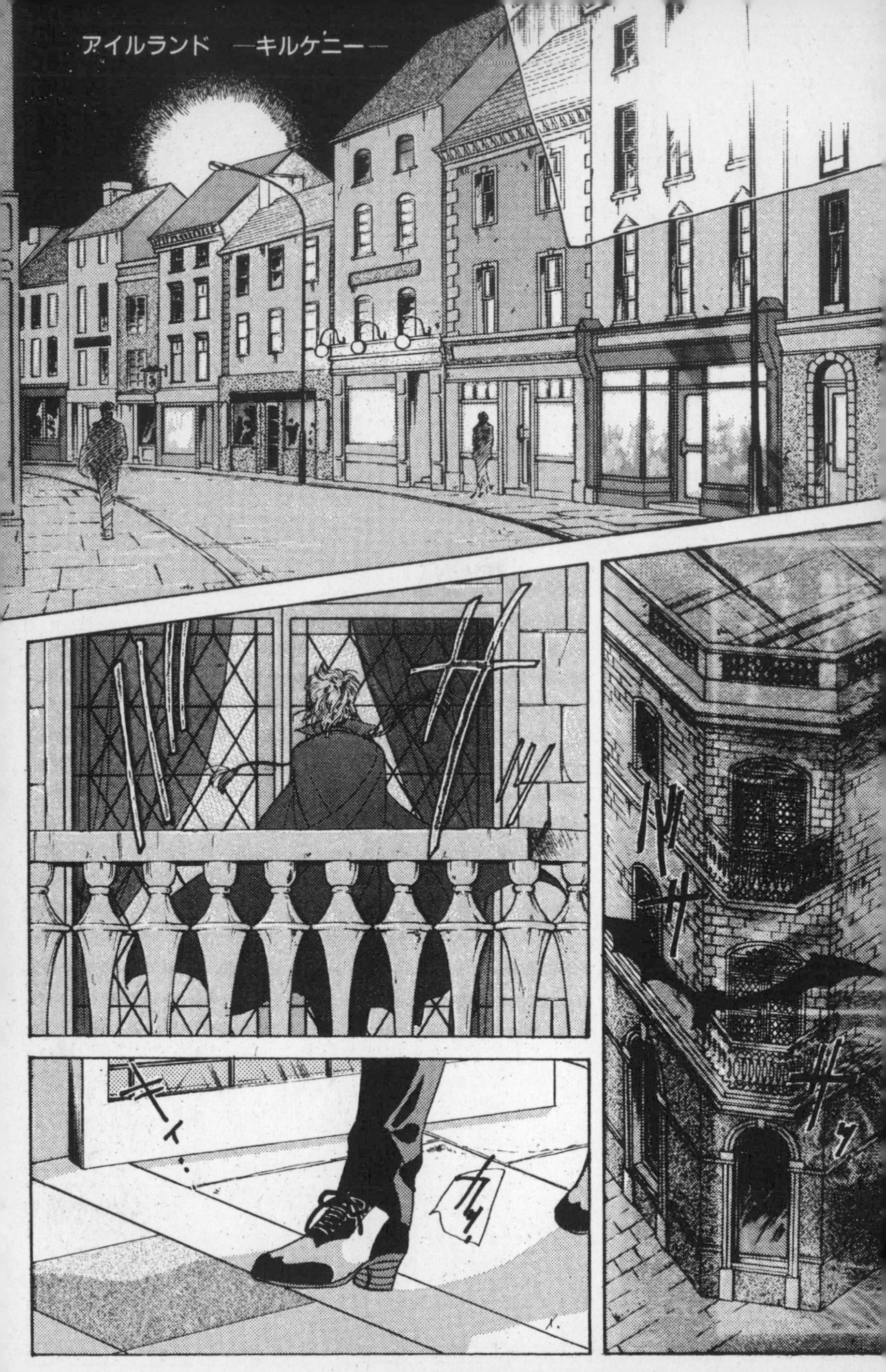
アイルランド —キルケニー—
キイ…
カッ

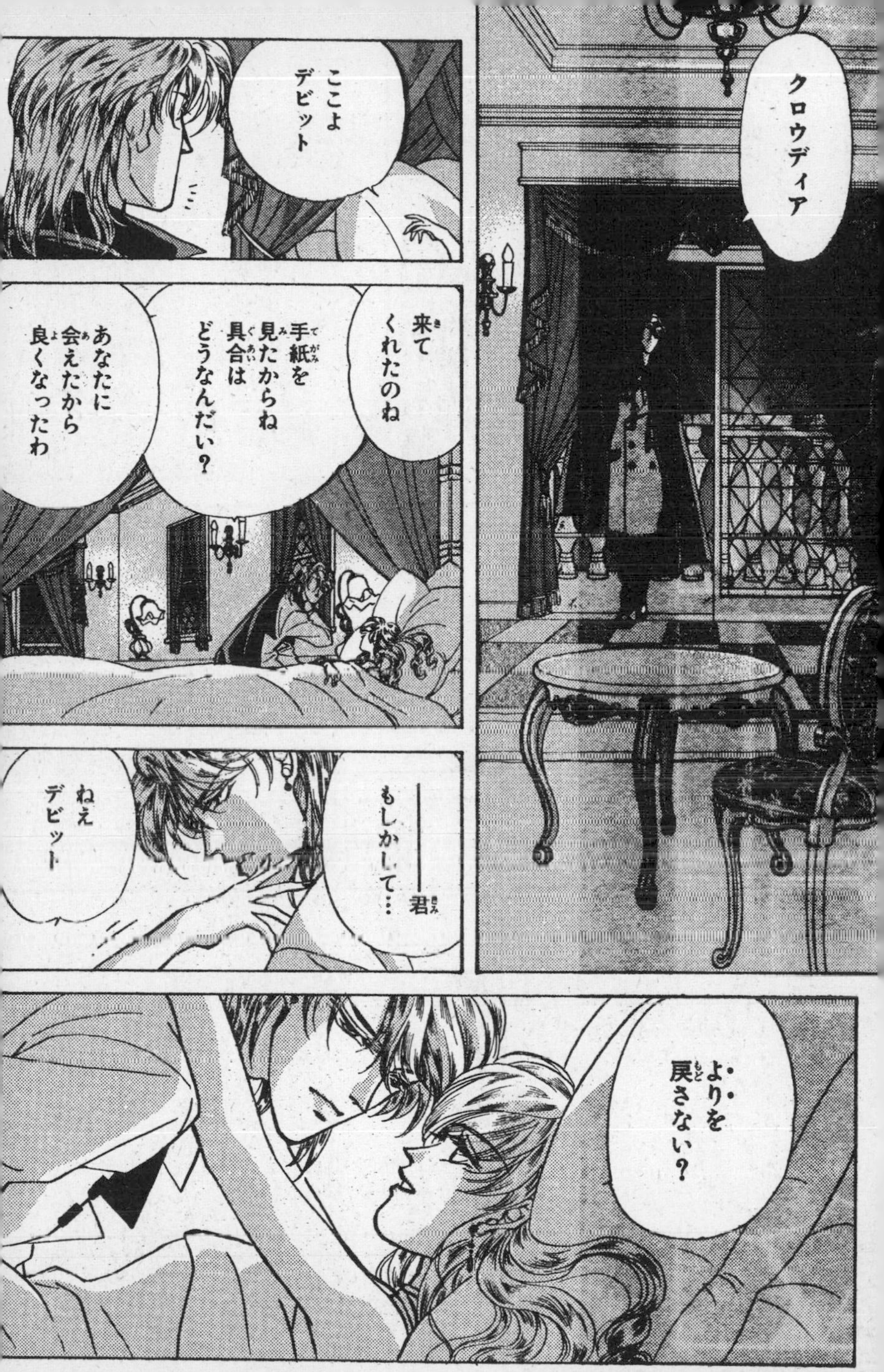
クロウディア
ここよ デビット
来てくれたのね
手紙を見たからね 具合はどうなんだい？
あなたに会えたから良くなったわ
――君 もしかして…
ねえ デビット
よりを戻さない？

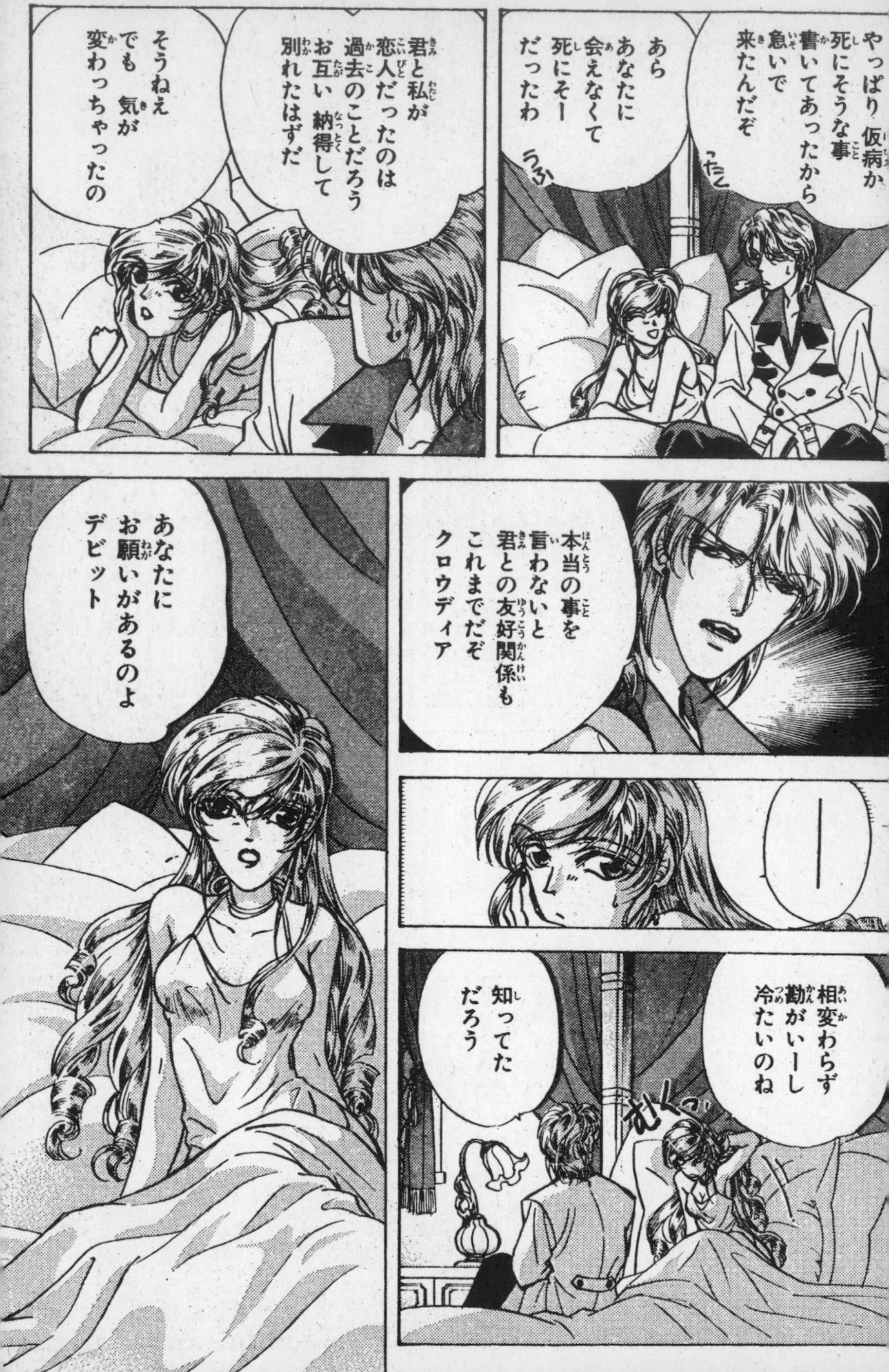
やっぱり仮病か
死にそうな事書いてあったから急いで来たんだぞ
ったく
あら あなたに会えなくて死にそーだったわ
うふ
君と私が恋人だったのは過去のことだろう お互い 納得して別れたはずだ
そうねえ でも 気が変わっちゃったの
本当の事を言わないと君との友好関係もこれまでだぞ クロウディア
――
相変わらず勘がいーし冷たいのね
むくっ
知ってただろう
あなたにお願いがあるのよ デビット

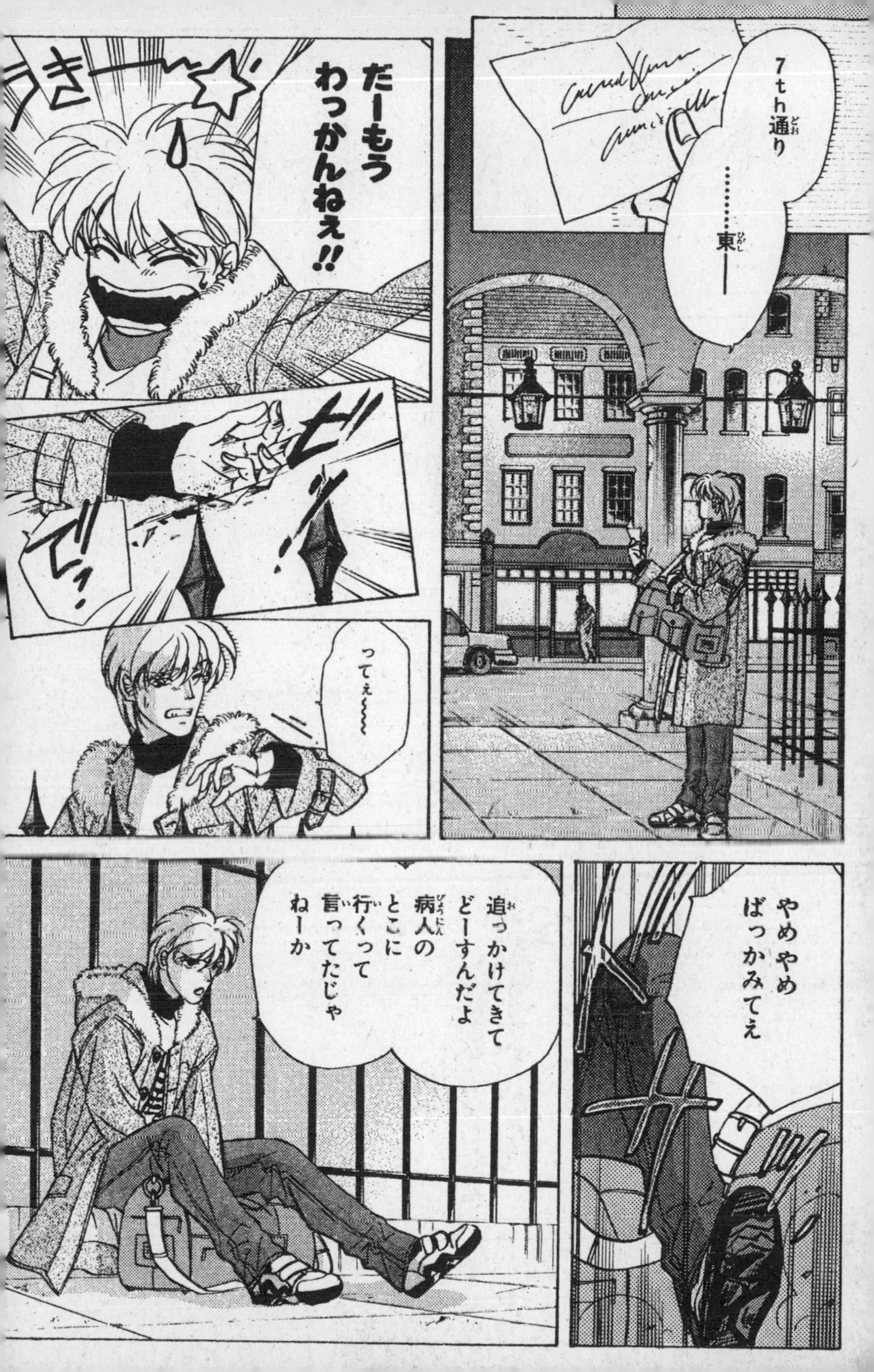
7th通り……東──
うきー
だーもう わっかんねえ!!
ってぇ〜〜〜
やめやめ ばっかみてえ
追っかけてきて どーすんだよ 病人の とこに 行くって 言ってたじゃ ねーか

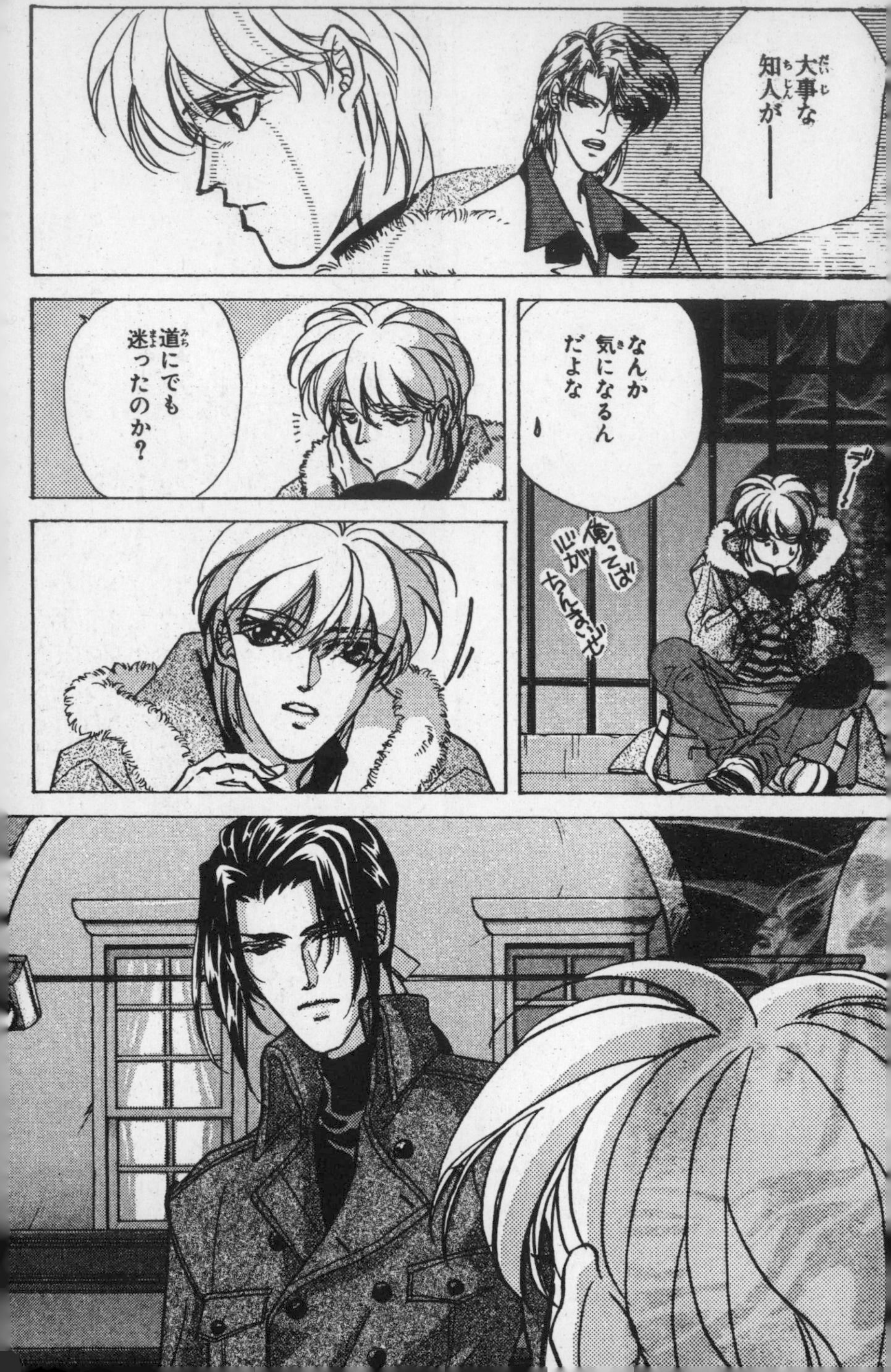
大事な知人が――
なんか気になるんだよな
ラ～
俺ってば心がちんまいぜ
道にでも迷ったのか？

BY TOMOKO HAYAKAWA

It's a beautiful, expansive mansion, and four handsome, fifteen-year-old friends are allowed to live in it for free! But there is one condition—within three years the young men must take the owner's niece and transform her into a proper lady befitting the palace in which they all live! How hard can it be?

Enter Sunako Nakahara, the horror-movie-loving, pock-faced, frizzy-haired, fashion-illiterate hermit who has a tendency to break into explosive nosebleeds whenever she sees anyone attractive. This project is going to take far more than our four heroes ever expected; it needs a miracle!

Ages: 16 +

Special extras in each volume! Read them all!

VISIT WWW.KODANSHACOMICS.COM TO:

• View release date calendars for upcoming volumes
• Find out the latest about new Kodansha Comics series

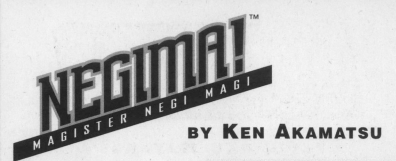

NEGIMA!™
MAGISTER NEGI MAGI

BY KEN AKAMATSU

1
FOR MATURE AUDIENCES AGES 16+
NEGIMA!
MAGISTER NEGI MAGI
by
KEN AKAMATSU
CREATOR OF *LOVE HINA!*

Negi Springfield is a ten-year-old wizard teaching English at an all-girls Japanese school. He dreams of becoming a master wizard like his legendary father, the Thousand Master. At first his biggest concern was concealing his magic powers, because if he's ever caught using them publicly, he thinks he'll be turned into an ermine! But in a world that gets stranger every day, it turns out that the strangest people of all are Negi's students! From a librarian with a magic book to a centuries-old vampire, from a robot to a ninja, Negi will risk his own life to protect the girls in his care!

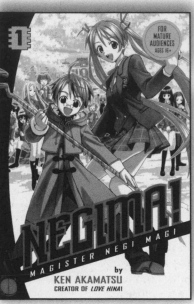

Ages: 16+

Special extras in each volume! Read them all!

KC KODANSHA COMICS

VISIT WWW.KODANSHACOMICS.COM TO:

- View release date calendars for upcoming volumes
- Find out the latest about new Kodansha Comics series

TOMARE!
STOP

You're going the wrong way!

Manga is a completely different type of reading experience.

To start at the beginning, Go to the end!

That's right! Authentic manga is read the traditional Japanese way—from right to left, exactly the opposite of how American books are read. It's easy to follow: Just go to the other end of the book and read each page—and each panel—from right side to left side, starting at the top right. Now you're experiencing manga as it was meant to be!